29

50 FABULOUS PLACES TO RETIRE IN AMERICA

THIRD EDITION

By

ARTHUR GRIFFITH

AND

MARY GRIFFITH

CAREER
PRESS
Franklin Lakes, NJ

50 FABULOUS PLACES TO RETIRE IN AMERICA, THIRD EDITION
EDITED BY ASTRID DERIDDER
TYPESET BY EILEEN MUNSON
Cover design by Johnson Design
Printed in the U.S.A. by Book-mart Press

To order this title, please call toll-free 1-800-CAREER-1 (NJ and Canada: 201-848-0310) to order using VISA or MasterCard, or for further information on books from Career Press.

CAREER
PRESS

The Career Press, Inc., 3 Tice Road, PO Box 687,
Franklin Lakes, NJ 07417
www.careerpress.com

Library of Congress Cataloging-in-Publication Data

50 fabulous places to retire in America.—3rd ed. / Arthur Griffith.
  p. cm.
Rev. ed. of: 50 fabulous places to retire in America / Lee & Saralee Rosenberg. 1st ed. c1991.
ISBN 1-56414-849-1 (paper)
  1. Retirement, Places of—United States. I. Title: Fifty fabulous places to retire in America. II. Griffith, Arthur. III. Rosenberg, Lee, 1952 – 50 fabulous places to retire in America.

HQ1063.R66 2006
646.7'909733—dc22

2005045696

► Acknowledgments

The authors wish to acknowledge with thanks the help and support of our families and friends, who gave us the space and time to complete the project. Then, thank you also, to Astrid deRidder, editor par excellence, whose expert eye kept us on track. Also, a big thanks goes to all the gracious Realtors who gave their valuable time and expertise. And last, and possibly most helpful, was the wait-staff of the Anchor River Inn in Anchor Point, Alaska—Ashley, Jen, Randy, Rebecca, Sam, and Shannie—who continually greeted us, supported us, and cheered us on. Thank you all!

CONTENTS

"Older Americans Month" originated with a presidential proclamation in May of 1963. It has been proclaimed by the president every year since then. President George W. Bush once stated, "Our seniors have cared for their families and communities, enhanced our economic prosperity, defended our nation, and preserved and protected the Founders's vision. Their commitment to our future sets an inspiring example for all."

Retirement for the elderly has been around forever, right? Wrong. Actually, the "elderly" haven't been around forever. Most folks didn't live nearly as long as we do now. The beginning of the 20th century marks the start of "retirement" as we know it. Before that time, a person worked until death or severe illness kept them from working. And because the majority of American families were engaged in some form of farming or industry, work meant food, clothing, housing, and community involvement. Retirement (if it ever came) was brief, measured in weeks or months, not years, and required no planning.

One turning point was the Great Depression, which began in 1929. One in every four workers was unemployed. Family stories abound, telling of "when the family lost the farm," companies (and executives) disappeared overnight, and many families split up, sending the children to live with relatives who were better off. During this time of unprecedented poverty, the government was gravely concerned about the survival of the economic life of the nation, and searched for ways to put younger workers into jobs. At the same time, it wanted to remove older workers, who were perceived to be of less value.

It wasn't until 1935 however that Social Security was created. It became the first retirement institution in the United States. The payments were relatively low, even for those times, and no automatic cost of living increases would be instituted until 1972. Nonetheless, it was something, and the citizens who lived through those difficult years saw hope for the first time. The first retirees worked until age 70, a far cry from the eligibility of 62 today.

As time moved on, so did the Social Security System. Retirement benefits were established by private industry, to provide employees with incentives to remain in their jobs over a long period of time. In 1960, for example, company retirement was provided for more than half the country's workers. These factors added to the ability of the average worker to retire and have time to enjoy life before "old age" set in. These were termed the "Golden Years." Nowadays we see folks getting bored with the endless "vacation" of retirement. And many people, because of increased strength and overall good health well into their 80s, need more than a sunny porch, an outdoor recliner, and a glass of iced tea.

Activity is what most retirees want, and plenty of it. Whether it involves a new job, getting an advanced educational degree, starting a business, or writing a book, seniors of today are planning and living out entirely new lives. If John Glenn can get back into space in his 70s, and any number of actors and actresses work well into their 80s, why can't the rest of us do similar things in our retirement?

Now that it's too late to do anything about the wrinkles and warts that are firmly in place, or the few extra pounds (that don't look bad), grandchildren, and great-grandchildren, you finally have some ideas about what to do in your retirement. Well, that's just great, because this book offers delicious choices to you concerning where to locate, if moving is in your plan. You may decide to travel the world after a lifetime of staying put, or you may throw caution to the wind and move. But to where?

That's where this book comes in. Here are the profiles of 50 truly fabulous places to live in the United States, and you have the option of moving to any one of them. But what's that you say? You haven't got all the money you need to buy into "fabulous" places? Well, some of the cities profiled are indeed for the well-financed retiree, but the majority of our "50 Fabulous Places to Retire in America" are for real people with real budgets.

We've all heard the old saying, "The Devil's in the details." Nowhere is that more true than in real estate, or in planning for retirement! There's another saying, too, that says "Heaven's in the details." I think they may be talking about the same details,

As you begin this adventure, you will find that this handy reference is a real friend. It is our hope that, dog-eared and tattered, it will become like your teddy bear of old—a faithful friend and happy companion. So many places in this country offer so much. And all the legwork has been done for you! Telephone numbers and Websites, which are peppered throughout the book, provide you with additional resources, should you choose to get more in-depth information. The fun part is reading, imagining, plotting a course, and planning your adventure!

Facts, Numbers, and Tips

Someone once said that we think of George Washington as "the father of our country." But in reality, we have modeled our society after the eternally enumerating Ben Franklin. We are not a country of statesmen, we are shopkeepers. We are not military geniuses, we are accountants. We are a people ruled by numbers. You disagree? How about your blood pressure numbers, heartbeats per minute, number of dollars you command, miles to the gallon, how fast can you get it done, your credit score, the distance from home to work and school, or ages of your children?

Because we love numbers, let's look at some that are important to senior citizens. What we have here are interesting and informative statistics to promote awareness of current trends. And while you might think that you are the only one anxious about aging, you may find that these numbers are reassuring. It's nice to know you're not alone in all this.

For example:

- As of July 1, 2004, 36.3 million people 65 years and older lived in the United States, and that was 12 percent of the total population.
- Between 2003 and 2004, 351,000 people graduated to the "Over 65" age group.
- Between 2003 and 2004, 9 million people were 85 years of age.
- The projected size of the 65-and-over population by 2050 is 86.7 million.
- The projected percentage increase in population of people over 65 from 2004 to 2050 is 147 percent. (Whew!)
- In 2005, 4.6 million of us 65 and over were still working. (Good for us!)

- Of the people between 65 and 69 years of age, 77 percent graduated from high school.

- Of the people between 65 and 69 years of age, 20 percent of folks have bachelors or masters degrees.

- Almost 19 percent of citizens between the ages of 70 and 74 have graduated college.

- Of the people over the age of 75, 15 percent are college graduates.

Marital Status:

- Approximately 44 percent of women age 65 and over are widows.

- Approximately 14 percent of men age 65 and over are widowers.

- Almost 41 percent of women age 65 and above are married and living with spouses.

- Women age 65 and older are three times more likely to be widowed than men in the same age group. (Sad, but true.)

- Almost three-quarters of men 65 and older are married and living with spouses.

- There were 100 women for every 71 men at age 65 and older as of July 1, 2003.

- There were 100 women for every 83 men between ages 65 and 74 as of July 1, 2003.

- There were 100 women for every 44 men over age 85 as of July 1, 2003.

Health:

- Approximately 12.4 million of those 65 and over walk at least six times a year. (Wait! We go more often than that, don't we?)

Military:

- We proudly boast 9.7 million military veterans. (Ten-hutt!)

Voting Record:

- We had 72 percent of citizens ages 65 to 74 vote in the last presidential election. (That is the highest rate of any age group!)

Financial:

- Can you believe that 81 percent of us own our own homes? (This is the American Dream; how nice for us that it still reigns.)

- We have a modest poverty rate of 10 percent. This is an interesting number that sheds light on how we stack up against our fellow citizens.

- In 2003, the median net worth for senior citizens is around $108,000, versus $7,240 for those under age 35.

- The senior citizens' median income for 2003 was $23,787.

Who Lives Where:

- More than 35 percent of Charlotte County, Florida, residents are 65 and over. (That's the highest percentage of any county in the nation!)
- Similarly, 21 percent of Clearwater, Florida, residents are 65 and over. (Among cities with populations of 100,000 or more.)

Here are the 50 U.S. towns with the highest average age of residents:

1. Laguna Woods, California: 78 years
2. Century Village, Florida: 77.7 years
3. Kings Point, Florida: 77.7 years
4. Rossmoor, Maryland: 76.9 years
5. Crestwood Village, New Jersey: 75.8 years
6. Holiday City-Berkeley, New Jersey: 75.8 years
7. Greater Sun Center, Florida: 75 years
8. Sun City, Arizona: 75 years
9. Sun City West, Arizona: 73.2 years
10. Hamptons at Boca Raton, Florida: 72.9 years
11. Green Valley, Arizona: 72.2 years
12. West Vero Corridor, Florida: 71.9 years
13. Timber Pines, Florida: 71.6 years
14. South Pasadena, Florida: 70.6 years
15. Sun Lakes, Arizona: 69.3 years
16. Venice, Florida: 68.8 years
17. Micco, Florida: 68.6 years
18. Lady Lake, Florida: 68.4 years
19. Longboat Key, Florida: 67.9 years
20. Zephyrhills West, Florida: 67.8 years
21. Beverly Hills, Florida: 67.8 years
22. Pelican Bay, Florida: 67.4 years
23. Hot Springs Village, Arkansas: 67.1 years
24. Palm Beach, Florida: 66.6 years
25. The Villages, Florida: 66.3 years
26. Sun City, California: 66.1 years
27. Whisper Walk, Florida: 65.8 years
28. Sugarmill Woods, Florida: 65.0 years
29. Punta Gorda, Florida: 63.6 years

30. Englewood, Florida: 63.0 years
31. Fortuna Foothills, Arizona: 62.9 years
32. Rotonda, Florida: 62.7 years
33. Rancho Mirage, California: 61.3 years
34. Bella Vista, Arkansas: 61.2 years
35. Estero, Florida: 61.2 years
36. Skidaway Island, Georgia: 61.0 years
37. Naples, Florida: 60.7 years
38. Pine Ridge, Florida: 60.5 years
39. Sanibel, Florida: 60.5 years
40. Pinehurst, North Carolina: 60.4 years
41. North Fort Myers, Florida: 60.2 years
42. Marco Island, Florida: 60.1 years
43. Siesta Key, Florida: 59.7 years
44. Iona, Florida: 59.4 years
45. Fort Myers Beach, Florida: 59.1 years
46. Seminole, Florida: 59.1 years
47. Bayonet Point, Florida: 59.0 years
48. Pine Island Ridge, Florida; 58.7 years
49. Laurel, Florida: 57.7 years
50. Hudson, Florida: 57.2 years

Reading this list makes you feel absolutely spritely, right? The previous statistics were gathered from the U.S. Census Bureau "Facts for Features" Webpage (*www.census.gov/Press-Release/www/releases/archives/facts_for_features/001626.html*).

Here are the Top 50 cities of populations over 5,000 with the highest median house value:

1. Montecito, California: $1,000,001
2. Hillsborough, California: $1,000,001
3. Palm Beach, Florida: $1,000,001
4. Tiburon, California: $1,000,001
5. Saratoga, California: $1,000,001
6. Atherton, California: $1,000,001
7. Beverly Hills, California: $1,000.001
8. Malibu, California: $1,000,001

9. Woodside, California: $1,000,001
10. Kings Point, New York: $1,000,001
11. Aspen, Colorado: $1,000,001
12. Los Altos Hills, California: $1,000,001
13. Los Altos, California: $983,000
14. Bronxville, New York: $959,600
15. Kentfield, California: $907,300
16. Cherry Hills Village, Colorado: $893,000
17. Stanford, California: $870,800
18. New Canaan, Connecticut: $831,000
19. Palo Alto, California: $811,800
20. Palos Verdes Estates, California: $795,600
21. Sausalito, California: $786,200
22. Los Gatos, California: $784,600
23. Greenwich, Connecticut: $781,500
24. Menlo Park, California: $778,500
25. Piedmont, California: $760,000
26. Winnetka, Illinois: $756,500
27. Mill Valley, California: $746,200
28. Weston, Massachusetts: $739,200
29. The Village of Indian Hill, Ohio: $738,800
30. Strawberry, California: $737,300
31. Alamo, California: $731,200
32. Paradise Valley, Arizona: $722,700
33. Blackhawk-Camino Tassajara, California: $716,00
34. Darien, Connecticut: $711,000
35. Newport Beach, California: $708,200
36. Scarsdale, New York: $708,000
37. San Marino, California: $690,800
38. Burlingame, California: $685,900
39. Highland Park, Texas: $685,700
40. Coronado, California: $683,400
41. Manhattan Beach, California: $672,600
42. Glencoe, Illinois: $667,000
43. Larkspur, California: $663,000

44. Lake Forest, Illinois: $662,400

45. Larchmont, New York: $656,300

46. Laguna Beach, California: $653,900

47. Cupertino, California: $649,000

48. Rolling Hills Estates, California: $637,800

49. Rye, New York: $635,700

50. Oak Brook, Illinois: $635,400

The National Association of Realtors fourth quarter survey found that for existing homes across the nation, the median price rose 8.8 percent from the fourth quarter of 2003 to the fourth quarter of 2004. What that means in actual prices is that the median price was $172,400 in the fourth quarter of 2003, versus $187,500 in the fourth quarter of 2004. As you know, the median price is not an average, rather it represents a typical selling price, where half of the houses sold for more, and half sold for less.

On to some tips for beating the odds and having a great time while your relatives marvel at your energy. Remember, what is good for the body is also good for the spirit. I'm not talking about excessive exercise, I'm talking about getting into the kind of shape it's going to take for you to move to a new city, enjoy life when you get there, and not injure yourself in the process.

Follow these tips, and with time and persistence, you'll feel more energy and be in better shape than ever before!

• Start your exercise slowly. (Check with the doctor to design a program that's right for you.)

• Exercise in the morning. (Statistics show that morning exercisers live longer than evening exercisers.)

• Exercise with a buddy. (Guilt is a great motivator.)

• Exercise only if it allows you to talk (This is an old rule of thumb for aerobic exercise.)

• Read the comics before you exercise. (Humor always lightens the load!)

• Dress for the weather, if going outdoors. (There's no sense in catching pneumonia.)

• Set goals. Make them small. (You will most likely achieve them faster than you think!)

• Record your progress. (There's nothing quite like hitting one goal to motivate you for the next.)

• Congratulate yourself and your partner on goals achieved. (Do it with chocolate!)

Most of us don't just want to live longer, we want to live healthy for as long as we can. That's not such a bad notion, and with a little effort, it's not such hard work either!

Friendly Internet Websites

More and more seniors are realizing the power of the Internet. We have some of the most awesome power ever imagined at our fingertips. Communications are virtually instantaneous, and whatever you want to learn is readily available. But what if you don't know anything about computers? Even the most inexperienced senior can learn how to use e-mail and the World Wide Web. If you don't have a precocious teenager available to teach you, then go to a local community college or senior center for a class. You will thank me!

A friend of mine swore that he would never learn how to use a computer. However, his son was after him to become "computer literate" so they could talk online. I said that he'd probably be purring into the screen before he was done, but I was wrong. He still dislikes computers, and he probably always will. But he has learned how to use them to communicate with his family. And he's happy with his new-found power. He has a lot of company in that. Research has shown that seniors are becoming more and more adept at maneuvering around the Internet. We are the fastest growing group online, gaining around 15 percent each year over the last 15 years. According to some experts, seniors own more than 50 percent of all home computers!

If you own a computer and browse the Web on a regular basis, you are probably aware that you can find useful information on any number of topics, including retirement plans, jobs in distant places, entertainment, general health, and healthcare options. Did you know that research has shown that those who regularly cruise the Internet are likely to be healthier and happier than those who do not?

Government Websites

When you had your first baby, there was no manual provided. And now that you're getting older, there's no manual for aging either. However, you can arm yourself by doing research. One of the best resources is a Website put up by the government. (Your tax dollars at work for you, how nice!) It's called "Eldercare" and is a public service of the U.S. Administration on Aging (*www.eldercare.gov/Eldercare/Public/Home.asp*). In addition to general information on aging, this Website displays links to sites that provide information to caregivers of the elderly. If you would rather call Eldercare, their phone number is 1-800-677-1116.

The official U.S. government portal (*http://firstgov.gov*) offers a multitude of general Websites for seniors, some of which deal with issues such as consumer protection, education, jobs, volunteerism, federal and state agencies, health, laws, regulations, retirement, taxes, travel, and leisure. For more information, and an afternoon's worth of surfing, check out their main Website (*http://www.firstgov.gov/Topics/Seniors.shtml*).

If you have the time, patience, and are interested, the Agency on Aging has a nifty Website for statistics and other information on aging *(www.aoa.dhhs.gov)*. Here are a few of the available statistics on aging up to July 1, 2004: The population of those 60 years and over is 48,883,408! For 65 years and over, it's 6,293,985. And for ages 85 and over, the population is 4,859,631.

Several helpful services and news items are linked to the Benefits Checkup Website (*http://ssl1.benefitscheckup.org/before_you_start.cfm*). The site features Benefit Checkup, a service to help people already enrolled in Medicare. It also helps other older adults learn about and sign up for government benefits.

Here are a few other Websites from the Administration on Aging:

- Alzheimer's resource room: *www.aoa.dhhs.gov/alz/index.asp*
- Elder rights and resources: *www.aoa.dhhs.gov/eldfam/Elder_Rights/Elder_Rights.asp*
- For caregivers: *www.aoa.dhhs.gov/eldfam/For_Caregivers/For_Caregivers.asp*
- Housing: *www.aoa.dhhs.gov/eldfam/Housing/Housing.asp*
- Money matters: *www.aoa.dhhs.gov/eldfam/Money_Matters/Money_Matters.asp*.
- Nutrition: *www.aoa.dhhs.gov/eldfam/Nutrition/Nutrition.asp*
- Promoting healthy lifestyles for seniors: *www.aoa.dhhs.gov/eldfam/Healthy_Lifestyles/Healthy_Lifestyles.asp*
- Volunteer opportunities: *www.aoa.dhhs.gov/eldfam/Volunteer_Opps/Volunteer_Opps.asp*

Women's Issues in Retirement

For specific, day-to-day living, you will find the best suggestions in the "Senior Services," "Medical," and "Let the Good Times Roll" sections of the city profiles later in this book. In this chapter, we offer a distillation of the best general sources of advice and information from governmental agencies, non-profit organizations, and commercial sites that we have found on the Internet.

First, there is the Women's Institute for a Secure Retirement (*www.wiser.heinz.org*), which offers information and links for women retirees. It also explores options for working women and offers suggestions for retirement planning. Another good source for women and retirement issues is the Woman's Guide to Retirement Planning (*http://retireplan.about.com/library/bl_women.htm*), an excellent discussion of several factors and special concerns for women regarding retirement. The U.S. Department of Labor's Website (*www.dol.gov/dol/audience/aud-women.htm#pensions*) gives another look at issues women face as retirement approaches.

The Women Matter Website (*www.womenmatter.com*) is where the rubber meets the road for women considering going to work, or already in the workforce, evaluating investments, approaching retirement, and beyond. The people behind this site are politically active and report on Congress and its treatment of issues critical to the well-being of American women. They suggest that our employment outside the home, the taxes we pay out of what we earn, and the benefits we earn, are linked together in a single critical life issue for women, because they set the minimum standard for quality of living for all of us.

The Older Women's League (*www.owl-national.org*) is the only national grassroots membership organization to focus solely on issues unique to women as they age. If you take a look at their Website, you will definitely learn something. The Women's Health Website (*www.womhealth.org.au*) will give you answers to questions you may have been carrying around for long time. This most useful Australian Website is uncluttered, easy to navigate, and clearly written.

An interesting side note: While researching women's issues, we found that a recent study shows that women who hold traditional jobs, such as clerical, food service, or manufacturing workers, fare better than their professional career sisters at retirement. It seems that those of us who hold high-salaried positions (engineers, managers, lawyers, and so on) are apt to feel a real sense of loss at retirement. On the other hand, the rest of the female workforce tends to feel relief and renewed enthusiasm at retirement.

Faith-Based Retirement

For those who are interested, Retirement with a Purpose has a Website that offers a wealth of information for retirees (*www.retirementwithapurpose.com*). Many topics have to do with living well, offering your time to others as a volunteer, and faith-based activities.

Business in Retirement

A Website that will inform on the best places in America to do business is sponsored by BizJournals (*www.bizjournals.com*), an outfit that labels itself "strictly business, strictly local." There you will find business news and success stories.

The Reasons for Starting a Small Business site (*http://craftandfabriclinks.com/busfocus/business_book_1.html*) is a free online booklet that asks you to look at your reasons and capabilities for, start your own business. Nobody there says you can't. They just ask you to put some serious thought into why you want to open a business.

The government site (*www.lep.gov*) provides essential information on guidance and resources for recipients of federal financial assistance dealing with individuals with limited English proficiency.

The HIPAA site (*www.hhs.gov/ocr/hipaa*) provides essential information about protection of the privacy of personal health information.

This Federal Disability Website (www.DisabilityInfo.gov) maintains a comprehensive listing of disability-related government resources.

Money Management

There are approximately 1.9 million Websites that claim to have something to do with money management in retirement. But how many of them are important to you? The following are a few suggestions of the available Websites that aren't too steeped in financial-babble.

This brief article helps explain options when planning on how to get money out of tax-deferred or other retirement funds: *www.advisortoday.com/archives/2000_june_mm.html*.

Consolidating funding sources sounds like a great idea. But how do you do that? Here's a Website that has the answers: *http://seniorliving.about.com/od/manageyourmoney/a/retirementfunds.htm*. And while you're there, check out the many links to such things as the Six Steps to Better Senior Sex, Senior Job Bank, Knee Exercise, 10 Date Ideas for Senior Dating, Four Exercises That Seniors Need, and more.

Talk about locking the barn door after the horse has been stolen! The wonderful Website from the American Savings Education Council (ASEC) (*www.choosetosave.org/asec*) offers advice to smart citizens about how to begin to save money for retirement and how to prioritize savings. The ASEC states that its mission is "to make saving and retirement planning a priority for all Americans."

Also, we all need to know a few facts about Social Security. Social Security currently replaces only about 52 percent of pay for individuals earning $15,000 a year, about 42 percent of pay for individuals earning $25,000 a year (the U.S. average), about 37.5 percent of pay for individuals earning $35,000 a year, and about 24 percent of pay for individuals earning $61,200 (the current maximum taxable earnings for which individuals are subject to the Social Security tax).

In addition, individuals need to be aware of what the Social Security normal retirement age will be when they retire. Do your children know, for example, that under current law, the normal retirement age will gradually rise to age 67 by the year 2027? (Ouch!)

Veterans' Information

The Veterans Affairs (VA) Website (*www.va.gov*) is for you veterans. Whatever the VA has online is available to you via links from this starting point. The online applications alone are worth a look. They include Compensation & Pension, Education, Health Eligibility, My Health, Vocational Rehab, and Employment Services. The VA has special programs (*www1.va.gov/accessible*) including Section 508 Accessibility, which is all about removing barriers to mobility for disabled vets.

Military Services (*www.vba.va.gov/bln/21/milsvc*) is an outreach to active duty service members and veterans. Minority Veterans (*www1.va.gov/ centerforminorityveterans*) provides and promotes the use of VA programs, benefits, and services by minority veterans. Women Veterans (*www1.va.gov/womenvet*) is a Website that works to ensure women veterans have access to VA benefits and services.

Finally, there are a few links under Today's VA: About the VA (*www.va.gov/ about_va*). The VA's goal is to provide excellence in patient care, veterans' benefits, and customer satisfaction.

The VA's Office of Congressional and Legislative Affairs (*www.va.gov/oca*) is the focal point for department management and coordination of all matters involving the Congress. In regard to job opportunities (*www.va.gov/jobs*), the VA can provide you with challenging, interesting, meaningful work, caring for the veterans who have risked their lives to protect our freedom.

The Public Affairs (*www1.va.gov/opa*) section presents news press releases, fact sheets, programs, issues, biographies of VA officials, feature items and information, faith-based and community initiatives, intergovernmental affairs, and special events. One of special interest to older veterans is the "Golden Age Games," held nationally in May of each year. From the U.S. Department of Veterans' Affairs (*www.va.gov/vetdata*) comes a Website of links to four categories of information: healthcare, benefits, memorial/burial, and miscellaneous topics of interest. It is quite possibly the most clear, concise, readable, and important site for veterans. The site provides social and economic information about veterans, demographic, and geographic veteran information, statistical information by veteran program areas, and veteran survey information, as well as references to other veteran information sites.

And there you have it. It is by no means a complete listing of Websites, but it may prove helpful as a jumping-off place in researching some aspects of retirement living that may have you stumped. You may find something of value in more than one of these Websites. The important thing to remember is that, even if the site itself looks less than helpful, a link on the site may answer just the question you are asking.

Moving: Worse than a root canal, but more fun than a water slide

Pretend moving is a party. No really, just humor me! How do you prepare for a party? You don't wait till a week before the bash to start making the guest list, right? Moving is the same thing, only a little different. Whether you call it "countdown" or "top-down," the method is the same. Start the planning as soon as you are certain you are going to move.

1. Before you do anything else, sit down and make a list. It doesn't have to be detailed at this point. Make columns with the headings "Before the Move" "During the Move" and "After the Move." Make sure you leave enough space to begin organizing your adventure.

2. As early as possible, but no later than three months prior to Moving Day, begin sorting the stuff that goes with you, and the stuff that doesn't. This doesn't mean just household stuff, it means sorting out all your possessions, and sometimes an attitude or two. Cheer up! This is going to be good. Here are some examples of things that must "earn" a place in the moving van: kitchenware, linens, appliances, shop tools, art objects (including paintings), exercise equipment, furniture, hobby materials, electronics, yard tools, office items, books, magazines, and clothing. Be thoughtful, but be thorough.

3. If you have things that you are planning to give to the kids or anyone else, now might be a good time.

4. Hold two garage sales. The first one should be as soon as you are done separating your household items. The second will come about 10 days before moving day. It's amazing how many things don't sell the first time, and how many other things will eventually end up in the "can do without" pile.

5. Get some help. You probably have a friend or relative who you can call on to help you with the sorting, tagging, and moving of things that should be sold. Be sure to feed this person well!

6. While you are sorting, remember that it may be smarter to get rid of your current stuff and buy new stuff once you've moved. For example, if you are moving from larger to smaller quarters, your old grand-sized furniture may not look right in the new place. It may not even fit! Some folks opt to leave a lot of stuff behind and furnish the new home when they get settled. Remember, moving companies charge not only by how far you're moving, but also by how heavy the load is.

7. Call the Salvation Army (or other favorite charity) to have them pick up what's left from the final garage sale. Be kind though, and take whatever is worn out or broken to the dump yourself. Do not do this before the garage sale! You may be surprised at what some people will buy.

8. Hire a mover. Sometimes this is a simple matter of calling around and asking for someone to come to your house and give an estimate of costs. These days it is wise to get more than one estimate. Three estimates are best. As you walk through each room with the moving company representative, ask for specific things that you need to have done. Remember, everything extra is going to cost extra. So be sure to specify exactly what you want, and have them give you the added costs. Also, be certain to ask the same questions of each representative. Otherwise, the differing estimates will be off and you will have to start over.

9. Unless you know the people well, it is generally unwise to use a "brother-in-law" mover. People lose belongings every year to "bargain" movers. On the other hand, if you have faith in an independent mover, you can sometimes save money, as they have more flexibility in pricing than the larger companies do.

10. If you choose to pack some items and let the movers pack others, be sure to purchase moving boxes. You can usually buy them from the moving company or from a packing and shipping retail outlet. The cost for you to pack a few boxes yourself will be close to that charged by the moving company, but sometimes the confidence that your fragile things are packed safely is worth the extra time and labor on your part. On Moving Day, the moving company personnel will probably mark the boxes you pack, for liability purposes. It isn't personal; it just keeps them out of hot water in case your Waterford crystal vase should arrive in more than one piece.

11. Ask the moving company representative about insurance, and make sure you understand your rights and liabilities. Again, you want this to be an adventure, not a negative learning experience.

12. Some things you won't have to worry about, because you have this book in hand, and we've included auto registration and driver's license information for your new home. Each city profiled gives you the specific requirements for the state, along with the different grace periods.

13. Get an expandable file, one with a flap and elastic fastener. This file will be your constant companion and best friend for the duration of the move. Put it in plain sight—the kitchen or dining table works well. This file will contain all the important paperwork that you'll need before, during, and after your move.

14. Contact your dentist and doctors to get all your records and prescriptions. It may take a while, so do this a month ahead of Moving Day. Put them in your file. If you would rather, you can simply have your medical records and prescriptions transferred.

15. Ask for referrals from your medical professionals.

16. If Fido Dog and Lady Kitty Kat are going with you, contact your veterinarian to obtain their medical records. This may take a while, too. When you get them, put them in your file.

17. Pet carriers are wonderful. Each animal needs his or her own space. Arrange for familiar blankets and cushions to be placed inside the carrier, because it will help your animal feel comfortable in unfamiliar surroundings.

18. If your pets have no experience with carriers, now is the time to introduce them. Do this well in advance. Moving is stressful for them, too. Your veterinarian can give you a better idea how to handle moving stress for your specific pets.

19. As early as possible, arrange for your pets to spend the night before the move with friends, away from the flurry of activity at your house. You will pick them up on your way out of town.

20. Plan your trip if traveling by car. Sketch out places to stay and make reservations ahead of time. Write it all down, and make two copies: one for the file, the other to be left with a friend.

21. Get to the post office for a change-of-address card. Fill them out and mail them a month in advance of your move. It can take six weeks to make the change with the post office. You can also mail cards to your friends and family to let them know your new address. If you're obsessive, or have some extra time, make a list of who you've sent them to. In the rush to move, you may forget who has been notified and who hasn't.

22. Notify your banks, financial planners, or anyone who handles your finances. Transfer funds and set up new accounts in your destination city.

23. Check into any refunds on deposits. This is big, not because of the amount of money involved, but because it's annoying if you don't apply for the refund in a timely manner, and then try to do it months later from a distant location.

24. If you are working, give notice. It is probably redundant, as most of us discuss retirement plans well ahead of time. But it does solidify the knowledge for everyone concerned that you are leaving. Enjoy the party!

25. Arrange for transfer of membership for civic, religious, or social organizations. This can be done well ahead of time. Keep any letters of introduction in your file.

26. As Moving Day gets near, make a list of services and utilities you use. Call each of them, noting on your list the date of your call. Give them the Moving Day, and ask what they need in terms of notification. Most will not require anything more than your phone call, but if there is a deposit (or pending charge) you should take care of it before you leave.

27. One week before Moving Day, unload the freezer. Defrost it. Use or give away extra food.

28. About three days before Moving Day, sit down and go over your lists. This will do two good things: first, reassure yourself that you are on track; and second, uncover anything that isn't yet completed.

29. Do not panic! You still have plenty of time to finish.

30. If you haven't done it already, get out a marker and number all the packed boxes that you have ready to go. For example, Ba-1 is bathroom-1, K-6 is kitchen-6.

31. Get a clipboard and list the numbered boxes and their contents.

32. Two days before Moving Day you should pack your travel gear. Remember, you will probably spend your last night in a local motel since your bedroom will be on the truck.

33. One day before Moving Day: You will probably be working with the movers now, as they go about the business of packing and loading your household.

34. Continue to number the boxes as they are sealed. Mark them on your list.

35. Confirm the time and place with the movers for delivery.

36. If possible, take a cell phone, and exchange numbers with the moving van driver.

37. Smile as they leave, and thank them for all their hard work.

38. Do a quick walk-through, checking drawers, closets, and cupboards.

39. Go to the place you will be staying overnight. Remember to take your file.

40. Get up early. Load your vehicle, leaving room for the pet carriers. Go out and treat yourself to a nice breakfast, and pick up your four-legged friends. Then take a deep breathe, because you've almost made it! Now all you have to do is unpack!

Congratulations!

Using the City Profiles

It is not possible to rank the cities in an order where one is "better" than another. They are all different. Which city you prefer depends on what you are looking for. This book includes large cities, small towns, rustic rural areas, and urban neighborhoods, places with lots of frantic activities, and other places with nice scenery and a slow life. It was done this way intentionally, so you can pick and choose from among the ones you like, according to the things you like to do and the life you'd like to lead.

The profiles are listed in alphabetical order by state and, within each state, by city. They are compiled in such a way that you can read the entire profile and get a snapshot of the principal features and characteristics of a city, or you can scan the subheadings and find just the information you want. This was designed to make comparisons between cities as easy to do as possible.

Some surprising information came to light as we were gathering data for the city profiles. The biggest surprise had to do with utilities. Things are changing everywhere! Compared to the previous edition of this book, most cities have increased in population. Tax rates seem to have gone up everywhere. Real estate costs have gone up everywhere, but more in some places than others. The number of airlines has come down, but the number of daily flights has gone up.

Websites

Throughout the text you will find Websites that should provide you with more information. But be prepared to find some of the links missing, since Websites appear and disappear constantly. The ones listed here contained good information at the time of writing.

Electric Company

The electric power industry in the United States has entered an era of dramatic change. Due to the Energy Policy Act of 1992, the industry is rapidly joining the deregulated natural gas, railroad, trucking, airline, and telecommunications industries in becoming intensely competitive. As Edwin Lupberger, CEO of Entergy Corporation, put it best when he addressed a group of economic development executives in Baton Rouge, "Nowadays, everywhere and everybody is our competition, whether we like it or not."

The way this affects you is that you may well be able to buy your electric power from more than one company. In some locations, you can switch from one power company to another with a simple phone call. In some places, you can buy your power from several companies at once. For example, you could buy 50 percent of your power from a local coal generation plant, and the other 50 percent from wind generators hundreds of miles away. If your town isn't this flexible yet, it probably will be soon.

Water and Sewer

Of all the utilities, the water and sewage services are the most stable. They are provided either by a city department or by a private company that has a contract with the city.

Telephone, Cable Television, and Internet

The telephone companies and cable television companies are the most dynamic of all. Merger mania is sweeping the country as companies get larger and larger. The names are constantly changing. Without a score card, it's impossible to tell whether multiple listings in a city are for multiple companies, or for the same company that has been visited with name changes and mergers. A couple of these changes occurred right in the middle of our research. In this book we have listed the telephone company on record for each city, if there was one at the time. In some places you will find more than one company listed as being actively available to you. Some cities have up to 50 local telephone providers!

Like electricity, you can call and change your local telephone company at any time. On top of all this, many people are not getting phone lines installed at all, but are using cellular phones instead. Some people are using their Internet connection for everything.

The same sort of thing is happening with cable television. You can get a small satellite dish and use it instead. Cable television suppliers are listed in this book where it was possible to do so. It is becoming more common for multiple companies to compete for your business. And even where a cable company is listed by the city, mergers and acquisitions often change the name.

Car Registration

The Departments of Motor Vehicles in various states differ in the way they do business, so we've listed the bigger differences for each city. But there are always more details. This private Website (*www.dmv.org*) contains links to extensive information for all states.

Real Estate Prices

If you're trying to get a feel for the way real estate prices may be going in a city, here are some questions to ask and some areas to explore. What can you find out about the local economy? Look into manufacturing growth, job growth, consumer spending, and the amount of construction that is going on. If all the indicators are up, then the local economy is on the rise and the prices will be following.

What can you find out about the population trend? If the population is shrinking, for whatever reason, there are going to be too many vacant houses for there to be much appreciation. On the other hand, if the population is increasing, then all those people are going to need places to live, and there could be a housing shortage. What can you find out about renting? There is a pattern here. If rent prices increase, housing purchase prices are sure to follow. When rent prices drop, higher house prices cannot sustain themselves for very long.

What can you find out about the luxury house market? If the most expensive houses are increasing in value, then the lower and mid-range houses are sure to follow. Price growth always seems to start at the top and work its way down through the price ranges until it eventually affects the most modestly priced houses.

The Problem With Statistics

As you read through the descriptions of the various cities in the book, you will find a lot of statistics. You should consider these as rules of thumb, not as the cold, hard facts they seem to be. They can be used as guidelines and comparisons for making up early possibility lists, but don't count on them for making any final decisions. Even the most intensely worked and closely studied sets of figures can be misleading.

The cost of living index is calculated on a national scale, where the average city is listed at 100. Some cities are more expensive (New York City is at 435) while others are less (Phoenix comes in at just over 98). The numbers here are composites, including averages about groceries, housing, utilities, transportation, healthcare, and miscellaneous.

If you find a city you like, but something seems to be wrong with it, investigate further. Crime statistics are often one of those misleading factors. Federal agencies scrupulously calculate the crime rates reported in different categories from the information turned in to them, but the officer on the beat can write down anything he or she wants.

Distance Learning

One of the things seniors love to do is go back to school. Luckily, it's getting easier to do just that! In gathering information on colleges and universities, an interesting trend came to light. Almost every school has a distance learning program of some kind, which is usually offered over the Internet. Some of the programs are in their beginning stages, and some have become quite sophisticated. Most of the distance learning programs offer a collection of non-credit courses, but work is proceeding on credit courses being offered online also.

If you would be interested in taking such a course, call more than one university in your area to check on what they offer, because the tuition and the rules vary. In fact, other than tuition and possible campus visits, there is no need to stick with the local schools. The Internet doesn't have geography, so taking a course from around the corner is often the same as taking one from 2,000 miles away! We've provided you the local listings for your convenience, but don't limit yourself. If you see an opportunity at a school across the country, you should pursue it!

Alaska	1. Anchorage
	2. Homer
	3. Palmer
Arizona	4. Prescott
	5. Scottsdale
	6. Tucson
Arkansas	7. Fayetteville
	8. Hot Springs Village
California	9. Palm Springs
	10. San Diego
	11. Santa Barbara
Colorado	12. Colorado Springs
	13. Fort Collins
Florida	14. Boca Raton
	15. Daytona Beach
	16. Fort Lauderdale
	17. Melbourne
	18. Naples
	19. Ocala
	20. Sarasota
	21. St. Petersburg
Indiana	22. Bloomington
Louisiana	23. Lafayette
	24. Ruston
Maryland	25. Annapolis
	26. Bowie
Minnesota	27. Rochester
Missouri	28. Branson
	29. Columbia
Montana	30. Bozeman
	31. Missoula
New Mexico	32. Las Cruces
	33. Santa Fe
North Carolina	34. Asheville
	35. Raleigh
Oregon	36. Eugene
	37. Klamath Falls
	38. Medford
Pennsylvania	39. Wayne
South Carolina	40. Charleston
Texas	41. Austin
	42. Plano
	43. San Antonio
Utah	44. St. George
Vermont	45. Burlington
Virginia	46. Charlottesville
Washington	47. Bellingham
	48. Everett
	49. Olympia
	50. Sequim

50 Fabulous

Places to Retire in America

1

Anchorage, Alaska

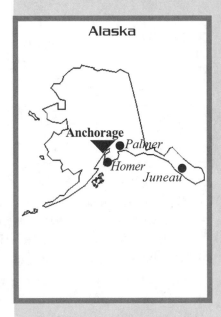

Alaska

Anchorage at a Glance

Located in south central Alaska on the shores of Cook Inlet, the Municipality of Anchorage is a unique urban environment situated in the heart of the wilderness. It is the largest city in Alaska and is home to nearly 42 percent of the state's population. Nearly 10 percent of the Anchorage population is comprised of members of the military and their dependents. The number of military retirees totals more than 44,000. Alaska remains on the Top 10 list for the percentage of veterans in the population. Anchorage is so isolated from other metropolitan areas that it has become almost entirely self-sufficient, so you will find a local source for every amenity and service that you need. It is the state's major media center with 26 radio stations, nine local television stations, pay television services, a major daily newspaper, several business publications, and a number of alternative newspapers. Approximately 90 percent of Anchorage's adults have high-school diplomas, 65 percent have attended one to three years of college, and 17 percent hold advanced degrees. Consequently, Anchorage is among the top metropolitan cities in educational attainment. You will have lots of space to yourself in Anchorage, which has a modest 153.4 people per square mile. And as soon as you leave the city limits, that drops to 1.1 persons per square mile. Alaska definitely has room for you!

Possible Drawbacks: You will be awfully far from friends and family residing in the lower 48 states. Also, there are fewer daylight hours in winter, but summer makes up for it with many hours of sunshine.

▶ Nickname: Los Anchorage

▶ Borough: Anchorage

▶ Area Code: 907

▶ Population: 268,983

▶ Borough Population: 270,951

▶ Percent of Population Over 65: 5.5%

▶ Region: South central Alaska

▶ Closest Metropolitan Area: Seattle, 1448 miles by air, 2360 miles by land

▶ Median Home Price: $190,152

▶ Best Reasons to Retire Here: Gorgeous scenery, close encounters with wildlife, and great hunting, fishing, and trapping. Also, the shock on the faces of your loved ones when you announce and discuss your plans to move to Alaska.

Climate

Latitude 61° N Longitude 149° W	Average High Temperature (°F)	Average Low Temperature (°F)	Precipitation (")	Sunshine (%)
January	20.1	16.6	1.1	34
April	42.3	28.4	0.5	50
July	64.2	52.2	2.0	43
October	38.7	27.9	1.7	36
YEAR	41.5	28.6	16.4	41

Utilities

Overview: The cost of living index places Anchorage well above average at 122.7, where the national average is 100. Healthcare has the highest rating at 162.3. Housing is at 130.6 and food cost is at 121.7. However, much of this cost of living is offset by the fact that there is no sales tax and no income tax. Utilities are surprisingly low at 87.8.

Gas Company: Contact the Enstar Natural Gas Company (907-277-5551; *www.enstarnaturalgas.com*).

Electric Company: Municipal Light & Power (907-279-767; *www.mlandp.com*); Chugach Electric Association, Inc. (907-563-7366; *www.chugachelectric.com*) ; and areas north of Anchorage are serviced by the Matanuska Electric Association (907-761-9300; *www.matanuska.com*).

Phone Company: GCI Cable, Inc. (907-265-5400; *www.gci.com*)

Water/Sewer Company: Anchorage Water and Wastewater Service, Solid Waste Services (907-343-6262; *www.muni.org/sws*).

Cable Company: GCI Cable, Inc. (907-265-5400; *www.gci.com*)

The Tax Axe

Car Registration: The Department of Motor Vehicles requires your car to be registered in Alaska within 10 days. Auto licenses renew every year. Depending on the age of the vehicle, it can run as high as $200 or as low as $0.

Driver's License: Your out-of-state license is good for 90 days. New licenses are $40, which includes testing. Driver's licenses need to be renewed every four years and cost $20.

Sales Tax: There is no sales tax in Anchorage.

State Income Tax: There is no income tax in Alaska.

Retirement Income Tax: There is no retirement income tax in Alaska.

Property Tax: Property is assessed in differing millage rates for different sections of Anchorage. There are 58 Tax Levy Districts with millage rates ranging from 10.94 mills to 16.29 mills. At this writing, the first $150,000 of assessed value of property is exempt from municipal taxes. Contact the Municipal Assessor's Office for Senior Citizen/Disabled Veteran Exemptions (907-343-6770).

Local Real Estate

Overview: The 2004 house-price appreciation ranking for Anchorage places the city in the 106th position with a 9.23 percent increase over the same time period in 2003. The five-year increase sits at a respectable 38.56 percent.

Average price of a three-bedroom/two-bath home: $241,000

Average price of a two-bedroom condo: $135,000

Common Housing Styles: Contemporaries, Ranch, modern multi-level (in higher-end homes), and log cabins. Lots of homes have attached/heated garages, decks, and full basements.

Rental Market: Rental availability changes like the weather in Anchorage, which can change on a dime. One day there will be a ready supply, and the next day, the market will dry up.

Average rent for a two-bedroom apartment: $1,350 per month

Communities Popular With Retirees: Eagle River, Chugiak, and Matanuska-Susitna

Nearby Areas to Consider: Wasilla, 50 miles from Anchorage, is in the heart of the fastest growing area in Alaska. It's large enough to have a few metropolitan amenities, yet small enough to preserve the charm, security, and familiarity that are unique to the Alaska small-town life. Wasilla is not out of the way, it's on the highway and railroad that links Anchorage and Fairbanks. Girdwood, 40 miles south of Anchorage, is nestled among the breathtaking Turnagain Arm fjord and spectacular Mt. Alyeska. It has evolved from a gold-mining town into Alaska's only year-round resort community. In this unique town, you will experience an authentic Alaskan adventure daily.

Earning a Living

Business Climate: Anchorage has enjoyed uninterrupted job growth for the last 16 years. While Alaska's economy is still largely based on resource extraction, there has been a steady increase in the number of service jobs in transportation and logistics, as well as the health-care, retail, and professional services. The oil and gas industry has a relatively small presence in Anchorage, but it is important throughout Alaska. There is a large military presence: Anchorage is home to Elmendorf Air Force Base, Fort Richardson Army Post, and Kulis Air National Guard base. Anchorage International Airport is one of the busiest cargo airports in North America, with more than 560 transcontinental cargo flights weekly. Travelers journeying to Alaska often use Anchorage as a gateway to the rest of the state, and Anchorage supports the tourism industry statewide.

Help in Starting a Business: The Anchorage Economic Development Corporation (907-258-3700; *www.aedcweb.com*) is your one-stop shop when you are considering Anchorage as a business location. The corporation maintains relationships with several local entities that can assist you in getting your business started, from commercial real estate agents and banks to utilities and insurance companies.

Job Market: The job market in Anchorage is good, and it usually stays that way. The unemployment rate is very low and there are a lot of jobs available. The large majority of jobs created in the last decade have been in the retail and service sector. One problem in recruiting workers is getting people to come this far north.

Medical Care

The cost of visiting doctors in Alaska can be expensive. According to a 2001 report, medical service costs 60 percent more in Alaska than it does across the rest of the nation. The U.S. average hospital room rate is $493 per day, but in Anchorage, it's $800. Providence Alaska Medical Center (907-261-2945; *www.providence.org*) is Alaska's largest hospital, and has 341 beds and more than 500 physicians on staff. It is a full-service facility, featuring the state's most advanced medical equipment and treatment systems available. Some features include heart and cancer centers, Alaska's largest emergency department with air ambulance transport, diagnostic, rehabilitation, and surgical services. Alaska Regional Hospital (907-276-1131; *www.alaskaregional.com*) has more than 1,000 employees and a medical staff of 450 independent practitioners. Alaska Regional offers cardiovascular services, a 24-hour emergency department, a comprehensive health-management center, cancer services, diagnostic imaging, and a wide range of surgical services, including neuro, spinal, and orthopedic. Other services include free prostate cancer screenings, health education seminars, and support groups for cancer and stroke survivors.

Services for Seniors

The SeniorCare Senior Information Office (907-269-3680; *www.hss.state.ak.us/dsds*) is your resource and referral for benefits and services for seniors in the state of Alaska, including an up-to-date directory of local physicians who accept Medicaid and Medicare clients. Available programs and services include SeniorCare, prescription drug information, and assistance for seniors. The Anchorage Senior Center (907-258-7823; *http://home.gci.net/~ancsrctr/*) offers referrals and assistance with federal and state programs, housing, and other services. The center has facilities and activities such as craft and exercise classes, weekly dances, and a nurse's station that provides monitoring for certain health conditions. The Older Persons Action Group (907-276-1059) is a private, nonprofit senior advocacy group, that publishes a weekly newspaper, has job-search assistance, training opportunities, income-tax assistance, financial planning, and general advocacy for senior and intergenerational issues.

Continuing Education

Alaska is a diverse state, and its universities offer many classes that are usually not seen in the lower 48 states. For example, there are several classes in Alaska Native studies, including language, culture, and Native perspectives, as well as Alaskan history, with some materials provided by the men and women who lived it. The University of

Alaska Anchorage (907-786-1480; *www.uaa.alaska.edu*) hosts more than 9,453 full-time students. Alaska residents 60 years or older may register for most classes and have tuition waived after they have been admitted to the university. Be aware that registration is on a space available basis only. Use of senior citizen tuition waivers is governed accordingly. The Student Government Fee and Student Media Fee are waived for senior citizens, while the Student Life Fees are mandatory for all students taking three or more credits on the Anchorage campus. Registration using a senior citizen tuition waiver for payment is permitted only during late registration. Alaska Pacific University (907-564-8428; *www.alaskapacific.edu*) is the only accredited private liberal-arts university in the state. Its enrollment currently stands at 504 full-time students.

Crime and Safety

In August 2002, Anchorage had a crime rate of 5,118 per 100,000 people. Property and violent crime has decreased in the municipality by more than 30 percent since 1997. The Anchorage Police Department supports specialized units, such as the K-9 and emergency-response teams, and also promotes the Crime Stoppers program. A Neighborhood Crime Watch program has been implemented to assist residential neighborhoods.

Getting Around Town

Public Transportation: The People Mover Bus (907-343-6544; *www.muni.org/transit1/bus.cfm*) is Anchorage's primary municipal transportation system. AnchorRIDES is a shared ride service providing curb-to-curb trips for people with disabilities and senior citizens. The municipality and its contractor provide the service as part of the Anchorage public transportation system.

Roads and Highways: You probably won't get lost, because there aren't that many highways in Alaska. All the highways have numbers, but most Alaskans can give you directions using names. For example, the Seward Highway (Highway 1) connects Anchorage and Seward, but, oddly, and for no particular reason, it becomes Highway 9 halfway down the Kenai Peninsula. The Glenn Highway (also Highway 1) connects Anchorage to Palmer, and points north. In town, most east-west streets are numbered, but several have names such as Dimond Boulevard and Tudor Road, and the north-south ones are alphabetical, such as Barrow and Cordova.

Airports: Anchorage International Airport (*www.dot.state.ak.us/anc*) earned the top rating of excellence in the airport category of "Over One Million Tons of Cargo" by *Air Cargo World*. The airport also has an enormous passenger service, with 4.8 million passengers served in 2004, and revenue of over $69.2 million. It has 17 domestic and five international airlines providing passenger services.

Ports: Alaska's Regional Port (907-343-6201; *www.muni.org/port*) has a five-berth terminal. More than five million tons of various commodities moved across the docks in 2005. Anchorage is served regularly by two major carriers that bring four to five ships weekly from the Pacific Northwest.

Let the Good Times Roll

Recreation: Alaska boasts some of the best fishing in the world, and Anchorage residents often fish within just 40 miles of the city. Trout fishing is excellent and the salmon fishing is unparalleled. Anchorage is one of the few cities in the world where fish can be caught safely in the heart of downtown. Ship Creek runs from the Chugach Mountains to Cook Inlet, and supports several species of salmon. More than 60 glaciers can be found within 50 miles of Anchorage. The most frequently visited is Portage Glacier, a mere 45 miles south of Anchorage. A trip to the glacier is a must for your family and friends when they come to visit. The municipality maintains 235 parks totaling 14,942 acres, 74 playgrounds, 48 tennis courts, 107 ball fields, 18 ice-skating areas (indoor and outdoor), 126 miles of ski trails, and 134 miles of paved bike trails. There are four community recreation centers, six pools, two campgrounds, and two municipal golf courses (in addition to military-owned and privately owned golf courses). Premier winter attractions in Anchorage include more than 124 miles of groomed cross-country ski trails, of which 25 miles are lighted for night skiing. Downhill skiing, sledding, hiking, snowboarding, dog sledding, and ice-skating are also popular winter activities. Mt. Alyeska, home to the state's largest ski resort, is just a 40-minute drive south of the city. For those who prefer to exercise indoors, Anchorage has several athletic clubs, including Gold's Gym and the Alaska Club, which offer indoor tennis, track, racquetball, swimming, weights, and aerobics. You can swim by visiting any of the municipal swimming pools located at the local high school.

Culture: The Anchorage Opera, the Anchorage Concert Chorus, and the Anchorage Concert Association currently top the classical music scene. Located next to Town Square Park in downtown Anchorage, the Alaska Center for the Performing Arts is a three-part complex that hosts many performing arts events. The Anchorage Museum of History and Art offers the opportunity to view splendid objects from Alaska's past and present. The collections and exhibits, lectures, films, children's programs, and special events attract more than 250,000 residents and travelers annually. The Alaska Native Heritage Center provides programs in both academic and informal settings including workshops, demonstrations, and guided tours of indoor exhibits and outdoor village sites.

Annual Events: January has the Great Alaska Beer and Barleywine Festival. The WinterFest, also in January, brings the Polar Bear Plunge, snowboard competitions, and Mountain Bike Slalom. The big February event is the Anchorage Fur Rendezvous, commonly known as the Fur Rondy. It's a wild, wacky, and truly Alaskan way to have fun every February. The Duct Tape Ball is also held in February. March has the ACVB Torchlight Ski Parade, which is a cross-country ski event for all ages and skill levels, and calls for you to BYOL (Bring Your Own Light). The Iditarod Trail Sled Dog Race runs from Anchorage to Nome, and is known as "The Last Great Race." The Alyeska Spring Carnival & Slush Cup is a festival of snowsports and music held in April. The Eagle River Nature Center Seymour Challenge in May is a 10K race for ages 12 and older, and starts the annual summer running season. The Visitor Industry Charity Walk, often referred to as the "5K Buffet," may be the only event where participants feast along the entire route! In June, the Three Barons Renaissance Fair steps back into time to the traditions and culture of the Renaissance. Spirit Days in June is the largest celebration of American Indian and Alaska Native cultures. The Mayor's Midnight Sun Marathon in June draws runners and walkers from all over the world to compete in five marathon events. The Alaskan Scottish Highland Games are also held in June. In July, the Girdwood Forest Fair is set in the forest along Glacier Creek. Many events are held on July Fourth, including a 5K fun run and Teddy Bear Picnic. August brings the Alyeska Blueberry & Mountain Arts Festival with great food, wine, creative arts, and crafts for all ages. The Great Alaska Salmon Bake and Flyby in August is complete with vintage aircraft and flyby's from around the state. During Humpy's Marathon, beautiful scenery will stimulate the senses, but the biggest concern may be encountering the local moose. In September, the Alaska State Fair has monster vegetables, local music, fun crafts, and the Alaska State Rodeo. In October, the Nye Frontier Hockey Classic consists of four top-ranked college teams competing in a fast-paced hockey tournament. In November, the Great Alaska Shootout brings a pre-season college basketball tournament. Thanksgiving weekend begins the Anchorage "City of Lights" holiday season, with the Town Square Tree Lighting Ceremony, the Cincinnati Ballet performing *The Nutcracker*, and the Annual Crafts Weekend at the Museum of History and Art. The Anchorage International Film Festival is held in December with a provocative showcase of some of the best independent film and video from around the world.

When the Grandkids Come: The Imaginarium is a hands-on science discovery center aimed at entertaining and teaching kids of all ages about science, nature, and space. Kid-friendly events are usually held at the beginning of the Iditarod and the Fur Rondy. In addition, try going fishing, the Musk Ox Farm, or a visit to the local reindeer.

More Information

Municipal

The Anchorage Chamber of Commerce

441 West 5th Avenue Suite 300

Anchorage, AK 99501

907-272-2401

www.anchoragechamber.org

Newspaper

The Anchorage Daily News

1001 Northway Drive

Anchorage, AK 99514

800-478-4200

www.adn.com

Realty

We do not have a Realtor recommendation for Anchorage. As an option, check out *www.realtor.com* or *www.homegain.com.* Select a Realtor with both CRS and GRI designations after their names, since it means that these folks have gone the extra mile and are both graduates of the Realtor Institute and Certified Residential Specialists.

2

Homer, Alaska

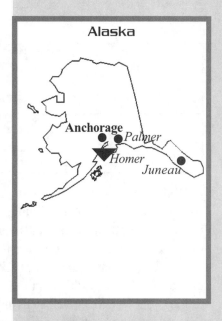

Alaska

Anchorage • • Palmer
▼ Homer Juneau

Homer at a Glance

Homer is one of the last truly great places in the country to exercise your pioneering spirit and sense of adventure. Add some of the most spectacular views imaginable, and you've got a thumbnail sketch of this part of Alaska. Geographically, it sits at the end of the Kenai Peninsula, almost due south of Anchorage. Locals have dubbed it "the end of the road," although it's also called "the banana coast" because of the great weather. The Sterling Highway, which was recently named one of the scenic byways of America, connects Homer to the rest of Alaska. The Homer Spit, a long, narrow finger of land that stretches halfway across Kachemak Bay, is home to a boat harbor with room for 700 charter and commercial fishing boats year-round, and upwards of 1,500 in summer. The Spit also has a luxury hotel/motel, as well as several summer diversions, including the Pier One Community Theatre, boardwalk, restaurants, as well as charter offices and a ship's chandler. Homer calls itself the home of the best halibut fishing in the world. It also has world-class salmon fishing, wildlife viewing, tours by boat or plane, kayaking tours, and the Kachemak Bay Shorebird Festival. For the artist, there are several art stores along Pioneer Avenue in addition to the Bunnell Street Art Gallery and the Pratt Museum.

Possible Drawbacks: Alaska can be "too far away" for many folks. It may be too quiet for some, or too dark in winter for others. And although the art and theatre are top-notch, the weather may cause some concern, as it makes getting around a little difficult.

▸ Nickname: The End of the Road
▸ Borough: Kenai
▸ Area Code: 907
▸ Population: 5,332
▸ Borough Population: 49,691
▸ Percent of Population Over 65: 8.9%
▸ Region: Kenai Peninsula
▸ Closest Metropolitan Area: Anchorage, 200 miles
▸ Median Home Price: $112,400
▸ Best Reasons to Retire Here: The spectacular natural scenery, lots of privacy, great fishing and hunting, strong arts community and a great senior center, and free community college opportunities for seniors.

Climate

59° N Latitude 151° W Longitude	Average High Temperature (°F)	Average Low Temperature (°F)	Precipitation (")	Sunshine (%)
January	27.3	14.7	2.4	34
April	39.6	25.7	1.2	50
July	60.8	44.1	2.4	43
October	40.5	28.6	3.9	36
YEAR	42.3	28.8	29.9	41

Utilities

Overview: The cost of living, according to the latest available data, is nearly 8.5 percent higher than the national average, with housing about 12 percent higher. Health care is average. However, groceries and transportation are an expensive 15 percent higher than the national average. Utilities are level with the national average with the exception of water, which is nine percent higher. However, savings can be made by drilling your own water well, or living just outside the city limits. In addition, many people shop in Soldotna, a larger city 70 miles to the north that provides reasonably priced groceries, clothing, and appliances.

Gas Company: At this time, there is no local natural gas service. Propane gas is available through Alaska Propane (907-235-8586) and is normally used for cooking stoves, and some auxiliary heating stoves. Tanks are leased from the company at less than $100 per year, and auto-fill is the most practical method for the average user. Yearly cost will vary according to usage, but the average monthly cost in 2003 to run a small heating unit as an auxiliary in a 2,000-square-foot house averaged $104 per month.

Electric Company: The Homer Electric Association, Inc. (907-235-8551) serves the Homer area. Initial installation runs $40, but is dependant on credit rating. The average monthly cost for electric power to a 2,000-square-foot house is $125.

Phone Company: You have choices here. Alaska Communications Systems (800-478-7121) offers local, long-distance, wireless, and Internet services. GCI (800-770-1212) offers local, long-distance, wireless, TV cable, and Internet services. In each case, the deposit is $50, but may be waived with a letter of credit.

Water/Sewer Company: Homer Public Works (907-235-3170) can answer all your questions regarding billing for these services. The sign-up fee is $100. Water costs can be expected to average about $150 per month inside the city.

Cable Company: GCI Cable (907-235-6366; *www.gci.net*)

The Tax Axe

Car Registration: The Department of Motor Vehicles requires your car to be registered in Alaska within 10 days. Auto licenses renew every year. Depending on the age of the vehicle, it can run as high as $200 or as low as $0.

Driver's License: Your out-of-state license is good for 90 days. New licenses are $40, which includes testing. Your driver's license needs to be renewed every four years and costs $20.

Sales Tax: 3.5 percent (city) and 2 percent (borough), making the overall sales tax 5.5 percent, which is modest by most standards.

State Income Tax: There is no income tax in Alaska.

Retirement Income Tax: There is no retirement income tax in Alaska.

Property Tax: 5 mills (City); 6.5 mills (Borough). So, for a $100,000 home, the taxes would amount to $1,150 per year.

Local Real Estate

Overview: You have many choices in Homer's growing housing market. "Little jewels" may be found on the main streets or tucked away along rural lanes. Imposing log homes, as well as traditionally constructed houses, are available throughout the area. The cost of materials shipped to the far north makes new construction prohibitive in some cases. But for many who move here, the opportunity to live in basically unspoiled grandeur makes up for the additional expense.

Average price of a three-bedroom/two-bath home: $168,000

Average price of a two-bedroom condo: $75,000

Common Housing Styles: Houses reflect the taste and budget of the owners in Alaska. From old-timers' cabins in the woods to mansions on the hillsides, and everything in between—you'll see it all in Homer. Gardens abound in summer, with flowers blooming in the ground, on decks, and in hanging baskets. Kachemak Bay, and the mountains beyond, provide food for meditation, home to wildlife, and one of the most spectacular scenes, which is commonly known as "the million dollar view."

Rental Market: Because there are many out-of-state landowners, some rentals are available throughout the year. Like housing styles, rentals can range from cabins with minimal luxuries to elegant homes with custom touches throughout.

Average rent for a two-bedroom apartment: $500 per month

Communities Popular With Retirees: Fritz Creek, Anchor Point, and Happy Valley, although unincorporated, offer options that are close to nature.

Nearby Areas to Consider: Kodiak Island, south of Homer in the Pacific, is famous for huge Kodiak brown bears, world-class sport fishing, and one of the largest commercial fishing ports in the nation. The island is affectionately called Alaska's Emerald Isle, because it turns a magnificent green during the summer. The Kodiak Island Borough, with a population of 13,900, includes the city of Kodiak, seven villages, the U.S. Coast Guard Base, plus several camps and lodges. Cooper Landing is located along the Kenai River in the mountains north of Homer. You can enjoy the scenic river as it winds to Cook Inlet, and see dall sheep and mountain goats along the hillside.

Earning a Living

Business Climate: The largest employers in Homer are the local hospital, school system, and government agencies. Small business owners provide the community with good restaurants, art galleries, retail operations, services, and a variety of entertainment.

Help in Starting a Business: Sundog Consultants (907-235-5971) is available to guide the new business entrepreneur from startup to bookkeeping, payroll to management, and tax to retirement planning. The Small Business Development Center in Soldotna (907-262-7497) provides several services to individuals seeking to start small businesses.

Job Market: Because Homer has a growing tourism economy, jobs are available primarily throughout the summer.

Medical Care

The South Peninsula Hospital in Homer (907-235-8101) is a 122-bed acute-care facility that serves Homer, Seldovia, Anchor Point, Fritz Creek, Nanwalek, and Ninilchik. The hospital has facilities for emergency services as well as surgery, radiology, physical therapy, and long-term care. It has a heli-pad on-site that links Homer with the larger Anchorage hospitals.

Services for Seniors

Contact Homer Senior Citizens, Inc. (907-235-7655; *www.homerseniors.com*) for information on services that include the Friendship Center (adult daycare), Friendship Terrace (assisted living), Independent Senior Housing for those over 55, as well as transportation to and from the center, or to doctors' appointments. In addition, hot meals are delivered to seniors unable to get to the center for lunch. Support is offered in housekeeping chores, Social Security, tax preparation, energy, weatherization, applications for assistance, and property taxes. Medicare/Medigap insurance counseling is available through the Senior Services Division of Alaska (1-800-478-6065). After age 60, seniors are issued permanent fishing, hunting, and trapping licenses by the state of Alaska.

Continuing Education

The Kachemak Bay Branch of Kenai Peninsula College (907-235-7743) offers academic and continuing education classes free to seniors if space is available. Some classes can be taken for credit. At any given time, you might find the following diverse classes offered: psychology, Alaska history, computer classes, creative writing, local biology, intercultural studies, small-aircraft pilot training, or ballroom dancing.

Crime and Safety

Homer's crime rate has dropped in recent years. Although it was never a high rate, the decline has probably been influenced by the increase in cooperation between the city police force and local citizens. Property crimes decreased from 49 to 38 incidents per

1,000 people between 2003 and 2004. In the surrounding areas the crime rate is approximately 55 incidents per 1,000 people.

Getting Around Town

Public Transportation: Homer boasts that it doesn't have a single stop light. Some residents fear that this situation will change. Others fear that it will not. In any case, getting around town is as easy as hopping on your bike, or calling one of the local cab companies: Chux (907-235-2489), Kache Cab (907-235-1950), or Kostas (907-399-8008). No other public transportation exists.

Roads and Highways: Homer really is at "the end of the road." There is only one road out of town, the Sterling Highway, which runs from Homer north to Tern Lake Junction. Turn left and the Seward Highway will take you all the way to Anchorage. Or turn right, and you will be on your way to the city of Seward. Watch out for bears!

Airports: The Homer Airport sits between Beluga Lake and Kachemak Bay. For short flights across the bay or inlet, Homer Air (907-235-8591) or Beluga Lake Float Plane Service (907-235-8256) offer single-engine transport. To fly to Anchorage International Airport, call Era Aviation (800-866-8394). You will also want to acquaint yourself with Alaska Airlines in Anchorage. The airline provides service to more than 100 locations in the lower 48 states.

Let the Good Times Roll

Recreation: Although Homer is in Alaska, the weather is milder than most of the Midwest. There are a number of things to do in the wintertime, including cross-country skiing, dog-sledding, snowmobiling, aquacize classes, or lap swimming in the Homer High school pool. Many opportunities for entertainment are available throughout the year, from concerts in the park to movies at the Homer Theater (907-235-6728), to plays at Pier One Theatre (907-235-7333), to foreign films at Kachemak Bay Campus (907-235-7743). There are also hiking trails, kayaking, boating, sight-seeing tours, and camping throughout the summer.

Culture: Homer is home to a number of local artists who work in many media. The Bunnell Street Gallery (907-235-2662), Homer Council on the Arts (907-235-4288), and several retail art stores display paintings, sculpture, and handmade jewelry, as well as Native art. The Pratt Museum (907-235-8635) is a distinguished natural history museum, which displays (in addition to a permanent collection) traveling shows that change every few months. World-class music lives in Homer in the musicianship of the Kenai Peninsula Orchestra.

Annual Events: New Year's is the time to celebrate with fireworks, because in July the sun doesn't set until way after bedtime for the children. Then in February, "Cabin Fever" brings everyone out for a Mardi Gras parade. In March, "World Cafe" allows Homer's singers and dancers to shine on stage in a variety show that's not to be missed. March also has the Homer Winter King Salmon Tournament. April has a home and garden show, and June brings the summer solstice, midnight games, food, and fun for the entire family, in Kenai, about 80 miles north of Homer. In July there are traditional celebrations on the Fourth. In August, the Kenai Peninsula presents the Kenai Peninsula State Fair, "Alaska's Biggest Little Fair." Oktoberfest takes care of October, while November is Thanksgiving and the beginning of the holiday season. Bridging November and December is *The Nutcracker*, a local tradition for more than 15 years.

When the Grandkids Come: Well, if they show up in the summer, they can participate in any number of art classes at the Council on the Arts (907-235-4288). Or, the kids can accompany an adult and tour the Alaska Islands and Oceans Visitor Center (907-235-6961). Pier One offers acting classes at the theater on the Spit, or The Fishing Hole provides excellent salmon fishing for the young, and not-so-young. Homer has horseback riding on East End Road at the Trails End Horse Adventures (907-235-6393). Do the kids like whales? Rainbow Tours (907-235-7272) can provide reasonable rates for half day or full day excursions.

More Information

Municipal
Homer Chamber of Commerce
201 Sterling Highway
Homer, AK 99603
907-235-7740
www.homeralaska.org

Newspaper
Homer News
3482 Landings Street
Homer, AK 99603
907-235-7767
www.homernews.com

Realty
Annie Whitney
Alderfer Group
1213 Ocean Drive #1
Homer, AK 99603
907-235-5299
www.alderfergroup.com

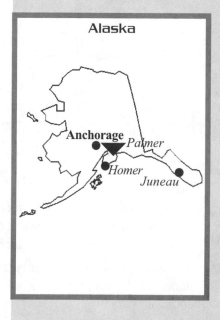

Alaska

3 ▶ Palmer, Alaska

Palmer at a Glance

If you're up for some rural living in the last frontier, it doesn't get better than this. Palmer is located in the center of the lush farmlands of the Matanuska Valley, 42 miles northeast of Anchorage. Palmer offers country-style living and recreation along with a distinctly modern community. Ringed by rugged mountains on three sides, the valley cradles the farms and dairy herds, which yield two thirds of Alaska's agricultural products. More than 40 bushels per acre of barley and oats are common. Major crops grown here include potatoes, lettuce, carrots, peas, squash, radishes, cauliflower, broccoli, and cabbage. (Some can grow up to 100 pounds!) Palmer is home to 200 musk oxen whose underwool (qiviut) is knitted into garments by Alaska Native women from 12 rural villages. Between 2,500 and 3,500 garments are created each year and sold by an Anchorage cooperative. The 75-acre musk ox farm just east of town is also a tourist attraction. If you want to grow a killer garden, this is the place to be. Palmer holds the Guinness World Record for "Biggest Broccoli," achieved in 1993 with a 35-pound specimen. You will find mild summers in the Matanuska Valley with long daylight hours and an average temperature of 60 degrees Fahrenheit. Winters on the other hand, are brisk, with moderate snowfall and an average temperature of 20 degrees Fahrenheit.

Possible Drawbacks: The temperature drops below freezing 194 days a year. The average temperature in January is 8 degrees Fahrenheit, and those cold nights are long.

▶ Nickname: Home of the Alaska State Fair

▶ Borough: Matanuska-Susitna

▶ Area Code: 907

▶ Population: 4,553

▶ Borough Population: 59,322

▶ Percent of Population Over 65: 9.1%

▶ Region: South central Alaska

▶ Closest Metropolitan Area: Anchorage, 42 miles

▶ Median Home Price: $110,100

▶ Best Reasons to Retire Here: Fantastic scenery and wilderness adventures. This is the place to grow a great garden during the endless summer!

Climate

61° N Latitude 149° W Longitude	Average High Temperature (°F)	Average Low Temperature (°F)	Precipitation (")	Sunshine (%)
January	21.0	5.5	0.9	34
April	44.4	27.1	0.5	50
July	66.2	48.4	2.3	43
October	41.4	26.2	1.6	36
YEAR	43.3	26.6	16.0	41

Utilities

Overview: The cost of living index puts Palmer at 111.6, which is above the national average of 100. The items that raise that cost are health care and food. Housing and utility costs are both below average.

Gas Company: There is currently no natural gas in Palmer. Heating is commonly done with delivered propane or heating oil, or by electricity. Wood burning stoves are common.

Electric Company: Matanuska Electric Association (*www.matanuska.com*) is part owner of the Alaska Electric Generation & Transmission Cooperative, Inc., which operates a gas turbine plant in Soldotna, and also purchases a percentage of electricity from Chugach Electric and the Bradley Lake Hydroelectric Project.

Phone Company: MTA Solutions (907-745-6600; *www.mtasolutions.com*)

Water/Sewer Company: Water is provided by three deep wells. It is treated and distributed throughout Palmer. Sewage is collected by pipe and treated in an aerated lagoon facility (*www.co.mat-su.ak.us/PublicWorks/talkeetna.cfm*).

Cable Company: There is no cable currently available in Palmer.

The Tax Axe

Car Registration: The Department of Motor Vehicles requires your car to be registered in Alaska within 10 days. Auto licenses renew every year. Depending on the age of the vehicle, it can run as high as $200 or as low as $0.

Driver's License: Your out-of-state license is good for 90 days. New licenses are $40.00, which includes testing. Your driver's license needs to be renewed every four years and costs $20. You should contact the Department of Motor Vehicles for more information about transferring your out-of-state license.

Sales Tax: The borough sales tax is 3 percent.

State Income Tax: There is no state income tax in Alaska.

Retirement Income Tax: There is no retirement income tax in Alaska.

Property Tax: The charges on assessed value are 3 mills by the city and 11.73 mills by the borough.

Local Real Estate

Overview: This area is growing, but you can still get a good-sized house on a larger lot for less money than in other places. There are great mountain-view lots and horse properties available. Lakefront properties usually run a bit more, depending on the area. The further away the house is from the city, the more you can get for your money.

Average price of a three-bedroom/two-bath home: $200,000

Average price of a two-bedroom condo: There are no condominium units available within 20 miles of Palmer.

Common Housing Styles: The styles vary from modern frame construction to rustic log. Most houses are custom-built by the owner, so many of them are unique and the styles vary widely.

Rental Market: A quarter of the residents in Palmer are renting. Most renting is seasonal. Many people live in Alaska part of the year and rent their houses the rest of the year, while others build cabins or simple houses to be inhabited only in the summer by renters.

Average rent of a two-bedroom apartment: $557 per month

Communities Popular With Retirees: Anchorage, the largest city in Alaska, is just 40 miles away. It offers a range of services, along with great entertainment, state-of-the-art health-care, convenient air travel, and good food in many international flavors!

Nearby Areas to Consider: Wasilla is also in the Mat-Su Valley to the west of Palmer. Wasilla has become the "restart" point of the Iditarod. The ceremonial start is in Anchorage, but the dogs ride in trucks to Wasilla to begin the long trail to Nome. The Iron Dog Race is a contest in which team's race snowmobiles from Fairbanks to Nome and finish in Wasilla. To the north of Palmer is Talkeetna, located in the shadow of Denali (Mt. McKinley) and at the junction of three rivers, with scenic vistas, salmon fishing, rafting, and boating excursions.

Earning a Living

Business Climate: Palmer's economy is based on a diversity of retail and other services, including tourism; agriculture; and city, borough, state, and federal government. Some light manufacturing occurs.

Help in Starting a Business: The Small Business Development program in Anchorage (907-269-8110; *www.dced.state.ak.us/*) helps individuals find the resources and information they need to pursue small business goals. Programs offered by the Palmer Chamber of Commerce throughout the year give businesses a chance to network, make new contacts, and make a difference in the community.

Job Market: The unemployment rate is 12.8 percent. More than half the jobs held by citizens of Palmer are in Anchorage, and the 45 mile commute is done by car. Currently, 79 residents of Palmer hold commercial fishing permits.

Medical Care

Valley Hospital in Palmer (907-746-8600; *www.valley-hosp.com*) is a 39-bed short-term hospital that is a Medicare and Medicaid participant, and has a full service emergency department and clinical laboratory. Nearby Anchorage has Providence Medical Center, (907-261-2945; *www.providence.org*), which is a 307-bed short-term facility, and is the largest hospital in Alaska, featuring the state's most comprehensive range of services and the most advanced medical equipment and treatment systems available.

Services for Seniors

The Palmer Senior Citizens Center (907-746-3374) provides a number of senior services and is the coordination point for many others, such as the Meals on Wheels program. Adult Day Services of the PSCC provides such services as meals and Alzheimer's support. The Alaska Food Coalition (907-222-3107; *www.alaskafood.org*) is a statewide group of more than 30 nonprofit and faith-based agencies working every day to help feed hungry Alaskans.

Continuing Education

The University of Alaska in Anchorage (*www.uaa.alaska.edu*) is the largest in the state. Alaska residents 60 years or older may enroll for most UAA credit classes and have tuition waived. Senior citizens must register and present a completed tuition waiver with proof of age during late registration.

Crime and Safety

The national index puts the Palmer violent crime rate at 748, where the national average is 495. The number of instances of property crime is below the national average of 4,325 at 3,760. The number of violent crimes recorded by the FBI in 2003 was 56. The number of murders and homicides was 0. The violent crime rate was 10.3 per 1,000 people.

Getting Around Town

Public Transportation: There is no public transportation in Palmer.

Roads and Highways: Palmer lies on the Glenn Highway, which goes south to Anchorage and north to the interior of Alaska. Close by is the intersection of the Parks Highway, which travels to Denali and on to Fairbanks. The Alaska Railroad connects Palmer to Anchorage, Whittier, and Seward to the south, and to Fairbanks in the north.

Airports: Several commercial airlines serve the Anchorage International Airport. The Palmer Municipal Airport supports private and chartered services. There are seven additional privately-owned airstrips in the vicinity. Float planes land at nearby Finger Lake and Wolf Lake.

Let the Good Times Roll

Recreation: State parks, historic landmarks, museums, and farms are but a few of the attractions gaining popularity among visitors to the Mat-Su Valley. The twin outdoor horse show-rings at the fairgrounds are busy for much of the summer. Up to 200 horses are entered in the larger shows, and top judges are often brought in to judge the competitions. Palmer has become the gateway to Alaska's foremost recreation area with campgrounds, glacier-carved valleys, and more than 50 resorts. On a typical weekend, Anchorage residents converge on the mountains, streams, and lakes of the Palmer-Wasilla-Big Lake area. Hatcher Pass, 20 miles north of Palmer, opens onto mountain summits that show you picturesque views of the valley. Hiking, biking, and year-round multiple-use trails are available to Hatcher Pass visitors. From July to September you can continue through Hatcher Pass to Willow (60 miles away) and return to Palmer via Big Lake. Nova Whitewater Rafting offers fantastic whitewater rafting on several rivers in the area. Nestled at the base of majestic Pioneer Peak in Palmer, Alaska Raceway Park supports a full season of drag race events. You can also visit the Independence Mine State Historical Park and catch a glimpse of Alaska's mining heritage.

Culture: About 20 percent of Alaskan citizens are descendants of natives, and this culture is everywhere and is part of daily life. Items from Palmer's pioneer era are displayed at the Palmer Visitor Information Center Museum, a rustic log cabin in the center of town, which is open year-round. Here you can also see and purchase items of some 100 local artists, much of which is on consignment. Several authors and artists are among Alaska's pioneer citizens, all of whom have interesting stories to tell. Nearby Anchorage has an active arts community, with a number of art galleries, active theatres, and a variety of concerts each year.

Annual Events: Each summer, from May through July, enthusiasts compete for prizes in the Mat-Su King Salmon Derby (*www.matsukingsalmonderby.com*). The Alaska State Fair is held at the Palmer Fairgrounds in the last week of August. The state's largest fair has craft booths, live entertainment, and farm exhibits, including 100-pound cabbages and other supreme agricultural products from Alaska's famous Matanuska Valley. Other attractions include a rodeo, a three-day state championship horse show, a well-rounded display of fair exhibits, continuous entertainment, as well as athletic contests. You can eat a variety of food, from turkey legs and crab cakes to cream puffs. Palmer Colony Days is a three-day event held in June to honor the first colonist who arrived in the Mat-Su area. There is an arts and crafts fair, horse-drawn wagon rides, shopping cart races, children's games and more.

When the Grandkids Come: Take them downhill skiing, snowboarding, cross-country skiing, dog sledding, snowmobiling (called snow-machining in Alaska), four wheeling, or whitewater rafting. The fishing, glaciers, state parks, and mountains all provide great opportunities for adventure, as do the eagles, moose, bear, and the musk-ox farm.

More Information

Municipal

Greater Palmer Chamber of Commerce
P.O. Box 45
Palmer, AK 99645
907-745-2880
www.palmerchamber.org

Matanuska-Susitna Valley Convention and Visitor's Bureau
HC 01 Box 6166 J21
Palmer, AK 99645
907-746-5000
www.alaskavisit.com

Newspaper

Anchorage Daily News
Box 149001
Anchorage, AK 99514
907-257-4547
www.adn.com

Realty

We do not have a Realtor recommendation for Palmer. As an option, check out *www.realtor.com* or *www.homegain.com*. Select a Realtor with both CRS and GRI designations after their names, since it means that these folks have gone the extra mile and are both graduates of the Realtor Institute and Certified Residential Specialists.

4 ▶ Prescott, Arizona

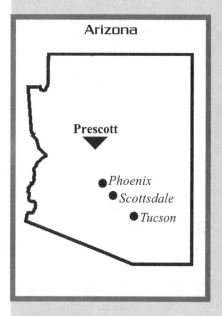

Arizona

Prescott

● *Phoenix*
● *Scottsdale*
● *Tucson*

Prescott at a Glance

Surrounded by the largest stand of Ponderosa Pines in the world, Prescott is the kind of town that steals your heart the first time you see it. Dubbed "Everyone's Hometown," Prescott is home to the downtown Courthouse Plaza, famous Whiskey Row, World's Oldest Rodeo, Prescott Fine Arts Association, Sharlot Hall Museum, Phippen Art Museum, Folk Arts Fair, Frontier Days, and Territorial Days. Prescott is smack in the middle of the Grand Canyon state of Arizona. It is located in the mountains of north central Arizona, approximately 96 miles northwest of Phoenix, and it borders the Prescott National Forest to the south and west. Prescott's average elevation is 5,400 feet, so the local climate is mild. The Courthouse Plaza, well known throughout Arizona as symbolizing the quintessential Mid-western downtown square, is located in the center of downtown and framed by towering elms. It is the focal point for many activities, including crafts fairs and antique shows. Five area lakes exist within 10 miles of downtown. The 1.2-million-acre Prescott National Forest contains numerous hiking trails and other outdoor recreational opportunities. The city places great emphasis on historic preservation, with more than 500 buildings on the National Register of Historic Places.

Possible Drawbacks: No matter what else it is, Prescott is still a small town, so shopping and cultural events are limited. Also, the altitude of 5,400 feet could cause breathing problems for some, so check with your physician.

▶ Nickname: Everyone's Hometown

▶ County: Yavapui

▶ Area Code: 928

▶ Population: 33,939

▶ County Population: 167,517

▶ Percent of Population Over 65: 26.8%

▶ Region: Central Arizona

▶ Closest Metropolitan Area: Phoenix, 99 miles

▶ Median Home Price: $297,000

▶ Best Reasons to Retire Here: Mild weather year-round and a small town western feel to the community. It's just big enough for medical services, shopping, and cultural events.

Climate

34° N Latitude 112° W Longitude	Average High Temperature (°F)	Average Low Temperature (°F)	Precipitation (")	Sunshine (%)
January	50.2	21.9	1.7	77
April	64.9	33.4	0.8	82
July	88.0	57.7	2.9	75
October	71.1	37.9	1.1	79
YEAR	68.2	37.4	19.2	78

Utilities

Overview: With the national cost of living index of 100, Prescott is slightly high at 103.6. In fact, it's slightly high in all categories, with groceries at 105.72, housing at 102.1, utilities at 100.08, transportation at 104.93, healthcare at 108.71, and the miscellaneous category at 104.08.

Gas Company: Natural gas is provided by Unisource Energy Services (928-445-2211). Propane can be provided by Amerigas, Ferrell Gas, and Flame Propane.

Electric Company: Arizona Public Service (800-253-9405)

Phone Company: Qwest Communications (800-244-1111)

Water/Sewer Company: The City of Prescott (928-777-129; *www.cityofprescott.net*)

Cable Company: Cable One (928-541-7530; *www.cableone.com*)

The Tax Axe

Car Registration: The car registration fee is $13.50. In addition, the state assesses a vehicle license tax. The amount is determined by the manufacturer's sticker price when the car was new. The value of the car is reduced 40 percent after the first year, and 15 percent each year thereafter. The tax is 4 percent of the car's value.

Driver's License: The driver's license fees get cheaper as you get older. Residents over 50 pay $10. If you have a current out-of-state driver's license, you will normally not have to take a written or road test. However, you may be required to take a written or road test any time that you apply for a license.

Sales Tax: City 2 percent, county 0.7 percent, state 5.6 percent—for a total of 8.3 percent.

State Income Tax: The state tax rate varies from 10 percent to 32 percent of your federal tax amount.

Retirement Income Tax: U.S. government and Arizona government pensions can be partially subtracted when figuring state income, but other pensions cannot.

Property Tax: $9.36 per assessed $100 of value

Local Real Estate

Overview: Much of the real estate here is organized and developed with retirees in mind. There are a number of communities designed specifically for retirement. The majority of retirees live here permanently, but some live here only in the winter and maintain summer homes further north.

Average price of a three-bedroom/two-bath home: $313,000

Average price of a two-bedroom condo: $205,000

Common Housing Styles: Prescott has a wide range of real estate options, from two-bedroom condos and town homes, ideal for second homes or weekend getaways, to established and respected neighborhoods and communities of single-family homes, and private gated golf-equestrian communities.

Rental Market: Prescott has a very active rental market, with the average for a two-bedroom home renting at $700 per month.

Average rent for a two-bedroom apartment: $575 per month

Communities Popular With Retirees: Hassayampa, Talking Rock Ranch, American Ranch, Granite Oaks, Pronghorn Ranch, Pinon Oaks, Forest Trails, Timberridge, Quailwood, Kingswood, Wildwood, Yavapi Hills, The Heritage, Crossroads Ranch, Williamson Valley Estates, Las Vegas Ranch.

Nearby Areas to Consider: Some of the oldest exposed rocks on earth are near Sedona, which has dramatic otherworld scenery with thousand foot formations surrounding a unique town. Sedona has western history in abundance, a thriving arts community, world-class hiking, golf, and the famous Jeep tours. Sedona is one of a kind. *USA Today* recently voted it the most beautiful city in the United States. The town of Payson is located in the rolling hills of the 200-mile-long escarpment named Mogollon Rim. Giant saguaros stand in the lower hills near Payson, forests cover the higher slopes, and rivers run through the surrounding canyons.

Earning a Living

Business Climate: The number one industry of Prescott is tourism. The city actively pursues environmentally clean industries. Prescott Connections (*www.prescottconnections.org*) is a local business networking group with the purpose of producing business-to-business referrals among members. The retirement community has become a significant portion of the population, and services are constantly being added for seniors.

Help in Starting a Business: Yavapai College Small Business Development Center (928-776-2008; 800-922-6787; *www2.yc.edu/content/sbdc*) is a small business support organization formed to counsel and train small businesses, and is an excellent resource for new business owners. The City of Prescott Economic Development Department

(866-878-2489; *www.prescotted.com*) assists in business relocation and expansion. The Small Business Counseling and Education (928-778-7438; 800-410-2260; *www.scorearizona.org/northern_az*) of northern Arizona offers face-to-face and other confidential business no-charge counseling services throughout the northern counties of the state. You can also check with the local Prescott chamber of commerce for more information.

Job Market: The unemployment rate is well below the national average at five percent. The major employers of the city of Prescott are: Sturm Ruger Manufacturing, County of Yavapai, Prescott Unified School District, Yavapai College, U. S. Forest Service, City of Prescott, Yavapai Regional Medical Center, Veterans Administration, State of Arizona, Embry-Riddle Aeronautical University, West Yavapai Guidance Clinic, Sears, Fortner & Gifford, and Exsil.

Medical Care

There are more than 150 practicing physicians in Prescott, as well as many dentists, chiropractors, opticians, and optometrists. The Yavapai Medical Center (928-445-2700; *www.yrmc.org*) is the largest hospital in central Arizona with 117 beds, and is fully accredited with 166 physicians on staff. Verde Valley Medical Center (928-639-6000; *www.nahealth.com*) about 34 miles away in Cottonwood, is a 99-bed hospital serving the Verde Valley, Sedona, and other Coconino County and Yavapai County cities and towns. The Northern Arizona VA Health Care System facility, located in Prescott, is one of the largest veteran's facilities in the Southwest. If you need anything more, Phoenix is only a short drive away.

Services for Seniors

The Adult Center of Prescott (928-778-3000; *www.adultcenter.org*) is all about adults on the move with dances, classes, and many other recreational, cultural, and educational opportunities. Prescott has at least eight long-term care and home-care facilities.

Continuing Education

Yavapai College (928-445-7300; *www.yavapai.cc.az.us*) is a two-year college with a variety of programs offered for adults and retirees. Prescott College (928-778-2090; *www.prescott.edu*) is a four-year institution in which students design their own programs. Northern Arizona University Yavapai (928-445-5231; *www.nau.edu*) is a four-year and graduate level institution with its main campus in Flagstaff, but instructors travel to Prescott to teach, and some courses are offered by distance learning.

Crime and Safety

The crime rate is above the national average. Violent crimes per 100,000 people are 347.5 compared to 276.28 nationally. Property crimes are 4979.1 compared to 2459.35

nationally. The overall crime index, per 100,000 people, is 5,326.6 as compared to 2,735.63 on a national level.

Getting Around Town

Public Transportation: The Prescott Transit Authority (800-445-7978; *www.prescotttransit.com*) runs a shuttle between Prescott and the Phoenix airport. The same agency operates Prescott Whipple Stage, Ace City Cab, Dial-A-Ride, and the Citibus.

Roads and Highways: 17, 69,169, 89, and 89A

Airports: The municipal airport of Prescott is the Ernest A. Love Field (928-445-7860), which is seven miles north of the city and provides local air service as well as daily air service to Phoenix Sky Harbor International Airport.

Let the Good Times Roll

Recreation: Prescott is home to some of the most amazing natural beauty and is a hub of state history, tradition, art, and culture. You will find outstanding recreational possibilities, including backpacking, mountain and street biking, golf, hiking, hunting, fishing, horseback riding, shooting, and swimming, to name a few. Prescott is well known as a popular golf destination, drawing thousands of golf enthusiasts each year. Boasting some of the state's most beautiful, affordable, state-of-the-art public and private golf facilities, Prescott has 108 cool holes of golf and offers year-round play. There are nearly 450 miles of scenic trails for hiking, backpacking, horseback riding, or mountain biking in Prescott National Forest. The forest also contains one National Recreational Trail (Granite Mountain Trail) and one National Historic Study Trail (General Crook Trail). With the mild climate, the trails can be enjoyed year-round. When the sun goes down, Prescott continues to shine. You can enjoy live music, theater, or simply stroll and gaze in wonder at the stars in the northern Arizona sky.

Culture: Prescott hosts several museums. You might be surprised at all the things there are to see and learn about Native American history and culture, the Grand Canyon, wild animals, spiders, trees and flowers, the original buildings that started Prescott, a Victorian house that was moved from one end of town to the other, a stagecoach and Conestoga wagon, theater productions and more. It's all there at the six cultural institutions: the Sharlot Hall Museum, Prescott Fine Arts Museum, the Smoki Museum, Phippen Museum, Heritage Park Zoo, and the Highland Center for Natural History.

Annual Events: The Street Faire is held every Thursday from June through August with live bands, Kidzone, Teenzone, the Dog Park and animal adoptions, vendors, crafters, and more. Nightly Entertainment in Courthouse Square is held June through August. The Prescott Farmers Market is held every Saturday morning from May to October. Also from May to October is the Wine Tasting and Chuckwagon BBQ Dinner at the Granite Creek Vineyards & Winery with their organic, sulfite-free wines. There is also the cowboy Chuckwagon BBQ dinner at the Old Red Barn in

Chino Valley. The Ghost Hunter University is held each April. It is an afternoon class followed by a detailed history of the haunted site over dinner and the guests are led on a truly interactive ghost hunt through the Hotel Vendome. In April is the Whiskey Row Marathon, a two mile fun run/walk. There is also the May in the Meadows Renaissance Faire that features jousting knights. With the weather almost perfect year-round, the list goes on and on.

When the Grandkids Come: Kids Club is held every second and fourth Tuesday with fun for children of all ages with music, songs, interactive educational programs, and a special guest each week. The entire area seems to have been built with kids in mind. And don't forget that the Grand Canyon is only 125 miles away!

More Information

Municipal

Prescott Valley Chamber of Commerce
3001 North Main Street, Suite 2A
Prescott Valley, AZ 86314
928-445-2000
www.pvchamber.org/

Chino Valley Area Chamber of Commerce
864 North U.S. Highway 89
Chino Valley, AZ 86323
www.chinovalley.org
877-523-1988

Newspaper

The Daily Courier
1958 Commerce Center
Prescott, AZ 86301
928-445-3333
www.prescottaz.com

Arizona Republic
6750 Inter-Cal Way
Prescott, AZ 86301
928-445-4181
www.azcentral.com

Realty

Ed Patterman
Windermere Real Estate
325 West Gurley Street
Prescott, AZ
928-778-1166

Scottsdale, Arizona

5

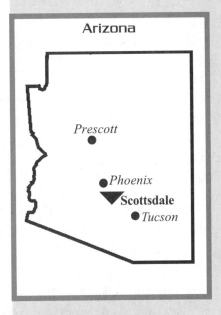

Arizona

Prescott
•

•*Phoenix*
▼**Scottsdale**
•*Tucson*

Scottsdale at a Glance

Scottsdale's relaxed lifestyle, rustic steakhouses, and passion for rodeos have given the city its nickname of "The West's Most Western Town." It has frequent events in a rawhide sort of style, including a replica cowboy town that offers a truly "Old Western" experience. Many shops sell Western clothes and Native American crafts and jewelry, while Fashion Square's designer boutiques and department stores provide a more cosmopolitan shopping scene. Nearby are the Sonoran Desert and McDowell Mountains, where you can enjoy camping, hiking, and other outdoor recreation. Set in the "Valley of the Sun," Scottsdale's climate is conducive to continuous outdoor activity, such as hiking, golfing, river rafting through the Sonoran Desert, and horseback riding in the mountains. You can go hang gliding or hot-air ballooning, which opens up fabulous views across the desert and mountains. Scottsdale has more than 200 golf courses. Downtown Scottsdale contains 585 unique shops, galleries, salons, restaurants, and night spots. There is plenty of free street-side parking and free trolley transportation. The facilities available are like those of a large city, yet the living is more like a small town or a resort. While Scottsdale is incorporated as its own city, it's actually a suburb of Phoenix, and so gives you access to many big city amenities.

Possible Drawbacks: The town fills up with tourists in the summer months, which can become quite hot!

▶ Nickname: The West's Most Western Town

▶ County: Maricopa

▶ Area Code: 480

▶ Population: 215,779

▶ County Population: 3,072,149

▶ Percent of Population Over 65: 12.4%

▶ Region: Central Arizona

▶ Closest Metropolitan Area: Phoenix, 13 miles

▶ Median Home Price: $600,000

▶ Best Reasons to Retire Here: There is warm weather year-round, a relaxed Western atmosphere, lots of golf, and other outdoor recreation.

Climate

33° N Latitude 111° W Longitude	Average High Temperature (°F)	Average Low Temperature (°F)	Precipitation (")	Sunshine (%)
January	65.8	41.2	0.8	78
April	84.8	55.2	0.2	89
July	105.8	81.0	0.8	85
October	88.8	60.8	0.6	88
YEAR	85.8	59.2	7.6	85

Utilities

Overview: The cost of living index is 115 with the national average being 100. Utilities and health-care costs in Scottsdale are higher than average.

Gas Company: Southwest Gas (800-873-2440; *www.swgas.com*)

Electric Company: Electricity is provided by Salt River Project (602-236-8888; *www.srpnet.com*) and by Arizona Public Service (602-250-1000; *www.aps.com*).

Phone Company: Qwest (480-968-0211; *www.qwest.com*)

Water/Sewer Company: Water is supplied by the city of Scottsdale (*www.ci.scottsdale.az.us*).

Cable Company: Cox Communications (623-594-1142; *http://phoenix.cox.net*) provides cable television service.

The Tax Axe

Car Registration: The state of Arizona imposes an annual motor vehicle license tax (VLT). The VLT is based on an assessed value of 60 percent of the manufacturer's base retail price reduced by 16.25 percent for each year since the vehicle was first registered in Arizona. As an example, the VLT for the first year's assessed value (say $15,000, which is 60 percent of a vehicle that costs $25,000) would be $420.

Driver's License: To get your Arizona Driver's License, just take your out-of-state license to the DMV, take the vision test (no written test is required), and, if you are age 50 or older, pay $10 and you'll be ready to go. You do have to supply one other form of identification in addition to your old license, such as a birth certificate, passport, social security card, or even a credit card. These must be originals, not photocopies.

Sales Tax: Arizona currently has a state sales tax of 5.6 percent (food and prescription drugs are exempt). The county adds a 0.7 percent tax. Scottsdale adds 1.69 percent for a total of 7.99 percent.

State Income Tax: The state has an accelerated income tax ranging from 2.87 percent, to 5.04 percent.

Retirement Income Tax: Social Security income is not taxed.

Property Tax: The taxes vary from one district to another, but they are generally low and average something like $11 per $1,000 of value. There is a lot of variation and you should check with the Maricopa County Treasurer (602-506-8511).

Local Real Estate

Overview: A housing boom has been adding value for buyers and profits for sellers. Planned communities are thriving, and offer amenities such as parks, recreation centers, and clubhouses. More of them are including commercial developments, such as office buildings and shopping centers. The village core concept, where people can live, work, and shop right in the immediate area, has become very popular.

Average price of a three-bedroom/two-bath home: $376,300.

Average price of a two-bedroom condo: $345,000.

Common Housing Styles: Tuscan, Santa Barbara, Spanish Mission, Spanish Revival, Mexican Colonial, Santa Fe Territorial, and various contemporary are popular.

Rental Market: Year-round home rental averages $1,200 per month, while seasonal rental is more like $2,500 per month.

Average rent for a two-bedroom apartment: $840 per month

Communities Popular With Retirees: Scottsdale Ranch, McCormick Ranch, and Old Town Scottsdale.

Nearby Areas to Consider: Cave Creek is located in northern Maricopa County and is also a suburb of Phoenix. It was once a sheep shearing station surrounded by open grazing lands, and still maintains that rustic look. Mesa, Arizona's third largest city, blends with Tempe and is 15 miles to the southeast. Mesa is the winter home of the Chicago Cubs and contains the Champlin Fighter Museum.

Earning a Living

Business Climate: Location is everything, so Scottsdale (and greater Phoenix) is blessed by its position in the middle of the largest and fastest-growing multi-state region in the country. It has a diverse economic base with a highly skilled workforce and strong business climate. Young, talented, and ambitious workers from across the nation move to Arizona, attracted by economic opportunity and the quality of life.

Help in Starting a Business: The Scottsdale Area Chamber of Commerce (480-945-8481; *www.scottsdalechamber.com*) provides small business counseling, guidance, and planning. The Arizona Department of Commerce (*www.azcommerce.com*) has business development services and other services to help you start a business.

Job Market: Jobs of all types are abundant in the area. In addition to the high-tech industry, a great number of health-care jobs are available.

Medical Care

Medical care in Scottsdale is excellent. Scottsdale Healthcare Shea (480-323-3000; *www.shc.org*) is a 305-bed facility, and Scottsdale Healthcare Osborn (480-882-4000) is a 285-bed short-term facility with 18 physicians on staff. Scottsdale Healthcare Thompson Peak (480-882-4636) is a 120-bed full-service hospital. The Healthsouth Meridian Point Rehab Hospital is a 46-bed rehabilitation facility. Samaritan Behavioral Health Center is a 60-bed psychiatric hospital. Senior Horizons is a 19-bed psychiatric hospital.

Services for Seniors

The City of Scottsdale Senior Center, (480-312-2375; *www.ci.scottsdale.az.us/seniors*) is housed in a multipurpose facility consisting of a dance hall, dining and kitchen facilities, office space, and classrooms. The Scottsdale Senior Center provides such a wide array of services and events that it is impossible to list them all. The Developing Older Adult Resources (602-285-0543) is a church and a synagogue group that helps seniors with home services, transportation, care-giver assistance, and other services. Scottsdale Civic Center Senior center and Elder Via Linda Senior Center offer recreational and social activities. The Scottsdale libraries have senior centers with magnifiers for those with poor vision, talking books, an eldercare library with books on senior health issues, and it provides library services free of charge for seniors. Seniors Choice at Home (480-946-4414; *www.seniorschoice.homestead.com)* provides in-home services for seniors.

Continuing Education

Seniors can take advantage of college courses offered through the Senior Adult Education Program, part of Scottsdale Community College (480-423-6000; *www.sc.maricopa.edu*). Arizona State University (*www.asu.edu*) has its main campus about 12 miles away in Tempe, and offers a number of continuing education programs. The University of Phoenix (*www.phoenix.edu*) is about 14 miles away, while the University for Working Adults provides online classes. The Gateway Community College (602-286-8686; *www.gatewaycc.edu*) is about 14 miles away in Phoenix. The Scottsdale senior centers offer a variety of computer programs and classes including Introduction to Computers, Intro to Windows, Word Processing, and Introduction to the Internet.

Crime and Safety

With 60 crimes per 1,000 people, this area's crime rate is slightly higher than the national average. This means that it's slightly more dangerous to live in Scottsdale than in other parts of the country, but you should be safe enough with a strong lock and a good alarm. Theft is the most common crime.

Getting Around Town

Public Transportation: The city of Scottsdale runs multiple bus routes. A downtown bus is known as the Scottsdale Trolley. Fares are reduced for senior citizens.

Roads and Highways: I-17 and I-10 are nearby, but no major highways directly enter the city.

Airports: Sky Harbor International Airport is in Phoenix, 10 miles away, and is served by 12 major airlines and schedules 1,000 flights a day.

Let the Good Times Roll

Recreation: A number of outfits will take you hot-air ballooning, or on desert or mountain expeditions. And, of course, there is no end to the golf courses. There is also no end to the restaurants! There are more restaurants than you can visit in a lifetime, and the variety is amazing. There is live entertainment somewhere every night. And there are the professional sports teams, including the Phoenix Suns basketball team, Phoenix Cardinals football team, Phoenix Coyotes hockey team, Arizona Diamondbacks baseball team, and the Phoenix Mercury basketball team. The weather is always on your side, and there are hundreds of spas, golf courses, tennis courts, fitness centers, racquetball courts, and swimming pools. You will find car races, boating, bowling, dancing, fishing, hiking, mountain biking, roller skating, snowboarding, and even scuba diving. Or just take a drive through the desert foothills and see the giant saguaro cactus in the sunset.

Culture: More than 125 galleries, studios, and museums are waiting. You can browse for antiques and collectibles, view a premier collection of American Impressionism, and select pieces from virtually every possible school of artistic thought. The performing arts are well represented, with theater, music, and dance performances at the Scottsdale Center for the Arts and Kerr Cultural Center. The world-renowned ArtWalk, which is held on Thursday evenings year-round, is sponsored by 120 art galleries. A recent survey of tourists indicated that art was the number one reason for visiting the area.

Annual Events: From December 10th through January 1st, Arizona's most unique holiday event is the Holiday Lights Extravaganza. Take a train ride through more than 100,000 lights, and featuring a variety of holiday displays that turn the Railroad Park into a winter wonderland. From the end of November through the first week of January, ZooLights is a unique event with nearly 2 million lights making it one of the largest light shows in the Southwest. You can also attend the annual Scottsdale Celebration of Fine Art and the Scottsdale Arts Festival.

When the Kids Come: The Arizona Cowboy College is a no-frills camp on a working cattle ranch. Fiddlesticks has a kids club with bumper boats, laser tag, batting cages, miniature golf, and more. At Rawhide the kids can ride a mechanical bull; visit the haunted house; and ride a stagecoach, camel, or miniature train.

More Information

Municipal

Scottsdale Area Chamber of Commerce
7343 Scottsdale Mall
Civic Center Mall Area
Scottsdale, AZ 85251-4498
480-945-8481
www.scottsdalechamber.com

Newspaper

East Valley Tribune
7525 East Camelback Road
Scottsdale, AZ 85251
480-970-2330
www.eastvalleytribune.com

The Arizona Republic
200 East Van Buren Street
Phoenix, AZ 85004
602-444-8000
www.azcentral.com

Realty

Russell Coffield
8079 North 85th Way
Scottsdale, AZ 85258
800-998-6012
www.russellcoffield.com

6

Tucson, Arizona

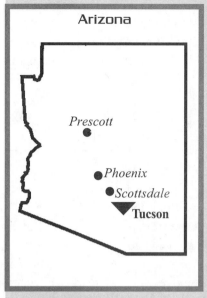

Arizona

Prescott

●*Phoenix*
●*Scottsdale*
▼**Tucson**

Tucson at a Glance

The city of Tucson offers retirees the advantages of big-city living with ultra-modern shopping centers, department stores, and everything from uptown boutiques to laid-back natural-food shops, bookstores that double as tea rooms, health services that are superb, a dry climate, more sunshine per year than just about any other place in the United States, and a wonderfully casual attitude. The University of Arizona is a top-notch university and research institution, and offers seniors and other life-long learners the advantages of ongoing academic and personal enrichment classes. Business flourishes and unemployment is low. And while it is a target for tourists, Tucson offers the same entertaining and informative pastimes for its own residents as it does for visitors. Even though it heats up in the day, every evening brings cool weather, which makes going out in the evening and sleeping a delight.

Possible Drawbacks: While Tucson is lucky because it has very few tornadoes and no earthquakes, sometimes the heat can be intense. And with all that sunshine, you should slather on the sunscreen, take your water bottle, and wear a straw hat! Also, the fauna are not always friendly. I would be less than responsible if I failed to mention spiders, snakes, and a scorpion species or two. You should remember the warning from your old biology teacher, "Everything in the desert either stings or sticks."

▶ Nickname: The Old Pueblo

▶ County: Pima

▶ Area Code: 520

▶ Population: 532,350

▶ County Population: 950,515

▶ Percent of Population Over 65: 12.3%

▶ Region: South central Arizona

▶ Closest Metropolitan Area: Phoenix, 115 miles

▶ Median Home Price: $175,000

▶ Best Reasons to Retire Here: The city is nestled in a beautiful desert valley ringed by mountain vistas. Tucson itself is a cosmopolitan mixture of cultures, architectural styles, and social events.

Climate

32° N Latitude 111° W Longitude	Average High Temperature (°F)	Average Low Temperature (°F)	Precipitation (")	Sunshine (%)
January	66.4	36.1	0.7	80
April	86.0	49.3	0.3	90
July	106.1	75.7	0.9	78
October	88.9	54.0	0.7	88
YEAR	86.5	53.4	8.5	85

Utilities

Overview: Several factors contribute to the growing economy, but the biggest factor is the population growth. Tucson has a dynamic population that moves in and out, and from house to house. Between 1999 and 2000, for example, almost 54,000 folks moved into the area, and 42,000 moved out. Only 23 percent of the newcomers moved in to accept a new job. And lots of folks just moved around. On average, Tucson citizens move every 3.5 years, while nationally, Americans move only every 5.2 years.

Gas Company: Southwest Gas (520-889-1888; 800-428-7324; *www.swgas.com*) has a connection fee for residential customers of $30 plus tax for the next available day. Also, a deposit will be charged based on the history of the account.

Electric Company: Tucson Electric Company (570-571-4000; *www.tucsonelectric.com*)

Phone Company: A number of companies and options are available within Arizona (520-628-6550; 800-535-0148; *www.cc.state.az.us/utility/telecom*).

Water/Sewer Company: City of Tucson Water Department (520-791-4331; *www.ci.tucson.az.us/water*). Pima County Wastewater Management (520-740-6609) operates the sewer system in the metropolitan Tucson area.

Cable Company: There are currently 46 cable companies operating in Tucson. A few examples are Comcast (520-744-1900), Cox Communications (520-748-1378), and Satellite Technology (520-326-2706).

The Tax Axe

Car Registration: The state of Arizona imposes an annual motor vehicle license tax (VLT). The VLT is based on an assessed value of 60 percent of the manufacturer's base retail price reduced by 16.25 percent for each year since the vehicle was first registered in Arizona. As an example, the VLT for the first year's assessed value (say $15,000, which is 60 percent of a vehicle that costs $25,000) would be $420.

Driver's License: To get your Arizona driver's license, just take your out-of-state license to the DMV, take the vision test (no written test is required), and if you are age 50 or older, pay $10.

Sales Tax: Arizona currently has a state sales tax of 5.6 percent. Food and prescription drugs are exempt. Tucson adds 2 percent, making local purchases add up to 7.6 percent above retail price.

State Income Tax: Tax rates for Arizona personal income range from 2.87 percent to 5.04 percent. Many exemptions exist, and you should seek the advice of a tax accountant. For example, Social Security and railroad retirement benefits are exempt. However, all out-of-state government pensions are fully taxed.

Retirement Income Tax: See the information listed. Even more complex are the rules for retired military disability pay. It is wise to seek the advice of a tax expert.

Property Tax: There is no Arizona state property tax other than real estate. Commercial real estate is assessed at 25 percent of fair market value. Residential real estate is assessed at 10 percent of fair market value. The average tax rate is $16 per $100 of assessed value. Property tax is calculated by applying the assessment ratio to the property's full cash value (80 to 85 percent of market value) to determine assessed value. Again, there are tax credits available to those 65 years old and older.

Local Real Estate

Overview: As a buyer, you will be impressed and delighted with the diversity in home styles available. You will also be pleased with the number of homes on the market. In a recent survey, the total of single-family dwellings numbered around 220,000, with a rate of vacancy at about 1.21 percent. You'll have a choice of more than 2,500 available homes at any given time. And if a new build is your choice, there are residential lots available in almost every area of Tucson. While real estate prices were flat several years ago, things have changed, and the prices have appreciated recently to about the national average.

Average price of a three-bedroom/two-bath home: $220,928

Average price for a two-bedroom condo: $185,000

Common Housing Styles: In older homes, you'll find lots of brick and lots of concrete. As newer homes are viewed, you'll see frame stucco, and elements which reflect styles from other parts of the country, including Cape Cod, Victorian reproductions, log cabins, and even an occasional castle.

Rental Market: About 66 percent of renters live in apartments.

Average rent for a two-bedroom apartment: $900 per month

Communities Popular With Retirees: Saddlebrook and Oro Valley

Nearby Areas to Consider: Green Valley is a booming Arizona retirement community. With nine golf courses, shopping plazas, dozens of clubs, volunteer organizations, medical facilities, and recreation centers, Green Valley is a destination for retirees seeking an active lifestyle. And while most of Green Valley is age-restricted, there are also areas with non-age-restricted communities where families with children live. This is a community with friendly neighbors, exciting activities, majestic surroundings, and true charm for seniors.

Earning a Living

Business Climate: The climate for business has never been better. With the population increasing for the foreseeable future, and with business and industry thriving, things look positive. Add to that an unemployment rate continuing downward (at last view, it sits at a respectable 3.4 percent of Pima County, 2 percentage points lower than the national average). And according to news from the local university, more students are electing to take jobs in the local market after graduation.

Help in Starting a Business: The Tucson Metropolitan Chamber of Commerce (520-792-1212; *www.tucsonchamber.org*) is a wonderful place to begin to explore business opportunities. Pima Community College has a Small Business Development Center (520-206-6404; *www.cc.pima.edu/sbdc*) where you can get a free business plan consultation. SCORE (520-670-5008; *www.scorearizona.org/tucson*) is the Service Corps of Retired Executives with confidential, one-on-one business counseling to meet the needs of business startups. The Tucson Urban League (520-791-9522; *www.tucsonurbanleague.com*) has a small business assistance program. The Microbusiness Advancement Center (520-620-1241; *www.mac-sa.org*) has small business plan consultations and loan packaging assistance.

Job Market: In the near term, the sectors that are expected to be strongest in the local economy are natural resources and mining, wholesale trade, construction, financial activities, and accommodation.

Medical Care

The University of Arizona at Tucson is home to the University Medical Centre, ranked in the Top 50 in nine different areas of competence, including geriatrics, by the 2004 U.S. News and World Report. It is a teaching hospital, so each patient receives the expertise and talents of a team of medical staff. This hospital really goes all out for its patients. In the area are 20 other medical and specialized health care facilities. You can find them all listed at the Help Line Database (*www.helplinedatabase.com/hospital-us/arizona-tucson.html*).

Services for Seniors

Many senior services are available. You can find an exhaustive list of senior services at the Tucson Pages (*http://emol.org/seniors/tucsonguideindex.html*). Also contact the Pima Council on Aging (520-790-7262; *www.pcoa.org*). The Tucson Learning Center (520-721-7591; *www.tucsonseniornet.org*) sponsors Senior Net, in which senior students can learn to use computers.

Continuing Education

The University of Arizona at Tucson provides two programs for seniors: Elderhostel, which provides weekly seminars on various topics in the liberal arts and sciences, and SAGE, the Seniors' Achievement and Growth through Education. Both programs are organized and led by members. Whether it's a discussion group, study session, creative workshop, or general social activity, this program offers both an avenue of expression, and an opportunity for intellectual stimulation rarely encountered.

Crime and Safety

Tucson is only 65 miles from the Mexican border, which means it experiences its share of drug traffic and related crime. Seniors quite often are targets for con artists and fraudulent schemes. The police try to inform the public, and to that end maintain a comprehensive Website (*www.ci.tucson.az.us/police*).

Getting Around Town

Public Transportation: The Department of Transportation (520-792-9222; *http://dot.ci.tucson.az.us*) operates the metropolitan transit system, including special transport vans and Sun Tran Buses (*www.suntran.com*), which were awarded the title of Outstanding Transit Organization of Arizona. Van Tran (520-791-5409; *www.vantran.org*) provides special transportation service.

Roads and Highways: I-10, I-19, I-8; US 80, 89; State Roads 86, and 93

Airports: Tucson is served by the Tucson International Airport where service is provided by at least 11 national and regional airlines.

Let the Good Times Roll

Recreation: You can marvel at the wonders of nature, from colorful desert flowers to flawless starlit skies, from majestic ribbed saguaro cacti to snow covered mountains. Close by is the Colossal Cave Mountain Park, a desert park listed on the National Register of Historic Places, as well as Kartchner Caverns State Park, Mt. Lemmon Ski Valley, Patagonia-Sonoita Creek Preserve, and the Saguaro National Park. The airtight Biosphere 2 Centre contains a tropical rainforest, a savanna, a desert, and a human habitat where research is ongoing. Kitt Peak National Observatory, open to the public during business hours. The Old Tucson Studios has more than 300 movies and television productions to its credit. San Xavier del Bac Mission was built between 1783 and 1797 by members of the Franciscan religious order. The mission is a historic landmark on the San Xavier Indian Reservation. Tombstone, known as "the town too tough to die," is a National Historic Site including the Bird Cage Theatre, Boot Hill graveyard, Camillus Fly Studio, and the OK Corral.

Culture: You will find a number of museums, art galleries, cultural centers, and more than a dozen theaters. You can save on tickets by having your own Tucson Attractions Passport (*www.tucsonattractions.com*). You can also visit the Arizona Opera, Arizona Theatre Company, and the Tucson Symphony Orchestra. The Amerind Foundation Museum features a collection of more than 25,000 Native American cultural items. The Pima Air and Space Museum is one of the largest aviation museums. Ruins from the 1600's are preserved in Tubac, the oldest European settlement in Arizona. Today the town is an internationally known art colony. The Tumacacori National Historical Park preserves the ruins of three Spanish Colonial missions.

Annual Events: January has the Quilt Fiesta, Family Arts Festival, Dillinger Days 1934 Street Festival, and the Coyote Classic Golf Tournament. During February you can enjoy the Mozart Festival and the Southwest Indian Art Fair. March and April have the Fourth Avenue Spring Street Fair and Festival of Hummingbirds. In May, enjoy the Cinco de Mayo celebrations and the Waila Festival. June has the Dia de San Juan Festia. In August, visit the Peach Mania Festival and Vigilante Days. September has the Dia de los Meurtos exhibit, Club Congress 20th Anniversary Celebration, and the Rex Allen Days. In October you should visit Buckelew Farm Pumpkin Festival and Corn Maze, or the Desert Thunder Professional Rodeo. In November, stop by the Culinary Festival or Celtic Festival. December has the Holiday Nights at Tohono Chul Park, Parade of Lights, Winterhaven Festival, and the Fourth Avenue Winter Street Fair.

When the Grandkids Come: The International Wildlife Museum features more than 400 animals from around the world, and most are mounted in dioramas representing their natural habitats. You should investigate Flandrau Center (*www.flandrau.org*) astronomy school's birthday party option where you can schedule a birthday party, and have a staff member provide a science demonstration. The Tucson Children's Museum (520-792-9985; *www.tucsonchildrensmuseum.org*) is housed in the historic Carnegie Library Building and offers hands-on exhibits. For scenery-rich hiking scaled to the size of young incredible energies and tastes, see the Picacho Peak State Park's Children's Cave Trail, Saguaro National Park's Signal Hill Petroglyphs Trail, and Westward Look Resort's Hummingbird Trail.

More Information

Municipal

Tucson Metropolitan Chamber of Commerce
P.O. Box 991
Tucson, AZ 85702
520-792-1212
www.tucsonchamber.org

Newspaper

Tucson Citizen
P.O. Box 26767
Tucson, AZ 85726
520-573-4561
www.tucsoncitizen.com

Realty

Sherie Broekema
5683 North Swan Road
Tucson, AZ 85718
520-299-2201
www.tucsonhomes.com

7

Fayetteville, Arkansas

Arkansas

Fayetteville

Little Rock

Hot Springs Village

Fayetteville at a Glance

Fayetteville's downtown square is home to unique shops, restaurants, historic buildings, and modern offices. You will always find a fanciful display of colorful flowers in the square gardens in the middle of town, carefully tended for each season. The scenery has to be one of the area's most enticing features. With four distinct seasons, you are always surrounded by nature showing off. What's equally pleasant is that the seasons are mild. The elevation of Mt. Sequoyah is 1,700 feet above sea level, the highest point in Fayetteville. Crossing to the west side of the mountain provides an overview of the city. You can travel back to Civil War times with a visit to Headquarters House, the Confederate Cemetery, and the Prairie Grove and Pea Ridge battlefield parks. The Arkansas Air Museum allows you to take flights of fancy among antique aircraft, or explore the exhibits at the University Museum. The sidewalks of the university invite walking, since they bear the engraved names of all of its more than 100,000 graduates. The walk begins in front of Old Main with the Class of 1876. Among the historical buildings are the Gunter House, the home of a colonel in the Confederate Army, and the Walker-Stone House, built in the late 1840s. All this, and the cost of living is still well below average.

Possible Drawbacks: Although the area has actively sought to keep its small-town flavor, the influx of business and residents continues to drive up property costs.

▶ Nickname: The Land of Opportunity

▶ County: Washington

▶ Area Code: 479

▶ Population: 58,047

▶ County Population: 169,683

▶ Percent of Population Over 65: 8.1%

▶ Region: Northwest Arkansas

▶ Closest Metropolitan Area: Little Rock, 192 miles

▶ Median Home Price: $166,068

▶ Best Reasons to Retire Here: Fayetteville has wonderful scenery, four distinct seasons, access to lots of lakes and rivers, and many cultural events.

Climate

36.1° N Latitude 94.2° W Longitude	Average High Temperature (°F)	Average Low Temperature (°F)	Precipitation (")	Sunshine (%)
January	44.3	24.2	2.1	50
April	68.5	46.2	0.2	60
July	89.1	68.6	0.8	73
October	70.4	47.3	0.6	65
YEAR	68.0	46.5	0.9	62

Utilities

Overview: The cost of living is 95.1 on a rating scale that puts the national average at 100, so living in Fayetteville is slightly cheaper than in other parts of the country.

Gas Company: Natural gas is supplied by Arkansas Western Gas (479-521-5330; *www.awgonline.com*).

Electric Company: Electricity is supplied by both Southwestern Electric Power Company (479-521-2871; *www.swepco.com*) and Ozarks Electric at (479-521-2900; *www.ozarksecc.com).*

Phone Company: Telephone service is provided by SBC (800-464-7928; *www.sbc.com*).

Water/Sewer Company: Water services are provided by the City of Fayetteville's water department (479-718-7600; *www.accessfayetteville.org*).

Cable Company: Cox Communications (479-751-2000; *www.cox.com*)

The Tax Axe

Car Registration: Automobile tags should be purchased as soon as the new resident is permanently located. Fees vary, depending on the make and model of the automobile. Bring the following when applying for tags: proof of assessment, proof of paid personal property taxes, and proof of current auto insurance.

Driver's License: Within 30 days you will need to apply for a driver's license. Bring identification in the form of social security card, birth certificate, military ID, or passport. You may want to contact the Arkansas Department of Finance and Administration (479-442-7691) for more information.

Sales Tax: The total sales tax is 11.25 percent, broken down as 6 percent state, 1.75 percent city, 1.5 percent county, 2 percent hotel/motel/restaurant.

State Income Tax: This ranges from 1 percent to 7 percent. Check with your local tax office for possible exemptions.

Retirement Income Tax: Social Security income is exempt. There are other exemptions, such as private pensions. Check with local tax office for specifics, as they can seem fairly complicated for the average taxpayer. Note that if you are retired military with a pension, the first $6,000 is exempt.

Property Tax: All property is assessed at 20 percent of market value. The city rate is 1 percent and the county rate is 6.3 percent. All property taxes are paid in arrears. All households are eligible for a refund up to $300 regardless of income or age. Homeowners 65 and older have their homestead assessment frozen.

Local Real Estate

Overview: As the area has grown, so have real estate prices. What in the mid-1990s was a $100,000 residence, is now close to $195,000.

Average price of a three-bedroom/two-bath home: $105,000

Average price of a two-bedroom condo: $122,300

Common Housing Styles: The newest architectural trends lean toward French Country and Old World styles.

Rental Market: While there are always apartments available, you need to remember that this is a college town, so call ahead for availability and rates.

Average rent for a two-bedroom apartment: $533 per month

Communities Popular With Retirees: Springdale, Bella Vista, Rogers, and Holiday Island are all popular communities.

Nearby Areas to Consider: Springdale is located in both Washington and Benton counties. The 2000 census showed a population of 45,798. Springdale is the location of the home office of Tyson Foods Inc., the largest meat company in the world. Eureka Springs has been named by the National Trust for Historic Preservation as one of America's Distinctive Destinations for being one of the best-preserved and most unique communities in the United States. The authentic 19th century Victorian resort is tucked in the Ozark Mountains of Arkansas, and encircled by two beautiful lakes and two scenic rivers.

Earning a Living

Business Climate: The business climate is, to coin an old cliché, bustling. The city's population has been growing at a rate of more than 3.2 percent annually, more than twice as fast as the state as a whole. According to the Milken Institute, an organization that publishes the "Best Performing Cities" according to the jobs created and maintained, Fayetteville ranked number one in the nation as recently as 2003. And the city didn't depend on the high-tech industry to do it either. Again, according to Milken, 2003's "leaders have all earned their high marks the old-fashioned way, with traditional businesses like retail, a growing population, and reliable growth industries such as government and health care."

Help in Starting a Business: The Arkansas Small Business Development Center (479-575-5148; *http://sbdc.waltoncollege.uark.edu*) is on the campus of the Sam M. Walton College. The center provides training, information, and consulting services to existing and potential business owners.

Job Market: Opportunities exist for full- and part-time employment in the areas of industry, manufacturing, human services, information technology, military applications, education, and government. Contact the chamber of commerce, the local newspapers, or the city of Fayetteville for more information.

Medical Care

Washington Regional is the only nonprofit community-owned and locally governed healthcare system in northwest Arkansas. They operate multiple facilities, including an acute-care hospital, a rehabilitation hospital, assisted living and long-term care facilities, an outpatient surgery center, and a network of clinics and services. One of these facilities is the Fayetteville City Hospital & Geriatric Care Center (479-442-5100; *www.wregional.com*), which operated from 1912 to 1950 as a general hospital. Its role was redefined in the 1960s as a center specializing in the unique needs of the elderly. Other hospitals in the Fayetteville area include the Healthsouth Rehabilitation Hospital (479-444-2200; *www.healthsouth.com*), the Vista Health System (479-521-5731; *www.vistahealthservices.com*), and the Willow Creek Women's Hospital (479-684-3000; *www.northwesthealth.com*).

Services for Seniors

The Office for Studies on Aging at the University of Arkansas in Fayetteville (*www.uark.edu/aging/gerontology.htm*) is a clearinghouse that provides links to a number of specialized resources having to do with care of the elderly, and self-help by senior citizens. The Area Agency on Aging of Northwest Arkansas (501-442-5194; 888-286-3611; *www.aaanwar.org*) provides a number of services, including adult daycare, caregivers' respite, and personal emergency response systems. They also organize Golden Excursions, which are tours designed especially for older adults. The Council on Aging (479-582-1604) provides supportive services for those in the county who are over 60. The Helping Angels (501-750-9900; 888-710-3456; *www.helpingangels.org*) takes on the fundamental task of connecting services with the people who need services.

Continuing Education

The University of Arkansas at Fayetteville has a Department of Continuing Education (479-575-3604; *www.uacted.uark.edu*), which provides both credit and non-credit courses in continuing education, as well as courses that can be taken off campus or online. The University of Arkansas also sponsors the Elderhostel program, which is dedicated to providing extraordinary learning adventures for people 55 and over. The North West Arkansas Community College (479-636-9222; 800-995-6922; *www.nwacc.edu*) has a "Golden-Age Waiver" in which students who have reached 60 years of age may have their tuition and course-related fees waived. Webster University (479-571-1511; 800-950-9945; *www.webster.edu/fayetteville*) is a small but well-accredited college, that offers both graduate and undergraduate degrees.

Crime and Safety

With a low crime incidence of 2,925 per 100,000 people, Fayetteville ranks well below the national average of 4,118.8 per 100,000. In 2003, *Forbes* magazine placed Fayetteville in the third spot of attractive places to live in the country. The low crime incidence played a major role in this ranking.

Getting Around Town

Public Transportation: Limited bus services is provided by Razorback Transit of the University of Arkansas (501-575-2551; *www.uark.edu*).

Roads and Highways: US 62 and 67; US Interstate Highway 540; Arkansas state highways 16, 45, 112, 156, 180, 265, and 471

Airports: The Fayetteville Municipal Airport is named Drake Field (479-718-7641; *www.accessfayetteville.org/aviation/drake_field*). Northwest Arkansas Regional Airport (479-205-1000; *www.flyxna.com*) is in Bentonville, 20 miles north of Fayetteville, and is served by six commercial airlines.

Let the Good Times Roll

Recreation: The Fayetteville Parks and Recreation Division (479-444-3471) has charge of more than 3,000 acres of parks, lakes, and recreational complexes in the city of Fayetteville. Sightseeing has to be among the top recreational pursuits for most residents, with miles of running and walking trails, plus a one-mile historic walking tour around the downtown district. Fishing, kayaking, and canoeing are also popular. And don't forget about the farmer's market, Air Museum, craft fairs, and shopping! Terra Studios will surprise even the most jaded world-weary traveler with exquisite glassblowing. The Northwest Arkansas Mall will fill your every shopping urge. In nearby Springdale, the Jones Center for Families provides a gymnasium, ice arena, and swimming pool for year-round physical fitness activities for the whole family.

Culture: The Walton Arts Center (479-442-3416) is the cultural hub of Fayetteville, and anchors the artistic life in the area. With more than 350 events each year, it's a wonder they have time to tidy up in between! There is also the Northwest Arkansas Orchestra and Symphony (479-521-4166). The Mount Sequoyah Retreat Center (479-443-4531), located in the highest point overlooking Fayetteville, has 70 acres of wilderness hiking trails, grassy lawns, and acres of flowers. In addition, Fayetteville is the home of some well-known former citizens: Senator W. Fulbright, and former President Bill Clinton, whose homes and haunts are part of historic tours.

Annual Events: In January, catch the Eagle Watch on Beaver Lake. In February, the Kiss a Pig Gala, Fat Saturday Parade of Fools, and Mardi Gras provide a lot of fun. In April, the Susan G. Komen Ozark Race for the Cure will help find a cure for breast cancer. May begins the season of craft and art fairs. June brings in farmers' market days, horse shows, truck shows, balloon festivals, BBQs, and cook-offs. There are too many art events to list, much less attend, in the 30 days of June. August heralds in the Washington County Fair and fine arts festival. September starts off with the Clothesline Fair, Antique engine and tractor show, and the quilt show. October celebrates the Mid America Nationals Car Show and Fly-In, and lots of Halloween events. November begins the holiday season with Razorback Football, and a kickoff to Christmas with town square lighting in neighboring Bentonville, including Christmas parades, carriage rides, *The Nutcracker Ballet*, and annual Open House tours of the 1895 Hawkins House. December's celebrations range from carriage rides to Santa-in-the-Park.

When the Grandkids Come: Take them to a football game at the Razorback Stadium. In the summer there are all kinds of water sports on Buffalo National River. And for fishing, you can't beat any of the five neighborhood rivers. Devil's Den State Park has excellent biking, camping, and hiking. If you haven't seen it, go to the Jones Center for Families in nearby Springdale. They feature indoor swimming, running tracks, weight room, and the only ice rink in northwest Arkansas.

More Information

Municipal

Fayetteville Chamber of Commerce
123 West Mountain
Fayetteville, AR 72701
479-521-1710
www.fayettevillear.com

Newspaper

Northwest Arkansas Times
212 North East Avenue
Fayetteville, AR 72701
479-442-1700
www.nwarktimes.com

Morning News of Northwest Arkansas
PO Box 7
Springdale, AR 72765
479-444-6397
www.nwaonline.net

Realty

Amy Kremer
4285 North Shiloh Drive, Suite 205
Fayetteville, AR 72703
479-236-8588
www.amymoves.com

Hot Springs Village, Arkansas

8

Arkansas

Fayetteville

Little Rock

Hot Springs Village

Hot Springs Village at a Glance

Hot Springs Village is a planned community on 26,000 acres of the Ouachita Mountains in the Diamond Lakes region. It is the largest gated community in the country. It has been extraordinarily well planned, and 25 percent of the village will remain green. Every house faces trees, lakeshore, or a golf course, of which there are six. Hot Springs Village was once described as a community of lakes surrounded by land. There are seven recreational lakes, with four additional recreational lakes currently in development or under construction. The amenities of Hot Springs Village are all owned and governed by the residents, not the developer. The property owners vote to elect a board of directors, who hire a city manager and staff, and set policy. The facilities, surroundings, and friendly neighbors have attracted retirees from all 50 states and from many foreign countries. The Property Owners Association has developed the infrastructure at a cost of $79 million. On top of that, Arkansas is one of the least expensive places in the country to live. Outside the village is one of the most lake-filled green mountain areas in the country. Only 22 miles away, in Hot Springs, is world-famous thoroughbred racing at Oaklawn.

Possible Drawbacks: Hot Springs Village is a small and somewhat remote town. Some people miss the big city, and the level of medical care is not always comparable.

▶ Nickname: The Other Hot Springs

▶ County: Garland/Saline

▶ Area Code: 501

▶ Population: 8,397

▶ County Population: 88,068/83,529

▶ Percent of Population Over 65: 56.6%

▶ Region: Central Arkansas

▶ Closest Metropolitan Area: Hot Springs, 22 miles

▶ Median Home Price: $203,800

▶ Best Reasons to Retire Here: It's a secure retirement community with lots of recreation. There are low taxes and four distinct seasons.

Climate

34° N Latitude 93° W Longitude	Average High Temperature (°F)	Average Low Temperature (°F)	Precipitation (")	Sunshine (%)
January	50.0	28.6	4.2	46
April	74.3	50.0	5.6	62
July	93.2	70.0	4.7	71
October	75.7	50.9	3.9	69
YEAR	73.0	50.0	55.5	62

Utilities

Overview: The cost of living in this area is one of the great attractions. On a national average of 100, the cost of living index is 68.

Gas Company: Natural gas is not available. Propane gas can be supplied to those residents wishing to use it for the fireplace or kitchen by Ferrell gas (501-623-8816) or by Aeropres (501-262-4300).

Electric Company: Electricity is available from Entergy Corporation (800-368-3749) in Garland County, or First Electric Co-Op (800-489-6716) in Saline County.

Phone Company: Telephone service is provided by Southwestern Bell (800-464-7928), and the monthly charge is $28.24 for basic service.

Water/Sewer Company: Water costs $8.75 a month for the first 8,000 gallons, and $2.12 per 1,000 gallons above that. Sewage charges are $13 per month. Sanitation is $11 per month.

Cable Company: Cox Communication (501-984-5010) charges $34.95 for enhanced basic monthly service.

The Tax Axe

Car Registration: Automobile registration is $17.25 for cars weighing 3,000 pounds or less. There is also a $5 annual auto decal fee. Contact the Department of Motor Vehicles for more information.

Driver's License: The cost is $14 for a regular noncommercial license.

Sales Tax: The state sales tax rate is 6 percent.

State Income Tax: Arkansas has an accelerated income tax with the rate varying from 1 percent to 6 percent, plus a 3 percent surcharge on all amounts due.

Retirement Income Tax: The first $6,000 of an IRA distribution is not taxed. Social Security income is exempt.

Property Tax: This is 20 percent of the appraisal valuation. Jessisville School District appraises at $34.80 per $1,000 value. Fountain Lake School District appraises at $34.80 per $1,000. Saline County appraises $40.70 per $1,000.

Local Real Estate

Overview: Existing-home sales hit a record high in 2005, defying expectations of a modest slowing trend. Multiple positive factors, including the lower interest rates, job market, and a shortage of houses being put up for sale, have all come together to coincide in a powerful demand for housing. The last time prices rose at a stronger pace was in November of 1980, when the median price rose 15.6 percent from a year earlier. Existing condominium and cooperative housing sales have also hit a record, increasing 4.8 percent.

Average price of a three-bedroom/two-bath home: $234,600

Average price of a two-bedroom condo: $160,000

Common Housing Styles: Popular styles include townhouses, garden villas, and single family houses, but a good variety is available.

Rental Market: The percentage of residents renting is significantly below that of the average for the rest of the state and the nation, but rental property is available year-round because people invest in property before they are prepared to retire and move.

Average rent for a two-bedroom apartment: $700 per month

Communities Popular With Retirees: Pine Bluff has a college campus, arts center, Delta Rivers Nature Center, and Jefferson Regional Medical Center. It has a population of 57,000, 13.7 percent of whom are 65 years or older.

Nearby Areas to Consider: Hot Springs Village is only 20 minutes from historic Hot Springs, known for thoroughbred racing and the natural thermal hot springs, which make it the only city in the nation to surround a national park. It is sometimes referred to as Spa City or America's First Resort. Arkadelphia, to the south, is home to two outstanding universities: Henderson State University and Ouachita Baptist University. From sporting events to theater and concerts to lectures, there is always something happening on the campuses of Arkadelphia.

Earning a Living

Business Climate: The community is small and the range of services is rather complete, so there is not much potential for businesses beyond those already established.

Help in Starting a Business: The University of Arkansas in Little Rock runs the Arkansas Small Business Development Center (501-324-9043; *http://asbdc.ualr.edu*). The center has training and seminars on every subject dealing with small businesses.

Job Market: A small town has a narrower range of jobs than a larger one. In Hot Springs Village, industries providing employment are mainly education, health and social services, retail trade, arts and entertainment, recreation, accommodation, food services, finance, insurance, and real estate.

Medical Care

Hot Springs Village residents have options for excellent healthcare both inside and outside the gates. Physicians and physician specialists, dentists, physical therapists, chiropractic services, natural healthcare, are all inside the gates, and two outstanding regional hospitals are in Hot Springs. St. Joseph's Mercy Health Center (*www.saintjosephs.com*) is a 292-bed short-term hospital on a 72-acre medical campus. St. Joseph's has complete cardiology and cancer care. National Park Medical Center (501-321-1000; *www.nationalparkmedical.com*) is a 166-bed short-term care hospital with such advanced techniques as image guided neuro-surgery. The Leo N. Levi National Arthritis Hospital (501-624-1281; *www.levihospital.com*) is an 89-bed rehabilitation hospital. Hot Springs Surgical Hospital is a 34-bed short-term hospital. Advance Care Hospital is a 27-bed long term care hospital. Hot Springs Rehabilitation Center is a 72-bed long-term facility.

Services for Seniors

With the majority of the population over 65, most services in Hot Springs Village are already designed and aimed for seniors. Super Senior property owners (those 80 years of age or older) may purchase an annual card good for greens fees, the Coronado Fitness Center, the DeSoto pool, tennis, and lawn bowling for half the regular property owner rate. Those 90 and over receive free greens fees and use of all recreation amenities free of charge.

Continuing Education

The National Park Community College (501-760-4222; *www.gccc.cc.ar.us*) offers adult education and continuing education. The Adult Education department assists adults to prepare for post secondary education. Instruction is conducted individually or in small groups. There is no charge for adult education classes. Non-credit continuing education courses are offered in computing, personal enrichment, professional development, and health and wellness. Also available in the continuing education program are corporate training and online courses.

Crime and Safety

The Village, a self-contained gated community, is extremely secure with 24-hour guards, plus the availability of the local police and fire departments. Crime statistics for Hot Springs Village are not kept. The violent crime rate in the city of Hot Springs is above average at 10.7 incidents per 1,000 people. Crimes of all types for Garland County are at the rate of 4,926 instances per 100,000 people.

Getting Around Town

Public Transportation: There is no public transportation in Hot Springs Village. You must have your own car.

Roads and Highways: State road 7 is adjacent to the village. I-70 is 15 minutes south and I-30 is about 30 minutes east.

Airports: Little Rock National airport is less than an hour to the south and is served by seven airlines.

Let the Good Times Roll

Recreation: There are nine championship golf courses open year-round. Beyond that, there are the tennis centers, boating on the lakes, miniature golf, basketball, swimming pools, a fitness center, lawn bowling, and bocce (Italian lawn bowling). In 1999, a 3,000 square foot games building was built to accommodate indoor activities such as Ping-Pong, pool, air hockey, foosball, computer games, movies, and board games. The Arkansas Game and Fish Commission stocks the lakes and monitors their progress. The result is abundant bass, crappie, catfish, and more. Some are so big you don't have to exaggerate their size! Just in case you forget your fishing supplies (or perhaps your boat) there are two marinas that rent pontoon, paddle, or fishing boats, as well as canoes, and they have plenty of equipment, bait, and fishing licenses for sale. The two beaches are also a popular attraction, especially in the summer. Fill your shoes with sand or dip your toes in the lake. Pavilions are popular gathering places for family reunions, picnics, barbecues, and other social gatherings. All of the facilities in the village are manned by professional staff, so you should always feel safe and securie in Hot Springs Village.

Culture: The arts district of Hot Springs Village is the best in Arkansas. Gallery walks are held the first Thursday and Friday of each month. The Ponce de Leon Auditorium presents symphonies, ballets, and other performing arts. Less than an hour away is Little Rock, with the Arkansas Symphony Orchestra, ballet, and frequent Broadway productions.

Annual Events: In May, the Hot Springs Music Festival is held with 18 concerts and 200 open rehearsals. June brings the Annual Shriner's Golf-A-Rama on the Village courses. In July are the Tennis Carnival, the Paddle Boat Races, and the Children's Olympics for 12 and under. July also brings a number of concerts along with tournaments for horseshoes, basketball, and miniature golf. In September are the Annual Hot Springs Blues Festival and the Arkansas State H.O.G. Rally. Also in September are the Arkansas Senior Olympics, a qualifying event for the National Senior Olympics. Oktoberfest is always held in Hot Springs, and December brings the Arkansas Symphony Orchestra Christmas Concert.

When the Grandkids Come: The children and youth programs of the village are constantly expanding. Summer activities have been incorporated into half-day camps for ages 3 to 12. Activities include group games, swimming, archery, miniature golf, crafts, and theatre. In Hot Springs, the Mountain Tower glass elevator rises 1,200 feet into the air. The National Park Aquarium has mule-drawn trolleys, and you can mine for diamonds at Crater of Diamonds State Park.

More Information

Municipal

Hot Springs Village Area Chamber of Commerce
4585 Highway 7 North, Suite 9
Hot Springs Village, AR 71910
877-915-9940
www.hotspringsvillagechamber.com

Hot Springs Village
100 Cooper Circle
Hot Springs Village, AR 71909
501-922-1541

Newspaper

Hot Springs Village Voice
P.O. Box 8508
Hot Springs Village, AR 71910
501-623-6397
www.hsvvoice.com

The Sentinel-Record
P.O. Box 580
Hot Springs National Park, AR 71902
501-623-7711
www.hotsr.com

Realty

Don Richardson
100 Cooper Circle
Hot Springs Village, AR 71909
800-553-6687
http://donsoldit.com

9 ▶ Palm Springs, California

Palm Springs at a Glance

Ah, Palm Springs! For those of us who have attained a certain age, the very name conjures images of glamour, luxury, and the possibility of rubbing elbows with America's rich and famous. The Palm Springs desert oasis has long been a place of rest and relaxation from the hassles of city living, regardless from which city you originally come! In Palm Springs you'll have plenty of room to roam. Imagine gorgeous, burnished colors of desert sunsets, the incredible green of challenging golf courses, sunshine dancing across the blue surface of the swimming pool, mountain breezes, and the wonderful abundance of services and entertainment that identify this fabulous city. Now, plop yourself down in the middle of all this. On a lounge chair by that beautiful pool, with a stimulating book and enough time to read more than a few pages. Or you might find yourself out on the back nine of an incredible golf course with three good friends, trading lies, making side bets, and then heading for the clubhouse.

Possible Drawbacks: The summer season can get really hot. But air conditioning is a wonderful thing, and Palm Springs is a great place to test it. Also, although everything you might desire is available, it can be very expensive. Sometimes the tourists can be a problem, but in my opinion, the beautiful surroundings more than make up for that potential drawback!

▶ Nickname: The Valley of Contentment

▶ County: Riverside

▶ Area Code: 760

▶ Population: 45,731

▶ County Population: 1,545,387

▶ Percent of Population Over 65: 35%

▶ Region: Southern California

▶ Closest Metropolitan Area: San Diego, 84 miles.

▶ Median Home Price: $182,695

▶ Best Reasons to Retire Here: Sunshine, country-club lifestyle, fun senior activities, great golf, hiking, fabulous shopping, state-of-the-art medicine, and internationally renowned entertainment.

Climate

33° N Latitude 116° W Longitude	Average High Temperature (°F)	Average Low Temperature (°F)	Precipitation (")	Sunshine (%)
January	70.2	42.4	1.1	84
April	86.9	54.0	0.2	85
July	108.7	75.2	0.2	88
October	91.4	59.4	0.3	81
YEAR	88.9	57.4	5.7	81

Utilities

Overview: The overall cost of living index is above average at 124.9, where the national average is 100. The cost of food is 120.9, housing is 131.1, healthcare is 140.4, and utilities are 149.3.

Gas Company: Southern California Gas Co. (800-427-2200; *www.socalgas.com*)

Electric Company: Southern California Edison (800-655-4555; *www.sce.com*)

Phone Company: Verizon (800-483-4000; *www.verizon.com*) provides local and long distance phone service in Palm Springs.

Water/Sewer Company: Desert Water Agency (760-329-6436; *www.dwa.org*) and Palm Springs Disposal (760-327-1351)

Cable Company: Time Warner (760-320-8810; *www.timewarnercable.com*)

The Tax Axe

Car Registration: Contact the Department of Motor Vehicles (800-777-0133; *www.dmv.ca.gov*). Residents of other states may operate their vehicles with current registration from their resident state for up to six months or until they accept gainful employment in California, otherwise become a resident, claim a homeowner's exemption in California, or enroll in an institution of higher learning as a California resident.

Driver's License: You may drive in this state without getting a California driver's license as long as your home state license remains valid. If you take a job or become a resident, you must get a California driver's license within 10 days. There's a $25 application fee, vision exam, traffic law exam, and a sign test.

Sales Tax: 7.75 percent

State Income Tax: The accelerated income tax ranges from 1 to 9.3 percent.

Retirement Income Tax: Social Security and Railroad Retirement benefits are exempt. There is a 2.5 percent tax on early distributions and qualified pensions. All private, local, state, and federal pensions are fully taxed.

Property Tax: Property is assessed at 100 percent of full cash value. The maximum amount of tax on real estate is limited to 1 percent of the full cash value. After taxes have been paid, homeowners 62 and older who earn $35,051 or less may file a claim for assistance on 96 percent of property taxes, up to $34,000 of the assessed value of their homes. Under the homestead program, the first $7,000 of the full value of a homeowner's dwelling is exempt. The state has a property tax postponement program that allows eligible homeowners (seniors, as well as blind and disabled residents) to postpone payments of property taxes on their principal place of residence. Interest is charged on the postponed taxes.

Local Real Estate

Overview: The prices and the number of houses and condos sold are up continuously over the past several years, and the trend is expected to continue.

Average price of a three-bedroom/two-bath home: $562,600

Average price of a two-bedroom condo: $484,500

Common Housing Styles: Palm Springs is a favorite place for stucco exteriors with red clay-tile roofs, and has an abundance of mid-century ultra-modern. Air conditioning, swimming pools, and fireplaces seem popular.

Rental Market: In Palm Springs there are excellent rentals available, especially from November through May. The season would be perfect timing to be on a golf course, enjoying a lake view, or even watching young folks play tennis.

Average rent for a two-bedroom apartment: $800 per month

Communities Popular With Retirees: Four Seasons, Trilogy in nearby La Quinta, and Del Webb's Sun City in Palm Desert

Nearby Areas to Consider: Cathedral City, in Riverside County, is between Palm Springs and Rancho Mirage, and derives its name from Cathedral Canyon to the south of town. The canyon was named because its rock formations were reminiscent of a cathedral. Several U.S. presidents have vacationed in Rancho Mirage, and Gerald Ford later bought a house there. The Betty Ford Center is located in the Eisenhower Medical Center of the town. Coachella is located at the eastern end of the beautiful Coachella Valley and is the gateway to the Salton Sea.

Earning a Living

Business Climate: Palm Springs employment is in education, health and social services, retail trade, and manufacturing. Tourism is such a strong employment element, it's in a class all by itself.

Help in Starting a Business: Among the organizations that can help you are the Riverside County Workforce Development Center (909-955-3148), the Palm Springs Workforce Development Center (760-327-0945), and the Jobs and Employment Services Department (909-945-4304). And don't forget the local chamber of commerce (760-325-1577).

Job Market: Palm Springs continues to welcome tourists for much of the year, so it's possible for locals to pick up part-time or full-time work in both tourist and retail trades.

Medical Care

The Desert Regional Medical Center (760-323-6498; *www.desertmedctr.com*) looks like an elegant Moorish castle, but is a 403-bed hospital with several areas of interest to seniors, including bariatric specialties, behavioral health/psych services, a comprehensive cancer center, emergency and trauma services, hospice, inpatient acute rehab, orthopedics, and transfusion-free medicine and surgery. For seniors specifically, Desert Regional has instituted a community program, Health Key Plus, which provides the 50 and over crowd with everything from help with insurance forms to travel discounts from participating vendors. Eisenhower Medical Center (760-340-3911; *www.emc.org/default.cfm*) is just a few miles away in Rancho Mirage. Its massive front is reminiscent of Frank Lloyd Wright's prairie homes. This 253-bed nonprofit hospital has garnered many honors throughout its history. Most recently, it was named in the Top 100 hospitals in the nation by Solucient, the leading source of healthcare business intelligence in the United States. They are best known for their excellent medicine in the fields of cardiology, orthopedics, and cancer care.

Services for Seniors

In Palm Springs, there are several services available, most of which are housed in one of the finest senior centers around. The Mizell Senior Center (760-323-5689; *www.mizell.org*) offers social programs, including bingo, fitness and dance, music, and space for community meetings and instruction. Among other opportunities at the center are computer instructions, health classes, special interest groups, and help with driving skills, taxes, insurance, and long-term care planning. Other senior centers in the area are in Cathedral City (760-321-1548), Joslyn Cove Communities Senior Center (760-340-3220), and Coachella (760-398-0104), which offers bilingual help, as well as the Desert Hot Springs (760-329-0222), Indio (760-347-5111), and La Quinta, (760-564-0096). In Palm Desert, the local senior center (760-340-3220) also serves the communities of Indian Wells and Rancho Mirage. They claim that the center is senior-focused, but its activities are not sedentary and the people who participate are interested in an active lifestyle.

Continuing Education

The Palm Springs Virtual University (760-416-5652) is the first of its kind nationwide. The University provides access to college courses, professors, and a classroom atmosphere via Internet connections and videoconferencing. Students need not step foot on campus. The city of Palm Springs joined the California Universities (Stanford, Cal Poly, and UCLA) and the public library, to establish life-learning for all. The visionaries involved transformed a multipurpose room inside the library to house computers, cameras, microphones, and a large-screened television to facilitate participation in distance learning.

Crime and Safety

The news is not particularly good. At almost double the national average, crime is a real problem in Palm Springs. On the bright side, it's mostly property crime, because violent crime is negligible. So, with a good security system, you should be okay. The reported incidents per 100,000 people are 6,096.6, compared to the national average at 4,532.

Getting Around Town

Public Transportation: Serving the area with transport services for those who have physical disabilities and for senior citizens are Sun Dial (763-43-3451), Desert Wheelchair (760-321-5601), and Disabled Trans. Services (760-320-2068). In Palm Desert service is provided by Dial-A-Ride (760-341-7433).

Roads and Highways: I-10, California Highway 111

Airports: The Palm Springs International Airport (760-318-3800; *www.palmspringsairport.com*) is served by 11 airlines and serves more than 1.3 million passengers annually.

Let the Good Times Roll

Recreation: Sparkling springs sheltered amid 13,000 acres of lush greenery provide a haven for a myriad of desert wildlife in the Coachella Valley Preserve (760-343-2733; *www.desertusa.com/wild/du_coachella.html*). In the center there is a 1,000-acre idyllic palm oasis. Joshua Tree National Park (760-367-7511; *www.nps.gov*) is a great place to escape and ponder the meaning of life. Living Desert Zoo and Gardens is a 1,200-acre interpretive center. Moorten Botanical Garden displays more than 3,000 varieties of desert plants, including prickly pears, agaves, and cacti. The Palm Springs Aerial Tramway starts in Chino Canyon near Palm Springs and takes passengers from a 2,643 foot elevation to the edge of the wilderness at 8,516 feet. Mount San Jacinto State Park has 54 miles of hiking trails with guided wilderness mule rides during snow-free months and cross-country ski equipment rentals during winter. This state park is only accessible by hiking or taking the tramway. At 1,500 feet above sea level, the Temecula Valley offers an ideal haven for growing premium grapes and has tours featuring 13 wineries. Among the Little San Bernardino Mountains, the desert oasis at Big Morongo Canyon is one of the 10 largest cottonwood and willow riparian habitats in California. The upstream end of the canyon lies in the Mojave Desert, while its downstream portion opens into the Colorado Desert.

Culture: There are performances by international stars in the Annenberg Theatre (*www.psmuseum.org/performances*) and in the McCallum Theater (*www.mccallumtheatre.com*), including ballet, classical piano, swing, blues nights, string quartets, soloists, opera, musical comedy performances, and much more. The cultural events in the city vary from the La Quinta Arts Festival and Native American Film and

Art in March, to International film festivals, jazz concerts, and film noir. In December, a wonderful holiday concert is performed by the Twenty-nine Palms Marine Corps Band.

Annual Events: In January, the International Film Festival is held and the Bob Hope Chrysler Classic is hosted by several area golf courses. In February the National Date Festival and County Fair is held at the Riverside County Fairgrounds. March brings the La Quinta Arts Festival and the Native American Film and Art Festival. April is the International Art Fair, the Swing'n Dixie Jazz Festival, and the annual White Party dance. May has the Smooth Jazz Festival and Will Clark's Bad Boys Pool Party. June has Jam Sessions at Melvyn's, the Film Noir Festival, and a Weekend with the King. July brings the VillageFest and the Street Fair. In August are the First Fridays at the Uptown Heritage Galleries and Antique District, and Guided Tours of the Palm Springs Desert Museum. September brings Rocktoberfest and an International Festival of Short Films. October has the International Hispanic Film Festival. November holds Art Affaire and the Golf Cart Parade. December includes the International Tamale Festival, Jazz Party, and Keys View in the Joshua Tree National Park.

When the Grandkids Come: Knott's Soak City Water Park (760-327-0499; *www.knotts.com*) on Gene Autry Trail is a fabulous water park with 13 waterslides, wave pools, and a lazy river. The Living Desert Zoo and Gardens is an interpretive center featuring mountain lions, wolves, javelina, bobcats, golden eagles, and much more. Balloon Above the Desert (760-776-5785; *www.caladventures.com/BalloonAbovetheDesert.htm*) will take you floating high above the desert.

More Information

Municipal
Visitor's Center
2901 North Palm Canyon Drive
Palm Springs, CA 92262
760-778-8418
www.palm-springs.org

Newspaper
The Desert Sun
P.O. Box 2734
Palm Springs, CA 92263
760-322-8889
www.thedesertsun.com

Realty
Fred S. Prescott
80519 Oaktree
La Quinta, CA 92253
760-771-0739
www.FredSPrescott.com

San Diego, California

San Diego at a Glance

Anyone who has ever visited this great city has fond memories. The sunshine, the beach, the mountain views, to say nothing of the friendly people, all draw you back. The city offers great medical care, transportation, sports, entertainment, shopping, and golf. About the size of the state of Connecticut, the San Diego region is home to more than 2.8 million people. Known for its year-round temperate coastal climate, the region stretches east into the mountains and south to the vast Anza Borrego Desert State Park. There are wonderful restaurants where every ethnic taste may be satisfied. You will, no doubt, find your own neighborhood coffee shop where you become a regular. There are numerous sit-down entertainments, from concerts in the park to on-stage performances in the several local theatres, where international artists come to play on a regular basis. And if it's business you're thinking of, this is definitely one of the most fabulous places to locate. Their programs for starting, relocating, and supporting businesses are phenomenal.

Possible Drawbacks: The crime rate is still above average. The good news is that most of it is non-violent. Also, prices are steep, even by today's standards, for real estate. But if you are prepared financially, go ahead and indulge your whims.

- ▸ Nickname: America's Finest City
- ▸ County: San Diego
- ▸ Area Codes:619, 858
- ▸ Population: 1,223,400
- ▸ County Population: 2,828,365
- ▸ Percent of Population Over 65: 9.9%
- ▸ Region: Southern California
- ▸ Closest Metropolitan Area: Los Angeles, 125 miles
- ▸ Median Home Price: $530,000
- ▸ Best Reasons to Retire Here: Fabulous weather, great healthcare, exotic scenery, and lots of recreational opportunities.

Climate

32° N Latitude 117° W Longitude	Average High Temperature (°F)	Average Low Temperature (°F)	Precipitation (")	Sunshine Percent
January	65.8	48.7	2.2	72
April	68.4	55.6	0.8	68
July	76.1	65.7	0.0	68
October	74.5	60.8	0.3	68
YEAR	70.7	57.6	9.9	68

Utilities

Overview: The cost of living is above the national average at around 136, with the national average figured at 100. The big cost is housing, which rises to 179, but everything is above average with food at 123. Healthcare and transportation are both at 121, and utilities are modestly above average at 103.

Gas Company: San Diego Gas and Electric (800-411-7343; *www.sdge.com*)

Electric Company: San Diego Gas and Electric (800-411-7343; *www.sdge.com*)

Phone Company: Vonage (877-486-6001; *www.vonage.com*)

Water/Sewer Company: San Diego Water Department (619-515-3500; *www.sandiego.gov/water*)

Cable Company: Time Warner Cable (858-695-3220; *www.timewarnercable.com*)

The Tax Axe

Car Registration: Contact the Department of Motor Vehicles (800-777-0133; *www.dmv.ca.gov*). Residents of other states may operate their vehicles with current registration in their names from their resident state for up to six months or until they accept gainful employment in California, otherwise become a resident, claim a homeowner's exemption in California, rent or lease a residence, or enroll in an institution of higher learning as a California resident.

Driver's License: You may drive in this state without getting a California driver license as long as your home state license remains valid. If you take a job or become a resident, you must get a California driver license within 10 days. There's a $25 application fee, vision exam, traffic law exam, and a sign test. Fees must be paid within 20 days of entry or residency to avoid penalties.

Sales Tax: 7.75 percent

State Income Tax: The accelerated income tax ranges from 1 to 9.3 percent.

Retirement Income Tax: Social Security and Railroad Retirement benefits are exempt. There is a 2.5 percent tax on early distributions and qualified pensions. All private, local, state, and federal pensions are fully taxed.

Property Tax: Property is assessed at 100 percent of full cash value. The maximum amount of tax on real estate is limited to 1 percent of the full cash value. After taxes have been paid, homeowners 62 and older who earn $35,051 or less may file a claim for assistance on 96 percent of property taxes on up to $34,000 of the assessed value. Homestead exemptions are handled at the county level. The first $7,000 of the full value of a homeowner's dwelling is exempt. The state has a property tax postponement program that allows eligible homeowners (seniors, as well as blind and disabled residents) to postpone payments on their principal place of residence. Interest is charged on the postponed taxes. Contact the California State Board of Equalization (800-400-7115) for more information.

Local Real Estate

Overview: The real estate market is definitely a seller's market. The city of San Diego is proud of its real estate, and the prices tell the tale. The average new detached home in San Diego County sells for more than three quarters of a million dollars. Resale single family homes have risen to a record high median price of more than half a million.

Average price of a three-bedroom/two-bath home: $781,000

Average price of a two-bedroom condo: $303,000

Common Housing Styles: San Diego is a big town, so it's no wonder you will find many different styles and features. One thing you can count on is that flowers bloom everywhere. As for styles, there are gracious adobe haciendas, contemporaries, ultramoderns, mid-western two-stories, one-story ranches, updated farm houses, upscale mansions, cute cottages, and bungalows of almost all the preceding styles. Front porches, second stories, pools, and great rooms continue to be popular.

Rental Market: Rental vacancies in San Diego have fluctuated between less than 1 and up to 4 percent between 1997 and 2004. The region's vacancy rate is currently 3.7 percent.

Average rent for a two-bedroom apartment: $1,210 per month

Communities Popular With Retirees: Santaluz, Otay Ranch, and Rancho Bernardo are all very popular communities.

Nearby Areas to Consider: Riverside is home to the University of California, Riverside. Riverside's downtown area is known as the "Mission Inn District." The Four Seasons Senior Community in Hemet has more than 1,100 single-story houses designed specifically for retirement and built around a golf club. Outdoor amenities include tennis courts, a lap pool and spa, barbecue, bocce court, horseshoe court, and a shuffleboard court.

Earning a Living

Business Climate: San Diego boasts an active and welcoming atmosphere for the new or relocating business. Described by *Forbes* magazine as "America's Best Place for Business and Careers" in 2002, San Diego continues to build on its advantages as a good business location. A thriving business base offering a multitude of services, coupled with unprecedented development during the past two decades, makes downtown an ideal location for anything from start-up ventures to well-established multimillion-dollar enterprises.

Help in Starting a Business: The city of San Diego (619-236-5555; *www.sandiego.gov*) provides organized, clear, and practical help for relocating and starting a business in San Diego. There are a variety of programs to directly assist small businesses, ranging from providing detailed information on city and regional services, to help with start-up questions and providing assistance with permitting issues. The city also provides matching grants to businesses in targeted areas for storefront renovation projects.

Job Market: Current unemployment sits at 3.8 percent. That said, there are opportunities in several areas. Most of the top 10 opportunities, according to California statistics for the county of San Diego, are in the area of service—retail sales, food preparation and serving, cashiers, office clerks, janitors, housekeepers, registered nurses, security guards, managers, and landscaping.

Medical Care

Alvarado Hospital Medical Center (619-287-3270; *www.alvaradohospital.com*) opened in 1972 as a 124-bed acute-care facility, and has grown to a 40-acre campus housing a 231-bed acute-care hospital and a 50-bed rehabilitation institute with more than 600 affiliated physicians. Aurora San Diego (858-487-3200; *www.aurorabehavioral.com/sandiego*) is a 55,000 square foot, two-story facility licensed for 80 acute-care beds and spreads over seven acres. Continental Rehabilitation Hospital (619-260-8300; *www.continentalrehab.com)* is a 110-bed hospital offering post-acute care and acute rehabilitation for patients who require intensive medical treatment or rehabilitation. Kindred Hospital (619-543-4500; *www.kindredsandiego.com*) is a 70-bed facility certified by Medicare and accredited by the Joint Commission on Accreditation of Healthcare Organizations. Scripps Acute Care Hospital (858-678-7000; *www.scrippshealth.org*) is a community-based healthcare delivery network. Sharp Memorial Hospital (858-541-3400; *www.sharp.com*) specializes in cardiac care, cancer treatment, pulmonary care services, rehabilitation, women's health, and multi-organ transplants. The University of California San Diego Medical Center (800-926-8273; *http:// health.ucsd.edu*) employs 4,364 staff at two hospitals and is licensed for a combined 531 beds. They have a program for older women called Senior Women's Care which offers the older woman medical attention and advice.

Services for Seniors

The city of San Diego (*www.sandiego.gov/seniorservices*) offers legal assistance, trips, special events, and employment services. They have published "The Senior Services Handbook," which is a reference guide to services provided by the city of San Diego. Also, Senior Citizens' Legal Services (858-565-1392; *www.seniorlaw-sd.org/*

metro.html) has free legal services for several areas of the city. The Salvation Army Senior Citizen Services and Centro Hispano Senior Center (619-283-2111; *www.salvationarmy.org*) provides services of several different types.

Continuing Education

The University of California San Diego (858-534-3150; *www.ucsd.edu*), with an enrollment of 25,000, permits individuals to audit courses with the consent of the faculty member in charge of the course. At the San Diego State University, with an enrollment of approximately 25,000, the College of Extended Studies (619-594-4707; *www.sdsu.edu*) has a new program for adults 50 years and older called the Osher Lifelong Learning Institute, in which people are given the opportunity to take academically rich courses that delve into topics that encourage discussion and intellectual stimulation. The Osher Lifelong Learning Institute is offering courses taught by emeritus faculty, subject matter experts, and other distinguished educators. The goal is to foster learning for the pure enjoyment of it. San Diego City College, (619-388-3400; *www.city.sdccd.cc.ca.us*), with more than 10,000 students, is a two-year community college. Other colleges in the same district are San Diego Mesa College and San Diego Miramar College. There are also six continuing education centers and the Educational Cultural Complex which offers both college and continuing education courses. The University of San Diego (619-260-4600; *www.sandiego.edu*), with 7,000 students enrolled, is a Catholic institution on 180 acres overlooking the city, Mission Bay, and the Pacific Ocean. The university campus is a community treasure, with Spanish Renaissance-inspired buildings. Recognized as one of the top 100 universities in the nation, the University of San Diego offers more than 60 undergraduate, graduate, and postgraduate degrees.

Crime and Safety

San Diego is an enormous city, and one can expect to run into a higher crime rate than in smaller places. On the positive side, there are fewer violent crimes than the overall average might indicate. According to *city-data.com*, the local crime index is 333.5, slightly above the national average of 330.6. However, the rate has fallen 4 points from the prior year, thanks in great measure to the quality of the local police department.

Getting Around Town

Public Transportation: Metropolitan Transportation Service really does a lot! From trains, trolleys, buses, and special deals for seniors, it's a nifty way to get around. As seniors, we can get not only reduced fares, but priority seating at the front or back door of the bus. And if you use a trained service animal, you are welcome on board all buses and rail vehicles at all times. The latest buses are "low floor," so you don't have to strain to get on. Wheel-chairs are accommodated where the international symbol of accessibility is at bus stops. If you have a question as to whether your information is acceptable to verify disability, please call the Transit Store (619-234-1060).

Roads and Highways: Interstate highways are 8, 15, 5, and 805. California highways going through San Diego are 52, 54, 56, 75, 76, 78, 94, 125, 163, 282, and 905.

Airports: San Diego International Airport, Lindbergh Field (619-400-2400; *www.san.org*) is the nation's busiest single runway commercial airport, serving more than 16 million passengers.

Ports: The Port of San Diego (619-686.6200; *www.thebigbay.com*) is fast becoming a major cruise port on the Pacific coast. In the past five years, San Diego has increased its cruise ship traffic by 300 percent and is the fastest growing cruise port on the West Coast.

Let the Good Times Roll

Recreation: With professional football and baseball teams, San Diego offers plenty of action in the sports arena: Downtown's PETCO Park, home to the San Diego Padres (*www.padres.com*) is America's newest urban Major League baseball stadium. Qualcomm Stadium (*www.chargers.com/stadium*) is home to the San Diego Chargers, San Diego State University Aztecs, and the Holiday Bowl. Two PGA tournaments, the Buick Invitational at Torrey Pines and the Accenture Match Play Championships at La Costa, tee off in San Diego each year. At 5,700 acres, Mission Trails Regional Park is one of the largest urban parks. Downtown offers more than a dozen parks ranging from the North and South Embarcadero Marina Park, to the Horton Plaza Park in the heart of the city. *Golf Digest* names San Diego one of its top 50 golf destinations in the world. Golfers can choose from 92 golf courses in San Diego County, offering everything from a seaside setting to challenging desert mountain terrain. Downtown's Balboa Park includes an 18-hole golf course. Cuyamaca Rancho State Park is a popular destination nearby for its 110 miles of hiking trails. Downtown's waterfront boardwalk and linear park along the railroad line are ideal urban trails. With 70 miles of Pacific Ocean coastline and 33 beaches, San Diego is a haven for swimming, surfing, boating, and sailing. Beautiful San Diego Bay is downtown's front porch and is filled with watercraft throughout the year. Free downtown bus tours are conducted the first and third Saturdays of the month. All tours begin at the Downtown Information Center (619-235-2222).

Culture: Balboa Park is one of America's premiere cultural complexes. The 1,400 acre park is home to more than 85 cultural institution, 15 museums and art galleries, four theaters, and the world-famous San Diego Zoo. Downtown includes 24 theaters and museums, art galleries, and 37 outdoor sculptures. Downtown arts organizations include Broadway San Diego (*www.broadwaysd.com*), where you can see the latest in Broadway entertainment; the San Diego Opera (*www.sdopera.com*), which produces world-class new and traditional opera; the San Diego Performing Arts League (*www.sandiegoperforms.com*), where music, dance, theater, and life come before you on the stage; the San Diego Repertory Theatre (*www.sandiegorep.com*), where plays range from Shakespeare to the latest word; as well as the San Diego Symphony (*www.sandiegosymphony.com*), a world-renowned group under the direction of Jahja Ling; the San Diego Theatres (*www.sandiegotheatres.org*); the Globe Theatre (*www.oldglobe.org*); and 4th & B (*www.4thandb.com*). Among the museums are the Museum of Contemporary Art San Diego, the Maritime Museum of the Star of India, the Maritime Museum at the Berkley, San Diego Chinese Historical Museum, Firehouse Museum, and the Midway Aircraft Carrier Museum.

Annual Events: In January catch the San Diego Marathon, Chinese New Year, Historical Society Holiday Homes Tours, and the Martin Luther King Jr. Day Parade and Festival. In February, see Accenture Match Play, World Golf Championship, Brazil Carnaval, Getty Center, Watts Towers, Borrego Springs Grapefruit Festival, Kumba Fest, and the Annual Jewish Film Festival. In March, you can attend the International Film Festival, Easter Bonnet Parade and Hat Contest, San Diego Latino Film Festival, and the Annual Kiwanis Ocean Beach Kite Festival. April brings in the following annual events: the Crew Classic Regatta, Adams Avenue Roots Festival of Music, Festival of Animation, Art Walk, Vintage Weekend, Del Mar National Horse Show, Linda Vista Multi-Cultural Fair and Parade, and the Fallbrook Avocado Festival. May brings the International Gem and Jewelry Show, Carlsbad Spring Fair, San Diego Sicilian Festival, Annual Ramona Air Fair, Gator by the Bay, Concerts on the Green, and the Annual Valley Center Western Days. June is the San Marcos Annual Chili Cook-Off, Imperial Beach Chili & Jazz Festival, Portuguese Fiesta, Camp Pendleton Rodeo, Naked Juice 5K Walk/Run, Mainly Mozart Festival, A Toast to Music, and the Annual Greek Festival. July celebrates with the San Diego Open Tennis tournament, San Diego LGBT Pride, Chula Vista Music in the Park, Harlem West Fest, and the Annual Humphrey's Concerts by the Bay. August has the U.S. Lifeguard Championships, Encanto Street Fair and Cultural Arts Festival, Comic-Con, Broadway San Diego, San Diego Blues Festival, and the Welk Resort Theatre. September brings Street Scene, YachtFest, Adams Avenue Street Fair, San Diego Zoo activities, Julian Bluegrass Festival & Banjo Fiddle Contest, and the Fiestas Patrias. In October there is the AIDS Walk and Fun Run, CONJECTURE (an annual science fiction and fantasy convention), Mum Festival at the Wild Animal Park, Autumn in Gaslamp Quarter, and Ghosts & Gravestones. In November, see the Baja 1000, Chrysler Classic Speed Festival, Fall Village Fair, Balboa Park Food & Wine Classes, Annual Welk Resort Theatre Musical Christmas, and the San Diego Thanksgiving Dixieland Jazz Festival. In December, celebrate with the Old Town Holiday, Parades of Lights, Quail Botanical Gardens, San Diego Bay Parade of Lights, and Holiday Jazz & Blues Fest.

When the Grandkids Come: First of all, take them to the world-famous San Diego Zoo, (*www.sandiegozoo.org*). It will take more than one day, so plan a weekend for it. Or you can visit the Children's Museum on West Island Avenue. Disneyland still enchants (*www.disneyland.com*), and so does Knotts Berry Farm (*www.knotts.com*). Because there are so many activities, check in with "San Diego Kids" online (*www.sdkids.com*).

More Information

Municipal

San Diego Chamber of Commerce
402 West Broadway
San Diego, CA 92101
619-544-1300
www.sdchamber.org

San Diego County Hispanic Chamber of Commerce
1250 6th Avenue
San Diego, CA 92101
619-702-0790
www.sdchcc.com

Newspaper

San Diego Union Tribune
P.O. Box 120191
San Diego, CA 92112-0191
619-718.5200
www.signonsandiego.com

North County Times
207 East Penn. Avenue
Escondido, CA 92025
760-745-6611
www.nctimes.com

Realty

Bill Johnston
643 G Street
San Diego, CA 92101
619-235-5447
www.billjohnston.com

Santa Barbara, California

California

Sacramento ●

Santa Barbara ◀ *Palm Springs* ●

San Diego ●

Santa Barbara at a Glance

Santa Barbara County is famous around the world for its breathtaking setting. Natural beauty shines from the dramatic mix of mountains, valleys, beaches, islands, and the sea. The cultural arts scene is one of the star attractions. You can enjoy world-class performances year-round. Few cities in the world boast as many restaurants per capita as Santa Barbara. Creative mouth-watering cuisine is prepared with fresh local produce and joined by superb wines from the Santa Barbara wine country. You can taste the fruits of sunny valleys as you sip your way through the products of more than 60 premium wineries. Enjoy a relaxing massage in one of the luxurious spas. Santa Barbara is famous for its beautiful beaches, most of which lie along a unique south-facing stretch of coastline that affords beach visitors sun all day long and greater shelter from winds and surf than many other coastal beaches. You can see the rich Spanish heritage in the city's distinctive architecture, the cobbled pathways, red tile roofs, and mission-style adobes. Explore the Western-style towns of Los Olivos and Santa Ynez. Visit the quaint Danish village of Solvang with its windmills and timbered Tudor facades. In Santa Barbara County, history whispers from every corner.

Possible Drawbacks: There are generally more buyers than sellers of real estate, which makes for expensive housing. There is also the earthquake risk. Finally, this is so close to paradise in so many ways, your relatives may all try to move in with you!

▶ Nickname: The American Riviera

▶ County: Santa Barbara

▶ Area Code: 805

▶ Population: 94,825

▶ County Population: 412,081

▶ Percent of Population Over 65: 8.4%

▶ Region: Southern California

▶ Closest Metropolitan Area: Los Angeles, 92 miles

▶ Median Home Price: $1,214,000

▶ Best Reasons to Retire Here: Santa Barbara enjoys ubiquitous flowering shrubs, towering palm trees, white sandy beaches, sunny days and cool nights, and a visible Spanish and Mexican heritage.

Climate

34° N Latitude 119° W Longitude	Average High Temperature (°F)	Average Low Temperature (°F)	Precipitation (")	Sunshine (%)
January	65.1	38.8	4.2	69
April	72.1	43.3	1.5	70
July	90.0	52.0	0.0	82
October	81.7	48.6	0.4	73
YEAR	76.5	45.7	19.6	73

Utilities

Overview: The cost of living index for Santa Barbara is 112.4 on a scale with the national average being 100. The largest cost jump is in housing.

Gas Company: Southern California Gas (800-427-2200; *www.socalgas.com*)

Electric Company: Southern California Edison (800-655-4555; *www.edison.com*)

Phone Company: Verizon (800-483-1000; *www.verizon.com*)

Water/Sewer Company: The city-owned Santa Barbara City Water District (805-564-5343; *www.santabarbaraca.gov*) gets its water primarily from reservoirs, but it also has a desalinization plant for emergencies.

Cable Company: Cox Cable (805-683-6651; *www.cox.com*)

The Tax Axe

Car Registration: Contact the Department of Motor Vehicles (800-777-0133; *www.dmv.ca.gov*). Residents of other states may operate their vehicles with current registration in their names from their resident state for up to six months or until they accept gainful employment in California, otherwise become a resident, claim a home-owner's exemption in California, rent or lease a residence, or enroll in an institution of higher learning as a California resident.

Driver's License: You may drive in this state without getting a California driver's license as long as your home state license remains valid. If you take a job or become a resident, you must get a California driver's license within 10 days. There's a $25 application fee, vision exam, traffic law exam, and a sign test.

Sales Tax: The state rate is 6.25 percent, and food and prescription drugs are exempt. Local areas can add to this, and they go as high as 8.75 percent.

State Income Tax: Personal income tax ranges from 1 to 9.3 percent.

Retirement Income Tax: Social Security and Railroad Retirements are exempt. There is a 2.5 percent tax on all early distributions and qualified pensions.

Property Tax: Property taxes are based on Proposition 13, which was passed by voters in 1978. Annual property taxes are approximately 1.2 percent of the purchase price of the property.

Local Real Estate

Overview: For 2004, house-price appreciation in the Santa Barbara and Santa Maria-Goleta areas ranked 11th among 265 metro areas evaluated, with an increase of 25 percent over 2003. Over a five year period, the increase comes in at a whopping 121 percent. Santa Barbara is a slow growth area.

Average price of a three-bedroom/two-bath home: $1,746,000

Average price of a two-bedroom condo: $941,000

Common Housing Styles: You are apt to see Spanish manor houses, one-story ranches, Tudor cottages, Mediterranean compounds, prairie houses, and adobe haciendas alongside contemporary houses and condominiums. Almost every house has a view of the mountains, and many have spectacular views of the Pacific Ocean.

Rental Market: There are lots of options in rental housing in Santa Barbara, from month-to-month rentals to one or two year leases. Week-by-week and fully furnished vacation accommodations are also available. A two or three bedroom house might cost between $1,800 and $3,000 per month.

Average rent for a two-bedroom apartment: $1,650 per month

Communities Popular With Retirees: Hope Ranch, Montecito, and the Mesa and Goleta areas are all popular with retirees.

Nearby Areas to Consider: The historic town of Santa Ynez is in the heart of the Santa Barbara wine country. The Danish village of Solvang is also in the wine country, where you can enjoy a picnic lunch in a vineyard or beside a waterfall. Twelve miles south of Santa Barbara is Carpinteria, a place with small town charm and breathtaking mountain views and a mile of state beach.

Earning a Living

Business Climate: Santa Barbara is often referred to as "Silicon South." Since the mid-90s there has been a 60 percent increase in the high-tech companies that are locally founded and call Santa Barbara home. Some large companies have left the area because of the high cost of doing business, and rumors abound that other companies may also pull up stakes, but they always seem to deny it. The city ranked 31st on *Forbes* magazine's "Best Places for Business and Careers." The best ratings were in crime rate and education, but it ranked much lower in the cost of doing business. State-mandated constraints, such as insurance and workers' compensation, are business concerns.

Help in Starting a Business: Before beginning, it would be wise to check out general information sources, such as Cuesta College's Small Business Development Center (805-549-0401; *www.smallbusinessinfo.org*). Also check the Delta College Small Business Development Center (209-943-5089; *www.deltacollege.edu*). Both are veritable gold mines of information for doing business successfully in the state of California. You can also take advantage of Santa Barbara's Chapter of Service Corp of Retired Executives (805-563-0084).

Job Market: Current unemployment sits at about 3.7 percent. Median household income is listed at $62,000. With services and retail making up 50 percent of employment, these sectors of the economy are the two places to look.

Medical Care

Cottage Health System (805-682-7111; *www.sbch.org*) formed in 1996 as a not-for-profit parent organization of Santa Barbara Cottage Hospital (including Cottage Children's Hospital), Goleta Valley Cottage Hospital, and Santa Ynez Valley Cottage Hospital. The system includes a combined total of 500 beds, and comprehensive services from anesthesiology to women's services. Because it is a teaching hospital system, some of the finest healing talent can be found on these campuses.

Services for Seniors

The best place to start a search for services in the Santa Barbara area in the Area Agency on Aging (805-925-9554; *www.cahf.org*). The Agency's purpose is to keep elders in their homes and out of institutions, for as long as possible. The California Registry (800-777-7575; *www.calregistry.com*) has information and provides qualified referrals to nursing homes, board and care homes, and Alzheimer's care. S.A.I.L. (805-884-9820) provides home maintenance and repairs for seniors who cannot afford to pay for it from standard sources. The fees charged depend on need. The Family Service Agency (805-965-1001; *www.fsacares.org*) are among other services that serves as coordinator for the Homemaker Program. For the numerous other senior services, check out the University of California, Santa Barbara Human Resources department.

Continuing Education

The UCSB Osher Lifelong Learning Institute (805-893-4200; *www.extension.ucsb.edu*) provides non-credit, no test, and no grade classes to those over the age of 50. Westmont College (805-565-6000; *www.westmont.edu*) is a Christian based, nonprofit liberal arts college. It was mentioned in *U.S. News & World Report's* "Best Colleges for 2005" issue. Santa Barbara Community College Continuing Education Division (805-687-0812; *www.sbcc.cc.ca.us/continuingeducation*) was founded in 1918 and is one of the nation's leading adult education programs. More than 42,000 people enroll in "Adult Ed's" 2,200 non-credit and community service courses annually. The Fielding Institute (805-687-1099; *www.fielding.edu*) is a graduate level college.

Crime and Safety

The overall crime index for Santa Barbara is a respectable 261.7 per 100,000 people. This is compared to the national average of 330.6. You are safer in Santa Barbara than in many other places in America.

Getting Around Town

Public Transportation: Santa Barbara Metropolitan Transit District (805-683-3702; *www.sbmtd.gov*) is a municipal bus system that transports passengers in and around Goleta, Santa Barbara, and Carpinteria. State Street Shuttle (805-683-3702) is an electric open-air bus that stops every 10 minutes on every block from Sola Street to the waterfront. The Waterfront Shuttle is an electric open-air bus that runs between the harbor and the Santa Barbara Zoo.

Roads and Highways: US 101; State Roads 144, 154, 192, 217, and 225

Airports: The Santa Barbara Airport (805-967-7111; *www.flysba.com*) is a small airport that is served by five airlines.

Ports: While strictly speaking it isn't a "port," the Santa Barbara Harbor is definitely challenging for sailors. It is home to more than 1,000 boats, and houses both the Santa Barbara Yacht Club and the Sailing Club. Stearns Wharf, the oldest working wooden wharf in California, is home to restaurants, shops, and free fishing. Bring a long line with your pole though, because it's high off the water!

Let the Good Times Roll

Recreation: The great weather opens up unlimited outdoor activities. You can hike to LaCumbre Peak (it's about a four-hour hike one way), or any of the other miles of trails around the area. Take your pick from a long list of activities, including cycling, kayaking, ocean swimming, canoeing, paragliding, rock climbing, running, sailing, skydiving, surfing, pool swimming, and even triathlon courses. For some of us diehard shoppers, there's marathon shopping any day of the week. The wide array of spectator sports even includes polo at the Santa Barbara Polo Club!

Culture: Historic sites and museums abound, and it is only possible to name a few of them here: Old Mission Santa Barbara (one of 21 California missions founded by Father Junipero Serra,) the Chumash Painted Cave State Historic Park, El Presidio de Santa Barbara State Historic Park, Santa Barbara Museum of Art, Museum of Natural History, Santa Barbara Historical Society Museum, Santa Barbara Dance Theatre, State Street Ballet, UCSB Department of Dramatic Art & Dance, Canticle A Cappella Choir, Concerts in the Park, Opera Santa Barbara, Santa Barbara Blues Society, Westmont College Music Department.

Annual Events: There's an event going on nearly every week, including the New Year's Day Hang Gliding and Paragliding Festival and the Santa Barbara International Film Festival. The International Orchid Show is held in March, Santa Barbara's Fair and Exposition is in April, and the Jewish Festival is held in May. The Semana Nautica Summer Sports Festival, Santa Barbara Writers Conference, and the Live Oak Festival are in June. July brings the French Festival, followed by a Greek Festival, Old Spanish Days Fiesta (generally celebrated at the full moon in August), and the Multicultural Dance and Music Festival comes to town the end of the month. The Danish Festival comes in September. October features the Santa Barbara Harbor and Seafood Festival, and later on, another festival for lemons. Mid-November begins Solvang's Winterfest (it continues right through early January). In December, the whole county turns out for the Holiday Parade and the Parade of Lights, a celebration of boats, decorated with Christmas lights, parading around in the harbor.

When the Grandkids Come: Among the things to do are a morning visit to the Santa Barbara Botanic Garden, feeding time at the Zoo, or prowling the halls of the Museum of Natural History. In addition, there are miles of hiking trails, boats, trains, and buses to ride, fish to catch, and whales to watch. Last, but not least, is the quirky Land Shark, an amphibious tour bus made of aluminum. It takes a look at the city from the road, then takes off into the ocean to get a sailor's-eye view of Santa Barbara.

More Information

Municipal

Santa Barbara Region Chamber of Commerce
924 Anacapa Street Suite 1
Santa Barbara, CA 93101
805-965-3023
www.sbchamber.org

Santa Barbara Conference and Visitors Bureau
1601 Anacapa Street
Santa Barbara, CA 93101
805-966-9222
www.santabarbaraca.com

Newspaper

Santa Barbara News Press
715 Anacapa Street
Santa Barbara, CA 93101
805-564-5200
www.newspress.com

Realty

Mark A. Moseley
3902 State Street
Santa Barbara, CA 93105
805-563-7232
www.coldwellbanker.com

12 Colorado Springs, Colorado

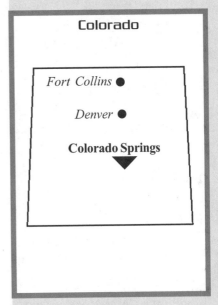

Colorado Springs at a Glance

The altitude of Colorado Springs is 6,000 feet. This is the land of adventure, inspiration, and relaxation. The city is home to world-class dining, shopping, lodging, unforgettable attractions, activities, and America's favorite mountain. Pikes Peak and the rest of the Rocky Mountains are just to the west of the city, and they provide a barrier that makes a heavy snowfall an unusual event. The mountains foster an outdoor lifestyle in a place where the cost of living is about the national average. The area is known for its many outdoor attractions, and that attracts lots of tourists. With more than 300 days of sunshine each year, the astounding view of Pikes Peak and the rest of the Rockies make it one of the premier living sites in the world. For those who are interested, the history of the Pikes Peak region is remarkably visible and accessible. The city provides breathtaking views—white in the winter, gold in the fall, and ablaze with the color of flowers in the summer and spring. The Cheyenne, Ute, Arapaho, and other Native American tribes hunted in the area. The town was formed in the 1800s when gold prospecting brought many settlers to the West. The words to the song "America the Beautiful" were inspired by the view from the top of Pikes Peak.

Possible Drawbacks: The altitude could cause breathing problems for some, so check with your doctor if you could be affected.

▶ Nickname: Jewel of the Foothills

▶ County: El Paso

▶ Area Code: 719

▶ Population: 380,567

▶ County Population: 535,117

▶ Percent of Population Over 65: 12.4%

▶ Region: Central Colorado

▶ Closest Metropolitan Area: Denver, 70 miles

▶ Median Home Price: $190,000

▶ Best Reasons to Retire Here: Stunning scenery, excellent climate, proximity to the Rocky Mountains, and a thriving arts community.

Climate

38° N Latitude 104° W Longitude	Average High Temperature (°F)	Average Low Temperature (°F)	Precipitation (")	Sunshine (%)
January	41.4	16.2	0.3	75
April	59.7	32.9	1.2	74
July	84.4	57.0	2.9	79
October	63.5	36.1	0.8	79
YEAR	61.5	35.2	15.8	71

Utilities

Overview: The cost of living in Colorado Springs is an exceptionally low 71, with the national average being 100.

Gas Company: Colorado Springs Utilities (719-448-4800; 800-238-5434; *www.csu.org*) provides natural gas to the Pikes Peak region.

Electric Company: Colorado Springs Utilities (719-448-4800; *www.csu.org*)

Phone Company: Verizon (*www.verizon.com*)

Water/Sewer Company: Colorado Springs Utilities (719-448-4800; 800-238-5434; *www.csu.org*) is owned by the city.

Cable Company: Contact Adelphia (719-633-6616; *www.adelphia.com*)

The Tax Axe

Car Registration: For registration and license plates, contact El Paso County (719-520-6240). Call ahead for required documents. New residents have 30 days after arriving to register their vehicles.

Driver's License: For adults between the ages of 21 and 61, driver's licenses expire on the birth date 10 years from the date of issue. Licenses for adults 61 years of age and older expire on the birth date five years from the year issued.

Sales Tax: The state sales tax is 2.9 percent. El Paso County adds 1 percent. The city of Colorado Springs adds 2.5 percent. The Pikes Peak Rural Transportation Authority adds 1 percent. The total is 7.4 percent.

State Income Tax: 4.63 percent

Retirement Income Tax: Taxpayers 55 to 64 years old can exclude a total of $20,000 for Social Security, state and local pensions, federal civil service pensions, military pensions, and private pensions. Those 65 and over can exclude up to $24,000 from the same pension programs.

Property Tax: Property is assessed by the county every other year, and the mill levy applied against this value is voted on by the citizens of the various neighborhoods of the county. In the Pikes Peak region, the rate is generally 0.005 percent of the value, so a $200,000 home would be charged a tax of about $1,000.

Local Real Estate

Overview: The Pikes Peak region includes El Paso County and Teller County, and the area has a wide variety of neighborhoods. Almost any situation you can imagine can be found, except perhaps oceanfront lots!

Average price of a three-bedroom/two-bath home: $230,000

Average price of a two-bedroom condo: $140,000

Common Housing Styles: Many houses have an open design to take in the scenery and the sunshine, so you will see plenty of glass and lots of porches, patios, and decks. The exterior is often stucco or stone, but brick and wood are also common. Solar heating is becoming common, but air-conditioning is rare because it is seldom needed.

Rental Market: The average rent for a two-bedroom home is in the range of $1,000 to $2,000 per month, and are readily available in a variety of styles.

Average rent for a two-bedroom apartment: $800 per month

Communities Popular With Retirees: The Pikes Peak region has several good neighborhoods. The Black Forest has horse property, and there is mountain property available in Crystal Park and Woodland Park. Lofts and Victorian houses can be found in Old Colorado City. Farms and ranches exist southeast of Colorado Springs. To the northeast of Colorado Springs is where you can find your horse ranch.

Nearby Areas to Consider: The city of Pueblo is 35 miles to the south. The Arkansas River cuts through the Rocky Mountains, creating a gorge with towering cliffs. And the cost of living in Pueblo is even lower than Colorado Springs. The city of Divide, 25 miles to the west and on the north slope of Pikes Peak at 9,260 feet, is the gateway to recreation in the Rocky Mountains.

Earning a Living

Business Climate: From 1993 to 2002, the total job growth was 34.6 percent. Government employment rose 20 percent and non-government employment rose 37.7 percent. Colorado Springs is within easy reach of cities such as Denver and Santa Fe. Recently, *Forbes* magazine named Colorado Springs the "13th Best Place for Business and Career" in the United States.

Help in Starting a Business: The Colorado Springs Small Business Resource Guide (*www.springssmallbiz.com*) is a listing of small business resources and is sponsored by the chamber of commerce. The Greater Colorado Springs Economic Development Corporation (719-471-8183; *www.coloradosprings.org*) is ready to help with fast-tracking the planning, site selection, and permit-acquiring process.

Job Market: The unemployment rate in Colorado Springs is 5.2 percent. The city is filled with businesses of all kinds, so many jobs are available. The city lost more than 5,000 manufacturing jobs and 4,000 high-tech jobs from 2000 to 2004, but this is not out of line with the national average.

Medical Care

Colorado Springs has three main hospitals. Memorial Hospital (719-365-5000; *www.memorialhospital.com*), which provides emergency/trauma services, a birth center, cancer services, occupational health services, and cardiovascular care. Penrose St. Francis Health Services (719-776-5000; *www.penrosestfrancis.org*), which was founded by the Sisters of St. Francis and is run jointly between Catholic Health Initiatives and Porter Care Adventist Health System. Sempercare Hospital (717-972-1100; *www.selectmedicalcorp.com*) offers services for long-term acute-care patients.

Services for Seniors

The Senior Resource Council (719-260-0744; *www.seniorresourcecouncil.org*) makes a wide range of senior services available to people in the Pikes Peak Region, including information on housing, medicare, transportation, home healthcare, legal matters, adult education, and more. The Colorado Springs Senior Center (719-385-5933) offers more than 150 different programs per week including arts, education, health/wellness, fitness, special programs, and cultural events. Silver Key Senior Service (719-632-1521; *www.silverkey.org*) helps to fulfill basic and social needs as well as promote independent living. Also contact the Pikes Peak Area Agency on Aging (719-471-7080) and the Family Caregiver Support Center (719-886-7526).

Continuing Education

Pikes Peak Community College (800-456 6847; *www.ppcc.cccoes.edu)* among other services, offers distance education with exams on campus. At the University of Colorado at Colorado Springs (*www.uccs.edu*) the individual colleges offer continuing education courses in their specific fields. Colorado College (719-389-6000; *www.coloradocollege.edu*) offers continuing education courses. Colorado Technical University (*www.ctucoloradosprings.com*) offers a range of degrees.

Crime and Safety

The crime rate is 4,713.4 incidents per 100,000 people. The crime index is 152, which is one and a half times the national average.

Getting Around Town

Public Transportation: The Colorado Springs Transit system (719-385-RIDE; *www.springsgov.com*) operates bus and van routes, as well as the Paratransit system for those unable to use the normal bus system. The Free Range Express (719-636-3739; *www.frontrangeexpress.com*) is a commuter service among the towns of Fountain, Colorado Springs, Monument, Castle Rock, and Denver. Amtrak and Greyhound run a connecting bus service between Colorado Springs, Denver, Fort Collins.

Roads and Highways: I-25; US 24, 85, and 87; state highways 83, 94, and 115

Airports: The City of Colorado Springs Municipal Airport (719-550-1972; *www.springsgov.com*) is about eight miles out of town and is served by eight major airlines.

Let the Good Times Roll

Recreation: You can spend a day, or just have a lunch, at Garden of the Gods campgrounds, and then take a short trip to Old Colorado Springs for shopping and dessert. The city's Adult Sports Program organizes sports leagues for adults and seniors in softball, volleyball, basketball, and flag football. The program serves more than 50,000 adults every year at various locations throughout the city. The Aquatics section of the City of Colorado Springs offers a variety of instructional and recreational programs for people of all ages and swimming abilities. They have two indoor pools and five outdoor pools. Echo Canyon River Expeditions guides tours where the Arkansas River tumbles out of the Rockies and carves its way through the Royal Gorge. It's an unforgettable rafting experience for everyone from family groups to experienced whitewater enthusiasts. The area is also filled with scenic golf courses. Not too far away, in the town of Cripple Creek, you will find a number of gambling casinos.

Culture: For 114 years, the Manitou and Pike's Peak Railway (the world's highest cog railroad and the highest train in the United States) has taken passengers to the 14,110 foot summit of Pikes Peak. Comedy, in some form or other, is always being presented on stage at Loonies. Young at Art is a monthly program for seniors at the Colorado Springs Fine Arts Center. The Garden of the Gods provides eduational tours, as well as a beautiful setting in which to learn about geology and history.

Annual Events: There is world-class racing in Colorado from June through September. See the Indy Racing League, NASCAR, USAC Silver Cup, Trans Am, and the AMA Superbike race on the newly built courses. For nearly two decades, astronomers from across the Uunited States and around the world have been gathering each summer in the mountains west of Colorado Springs. What draws them here each year? These gazers of the stars are enjoying Rocky Mountain Star Stare! Held in July in Pike National Forest, the event is one of this nation's premier star parties. Average attendance is usually 300 astronomers. Take 300 astronomers, spread them around a couple hundred acres, and it doesn't take much math to figure you can camp just about anywhere you want. Even better, set up your telescope and equipment right next to your tent or RV.

When the Grandkids Come: The Rocky Mountain Outdoor Center has a kayak instruction facility on the banks of the famous Arkansas River. Mountasia Family Fun Center has two 18-hole miniature golf courses, a batting range, bumper boats, a game room, and water wars. Joyrides Family Fun Center has go-karts, bumper boats, an arcade, mini golf, kiddie rides, treats and eats, and more. Don't forget to visit America's only mountain zoo, the Cheyenne Mountain Zoo.

More Information

Municipal

The Greater Colorado Springs Chamber of Commerce
2 North Cascade Avenue, Suite 110
Colorado Springs, CO 80903
719-635-1551
www.coloradospringschamber.org

Colorado Springs Convention and Visitors Bureau
515 South Cascade Avenue
Colorado Springs, CO 80903
877-PIKESPEAK
www.coloradosprings-travel.com

Newspaper

The Gazette
30 South Prospect Street
Colorado Springs, CO 80903
719-632-5511
www.gazette.com

Realty

Mary Calvert
2230 West Colorado Avenue
Colorado Springs, CO 80904
888-656-4712
www.marycalvert.com

Fort Collins, Colorado

13

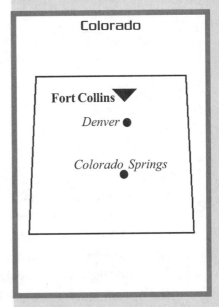

Colorado

Fort Collins ▼

Denver ●

Colorado Springs ●

Fort Collins at a Glance

Fort Collins takes more than a glance. It takes a lot of time (and more than one pair of good walking shoes) to explore this great city. Even though the city is relatively modest in size, there is fabulous biking, hiking, horseback riding, river-rafting, and cross-country skiing for the active senior. Beyond that are museums that feature classic and modern art, live theater, music performances, shopping centers, and art shows. Colorado State University, which offers attractive and challenging classes to the life learner, is consistently rated as one of the best agricultural schools in the United States. National rating services always rate Fort Collins in their "much preferred" category, and it's no wonder! You don't have to leave the neighborhood to see sheer cliffs, waterfalls, and an occasional lake. The beautiful Rocky Mountains are in your backyard, and provide numerous recreational opportunities for both summer and winter. The Cache la Poudre River runs through the city, providing excellent river rafting opportunities. And with more than 300 days of sunshine every year, there's no excuse to be gloomy!

Possible Drawbacks: Well, your family may want to stay with you forever! Also, there seems to be a lack of medical care for Medicare folks.

▶ Nickname: America's Choice City

▶ County: Larimer

▶ Area Code: 970

▶ Population: 126,548

▶ County Population: 273,965

▶ Percent of Population Over 65: 10%

▶ Region: Northern Colorado

▶ Closest Metropolitan Area: Denver, 66 miles

▶ Median Home Price: $235,722

▶ Best Reasons to Retire Here: Beauty of the surroundings, education, recreation, art, and shopping.

Climate

40° N Latitude 105° W Longitude	Average High Temperature (°F)	Average Low Temperature (°F)	Precipitation "	Sunshine (%)
January	45.1	19.9	0.7	71
April	62.8	35.6	2.5	67
July	87.4	58.5	1.6	71
October	66.7	38.7	1.2	72
YEAR	64.8	37.9	18.5	69

Utilities

Overview: The cost of living in Fort Collins is just a point or two above the national average. Housing for new single-family dwellings averages around $272,500, and resale averages $236,000.

Gas Company: XCel Energy (800-895-4999; *www.xcelenergy.com*) serves the area. There is no deposit. Gas/heat appliances average about $60 per month.

Electric Company: Contact the city of Fort Collins Electrical Utilities (970-212-2900). All-electric homes average $110 per month, while partial electric service is $50.

Phone Company: McLeod USA (970-207-0000) or Quest (800-244-1111) both offer service in northern Colorado. Hook-up costs are $35, and a deposit is required, depending on the credit check. Basic monthly service is $18.50.

Water/Sewer Company: The City of Fort Collins (970-212-2900)

Cable Company: Comcast Cable (888-824-4010)

The Tax Axe

Car Registration: For registration and license plates, contact El Paso County (719-520-6240). Call ahead for required documents. New residents have 30 days after arriving to register their vehicles.

Driver's License: For adults between the ages of 21 and 61, driver's licenses expire on the birth date 10 years from the date of issue. Licenses for adults 61 years of age and older expire on the birth date five years from the year issued.

Sales Tax: City sales tax is 3 percent, state sales tax is 2.9 percent, and Larimer County sales tax is just under 1 percent.

State Income Tax: 4.63 percent of federal taxable income

Retirement Income Tax: Taxpayers 55 to 64 years old can exclude a total of $20,000 for Social Security, state and local pensions, federal civil service pensions, military pensions, and private pensions. Those 65 and over can exclude up to $24,000 from the same pension programs. All out-of-state government pensions qualify for the pension exemption.

Property Tax: Property taxes are assessed on a percentage of the property's actual value. You can determine your property tax bill by multiplying the assessed value by the local tax rate. A Homestead exemption for qualifying seniors and the surviving spouse of a senior who previously qualified is available. Seniors must be at least age 65. It allows 50 percent of the first $200,000 in actual value of a primary residence to be exempt. The state pays the tax on the exempted value. The person must have owned and lived in the home for at least 10 years. The senior property tax exemption was suspended but becomes available again for 2006.

Local Real Estate

Overview: Real estate seems to be very big business in Fort Collins these days. The prices are above the national average, and there are several areas that actively solicit retirees. Because much of northern Colorado lends itself to riding, many homes are listed as horse properties.

Average price of a three-bedroom/two-bath home: $235,722

Average price of a two-bedroom condo: $121,000

Common Housing Styles: The sky's the limit! From traditional Cape Cod to passive solar homes, Fort Collins can accommodate you. If you desire a wood-stove-heated cabin in the woods, that is available too.

Rental Market: Fort Collins folks move here to stay, so most properties are owner-occupied. That said, there is an ample market in the rental category, with townhouses, condos, homes, and apartments in many price ranges.

Average rent for a two-bedroom apartment: $700 per month

Communities Popular With Retirees: Linden Park, Lofts Pine Street (Old Town), and Sunflower, which is a gated active adult community.

Nearby Areas to Consider: Windsor is located on the plains of northern Colorado and enjoys spectacular views of the Rocky Mountains and a diverse seasonal climate. Residents of Windsor enjoy a peaceful Colorado lifestyle, with convenient amenities and activities for seniors. You can enjoy a tremendous variety of outdoor activities including biking, hiking, golf, and ice skating. Berthoud is a town in the Fort Collins metro area. Berthoud straddles Larimer and Weld counties, and the estimated population in 2003 was 5,098. It is a small, progressive community that endeavors to provide the quality of life enjoyed by past and present generations while ensuring its position for the future within the dynamic Front Range economic corridor.

Earning a Living

Business Climate: The economic climate of Fort Collins has climbed along with the national level, which has encouraged a broadening commercial base in and around Fort Collins. Colorado State University actually leads the current list with almost 8,000 employees. In addition to government and education, Hewlett Packard, Agilent Technologies, Kodak, Wal-Mart, Advanced Energy, and Anheuser Busch all have a significant presence in the area.

Help in Starting a Business: Jared S. Polis (970-381-0681) develops new businesses. However, if you have it in mind to purchase an existing one, the Citadel Advisory Group, headed by John Smith (970-267-0802; *www.citadeladvisory.com*), and Sunbelt Business Brokers (970-221-9950; *www.cobizbrokers.com*) can help. Donna Beaman of Action International (970-402-9260; *www.action-international.com*) can provide coaching to a new business owner.

Job Market: The local economy is rebounding, and with it is coming a more favorable job market than has existed in the recent past. The continued decline in unemployment means, for seniors, that the job market in Fort Collins is going to be strong in a number of areas where individual expertise may be put to good use. Openings can be expected over the next few years in service, government, retail, construction, finance, and wholesale trade, to name just a few.

Medical Care

Poudre Valley Hospital (970-495-7000; *www.pvhs.org*) is a 285-bed hospital that contains the regional trauma center and is fully equipped with emergency, operating, and critical-care services. The heart center is for medical and surgical care of heart disease and the cardiovascular system, open-heart surgery, and has a rehab program for heart failure. It was named as a "Top 50 US Hospital" by *U.S. News & World Report* for excellence in orthopedic surgery. It provides complete medical and surgical care for patients with cancer.

Services for Seniors

More than 13,000 adults aged 50 and above belong to Poudre Valley Health System's Aspen Club. The organization was established in 1989 to provide a wide range of health education, screenings, hospital discounts, and social opportunities to residents from Fort Collins and surrounding communities. Membership is free. The Aspen Club also works with other senior programs such as AARP, local Retired Senior Volunteers Program, Medicare forums/training, the Mall Walkers Club, the Fort Collins Senior Center, and the Larimer County Office on Aging. The club is a useful resource when you need information about hospital and community services available for older adults—an Aspen Club card speeds admission for inpatient and outpatient services. Educational programs are given on health, wellness, nutrition, and senior lifestyles. For more information, contact the Poudre Valley Health System Senior Services/Aspen Club staff (970-495-8560; *www.pvhs.org*).

Continuing Education

Colorado State University in Fort Collins (*www.colostate.edu*) is among the nation's best in *U.S. News & World Report*'s rankings of "America's Best Colleges and Universities." The university offers multiple continuing education options. The Larimer campus of the Front Range Community College (970-204-8686; *www.frcc.cc.co.us*) is a two-year college offering many continuing education classes. The Fort Collins campus of Aims Community College (*www.aimsced.com*) offers a wide-ranging continuing education program. The University of Colorado Senior Auditor Program (*www.cualum.org/seniorauditor*) was created in 1973 by the Board of Regents, and gives Colorado's senior citizens the opportunity to attend classes on the CU-Boulder campus, 40 miles to the southwest. Any Colorado resident, age 55 or older, may sit in on most regularly scheduled daytime classes, tuition-free. The program is available for both the fall and spring semesters. You do not have to be an alumnus of CU to participate. Auditors do not receive academic credit for courses taken.

Crime and Safety

Fort Collins boasts a declining crime rate. The latest statistics available list a reduction between years 2003 and 2004. For year 2003, the total crime incidents was 4,574, and for 2004, it dipped to 4,014, making the reduction rate a healthy 12 percent overall.

Getting Around Town

Public Transportation: Transport (970-221-6620) is the city of Fort Collins's local bus service. It serves seniors, kids, persons with disabilities, and the general public. Express Charters (970-482-0629) provides excursion bus transportation services through Fort Collins and to other destinations around Colorado.

Roads and Highways: I-287, I-25, and US 87

Airports: The Fort Collins/Loveland Airport (970-962-2852) provides access to Colorado's many recreational sites. Denver International Airport (*www.flydenver.com*) is 55 miles to the south and is one of the largest airports in the world.

Let the Good Times Roll

Recreation: Fort Collins is known as "The Choice City" for many reasons. Let's begin with the senior center (970-221-6644), where seniors can swim laps in the 25-yard lap pool, and enjoy the spa, gymnasium, track, pool tables, and multi-use area. Then there's hunting, fishing, camping, picnicking, hiking, biking, horseback riding, cross-country skiing, snowmobiling, snowshoeing, white-water boating, rafting, canoeing, kayaking, and wildlife watching, in addition to such indoor pursuits as mall-walking. There's a lot of tennis and golfing going on, too! Just check in with the chamber of commerce (*www.ftcollins.com*). Rocky Mountain National Park is only one hour away. The Edora Pool Ice Center has indoor swimming and an ice arena. By the way, Horsetooth Reservoir and Horsetooth Mountain both take their distinctive name from a tooth-shaped piece of granite that dominates the skyline to the west.

Culture: Visit the Gardens of Spring Creek, the city's new community-oriented botanic gardens on an 18-acre site. Then go see the Anheuser-Busch Tour Center (970-490-4691), the Avery House Historic District (970-221-0533), and Discovery Science Center (970-472-3990), to name just a few of the choices. Then, for evening cultural fun, check Bas Bleu Theatre Company, Canyon Concert Ballet, Fort Collins Symphony Orchestra, Front Range Chamber Players, the Larimer Chorale, and OpenStage Theatre and Company.

Annual Events: In April is the Spring Contest, and the Pow-wow and Indian Market. In June, visit the Junior League Garden Tour, or Colorado Brewer's Festival. In July, see the Fabric of Legacies Quilt Show. August brings in the Larimer County Fair and New WestFest. September has the Museum of Contemporary Art Studio Tour. In November, see the Great Christmas Hall and Hall of Trees at Lincoln Center, the Holiday Craft Sale at the senior center, the Northern Colorado Woodcarvers show/competition, and the Fort Collins Annual Depot tour. In December, see the Canyon Concert Ballet's *The Nutcracker,* and Larimer Chorale's *Messiah and Carols.*

When the Grandkids Come: Depending on how young the kids are, you can start them out at the city pool. Visit the Rolland Moore Park Racquet Complex for tennis and racquetball, horseback riding at Cottonwood Hollow, Red Feather Guides, Sylvan Dale Guest Ranch, or Tip Top Guest Ranch, or the Fossil Creek Park, with its playground featuring fossils.

More Information

Municipal
Chamber of Commerce
Fort Collins Area Chamber of Commerce
225 South Meldrum Street
Fort Collins, CO 80521
970-482-3746
www.fortcollinschamber.com

Newspaper
Fort Collins Coloradoan
1212 Riverside Avenue
Fort Collins, CO 8052
www.coloradoan.com

Realty
We do not have a Realtor recommendation for Fort Collins. As an option, check out *www.realtor.com* or *www.homegain.com.* Select a Realtor with both CRS and GRI designations after their names, since it means that these folks have gone the extra mile and are both graduates of the Realtor Institute and Certified Residential Specialists.

14

Boca Raton, Florida

Boca Raton at a Glance

Think country club. Seriously. This is truly an upscale place to retire. From exciting nightlife to family fun, Boca Raton has it all. Did we mention that it's beautiful? The homes here are set in lovely neighborhoods, many of which feature incredible xeriscape (water conservation) landscaping. The city actively recycles waste and protects environmentally sensitive areas. This just may be the relaxed and gracious retirement you envisioned during all those years of working long hours, and watching your portfolio grow. Palm Beach County has more than 47 miles of white sandy beaches. We'd be foolish not to mention the Boca Raton Resort and Club. It's America's most exclusive premier resort, set on 356 acres. The main building was built in 1926 by Addison Mizner and is an architectural curiosity with its Moorish and Gothic influences, hidden gardens, archways, intricate mosaics, and fountains. The rest of the city of Boca Raton also echoes Mizner's taste and revels in a lush, plush, lifestyle. Palm Beach County enjoys mild tropical temperatures year-round. The name "Boca Raton" literally means "rat's mouth" in Spanish, but the name loosely translates into "thieves inlet," where dishonorable robbers hide.

Possible Drawbacks: It gets fairly warm in the summer. Okay, it gets really hot. Also, one blushes to mention the cost of living.

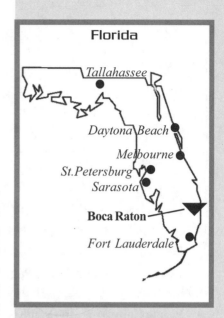

Florida

- Nickname: City for All Seasons
- County: Palm Beach
- Area Code: 561
- Population: 77,411
- County Population: 1,131,184
- Percent of Population Over 65: 19.8%
- Region: Southeast Florida
- Closest Metropolitan Area: Fort Lauderdale, 21 miles
- Median Home Price: $230,000
- Best Reasons to Retire Here: Exclusive lifestyle, fabulous housing, diverse recreational opportunities, excellent healthcare, low crime rate, and beautiful beaches.

Climate

26° N Latitude 80° W Longitude	Average High Temperature (°F)	Average Low Temperature (°F)	Precipitation (")	Sunshine (%)
January	74.3	51.1	2.3	66
April	83.3	59.0	2.9	76
July	90.5	70.9	7.7	72
October	85.3	65.1	4.6	70
YEAR	83.3	61.7	55.8	70

Utilities

Overview: The utilities cost sits at an average of 105, as opposed to the national average of 100. You can expect to pay a little more for everything here.

Gas Company: Florida Public Utilities (561-278-2636; *www.fpuc.com*)

Electric Company: Florida Public Utilities Company (561-278-2636; www.fpuc.com) or Florida Power & Light (561-994-8227; *www.fpl.com*)

Phone Company: Bell South is in Boca Raton (561-780-2355) and Pompano Beach (954-943-9023; *www.bellsouth.com*)

Water/Sewer Company: The residential charge by City Utility Service (561-338-7300) is $13.19 for the first bathroom and $6.59 for each additional one. Residents are billed bimonthly along with the water charges. There is a 25 percent surcharge on accounts outsides the city limits.

Cable Company: Adelphia (888-683-1000; *www.adelphia.com*)

The Tax Axe

Car Registration: This must be completed within 10 days of reporting to work, registering children in school, or registering to vote. A word of caution: There are differences in the amounts of taxes assessed, and they change at six months' of ownership. Best advice? Do not purchase a new car and then relocate to Florida within six months. Otherwise, you will be assessed at least 6 percent sales and use tax on that vehicle. You should wait and buy new when you get to Florida.

Driver's License: Contact Florida's Department of Highway Safety and Motor Vehicles for information (954-765-4697; *www.hsmv.state.fl.us*).

Sales Tax: 6.5 percent state sales tax. Check with the state for exemptions.

State Income Tax: There is no state income tax.

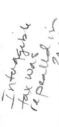

Intangible tax was repealed in 2007

Retirement Income Tax: Retirement income is not taxed. However, there is an intangibles tax of $1 per $1,000 of the value of investments such as stocks, bonds, notes, and mutual funds. As of 2004, the first $250,000 (individual filers) or $500,000 (married, filing jointly) of taxable assets are exempt.

Property Tax: All property is taxable at 100 percent of its valuation. Exemptions exist, but are complicated. For example, there is a senior citizens' exemption, but it only applies to the county or city millage, not to millage of school districts or other taxing authorities. Check with a local tax expert regarding your situation.

Local Real Estate

Overview: Boca Raton is unbelievably beautiful, but also has rapidly climbing prices. With the range of prices comes a unique diversity of residential choices, from basic contemporary homes to extraordinary dream estates, complete with tennis courts and heli-pads. Older coastal communities, many of which feature ocean views, will be more upscale, particularly around the Boca Raton Resort & Club, where condominium units in a building such as the Addison start at $1.5 million.

Average price of a three-bedroom/two-bath home: $255,462

Average price of a two-bedroom condo: $173,935

Common Housing Styles: There are lots of Mediterranean houses, clay tile roofs, and stucco. Bright and pastel color is everywhere. Most homes have pools, and a good percentage have porches (either screened or not). The Old Floresta Historic District is a small residential area full of Mizner-designed homes.

Rental Market: Rental availability can be very tight. According to one expert we consulted, at the end of 2004, rentals were saturated to the tune of about 96 percent in the Boca Raton area.

Average rent for a two-bedroom apartment: $1,000 per month

Communities Popular With Retirees: Century Village, Palm Springs, Broken Sound, and Stonebridge.

Nearby Areas to Consider: The City of Delray Beach won the title of All American City in 1993-1994. It has been recognized as a Florida Main Street Community, and was named the "Best Run Town in Florida" by *Florida Trend* magazine. There is also spectacular scuba diving at the wreck of the *S.S. Inchulva*, a few hundred yards from shore. Jupiter is a small town in Palm Beach County, approximately 12 miles north of Palm Beach Shores. It is one of the few towns in the area that does not have an island in front of it, so the beaches are part of the mainland.

Earning a Living

Business Climate: The average household income is high at $62,594, and the median age is 42.2. According to the Milken Institute's "Best Performing Cities" list, Boca Raton-West Palm Beach ranks fourth overall for 2004. What this means is that Boca Raton has proven itself capable of creating and sustaining jobs better than most.

Help in Starting a Business: Ten resources that can be helpful to business startups are the Small Business Administration (*www.sba.gov*), the Small Business Development Center (*www.fausbdc.com*), the U.S. Chamber of Commerce Small Business Center (*www.uschamber.com/sb*), the Florida Small Business Group (*www.floridasmallbusiness.com*), Enterprise Florida (*www.eflorida.com*), the Florida

Venture Forum (*www.flvencap.org*), SCORE Counselors to America's Small Business (*www.score-chapter412.org*), the Odeon Group (305-681-9600), Micro Business USA (305-438-1407), and First Florida Capital at (888-320-5504).

Job Market: Jobs are available on a full-time or part-time basis, depending on skill levels. In the first eight months of 2004, almost 82,000 jobs for Floridians were created across the state. Boca Raton certainly had its share.

Medical Care

The Boca Raton Community Hospital (561-395-7100; *www.brch.com*) is a non-profit hospital that was founded 30 years ago. It has 394 beds, making it the largest hospital in the southern part of Palm Beach County. The Delray Medical Center (561-498-4440; *www.tenethealth.com/Delray*) specializes in cardiac care. It has been honored as one of the Top 100 orthopedic hospitals in the United States. The North Broward Medical Center (954-786-6400; *www.browardhealth.org*) is a comprehensive, 409-bed healthcare facility. The Senior Research Center, classrooms and 250-seat conference center, provide space for lectures, meetings, support groups, and screenings. The North Ridge Medical Center (954-776-6000; *www.northridgemedical.com*) houses 391 beds, and is the largest open heart surgery provider in both Broward and Palm Beach Counties. The West Boca Medical Center (561-488-8000; *www.westbocamedctr.com*) is a 185-bed, fully accredited acute care facility. A Senior Outreach Center is located in the Boca Hamptons Shopping Plaza and offers classes addressing health issues of interest to the mature adult, as well as programs and services for children and their parents.

Services for Seniors

The Mae Volen Senior Center (561-395-8920; *www.maevolen.com*) has the mission of primarily serving the older population of Palm Beach County in appropriate areas of health and human services, with special emphasis and attention to the low-income senior citizens of the southern portion of Palm Beach County. Among the many services offered are planned excursions, lectures, trips, meals, access to social activities, bus rides, and a nifty library complete with tape players for the vision impaired and dyslexic. Sunshine Senior Services Inc. (561-368-8101) is a fee-for-service agency that can provide information and expert help for adults going through life's transitions and changes. Owned by Sunrise Senior Living, Stratford Court (561-392-2772; *www.martinaia.com*) is for seniors who want to maintain their rewarding lives without the responsibilities of running a household.

Continuing Education

The Center for Lifetime Learning at Palm Beach Community College (561-868-3556; *www.pbcc.edu/lifetimelearning*) charges a membership fee of $155, which entitles a member to unlimited admission to all classes from November through April, based on seating availability. The program is unique in that it allows for classes to begin on a daily, weekly, and monthly basis. The center offers more than 130 courses, forums, and lectures taught by 100 volunteer faculty members.

Crime and Safety

The crime rate in the city of Boca Raton is lower than the national average. The crime index is 245.3 per 100,000 people (the national average is 330.6). In addition to a low crime rate, Boca Raton boasts an Elder Crime Specialist (561-338-1239). This office serves as a liaison between the police department and the elder community. This is part of the police department's commitment and resources necessary to make Boca Raton a safer place for its elders.

Getting Around Town

Public Transportation: The Palm Tran (Palm Beach County Bus Line) (561-930-4BUS; *www.co.palm-beach.fl.us/palmtran*)

Roads and Highways: I-85, Florida Turnpike, Sawgrass Expressway, A1A, US 1, and US 441

Airports: Palm Beach International Airport (*www.pbia.org*) is 30 miles to the north, and is served by 20 major airlines that serve almost 6 million passengers annually. Fort Lauderdale International Airport (*www.broward.org/airport*) is 20 miles to the south, and is served by 29 major airlines.

Ports: Port Everglades in Fort Lauderdale/Hollywood, the Port of Palm Beach, and Port of Miami-Dodge Island all serve the Boca Raton area.

Let the Good Times Roll

Recreation: Family attractions in Boca Raton include Boomer's Family Recreation Center, an Australian-theme fun park; and the Buehler Planetarium, which offers various laser-light shows and educational programs. For outdoor aficionados, there are several golf courses, fishing tournaments, polo matches, horse shows, fiestas, spectator sports events year-round, boating, swimming pools, parks for picnics, scuba diving near coral reefs, and superb shopping.

Culture: For a complete overview of cultural opportunities, check with the Boca Raton Cultural Consortium (*www.artsinboca.org*). Offerings include the ballet, chorale music, a historical society, philharmonic orchestra, science museum, and various theaters. The Boca Raton Museum of Art hosts a number of exciting annual events and exhibitions. The Annual Auction is one of the museum's most popular fund-raising events, with more than 700 premier items. The Annual Outdoor Juried Art Festival, held outdoors in beautiful Mizner Park, showcases the works of more than 250 artists from around the world, and the Annual Gala is the museum's most elegant affair.

Annual Events: There is at least one event scheduled for each day of the year. January has the Children's Winter Fair, Monte Carlo Night, and the Martin Luther King Jr. celebration. February has the Fiesta of Arts, the Annual Arts Festival, and the Collector Car Auction. March has the Children's Fair and the Spring Fling. April has the Gail Hayward 5K Run/Walk, Fun Day at the Library, and Cinema in the Park. May brings the Make-A-Wish Annual Golf Classic and Summer Music in the Park. June has the annual summer extravaganza and the Summer Luau. July has the Fabulous Fourth and the Farewell to Summer party. For a complete list of events, see the Community Event Calendar (*www.bocaraton.com*).

When the Grandkids Come: The Children's Museum of Boca Raton (*www.cmboca.com*) teaches children local history and folklore through exhibits inside a 1912 wooden house. Two of the more popular exhibits in the museum (a mini-market and a pretend bank) demonstrate to children our economic system. Kid Fest, held in the spring, combines puppet shows and historical demonstrations to educate and entertain the young visitors.

More Information

Municipal
Greater Boca Raton Chamber of Commerce
1800 North Dixie Highway
Boca Raton, FL 33432
561-395-443
www.bocaratonchamber.com

Newspaper
Boca Raton News
5140 Congress Avenue
Boca Raton, FL
561-893-6549
www.bocaratonnews.com

Realty
Petrolia Team
6070 North Federal Highway
Boca Raton, FL 33487
561-997-9090
www.boca-delray-realestate.com

15

Daytona Beach, Florida

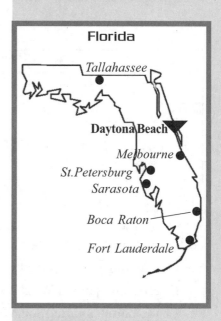

Florida

Daytona Beach at a Glance

Daytona Beach has been labeled the most gorgeous stretch of beach on the planet. That's a nice thing to discuss as you sit under your beach umbrella, sipping a cold drink, with the sunset behind you, digging your toes into warm, white sand. Once home to presidents and wealthy entrepreneurs, downtown Daytona Beach is now the core of the city. Downtown's main promenade, Beach Street, boasts a mile-long riverfront park lined with shops, eateries, and a professional baseball team—the Daytona Cubs—which plays in the Jackie Robinson Stadium on the waterfront. A new center for the arts in Volusia County, the News-Journal Center, was completed in 2005. Although the beach is still the biggest attraction, the Ocean Center convention complex, the new Daytona Beach International Airport, the new Ladies Professional Golf Association golf course, and the Halifax Marina are all involved in the renaissance that has been going on in Daytona Beach. Historical sites such as the Main Street Pier, the Oceanfront Boardwalk, and the Clock Tower add to the appeal. *U.S. News & World Report*'s "2005 Best Colleges" guide named Embry-Riddle a number one school in the Aerospace/Aeronautical/Astronautical Engineering category.

Possible Drawbacks: The crush of tourists can be daunting. Add to that the Florida summer heat, Spring Break students at the beach, and traffic, and you could have issues with life in the fast lane.

- ▸ Nickname: The World's Most Famous Beach
- ▸ County: Volusia
- ▸ Area Code: 386
- ▸ Population: 71,635
- ▸ County Population: 478,670
- ▸ Percent of Population Over 65: 17%
- ▸ Region: Eastern Florida
- ▸ Closest Metropolitan Area: Orlando, 45 miles
- ▸ Median Home Price: $162,600
- ▸ Best Reasons to Retire Here: Not only do you have abundant sunshine and white, sandy beaches, you also have seven golf courses within easy reach. And you're even close to Orlando!

Climate

29° N Latitude 81° W Longitude	Average High Temperature (°F)	Average Low Temperature (°F)	Precipitation (")	Sunshine (%)
January	68.0	46.8	2.5	58
April	79.9	58.5	2.6	73
July	89.8	72.5	5.6	65
October	81.5	65.1	4.8	60
YEAR	79.7	61.0	49.3	63

Utilities

Overview: The utilities in Daytona Beach are a pleasant surprise. The average cost of living in the city is a modest 66, with the national average at 100.

Gas Company: Florida Public Utilities Company (386-668-2600; *www.fpuc.com*)

Electric Company: Florida Public Utilities (386-668-2600; *www.fpuc.com*)

Phone Company: Bell South (386-780-2800; *www.bellsouth.com*)

Water/Sewer Company: Daytona Beach Water and Sewer (386-258-3172; *www.daytonachamber.com/relocation*)

Cable Company: Cable Connections (386-252-2707)

The Tax Axe

Car Registration: This must be completed within 10 days of reporting to work, registering children in school, or registering to vote. A word of caution: There are differences in the amounts of taxes assessed, and they change at six months' of ownership. Best advice? Do not purchase a new car and then relocate to Florida within six months. Otherwise, you will be assessed at least 6 percent sales and use tax on that vehicle. You should wait and buy a new car when you get to Florida.

Driver's License: Contact Florida's Department of Highway Safety and Motor Vehicles for information (954-765-4697; *www.hsmv.state.fl.us*).

Sales Tax: There is a 6.5 percent sales tax. Check with the state for exemptions.

State Income Tax: There is no state income tax.

Retirement Income Tax: Retirement income is not taxed. However, there is an intangibles tax of $1 per $1,000 of the value of investments such as stocks, bonds, notes, and mutual funds. As of 2004, the first $250,000 (individual filers) or $500,000 (married, filing jointly) of taxable assets are exempt.

Property Tax: All property is taxable at 100 percent of its valuation. Exemptions exist, but are complicated. For example, there is a senior citizen exemption, but it only applies to the county or city millage, not to millage of school districts or other taxing authorities. Check with a local tax expert regarding your situation.

Local Real Estate

Overview: The real estate market is tight, with prices reflecting the continuing popularity of Daytona Beach, and all of Florida. Bargains are few, but can be found if you are willing to look.

Average price of a three-bedroom/two-bath home: $325,000

Average price of a two-bedroom condo: $125,000

Common Housing Styles: Concrete block, ranch, Spanish, and Moorish

Rental Market: There are lots of rentals, but like housing all over Florida, it is becoming more expensive, with modest homes renting for $1,500 per month.

Average rent for a two-bedroom apartment: $850 per month

Communities Popular with Retirees: Deland and Holly Hill both cater to seniors, particularly when the time comes for moving into independent living or nursing home facilities.

Nearby Areas to Consider: Ormond-by-the-Sea and Ormond Beach are located at the north end of Daytona Beach. Ormond Beach, a lovely seaside community often called the "sparkling city by the sea," is known for an exceptional quality of life. Holly Hill is situated on the west bank of the Halifax River in Volusia County. It is bounded on the north by Ormond Beach, on the south by Daytona Beach, on the east by the Halifax River, and on the west by Nova Road. The city's area of four square miles occupies a ridge land along the Halifax River.

Earning a Living

Business Climate: According to the Milken Institute's "Best Performing Cities," which logs job creation and sustainability, Daytona Beach is currently fifth in the country. The research includes, among other things, employment and salary growth. This means you are very likely to land a fine job in an industry that's doing well. There is no guarantee, of course, but Daytona Beach looks very good for moving your business or finding a job.

Help in Starting a Business: The University of Central Florida Small Business Development Center (*www.bus.ucf.edu/sbdc*) sponsors seminars and workshops on a variety of topics. You do not have to be in business already to attend these programs. All seminars and workshops are offered at low cost with additional discounts for taking a series of related programs. They also provide information on numerous sources of small business assistance and other information.

Job Market: The Daytona Beach Chamber of Commerce (386-255-0981; *www.daytonachamber.com*) boasts the area's biggest networking event, Business After Hours. Hundreds of people attend these business-card exchange events, which are held bimonthly throughout the area. Call the chamber for details.

Medical Care

Columbia Medical Center in Daytona (386-239-5000) is a 214-bed hospital and is rated in the Top 10 Columbia facilities in Florida in patient satisfaction surveys. It is a general- and acute-care hospital. Columbia Medical Center in Ormond Beach (386-672-4161) is a 119-bed hospital and is noted for its Peninsula Regional Rehabilitation Center (inpatient rehab), medical surgery unit, and outpatient services. The Halifax Community Health Center, (386-254-4000; *http://hfch.org/index.html*) is a 764-bed full-service tertiary care hospital that serves Volusia and Flagler Counties and offers a continuum of care through affiliated organizations. Memorial Hospital (386-676-6000; *http://hfch.org*) has more than 400 beds.

Services for Seniors

The Council on Aging of Volusia County (386-253-4700; 888-252-6110; *www.coaiaa.org*) acts as a gatekeeper for most elder services in the Volusia County area. They provide access to in-home services, emergency assistance, special events, and more. The Social Security Administration provides a senior citizens information line (386-255-7543) if you have any questions.

Continuing Education

The Daytona Beach Community College (*www.dbcc.cc.fl.us*), with an enrollment of 6,257, offers a multi-faceted continuing education program. Bethune Cookman College (*www.bethune.cookman.edu*), with an enrollment of 2,638, offers courses online as well as on campus. Keiser College-Daytona (*www.keisercollege.cc.fl.us*) has a department of Continuing Education that offers courses online and at convenient hours. Embry-Riddle Aeronautical University Generations (*www.db.erau.edu*) is for those of us who love aviation. Here is a chance to do it all again with a week-long program. You can review, while your young one learns about, flight training, air traffic control, meteorology, aircraft maintenance, and space technology. The tuition is $1,800 per pair and includes flight fees, simulator sessions, classroom instruction, on-campus meals, materials, and field trips.

Crime and Safety

The total number of violent crimes in Daytona Beach in 2003 was 1,214. The number of murders and homicides was five. The violent crime rate was 18.5 per 1,000 people. The *www.city-data.com* crime index is 928.9, with the national average at 330.6.

Getting Around Town

Public Transportation: VOTRAN (386-756-7496; *www.votran.org*) is Volusia County's public transit system. It provides busses that run on scheduled routes throughoute Volusia County.

Roads and Highways: US 95, US 4; Hwy 1, 92, and 40, 483, and 415

Airports: The Daytona Beach International Airport (386-248-8069; *www.flydaytonafirst.com*) provides service to more than 150 destinations worldwide. Orlando International Airport, (*www.orlandoairports.net*) is 50 miles to the south-west and is served by 62 airlines.

Let the Good Times Roll

Recreation: Daytona USA (386-947-6800; *www.daytonausa.com*) is a 60,000-square-foot interactive motor sports attraction that is the world-class showplace of America's fastest sport. Here you will find the heart-pounding thunder of bumper-to-bumper competition on the high banks of the Daytona International Speedway. You can also experience the thrills and spills of high-tech motion simulators. See some great baseball as the local minor league Daytona Cubs (*www.daytonacubs.com*) show it off in the Jackie Robinson Ballpark. These players, part of the Cubs farm club, took the State Championship in 2004. Nearby attractions include Walt Disney World, Kennedy Space Center, St. Johns River Country (DeLand area), St. Augustine, Silver Springs, Sea World, Universal Studios Florida, and Cypress Gardens. For information on hunting and fishing licenses, call the state of Florida (386-254-4635).

Culture: The News-Journal Center (*www.news-journalcenter.com*), a facility for performing and visual arts and education, offers professional performances, educational outreach, and community-wide involvement. Also visit the Halifax Historical Museum (*www.halifaxhistorical.org*), Museum of Arts and Sciences, and the Center for Florida History (*www.moas.org*), the Southeast Museum of Photography (*www.smponline.org*), and the Ponce de Leon Inlet Lighthouse (*www.ponceinlet.org*).

Annual Events: This is a city known for its wonderful raceway and year-round outdoor activities. A short list of events might include the Rolex 24 Hour Race, the Daytona 500, Bike Week, the Daytona 200, the Garden Show, the Spring Car Show & Swap, Spring Break Nationals, National Cheerleading Championship, the Pepsi 400, Florida International Festival-LSO, and Biketoberfest. For a comprehensive list of annual events, check out the community calendar (*http://daytonabeachcvb.org/community.cfm*).

When the Grandkids Come: There are several options right in the center of the city, beginning with the Daytona Lagoon at Ocean Walk Village. The lagoon also has Grand Prix go-kart racing, mini-golf, an awesome arcade, laser tag, rock climbing, and a play center, which should keep the kids entertained for awhile. For a continued listing that includes such diverse activities as skating, surfing, swimming rock climbing, para-sailing, Hawaiian luaus, and a tour of an honest-to-goodness chocolate factory, check out the Daytona Beach online event calendar (*http://daytonabeach.com/AtFamilyFun.asp*).

More Information

Municipal

City of Daytona Beach
P.O. Box 2451
Daytona Beach, FL 32115
386-671-8000
www.ci.daytona-beach.fl.us

Daytona Beach Chamber of Commerce
126 East Orange Avenue
Daytona Beach, FL 32114
386-255-0981
www.daytonachamber.com

Newspaper

Daytona Beach News-Journal
901 Sixth Street
Holly Hill, FL 32117
386-252-1511
www.news-journalonline.com

The Avion
Embry-Riddle Aeronautical University Student Newspaper
600 South Clyde Morris Boulevard
Daytona Beach, FL 32114
800-862-2416
www.avionnewspaper.com

Realty

We do not have a Realtor recommendation for Daytona Beach. As an option, check out *www.realtor.com* or *www.homegain.com*. Select a Realtor with both CRS and GRI designations after their names, since it means that these folks have gone the extra mile and are both graduates of the Realtor Institute and Certified Residential Specialists.

16 ▶ Fort Lauderdale, Florida

Florida

Tallahassee

Daytona Beach

Melbourne

St.Petersburg

Sarasota

Boca Raton

Fort Lauderdale

Fort Lauderdale at a Glance

Fort Lauderdale is located directly against miles of beaches on the Atlantic Ocean. Miami and Miami Beach are its neighbors to the south, while Boca Raton and West Palm Beach are to the north. Some of the highlights of Fort Lauderdale, other than the beautiful beaches, must include the coastal-waterway, Las Olas Boulevard, and the Riverwalk. Fort Lauderdale earns its "Venice of America" title from all the different kinds of traffic by watercraft. The Broward Center for the Performing Arts offers numerous excellent performances. Museums and parks exist throughout the city. Fort Lauderdale has more than 300 miles of navigable waterways and 40,000 resident yachts. But you need not have a yacht, because the Water Taxi of Fort Lauderdale provides a scenic, affordable mode of transportation to and from many restaurants, shops, and theater. For entertaining trips through the canals and waterways, the Jungle Queen, Carrie B, and Riverfront Cruises offer day tours and dinner cruises. These water taxis also provide entertaining and informative commentaries on the sights, and information about some of Fort Lauderdale's celebrity residents.

Possible Drawbacks: Fort Lauderdale has lots of water! If you are expecting a simple country setting, this isn't it. With the population increasing at the rate of 2.6 percent per year, all the elements that go along with that are here, including higher than average prices.

▶ Nickname: The Venice of America

▶ County: Broward

▶ Area Code: 954

▶ Population: 170,857

▶ County Population: 1,623,018

▶ Percent of Population Over 65: 40%

▶ Region: Eastern Florida

▶ Closest Metropolitan Area: Miami, 26 miles

▶ Median Home Price: $296,800

▶ Best Reasons to Retire Here: Fort Lauderdale is a cosmopolitan city, as well as a coastal-waterway city. The sunshine is wonderful too! Just be sure to wear your sailor cap.

Climate

26° N Latitude 80° W Longitude	Average High Temperature (°F)	Average Low Temperature (°F)	Precipitation (")	Sunshine (%)
January	74.3	51.1	2.3	66
April	83.3	59.0	2.9	76
July	90.5	70.9	7.7	72
October	85.3	65.1	4.6	70
YEAR	83.3	61.7	55.8	70

Utilities

Overview: The overall cost of living in Fort Lauderdale is higher than the national average. Housing and health care are above the national average. Groceries are also slightly higher. However, the cost of for utilities is below the national average.

Gas Company: Atlantic Gas Corp (954-733-9936)

Electric Company: Florida Power and Light (*www.fpl.com*)

Phone Company: Bell South (954-491-0158; *www.bellsouth.com*)

Water/Sewer Company: The services of the Public Service Department include all water, wastewater, and storm water activities throughout the city (954-828-8000; *http://ci.ftlaud.fl.us/public_services/*).

Cable Company: Cable television is available from Comcast (*www.comcast.com*).

The Tax Axe

Car Registration: This must be completed within 10 days of reporting to work, registering children in school, or registering to vote. A word of caution: There are differences in the amounts of taxes assessed, and they change at six months' of ownership. Best advice? Do not purchase a new car and then relocate to Florida within six months. Otherwise, you will be assessed at least 6 percent sales and use tax on that vehicle. You should wait and buy new when you get to Florida.

Driver's License: Contact Florida's Department of Highway Safety and Motor Vehicles for information (954-765-4697; *www.hsmv.state.fl.us*).

Sales Tax: 6.5 percent state sales tax. Check with the state office for exemptions.

State Income Tax: There is no state income tax.

Retirement Income Tax: Retirement income is not taxed. However, there is an intangibles tax of $1 per $1,000 of the value of investments such as stocks, bonds, notes, and mutual funds. As of 2004, the first $250,000 (individual filers) or $500,000 (married, filing jointly) of taxable assets are exempt.

Property Tax: All property is taxable at 100 percent of its valuation. Exemptions exist, but are complicated. There is a senior citizen exemption, but it only applies to the county or city millage, not to millage of school districts or other taxing authorities.

Local Real Estate

Overview: As in so many other places in Florida, prices continue to climb, developers continue to build, and people continue to move in. The sky seems to be the limit on real estate, but reasonably priced housing can still be had, if you're willing to look around. You should probably contact a Realtor for the best deals.

Average price of a three-bedroom/two-bath home: $585,000

Average price of a two-bedroom condo: $525,000

Common Housing Styles: Fort Lauderdale's European influence can be felt in many areas with Mediterranean villas and Spanish-flavored architecture. On the other hand, many new developments are opting for simpler, stucco bungalows, featuring single-story floor plans and screened-in porches.

Rental Market: In addition to all the wonderful amenities in the community, apartments are available for every taste. There are more than 50 complexes with apartments that range from $600 to $6,000 per month, depending on the lifestyle for which you are looking.

Average rent for a two-bedroom apartment: $1,800 per month

Communities Popular With Retirees: Pompano Beach and Deerfield Beach

Nearby Areas to Consider: Coconut Creek, the butterfly capital of the world, is located in south Florida about 20 minutes northwest of Fort Lauderdale. The city is 11.3 square miles with approximately 48,000 residents. Housing is primarily single-family homes, condominiums, and townhouses within professionally landscaped communities.

Earning a Living

Business Climate: From software technology to international trade, Fort Lauderdale is the center of a robust and diversified business climate. In recent years, Broward County has substantially outpaced the national economic growth rate, while the county population has climbed to nearly 1.7 million.

Help in Starting a Business: The Small Business Development Center Fort Lauderdale (954-771-6520) works with start-up and existing business owners providing free counseling services on issues such as business planning, registering a business, financing, regulations, licensing, training, workforce, manufacturing, environmental, and various other business management disciplines. The SCORE Counselors to America's Small Business Fort Lauderdale Beach (954-356-7263) is a national, nonprofit association and resource partner with the U.S. Small Business Administration. With 12,400 volunteer members and 389 chapters, SCORE offers a seasoned source of professional business counseling at no charge for business owners and start-up ventures.

Job Market: According to the U.S. Department of Labor, the July 2005 preliminary unemployment rate was at a reasonable 3.8 percent. This means that there are lots of opportunities here. A second career is definitely possible in Fort Lauderdale.

Medical Care

North Broward Hospital District (954-759-7400; *www.browardhealth.org*) is a medical information center, plus a registration service for Senior Supper Clubs or Mall Walkers groups. The Broward General Medical Center (954-355-4400) is a general and surgical service hospital and currently offers 560 beds. For seniors, there are such tangent services as elderly/disabled intermediate nursing care and Alzheimer's care. With a full-time, paid staff of more than 2,200, you're sure to find answers to your questions. The Imperial Point Medical Center (954-776-8500) is a general and surgical facility with 180 beds. It offers several inpatient and outpatient services, among which are: hospice, pain alleviation and palliative care, arthritis centers, and geriatric services. The Clinica de las Americas (954-761-1020) is situated in the center of a well-established Hispanic community and seeks to reach the under served as well as provide an ambient air of cultural respect. For those of Hispanic background, the clinic hopes to provide a comfort zone within which to receive primary medical care.

Services for Seniors

The Area Agency on Aging of Broward County (954) 714-3456; *www.seniorsummit.org*) is a gold mine of information and can link seniors to many services available in Broward County, including wheelchair service, Meals on Wheels, or the name of a senior group in your neighborhood. Senior Connection (954-714-3464) links seniors to a series of community-based services to maximize the independence of elders, allowing them to remain in the community and their homes. Assistance is available in English, Spanish, and Creole. The Nova Southeastern University Counseling Center for Older Adults (954-262-5843; *www.nova.edu/nccoa*) is in the Maxwell Maltz Psychology Building.

Continuing Education

Contact the Institute for Learning in Retirement in Fort Lauderdale (954-262-8471; *www.nova.edu*). The Nova Southeastern University is the biggest independent higher education facility in Florida, and is the eighth largest in the nation. Many opportunities are offered for seniors, among which is the Institute for Learning in Retirement and while not specifically aimed at seniors, the Interdisciplinary Arts Program, which begins at the graduate level, is a fascinating notion. The School of Adult & Continuing Education (954-493-8892; *www.barry.edu*) has the mission to "provide adult students with undergraduate/graduate credit, non-credit, and certificate programs which recognize the educational needs of adult learner and promote lifelong learning."

Crime and Safety

According to the Fort Lauderdale Police Department's Uniform Crime Report, the overall crime rate fell between 2000 and 2003. However, between 2003 and 2004, the crime rate began climbing, and, for the first quarter of 2005, has risen some 20 percent over 2004. Fort Lauderdale has historically suffered a high rate of criminal activity.

Getting Around Town

Public Transportation: With Broward County Transit (*www.co.broward.fl.us/bct/welcome.htm*), persons 65 years and older have the option of obtaining a reduced fare card or showing another acceptable form of identification with proof of age. The senior fare currently sits at 50 cents per ride.

Roads and Highways: I-95, Florida's Turnpike; I-595, I-75 (Port Everglades Expressway); Sawgrass Expressway, and A1A

Airports: Fort Lauderdale-Hollywood International Airport serves more than 40,000 passengers each day in four modern terminals (*www.fort-lauderdale-fll.com*).

Ports: Once known as Bay Mabel Harbor (*www.broward.org/port.htm*), Port Everglades serves Fort Lauderdale, Hollywood, and Dania. In addition to servicing in excess of 2,700 freight ships in 2004, this port welcomed well over 2.3 million cruise passengers, and operates with an annual budget of more than $112 million.

Let the Good Times Roll

Recreation: Fort Lauderdale is home to Boomers, St. Tropez Casino Cruises, Stanahan House, Dania Beach Hurricane, and My Jewish Discovery Place. Tourists also enjoy Graves Museum of Archaeology & Natural History, the Fort Lauderdale Antique Car Museum, Old Fort Lauderdale Village and Museum, Everglades Holiday Park, and Sawgrass Recreation Park. Don't forget Flamingo Gardens! Take a cruise with Jungle Queen Riverboat Cruises. Also available are Hugh Taylor Birch State Park, Port Everglades, and Pro Dive. Another water outlet is Fort Lauderdale Aquatic Club. Port Everglades, Carolina Golf Club, Tournament Players Club, and Jacaranda Golf Club are still more attractions. And if you run out of things to do, the beaches around here are great for swimming, surfing, or just soaking up the sun.

Culture: Fort Lauderdale has the well-known Broward Center for the Performing Arts (*www.browardcenter.org*). Visitors can enjoy Bonnet House Museum and Gardens, Young at Art Children's Museum, Regal Cypress Creek Station, Butterfly World, IFGA Fishing Hall of Fame & Museum, and the Old Dillard Museum. Don't forget about the Wray Botanical Collection, the Buehler Planetarium, or the Museum of Discovery and Science.

Annual Events: Fort Lauderdale hosts numerous annual events, including art festivals, antique car shows, fiestas, air fairs, boat shows, film festivals, thoroughbred racing, Renaissance festivals, chili cook-offs, Seminole tribal fairs, craft fairs, and more. Be sure to check out the community calendar for more information (*http://fort.lauderdale.eventguide.com*).

When the Grandkids Come: March them down to the Ah-Tah-Thi-Ki Museum (863-902-1113), where they will learn all about the Seminole Indians. The museum name means "to learn" in the Seminole Mikasukee language. While you are there, you can take in air-boat ride on a Billie Swamp Safari. Also, be sure to check in with the Broward Center for the Performing Arts (954-462-0222) for children's theater productions.

More Information

Municipal

Fort Lauderdale Chamber of Commerce
512 North East 3rd Avenue
Fort Lauderdale, FL 33301
954-462-6000
www.ftlchamber.com

Newspaper

New Times Broward-Palm Beach.
P.O. Box 14128
Fort Lauderdale, FL 33302
954-233-1600
www.newtimesbpb.com

Realty

Randy and Jerry Spano
Bluewater International Properties, LLC
258 Commercial Boulevard
Fort Lauderdale, FL 33308
954-802-1010
www.condosbythesea.net

17   Melbourne, Florida

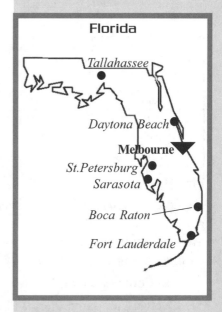

Florida

Melbourne at a Glance

There is energy in Melbourne that tells you right away that this is not your average town. A lot of independent and original American thinking goes on here, and the lucky new residents benefit from it. The city is part of Florida's "Space Coast," so-called because of its close proximity to NASA's Kennedy Space Center. This is the place to watch the shuttles launch! Melbourne is also one and a half hours due east of Orlando and the attractions at Disney World. While most of Melbourne is located on the Florida mainland, a small portion is located on a barrier island, which gives you lots of choices for relocating to ocean views, as well as some protection from approaching storms. The Indian River Lagoon separates the mainland from the island. Spanning the Indian River Lagoon is a pair of four-lane, high-rise bridges, known as the Melbourne Causeway and the Eau Gallie Causeway, both of which are quite stunning! MacMillan Travel recently ranked Melbourne the 10th most popular place in the nation for retirees.

Possible Drawbacks: There really aren't too many. Melbourne is one of those golden, small-town America places, but that kind of life bothers some city dwellers. Also, the crime rate continues to be higher than average. The summer's tend to be hot, but you can always cool off at the beach!

▶ Nickname: The Space Coast

▶ County: Brevard

▶ Area Code: 321

▶ Population: 71,382

▶ County Population: 519,387

▶ Percent of Population Over 65: 19.7%

▶ Region: Eastern Florida

▶ Closest Metropolitan Area: Orlando, 67 miles

▶ Median Home Price: $85,400

▶ Best Reasons to Retire Here: Lots of sunshine, quality entertainment, ocean views, and a relatively good cost of living.

Climate

28° N Latitude 80° W Longitude	Average High Temperature (°F)	Average Low Temperature (°F)	Precipitation (")	Sunshine (%)
January	70.9	50.5	2.2	58
April	80.6	60.4	2.2	73
July	90.0	72.1	5.3	65
October	82.6	67.1	4.8	60
YEAR	81.0	62.6	48.8	63

Utilities

Overview: The National Association of Home Builders ranked Melbourne as one of the most affordable cities in the nation. The cost of living is 99.8, with the national average of 100. Transportation costs show up as the most expensive, while utilities are the biggest bargain.

Gas Company: Florida City Gas (321-636-4757; *www.floridacitygas.com*)

Electric Company: Florida Power & Light (321-723-7795; *www.fpl.com*)

Phone Company: Bell South Residential (321-780-2355; *www.bellsouth.com*)

Water/Sewer Company: City of Melbourne Utilities (321-727-2900)

Cable Company: Time Warner (321-631-3770; *www.timewarnercable.com*)

The Tax Axe

Car Registration: This must be completed within 10 days of reporting to work, registering children in school, or registering to vote. A word of caution: There are differences in the amounts of taxes assessed, and they change at six months' of ownership. Best advice? Do not purchase a new car and then relocate to Florida within six months. Otherwise, you will be assessed at least 6 percent sales and use tax on that vehicle. You should wait and buy a new car when you get to Florida.

Driver's License: Contact Florida's Department of Highway Safety and Motor Vehicles for information (954-765-4697; *www.hsmv.state.fl.us*).

Sales Tax: 6.5 percent state sales tax. Check with the state for exemptions.

State Income Tax: There is no state income tax.

Retirement Income Tax: Retirement income is not taxed. However, there is an intangibles tax of $1 per $1,000 of the value of investments such as stocks, bonds, notes, and mutual funds. As of 2004, the first $250,000 (individual filers) or $500,000 (married, filing jointly) of taxable assets are exempt.

Property Tax: All property is taxable at 100 percent of its valuation. Exemptions exist, but are complicated. For example, there is a senior citizen exemption, but it only applies to the county or city millage, not to millage of school districts or other taxing authorities.

Local Real Estate

Overview: There is an abundance of properties for sale in and around Melbourne, whether you are looking for a mansion, bungalow, or condo. For every comfort zone, there are many options, from an ultra-extravagant $6.7 million palatial Spanish-style estate, to modest condos priced in the low $100,000's.

Average price of a three-bedroom/two-bath home: $166,200

Average price of a two-bedroom condo: $250,000

Common Housing Styles: Contemporaries, Mediterranean, and Spanish styles abound. You'll commonly find lanais (covered porches ideal for socializing in the evenings) and swimming pools, but you won't find basements so near the water, because there is a danger of flooding.

Rental Market: Availability is high, with new construction on the rise. You should have many choices and amenities from which to choose.

Average rent for a two-bedroom apartment: $1,200 per month

Communities Popular With Retirees: Palm Bay, West Melbourne, Indialantic, Melbourne Beach, Indian Harbour Beach, and Satellite Beach. Also Viera and Suntree. Rockledge and Viera both feature retirement complexes that offer small-town atmosphere with the convenience of the big city.

Nearby Areas to Consider: The city of Palm Bay is a mostly residential metropolitan area adjacent to other municipalities, and has the Indian River to the east and large regional parks to the west. For three years in a row, Palm Bay was one of the 30 finalists to be the "All American City." Satellite Beach is a small town cradled between a warm Atlantic beach to the east and the Indian River Lagoon to the west. Satellite Beach is a favorite of military families and those who love the beach.

Earning a Living

Business Climate: Talk about dynamic! This place is wonderful for starting, sharing, running, buying into, or directing your own business destiny. Contact the local chamber of commerce *(www.melpb-chamber.org)* for more information regarding starting a business or relocating to Melbourne.

Help in Starting a Business: Brevard Community College Regional Small Business Development Center (321-632-1111; *www.brevard.cc.fl.us*), can help with getting a business started, navigating local and state ordinances, and getting the right financial assistance. Also check out the chamber of commerce (*www.melpb-chamber.org*) for help getting started in business.

Job Market: Industries providing employment include education, health, and social services; retail trade; manufacturing; arts; entertainment; recreation; accommodation and food services. There is a lot of opportunity, and there are many jobs out there.

Medical Care

Holmes Regional Medical Center (321) 434-7000; *www.health-first.org*) is a full-service, nonprofit, 514-bed hospital located in Melbourne. With more than 500 physicians on staff, the center offers a full range of services including cancer, heart, emergency and trauma, laboratory, orthopedics, and women and children's programs. Healthsouth (321-984-4600) is an 80-bed, inpatient rehabilitation facility that participates both in Medicare and Medicaid. Circles of Care (321-676-6650; *www.circlesofcare.org*) provides mental-health care for Brevard County.

Services for Seniors

Through the auspices of the Brevard County Parks and Recreation Department, seniors are well served by several senior centers (321-268-2333). The number of activities is impressive, including line-dancing, billiards, morning coffees, lunches with other seniors, tap/aerobics, canasta, duplicate bridge, jazz dance, pinochle, book of the month club, shuffleboard, socials, and dances.

Continuing Education

Brevard Community College, Melbourne Campus (321-433-5513; *www.brevardcc.edu*) has an enrollment of more than 6,000 students, and retirees make up a significant percentage of the enrollment. Applicants who are senior citizens (age 55 or older) will receive a waiver of the application fee and tuition discount of $5 per credit hour for college credit courses.

Crime and Safety

The crime rate is above average. On one scale of measurement, the crime rate is 136, where the national average is 100 and the Florida crime rate is 129. The *www.city-data.com* crime index is 620.3, as compared against the national average of 330.6. Murder, rape, robbery, burglary, larceny, and car theft are all down, while assault is the single crime that has grown. Nonetheless, statistics indicate that Melbourne carries a crime index across the board that is almost double the national average.

Getting Around Town

Public Transportation: Space Coast Area Transit (SCAT) (321-633-1878; *www.ridescat.com*) is a unique system that blends traditional fixed-routes with individualized special-needs transportation services. For example, SCAT oversees Volunteers in Motion, which uses volunteer drivers and escorts to provide trips and personalized services for frail and elderly residents of Brevard County. This way, SCAT can overcome the cost barriers for those who have very limited mobility options. In addition, Melbourne residents can use two bus routes free of charge thanks to a subsidy from the Melbourne City Council.

Roads and Highways: I-95, US 1, 192, A1A, and Beeline Expressway

Airports: The Melbourne International Airport (321-723-6227; *www.mlbair.com*) is served by Delta Airlines plus several regional carriers. The airport also provides services such as charter passenger flights, private aviation, and air freight flights. International services include U.S. Customs, I.N.S., and U.S.D.A.

Ports: The Canaveral Port Authority (321-783-7831) is a governmental agency created by the Florida legislature. The place is gorgeous! Imagine glimmering cruise liners stretched out beneath a tropical blue sky. Fishing boats sometimes dot the horizon as they compete in one of several annual tournaments.

Let the Good Times Roll

Recreation: Melbourne's Leisure Services Department consists of numerous Parks and Recreational Facilities, including the Melbourne Municipal Golf Course and Harbor City Municipal Golf Course, as well as the Melbourne Auditorium, the Eau Gallie Civic Center, and several parks that offer tennis courts, swimming pools, and much more. Seniors can join the younger crowd in Melbourne to watch stunning events such as the launching of satellites and shuttles from Cape Kennedy. Of course, there is an abundance of sunning to be done on the beaches, as well as dancing, yoga, language classes, culinary classes, and more.

Culture: The Liberty Bell Memorial Museum (321-727-1776) is for the patriots among us. If you can't make a visit to the original in Philadelphia, this full-size replica of the Liberty Bell is an appealing alternative. Housed in a former water plant, the Liberty Bell Memorial Museum showcases war artifacts, model warships, airplanes, and a gallery of U.S. flags and reproductions of documents from the Mayflower Compact to Thomas Jefferson's rough draft of the Declaration of Independence. Melbourne and the surrounding areas combine information on their art shows and events in an impressive, year-long calendar (*www.artsbrevard.org*) that includes classes in both fine and performing arts, concerts by orchestras, combos and solo artists, and a full schedule of theatrical performances.

Annual Events: There's always the Mothers Day Celebration and Mother/Son Western Roundup in May, as well as the Daddy/Daughter Day in June. The Independence Day Fireworks in Cocoa on July Fourth are quite memorable, as is the CrackerFest and Paws in the Park, a celebration of dogs and their best friends in October. Fox Lake has a Christmas Festival of Crafts in November, and Moore has a Christmas Craft Festival in December.

When the Grandkids Come: First, go see the Andretti Thrill Park. Then visit the nearby BCC Planetarium and Observatory. It hosts events nightly, so nobody is ever disappointed. Go see the animals at the Brevard Zoo (321-254-3002). Orlando is less than an hour away, and you can take the kids there to enjoy Disney World, Universal Studios, Sea World, and much more.

More Information

Municipal

Melbourne Chamber of Commerce
1005 East Strawbridge Avenue
Melbourne, FL 32901
321-724-5400
www.melpb-chamber.org

Newspaper

Florida Today
P.O. Box 419000
Melbourne, FL 32941-9000
321-259-5000
www.floridatoday.com

Realty

We do not have a Realtor recommendation for Melbourne. As an option, check out *www.realtor.com* or *www.homegain.com.* Select a Realtor with both CRS and GRI designations after their names, since it means that these folks have gone the extra mile and are both graduates of the Realtor Institute and Certified Residential Specialists.

18 ▶ Naples, Florida

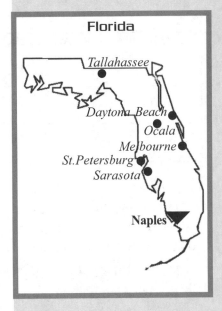

Florida

Tallahassee

Daytona Beach
Ocala
Melbourne
St.Petersburg
Sarasota

Naples

Naples at a Glance

Are we in paradise, yet? Honestly, this place is truly fabulous! The sun, the sea, and the beautiful beaches are guaranteed to seduce the most world-weary traveler with quiet elegance and a restful lifestyle. Don't get me wrong, there is a lot to do if you're feeling energetic, including swimming, sunning, surfing, biking, sailing, golf, and many other activities. But for those interested in a more relaxed lifestyle, this town offers breathing space and opportunities to relax. You can forget all about the busy city life as you sip a cool drink on your porch. Naples is a year-round resort destination fronting the Gulf of Mexico on Florida's southwestern tip. It is the county seat for Collier County, and offers many services for seniors. There are many city and county parks available for you to explore, or several public beaches where you can relax and enjoy the sunshine. The area is renowned for a multitude of activities, including golf, sailing, sport fishing, beach combing, as well as many cultural and shopping experiences. And don't forget about the Florida Everglades, which offer many opportunities for wildlife watching, volunteering, and conservation efforts. From sand traps to Saks trips, Naples has it all!

Possible Drawbacks: Well, it isn't cheap, and some find it a little too quiet. Also, the intense summer heat gets to some folks.

▶ Nickname: The Paradise Coast

▶ County: Collier

▶ Area Code: 239

▶ Population: 20,976

▶ County Population: 251,377

▶ Percent of Population Over 65: 42.3%

▶ Region: Southwest Florida

▶ Closest Metropolitan Area: Fort Meyers, 30 miles

▶ Median Home Price: $416,000

▶ Best Reasons to Retire Here: Lots of golf in a paradise-like atmosphere. Sandy beaches, great recreation and shopping, plus a low crime rate.

Climate

26° N Latitude 81° W Longitude	Average High Temperature (°F)	Average Low Temperature (°F)	Precipitation (")	Sunshine (%)
January	76.3	53.1	2.0	67
April	84.6	61.0	1.9	77
July	91.4	72.1	8.2	72
October	87.3	67.1	3.3	70
YEAR	84.7	63.5	52.9	72

Utilities

Overview: The cost of living in Naples is well above the average of 100 at 113.1. This is mostly because of the housing cost, which is at 138.3. Food is slightly high at 104.2, but utilities are quite low at 89.3.

Gas Company: Peoples Gas (*www.peoplesgas.com*)

Electric Company: Florida Power and Light (*www.fpl.com*)

Phone Company: Sprint (800-699-0728; *www.ConnectMyPhone.com*)

Water/Sewer Company: Water is provided by the city (239-213-4700).

Cable Company: Comcast Cable (239-793-3577; *www.comcast.com*) and Time Warner Cable (239-598-1104; *www.timewarnercable.com*)

The Tax Axe

Car Registration: This must be completed within 10 days of reporting to work, registering children in school, or registering to vote. A word of caution: There are differences in the amounts of taxes assessed, and they change at six months' of ownership. Best advice? Do not purchase a new car and then relocate to Florida within six months. Otherwise, you will be assessed at least 6 percent sales and use tax on that vehicle. You should wait and buy new when you get to Florida.

Driver's License: Contact Florida's Department of Highway Safety and Motor Vehicles for information (954-765-4697; *www.hsmv.state.fl.us*).

Sales Tax: 6.5 percent state sales tax. Check with the state office for exemptions.

State Income Tax: There is no state income tax.

Retirement Income Tax: Retirement income is not taxed. However, there is an intangibles tax of $1 per $1,000 of the value of investments such as stocks, bonds, notes, and mutual funds. As of 2004, the first $250,000 (individual filers) or $500,000 (married, filing jointly) of taxable assets are exempt.

Property Tax: All property is taxable at 100 percent of its valuation. Exemptions exist, but are complicated. For example, there is a senior citizen exemption, but it only applies to the county or city millage, not to millage of school districts or other taxing authorities.

Local Real Estate

Overview: Some of the most expensive and sought-after real estate in all of Florida is in this area. So, good luck! Naples was ranked first in the "Top 10 Second Home Markets for 2005" (*www.escapehomes.com*). Before you purchase, check with the flood-plain folks at the Naples Floodplain Information Office (239-213-5039), to be sure your dream home is on solid ground.

Average price of a three-bedroom/two-bath home: $838,747

Average price of a two-bedroom condo: $458,932

Common Housing Styles: There are lots of Mediterranean and Spanish-style mansions, and even one or two that look like medieval castles. But you might have to look around for something truly unique, because the more conventional styles dominate some of the understated, but still impressive, neighborhoods.

Rental Market: The rental market is partly seasonal, and partly year-round. There are always apartments available, and they aren't as expensive as you might think. Contact a Realtor to learn about the bset deals that are currently available.

Average rent for a two-bedroom apartment: $1,100 per month

Communities Popular With Retirees: Barefoot Beach, North Naples, Immokalee, and Marco Island

Nearby Areas to Consider: Bonita Sprints, along the coast to the north, has postcard-perfect beaches, neighborhoods shaded under grand gnarled oaks, wild orchids and swaying palms, championship golf courses, world-class performing arts centers, bustling restaurants and shops, lush parks, pristine preserves, and a thriving economy. Marco Island, off the coast to the south, is the largest of Florida's Ten Thousand Islands. The attraction is tropical sun-washed white beaches and a casual, easy-paced life-style.

Earning a Living

Business Climate: We can put your minds at ease on this one. According to the *American City Business Journal*, Naples has earned second place in the National Dynamic Small-Business Climates category. In addition, the latest statistics showed the unemployment figures at a low 2.2 percent.

Help in Starting a Business: Call the chamber's newly formed Business Education Program (239-262-6376). The Small Business Committee is dedicated to improving the business environment in the Greater Naples Area through a series of seminars, workshops, and roundtables.

Job Market: Naples is unique in that the opportunities for employment are spread over many categories, with none capturing more than 20 percent of the marketplace. Opportunities for jobs are in finance, insurance, real estate, education, healthcare and social services, retail trade, professional, and scientific fields, management, administrative, waste management services, arts, entertainment, recreation, accommodation, and food services.

Medical Care

Naples not only boasts a strong healthcare system, it gives you choices for however much coverage you request or require. Naples Community Hospital (239-436-5000; *www.nchmd.org*) is a 390-bed not-for-profit hospital with more than 500 physicians, 4,000 trained employees, and 1,900 volunteers. North Collier Hospital (239-513-7000; *www.collierdocs.com*) is an 88-bed acute-care facility and is an affiliate of the Naples Community Hospital. North Collier has three operating rooms and an endoscopy room for examining the stomach and colon. Emergency patients are seen in the 24-hour, 7-day emergency department. Cleveland Clinic Hospital (239-348-4000; *www.clevelandclinic.org*) is a fully integrated medical campus that includes a new 70-bed hospital.

Services for Seniors

This is one area where this town shines. If you have any questions about programs, the best possible source to contact is the regional Area Agency on Aging, which is Senior Solutions of Southwest Florida in Fort Myers (239-332-4233; *www.seniorsolutions.org*). Florida has a Long Term Care Ombudsman Council (813-338-1493; *http://ombudsman.myflorida.com*) in each district to investigate resident complaints pertaining to long-term care facilities. Social, educational, and nutritional programs designed for older Floridians are administered by the Department of Children & Families or the Department of Elder Affairs (941-332-4233; *www.state.fl.us/cf_web*). Senior Assist (239-437-1447; *www.seniorcaremanager.com*) has experience helping people with special problems. The Retired Senior Volunteer Program (239-774-8833; *www.swflorida.com)* serves persons 55 and over who wish to volunteer their time.

Continuing Education

The Institute for the Development and Enhancement of Adult Learning (239-643-2700; *www.acenet.fau.edu*) is housed at Florida Atlantic University. Florida Gulf Coast University (800-590-3428; *www.fgcu.edu*) is just 20 minutes from Naples and offers 17 undergraduate and nine graduate programs with an emphasis on the integrated use of technology. Edison Community College (800-749-2322; *www.edison.edu*) has expanded to include a 50-acre campus in Collier County offering study facilities for an associate's degree in the arts and sciences. International College (239-513-1122; *www.internationalcollege.edu*) is a four-year college with degrees in accounting, computers, and business. Walden University (312-263-0456; *www.waldenu.edu*) is based in Naples and offers online undergraduate, graduate, and postgraduate programs.

Crime and Safety

The low crime rate in Naples is a credit to the local law enforcement and to the citizens who look out for one another. For the year 2002, the index was 327.9, which is below the national average of 330.6. The total number of reported crimes per 100,000 people is 3,704.5, which is below average.

Getting Around Town

Public Transportation: Collier Area Transit (239-774.8192; *www.co.collier.fl.us/ transadmin*) provides bus service throughout the city and has vehicles able to accommodate wheelchairs and electric scooters.

Roads and Highways: I-75, State 84, US 41

Airports: The Southwest Florida International Airport (941-768-4383; *www.flylcpa.com*) is 27 miles from Naples and is served by 21 major and regional airlines. Naples Municipal Airport (239-643-0733; *www.flynaples.com*) is located within minutes of downtown Naples and provides regional service.

Let the Good Times Roll

Recreation: There are 50 miles of coastal beaches, some of which have interesting names, such as Barefoot, Clam Pass, Delnor-Wiggins Pass, and Lowdermilk. With more than 50 golf courses, Naples is sometimes known as the Golf Capital of the United States. The list of marinas is extensive, but here are a few memorable ones: Boat Haven, Calusa Island Yacht Club & Marina, Mid-Island Marina of Naples, and the Naples Marina. There are five Florida state parks, two National parks, and numerous Collier County and Naples parks. There is even a casino in nearby Immokalee, called the Seminole Casino.

Culture: The fourth edition of the *100 Best Art Towns in America* by John Villani calls Naples "an arts powerhouse overdue for national attention" and ranks it number one in America. Naples is home to the Philharmonic Center for the Arts, which was opened in late 1989 with several art galleries. The Philharmonic Center for the Arts also offers the full range of activities from opera to pop to Broadway plays and lectures. And just in case you think all the shows are imported, check out the Naples Dinner Theater and the Sugden Community Theatre.

Annual Events: The beginning of the year sees Art in the Park and the Naples Invitational Art Fest. In February, visit the Home & Design Expo, plus the Annual Naples National Art Festival. In March, you can enjoy more Art in the Park. April, in addition to showers, brings Mike Ditka & Jim Hart Celebrity Golf. Also, there's the Concord Jazz Festival, a recital by jazz musicians who have appeared on the Concord label at Hayes Hall. Finally, April gives Neapolitans the Artescape Naples. In May, the Taste of Collier will get you off your recliner and into the sunshine. Then there's the Great Dock Canoe Race and another art fest, the Outstanding Artists of Florida Exhibition. June ushers in The Back Country Classic, one of the Caloosa Catch & Release Tournaments. In July you can participate in an Ice Cream Social. Then there is the Big Cypress Gallery Annual Labor Day Open House. You can explore the Big Cypress Swamp with a series of swamp walks, lectures, gallery exhibits, and live music. September sees Summer Jazz on the Gulf, when the Naples Beach Hotel and Golf Club hosts live jazz entertainment. September also offers the Florida Watercolor Society Annual Exhibition. October includes the American Musical Heritage Lectures Fall Series. Swamp

Buggy Races are held at Florida Sports Park on the third and last weekend in late October, culminating in the Queen's Mud Bath. The Beach Treasure Sale is on the first Saturday in November, as is the Old Florida Festival, celebrating the history of Florida, complete with pirates, conquerors, and early settlers. The Fall Theatre Festival is one-act plays produced by local theater groups, hosted by the Koreshan State Historic Site. At the end of November is the American Indian Arts Celebration. The Ah-Tah-Thi-Ki Museum sponsors a celebration of Native American culture and heritage on the Seminole Big Cypress Reservation. During the last week in December, 5th Avenue South is filled with the paintings, sculptures, and crafts of local artists, complete with all kinds of food booths and nationally recognized live musicians.

When the Grandkids Come: There's the Teddy Bear Museum, where more than 5,000 teddy bears reside. The Conservancy of Southwest Florida's Natural Science Museum has the marine exhibit, serpentarium, sanctuary, nature trail walks, and mini-boat rides. Then there's the Caribbean Gardens & Jungle Larry's Zoological Park, featuring tropical gardens, endangered species, boat rides, live shows, a petting farm, and live alligators. There's King Richard's Family Fun Center, which has a medieval castle housing video games, pinball, batting cages, go-kart track, kiddie train, bumper boats, batting cages, and miniature golf. The Naples Horse and Carriage Company is an enchanting way to tour Naples. And if that's too old-fashioned, try the Naples Trolley Tours, a unique two-hour sightseeing tour of Naples in a replica 1907 Cincinnati Trolley.

More Information

Municipal

Chamber of Commerce
2390 Tamiami Train North
Naples, FL 34103
239-262-6141
www.napleschamber.org

Newspaper

Naples Daily News
1075 Central Avenue
Naples, FL 34102
239-262-3161
www.naplesnews.com

Realty

We do not have a Realtor recommendation for Naples. As an option, check out *www.realtor.com* or *www.homegain.com*. Select a Realtor with both CRS and GRI designations after their names, since it means that these folks have gone the extra mile and are both graduates of the Realtor Institute and Certified Residential Specialists.

19 Ocala, Florida

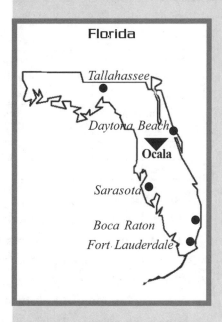

Ocala at a Glance

Marion County's location in the center of the state makes it almost unavoidable to travelers. Ocala is crisscrossed by a number of major thoroughfares, and is little more than an hour north of Orlando. Many travelers passing through the area fall in love with the majestic farms and scenic rolling hills, and end up becoming full-time residents. Ocala has been recognized as an "All-American City" and the fifth best place to live in America as well as the 11th "Most Livable Small City" by *Money* magazine. Housing is perhaps the main reason Marion County residents enjoy such a high quality of life. A modest cost of living helps keep down the cost of doing business. The cost of living index is listed below the national index record at 93.75. The mild climate allows businesses and schools to experience a minimum of lost productivity due to inclement weather. The summer days average 90 degrees Fahrenheit, and the other six months of the year average a very pleasant 53 degrees Fahrenheit. The warmth and sunshine let folks get outside to play year-round. The Ocala National Forest makes up almost one-third of the landmass of Marion County and offers a vast range of outdoor activities including hunting, fishing, hiking, canoeing, and camping.

Possible Drawbacks: The increase in price of real estate was second-highest in the south in the second quarter of 2004, at 29.9 percent. The heat might be a drawback for some, because it regularly climbs to over 90 degrees Fahrenheit in the summertime.

▸ Nickname: Brick City
▸ County: Marion
▸ Area Code: 352
▸ Population: 47,643
▸ County Population: 280,288
▸ Percent of Population Over 65: 20.4%
▸ Region: Northern Florida
▸ Closest Metropolitan Area: Gainesville, 35 miles
▸ Median Home Price: $114,000
▸ Best Reasons to Retire Here: If you like horses, beautiful surroundings, small-town atmosphere, friendly folks, a solid business community, good local health care, and lots of recreation, this could be the place for you.

143

Climate

29° N Latitude 82° W Longitude	Average High Temperature (°F)	Average Low Temperature (°F)	Precipitation (")	Sunshine (%)
January	69.8	45.0	2.8	58
April	83.8	56.7	3.3	73
July	92.1	70.7	7.9	65
October	84.4	60.6	2.9	60
YEAR	82.8	58.5	52.9	63

Utilities

Overview: Ocala's cost of living index is 66, well below the average of 100.

Gas Company: Natural gas is available from Teco/Peoples Gas (352-622-0111; *www.peoplesgas.com*) and propane is supplied by Teco Propane (352-671.8290; *www.tecoenergy.com*).

Electric Company: Ocala Electric Utility (352-629-8411; *www.ocalaelectric.com*)

Phone Company: BellSouth (*www.bellsouth.com*) or Sprint Florida (800-339-1811; *www.everythingdsl.com*).

Water/Sewer Company: The city of Ocala Water and Sewer (352-351-6770; *www.ocalafl.org/water*)

Cable Company: Galaxy Cable Company (800-365-6988) and Cox Cable (352-867-4010) provide cable TV in Marion County.

The Tax Axe

Car Registration: Must be completed within 10 days of reporting to work, registering children in school, or registering to vote. A word of caution: There are differences in the amounts of taxes assessed, and they change at six months' of ownership. Best advice? Do not purchase a new car and then relocate to Florida within six months. Otherwise, you will be assessed at least 6 percent sales and use tax on that vehicle. You should wait and buy new when you get to Florida.

Driver's License: Contact Florida's Department of Highway Safety and Motor Vehicles for information (954-765-4697; *www.hsmv.state.fl.us*).

Sales Tax: 6 percent state sales tax, 1 percent city

State Income Tax: There is no state income tax.

Retirement Income Tax: Retirement income is not taxed. However, there is an intangibles tax of $1 per $1,000 of the value of investments such as stocks, bonds, notes, and mutual funds. As of 2004, the first $250,000 (individual filers) or $500,000 (married, filing jointly) of taxable assets are exempt.

Property Tax: All property is taxable at 100 percent of its valuation. Exemptions exist, but are complicated. For example, there is a senior citizen exemption, but it only applies to the county or city millage, not to millage of school districts.

Local Real Estate

Overview: The real estate bubble is definitely still expanding. Sellers are currently in the driver's seat, and buyers have to bring full-price offers to the table.

Average price of a three-bedroom/two-bath home: $167,900

Average price of a two-bedroom condo: $97,900

Common Housing Styles: Ocala has lots of ranch style homes, as well as the occasional Mediterranean and Spanish style. Many homes feature swimming pools and screened-in porches.

Rental Market: Of all the housing units in Ocala, 21 percent are rentals. That means that a little over one in five houses, condos, or apartments are available to rent. Ocala has a 90-percent occupancy rate, so it would be best to arrange housing before you move there.

Average rent for a two-bedroom apartment: $900 per month

Communities Popular With Retirees: On Top of the World, Spruce Creek, and Oak Run

Nearby Areas to Consider: Ocala Palms is a beautiful, planned, country club community quietly nestled on rolling hills with the city of Ocala just minutes away. Once a 500-acre cattle ranch, Ocala Palms has become an idyllic retirement lifestyle for retirees. Much of nature remains, such as live oak, hickory nut; and magnolia trees; blue herons and egrets; and of course the resident swans swimming in the pond at the welcome center. Dunnellon has something to offer everyone, such as the Rainbow Springs State Park; crystal clear Rainbow River to canoe, kayak, or tube; and a fisherman's paradise on the Withlacoochee River and Lake Rouseau.

Earning a Living

Business Climate: Service and manufacturing provide the majority of employment opportunities, although agriculture is also important to the area. The horse farms of Marion feature more horses than any other county in the nation, including any in the famed Bluegrass state. Over 29,000 of Marion County residents are employed in the thoroughbred industry. Ocala also hosts many national and international industries, including Lockheed Martin, Clarison International, Golden Flake, K-Mart, Dayco, Microdyne, Townley Manufacturing, Signature Brands, LLC, and Associated Grocers. As of February 2005, the U.S Bureau of Labor Statistics reports that the unemployment rate in Ocala sits at a modest 4.5 percent.

Help in Starting a Business: The city and county have good incentives for new or relocating businesses to choose the area. The University of Florida (800-450-4624; *www.sbdc.unf.edu*) assists in starting or buying a business. Also see the Small Business Trends (*www.floridasmallbusiness.com*) for more information.

Job Market: With business growing, you'd think the business market would be favorable to finding a job. From all accounts, however, one of the greatest selling points to the business communities around Ocala is the available workforce. If you need or want to work, it might be best to check out the opportunities beforehand.

Medical Care

Munroe Regional Medical Center (*www.munroeregional.com*) is a 421-bed acute-care hospital. It accepts Medicare and Medicaid patients. Through the center's Senior Focus with lifestyle changes, early detection, and improved treatments, seniors can lead active, healthy, and productive lives. For the second year in a row, Munroe Regional's Heart Center has been recognized among the "Top 100 in the Nation" by a healthcare information company that ranks hospitals throughout the country. The Ocala Regional Medical Center (352-401-1000; *www.ocalaregional.com*) is a 200-bed facility, and was named one of the nation's "100 Top Hospitals" for cardiovascular care. It accepts Medicare and Medicaid patients. West Marion Community hospital (*www.westmarion.com*) is the newest hospital. It opened as a private 70-bed hospital, fully accredited by the Joint Commission on Accreditation of Healthcare Organizations.

Services for Seniors

The Prestige 55 program (352-671-2114; *www.munroeregional.com*) is one of Munroe Regional's commitments to serve Marion County's mature adults. Prestige 55 is "a little something extra" for those in the community age 55 and over. Members receive medical screenings, education, counseling, special events, and numerous other privileges. Ocala Regional Medical Center maintains a comprehensive online Senior Health Guide that lists all the diseases, conditions, syndromes, and ills one can imagine, along with symptoms and treatment options (*www.ocalaregional.com*). The Golden Friends (352-401-1338; *www.ocalaregional.com/SeniorFriends.asp*) was formed to encourage members to live a healthy lifestyle with "activities for fellowship and fun." If you're into volunteering, here's an opportunity: contact the Retired and Senior and Volunteer Program (352-291-4444; *www.cfcc.cc.fl.us/about/rsvp*).

Continuing Education

Central Florida Community College in Ocala (352-854-2322; *www.cfcc.cc.fl.us*) offers distance learning and online courses, as well as a number of credit and non-credit programs. The new Hampton Center (352-873-5881; *www.cf.edu/about/hampton.htm*) is also part of the community college system. The president is authorized to approve fees for lifelong learning programs on a course-by-course basis.

Crime and Safety

Serious crimes known to police per 100,000 people is 5,695. Property crimes known to police per 100,000 people is 2,028. Violent crimes known to police per 100,000 people is 900.

Getting Around Town

Public Transportation: SunTran Ocala/Marion County Public Transit System (352-401-6999; *www.suntran.org*).

Roads and Highways: I-75, US 27, 301, 441; SR 40, 35, 484, 464, 326 and 200

Airports: Local air service is provided by the Ocala International airport. Commercial airline service is available at Gainesville, 40 miles to the north, and Orlando, 75 miles to the south.

Let the Good Times Roll

Recreation: Ocala is fabulous if you enjoy the outdoors. You will find yourself looking around at parks for camping, hiking, fishing, watching (or riding) the horses, hunting, golfing, playing tennis, and on and on. The Silver River State Park (352-236-7148; *www.floridastateparks.org/silverriver*) has kayaking, canoeing, hiking, and picnicking, or you can visit the Silver River Museum and Environmental Education Center. There is a playground for the children, too. The 383,573-acre Ocala National Forest is incredible—for its size, number of different ecological sites, and variety of possible activities. You can camp, horseback ride, hunt, hike, or just hang out and enjoy the scenery. If you want to visit the water, the Atlantic is only 70 miles away and the Gulf of Mexico is only 40 miles away.

Culture: The Appleton Museum of Art (*http://appletonmuseum.org*) is touted as the "Crown Jewel" of Ocala's cultural life. It is large and active, with at least three seasons of traveling exhibitions each year. It boasts an active program for children as well as adults. Other cultural pursuits are numerous, and growing in size and quality. The Ocala Civic Theatre (*www.ocalacivictheatre.com*) produces professional-quality, live theater. For music and dance, check out the performances of the Marion Performing Ballet and the Ocala Dance Theatre, which are staged throughout the year. The Central Florida Community College (CFCC) is the home of the Central Florida Symphony, a 60-member orchestra that plays a wide range of music. Also performing on the music scene are the CFCC students' Variations Jazz Band, the Ocala Festival Orchestra, the Marion Chamber Music Society, and the Marion Civic Chorale. All may be reached through the chamber of commerce.

Annual Events: January has the Gainesville Brass Quintet, presented by the Marion Chamber Music Society, and Ma Barker Day, a re-enactment of the famous shoot-out between Ma Barker and her gang and federal agents in the mid-1930s. February has the Greek Festival, while March has the Historic Ocala Preservation Society's Antique Show. In April you can catch the Dunnellon Boom Town Days, Ocala Marion County Day, and the Annual Heritage Home and Secret Garden Tour. May has the annual Belleview Founder's Day and Symphony Under the Stars. During June, July, and August, tourists and locals both camp out at the beach for the summer. September has the annual Autumn Gift Market, National Public Lands Day, Chili Cook-Off, and the Fort

King Festival. In October, check out the Ocala Cultural Festival. November brings the Steel Horse Stampede and Peanut Festival. December brings the Festival of Trees and Festival of Lights.

When the Grandkids Come: There are plenty of family activities for indoor and outdoor adventures. A selection of movie theaters, arcades, roller skating rinks, and bowling centers await the youngsters. There's even a 350-acre nature theme park in the county and a water park featuring a wave pool and eight waterslides. Orlando, with its Disney World, MGM Studios, Universal Studios, and Sea World, is just over an hour's ride by car.

More Information

Municipal

Ocala/Marion County Chamber of Commerce
110 East Silver Springs Boulevard
Ocala, FL 34470
352-629-8051
www.ocalacc.com

Newspaper

Ocala Star Banner
P.O. Box 490
Ocala, FL 34478
352-867-010
www.ocala.com

Realty

We do not have a Realtor recommendation for Ocala. As an option, check out *www.realtor.com* or *www.homegain.com*. Select a Realtor with both CRS and GRI designations after their names, since it means that these folks have gone the extra mile and are both graduates of the Realtor Institute and Certified Residential Specialists.

20

Sarasota, Florida

Florida

Tallahassee

Daytona Beach

Ocala

Sarasota

Boca Raton
Fort Lauderdale

Sarasota at a Glance

Sarasota has long been a destination for re-tirees. It's very attractive, with approximately 300 days of sunshine per year; beautiful white sandy beaches; access to swimming, snorkeling, water-skiing, and fabulous golf courses. You can stroll the parks and shopping centers, malls, and boutiques, and enjoy the restaurants, and, and...okay, okay, we'll stop! But you get the picture. Sarasota has many opportunities for recreation, education, culture, and culinary adventures. Incidentally, this is the first place I heard the word "Floribbean" to describe a unique Florida cuisine. You'll just have to try it; it's wonderful! For more educational entertainment, you can spend days investigating the Mote Marine Laboratory and the famous shark-research facility, as well as Marie Selby Botanical Gardens, Pelican Man's Bird Sanctuary, Myakka River State Park, Historic Spanish Point, Sarasota Jungle Gardens, and Warm Mineral Springs. Sarasota is located on the western shore of Florida, and basks in the warm waters of the Gulf of Mexico.

Possible Drawbacks: It gets really hot in June, July, and August. Flooding can sometimes be an issue, because there is the occasional storm or hurricane.

▶ Nickname: The Culture Coast
▶ County: Sarasota
▶ Area Code: 941
▶ Population: 53,637
▶ County Population: 349,400
▶ Percent of Population Over 65: 31.5%
▶ Region: Western Florida
▶ Closest Metropolitan Area: Tampa, 50 miles
▶ Median Home Price: $264,000
▶ Best Reasons to Retire Here: Gulf Coast location, beautiful city, amazing cultural and sports events, and lots of outdoor recreation.

Climate

27° N Latitude 82 ° W Longitude	Average High Temperature (°F)	Average Low Temperature (°F)	Precipitation (")	Sunshine (%)
January	71.2	48.9	2.6	63
April	81.7	58.6	1.5	75
July	90.7	71.8	8.8	62
October	84.6	64.4	2.6	65
YEAR	82.0	61.3	54.4	66

Utilities

Overview: Sarasota sits at a composite index of 103.4, which is 3.4 points above the national average for costs in most areas. Our thanks to the Greater Charlotte Harbor Economic Development office for this data, which, in the fourth quarter of 2004, puts Sarasota grocery bills at 100.7, housing at 110.4, utilities at 91.9, and healthcare at 102.1 of the national average.

Gas Company: Teco Peoples Gas System (94-366-4277; *www.peoplesgas.com*)

Electric Company: Florida Power and Light (*www.fpl.com*)

Phone Company: Verizon (941-365-0054; *www.verizon.com*)

Water/Sewer Company: Sarasota County (941-861-6790; *www.scgov.net*)

Cable Company: Comcast Cablevision (888-793-4800; *www.comcast.com*)

The Tax Axe

Car Registration: This must be completed within 10 days of reporting to work, registering children in school, or registering to vote. A word of caution: There are differences in the amounts of taxes assessed, and they change at six months' of ownership. Best advice? Do not purchase a new car and then relocate to Florida within six months. Otherwise, you will be assessed at least 6 percent sales and use tax on that vehicle. You should wait and buy new when you get to Florida.

Driver's License: Contact Florida's Department of Highway Safety and Motor Vehicles for information (954-765-4697; *www.hsmv.state.fl.us*).

Sales Tax: 6 percent state sales tax and 1 percent city tax

State Income Tax: There is no state income tax.

Retirement Income Tax: Retirement income is not taxed. However, there is an intangibles tax of $1 per $1,000 of the value of investments such as stocks, bonds, notes, and mutual funds. As of 2004, the first $250,000 (individual filers) or $500,000 (married, filing jointly) of taxable assets are exempt.

Property Tax: All property is taxable at 100 percent of its valuation. Exemptions exist, but are complicated. For example, there is a senior citizen exemption, but it only applies to the county or city millage, not to millage of school districts or other taxing authorities.

Local Real Estate

Overview: Sarasota has just about every kind of housing development, neighborhood, and city accommodation imaginable. The costs are rising, but are doing so slowly.

Average price of a three-bedroom/two-bath home: $194,500

Average price of a two-bedroom condo: $162,000

Common Housing Styles: You can find bungalows and cottages that back to golf courses, and entire neighborhoods dotted with Spanish-style homes.

Rental Market: A representative of the National Association of Home Builders, which issues the Multifamily Market Index, recently stated that the improving job market is driving a rebound in apartment rentals in the Sarasota area.

Average rent for a two-bedroom apartment: $910 per month

Communities Popular With Retirees: Bradenton, Ellenton, and Valrico

Nearby Areas to Consider: Bradenton, 15 miles north of Sarasota, is known as the friendly city and has a population of 50,000. The city is just south of Tampa, and the citizens enjoy the beach and all types of water and boat adventures, plus it is a golfer's paradise. Venice abounds in natural beauty and splendor. The city sits 20 miles along the coast to the south of Sarasota, and offers something for everyone including beautiful beaches, its quaint downtown shopping area, and the old Florida scenery along the Myakka River.

Earning a Living

Business Climate: With a wealth of options and plenty of resources, Sarasota County is a good place to do business. From relocation and expansion assistance to workforce development and financial incentives, Sarasota County has earned rave reviews from the business community for fostering strategic alliances between the public and private sectors. A record number of companies relocated or expanded in Sarasota County in 2002, adding more than 472 jobs and $37 million in capital investment to the local economy.

Help in Starting a Business: Check in with the very active and competent services of the Sarasota Chamber of Commerce and the Sarasota County Committee for Economic Development (*www.sarasotachamber.org*). SMART (Sarasota Means Action Response Team) in cooperation with Sarasota County government and the Sarasota County Committee for Economic Development, has developed a rapid response process that assists targeted industry companies. The SCORE (*www.score-suncoast.org*) Counselor-in-Residence program is available to both current chamber members and those looking to start new businesses.

Job Market: According to the Milken Institute's list of "Best Performing Cities," 2004 found Sarasota ranking sixth in the nation. In rating cities, the Milken Institute factors in costs of living, growing populations, and stability in such areas as government and healthcare. So, the job market is blooming in Sarasota. Unemployment is down to only 3.8 percent, and there is room for folks who want to work. Part-time work is available much of the year, and above-entry level jobs are available.

Medical Care

Sarasota Memorial Health Care System (941-917-9000; 800-764-8255; *www.smh.com*) is an 828-bed regional medical center and the second largest public hospital in Florida. The 3,000 staff members make it Sarasota County's second largest employer. Sarasota Memorial's North County Health Center is a not-for-profit primary care practice. Services include family practice, internal medicine, pediatrics, dentistry, and pharmacy. Specialist referrals also are provided. Patients are charged for services on a sliding fee scale, based on federal poverty guidelines and their ability to pay. The Doctors Hospital of Sarasota (941-342-1100; *www.doctorsofsarasota.com*) is a 168-bed acute and general care facility that does not accept Medicaid/Medicare patients at this time.

Services for Seniors

The Sarasota Memorial Health Care System has three programs specifically aimed at seniors and other adults who experience various conditions associated with aging, such as emotional and/or mental issues, and addiction issues. Senior Friendship Center (941-955-2122; *www.seniorfriendship.com*) offers help with government forms to encouraging you to volunteer and offering a good word when it's needed. If you ever need to get from here to there, and you are without wheels, give these folks a call. The Sarasota County Sheriff's Office (*www.sarasotasheriff.org/seniorservices.asp)* is dedicated to improving the quality of life for senior citizens.

Continuing Education

The Sarasota Institute of Lifetime Learning (941-365-6404; *www.sillsarasota.org*) offers college-level lectures by leaders in academia, media, arts, think tanks, and the U.S. Foreign Service. The University of Southern Florida (941-379-0404; *www.usf.edu*) offers an undergraduate, graduate, and postgraduate degree. The university also has valuable programs for seniors as part of the Continuing Education department. Senior programs offer hands-on computer training through the SeniorNet program, and programs in the liberal arts through Learning in Retirement. There is a Senior Citizen Tuition Waiver Program that allows Florida residents age 60 and over to take credit courses at the university on a space-available basis and, in most cases, without payment of tuition. The Pierian Spring Academy (941-716- 2471; *www.pierianspringacademy.org*) is a place where adults and retired persons can delve into discussions about art, music, international relations, science, philosophy, and history, all under the guidance of highly qualified experts. In 2005, the fee per course was $110, with the third course at only $55.

Crime and Safety

The news is good. Even with a 9.2 percent poverty rate, Sarasota's crime rate overall is down by more than 10 percent across the board. According to the Sarasota County Sheriff's Office, violent crime went down by 10.45 percent over the previous year, and non-violent crime dropped by 10.74 percent.

Getting Around Town

Public Transportation: Sarasota County Area Transit (941-861-1234; *www.scgov.net*) provides local bus service throughout the city. Sarasota Tampa Express (941-355-8400; *www.stexps.com*) is a shuttle service between Sarasota and Tampa.

Roads and Highways: I-75, US 41, and 301

Airports: Sarasota Bradenton (*www.srq-airport.com*) is served by six major airlines and two commuter airlines. The service fluctuates with the seasons. Tampa International (*www.tampaairport.com)* is served by 22 airlines, and St. Petersburg-Clearwater International (*www.fly2pie.com*) is served by seven airlines.

Ports: Port Manatee (*www.portmanatee.com*) is the fifth largest of Florida's 14 deep water seaports.

Let the Good Times Roll

Recreation: There are some serious golf courses (60 at this counting), 35 miles of beautiful white-sand beaches, and many parks in the area. One other thing that you may have never heard of is the Sarasota County Games for Life competition, held in November. For professional couch potatoes, there are several professional football teams, including the Tampa Bay Buccaneers (*www.buccaneers.com*), Miami Dolphins, (*www.miamidolphins.com*), Jacksonville Jaguars (*www.jaguars.com*), and a professional baseball team, the Florida Marlins (*florida.marlins.mlb.com*).

Culture: Sarasota County is called Florida's "Cultural Coast." Offerings include an opera company, two symphonies, a ballet, a performing arts hall, professional theaters for every taste, and innovative architecture, as well as architectural seminars and programs. Visual arts lovers can roam through the sophisticated galleries, antique shops, artists' studios, and fine crafts boutiques. The cultural arts season is 365 days long, filled with festivals, performance events, and visual art exhibitions. The Sarasota County Arts Council (941-365-5118; *www.sarasota-arts.org*) is what every arts council should be. It maintains an up-to-date registry of events, artists, opportunities for artists, grants, organizations, foundations, contests, training programs, and arts news.

Annual Events: The Florida Winefest and Auction is held in April each year. The Cine World Film Festival is a November event. The Sarasota Reading Festival is downtown each November. Empty Bowls is an annual benefit held just before Thanksgiving.

Giving Hunger the Blues is an annual food and music event held each April. The Suncoast Offshore Grand Prix is a powerboat event held around the Fourth of July. Taste of the Nation is held each April. The Florida International Air Show is also held each April. The Venice Sharks Tooth Festival is held each April on Venice Beach. The Venice Holiday Parade is held at the end of November. The Sarasota Christmas Boat Parade occurs each December. The Sarasota Comedy Festival is held in May. You can find more, and get all the details, at the Sarasota community calendar (*www.sarasotacalendar.com*).

When the Grandkids Come: First, of course, take them to the beach! Then visit the Circus Sarasota, a not-for-profit performing arts organization featuring acts in the European style. Or you can take them to the G. WIZ Science Museum. This hands-on interactive facility is home to many wonders of science and technology.

More Information

Municipal
Sarasota Visitor Information Center
655 North Tamiami Trail (US 41)
Sarasota, FL 34236
941-957-1877
www.sarasotafl.org

Newspaper
Sarasota Herald-Tribune
801 South Tamiami Trail
Sarasota, FL 34236
941-953-7755
www.heraldtribune.com

Weekly Planet
1383 5th Street
Sarasota, FL 34236
941-308-0257
www.weeklyplanet.com

Realty
We do not have a Realtor recommendation for Sarasota. As an option, check out *www.realtor.com* or *www.homegain.com.* Select a Realtor with both CRS and GRI designations after their names, since it means that these folks have gone the extra mile and are both graduates of the Realtor Institute and Certified Residential Specialists.

St. Petersburg, Florida

21

Florida

Tallahassee
Daytona Beach
Ocala
St. Petersburg
Sarasota
Boca Raton
Fort Lauderdale

St. Petersburg at a Glance

The *Guinness Book of World Records* credits St. Petersburg with the longest run of consecutive sunny days: 768. Such a record-setting sunshine streak makes it easy to enjoy the areas beaches, which include two of the Top 10 rated beaches in the nation. St. Petersburg shares one of Florida's best public universities, has world-renowned medical facilities, and a world-class marine science research complex. It is home to one of the world's finest year-round climates, offers a stunning array of attractions including world-class museums, major league sports activities, boating, fishing, and just pure enjoyment. You can't beat Pinellas County's 35 miles of beaches and nearly 588 miles of coastline. It has 234 miles of waterfront properties. *Realtor* magazine listed St. Petersburg as one of the "Top 10 Golfing Destinations" for home buyers. St. Petersburg has the largest city marina in Florida. It also has the largest water reclamation system in the United States, delivering more than 20 million gallons per day to 6,500 customers for lawn irrigation.

Possible Drawbacks: If you are new to thunderstorms, ask the locals. Every day from June through September you can count on one. And it's a mixed blessing, because although they can be noisy, they do bring down the soaring heat. Florida is the lightning capital of the country, and this area can count on about 90 days of lightning a year.

- ▶ Nickname: The Suncoast
- ▶ County: Pinellas
- ▶ Area Code: 813
- ▶ Population: 248,232
- ▶ County Population: 921,482
- ▶ Percent of Population Over 65: 17.4%
- ▶ Region: Central Florida
- ▶ Closest Metropolitan Area: Tampa, 10 miles
- ▶ Median Home Price: $275,000
- ▶ Best Reasons to Retire Here: Year-round sunshine, outdoor recreation, affordable living, top-notch healthcare, fabulous beaches, and progressive employment opportunities.

Climate

27° N Latitude 82° W Longitude	Average High Temperature (°F)	Average Low Temperature (°F)	Precipitation (")	Sunshine (%)
January	68.4	52.9	2.5	63
April	80.2	64.8	2.4	75
July	89.8	76.3	8.2	62
October	82.9	69.1	3.2	65
YEAR	80.4	65.8	52.1	66

Utilities

Overview: According to the latest figures available, St. Petersburg can boast of having most of its cost-of-living scores under 100, the average for cost-of-living comparisons for 317 urban areas.

Gas Company: The TECO/Peoples Gas System (877-832- 6747)

Electric Company: Progress Energy (800-700-8744)

Phone Company: Verizon (800-483-4200)

Water/Sewer Company: The City of St Petersburg (727-893-7261)

Cable Company: The cable companies are Bright House Networks (727-579-8600; *http://mybrighthouse.com*) and Knology (850-215-1000; *www.knology.com*).

The Tax Axe

Car Registration: This must be completed within 10 days of reporting to work, registering children in school, or registering to vote. A word of caution: There are differences in the amounts of taxes assessed, and they change at six months' of ownership. Best advice? Do not purchase a new car and then relocate to Florida within six months. Otherwise, you will be assessed at least 6 percent sales and use tax on that vehicle. You should wait and buy new when you get to Florida.

Driver's License: Contact Florida's Department of Highway Safety and Motor Vehicles for information (954-765-4697; *www.hsmv.state.fl.us*).

Sales Tax: 6 percent state sales tax, plus 1 percent city tax

State Income Tax: There is no state income tax.

Retirement Income Tax: Retirement income is not taxed.

Property Tax: All property is taxable at 100 percent of its valuation. Exemptions exist, but are complicated. For example, there is a senior citizen exemption, but it only applies to the county or city millage, not to millage of school districts or other taxing authorities.

Local Real Estate

Overview: Like so many places in Florida, good housing is available, no matter your taste or pocketbook. There are beginner homes to suit the individual or couple, beach-front family homes with private boat docks, and high-rise condos.

Average price of a three-bedroom/two-bath home: $159,700

Average price of a two-bedroom condo: $130,000

Common Housing Styles: Single-family homes comprise the largest selection of real estate in this region. Textured concrete block, wood exteriors, and Spanish styles each influence local neighborhoods.

Rental Market: Rentals are moderate to strong across the board. As you might expect, rentals have kept pace with inflation. If relatives come to visit, remember that costs associated with short-term rentals are substantially higher.

Average rent for a two-bedroom apartment: $900 per month

Communities Popular With Retirees: The Snell Isle district and Kenneth City

Nearby Areas to Consider: If Florida's beach is where you want to be, check out Clearwater, north of St. Petersburg, which is close to everything. It is a beautiful peninsula bordered by the Gulf of Mexico to the west and Tampa Bay to the east. Ocala, although a growing community, has maintained a warm and friendly hometown atmosphere. Sarasota is one of America's best places to live, work, and raise a family.

Earning a Living

Business Climate: The major industries of Pinellas County are tourism, services, retail, manufacturing, finance, insurance, and real estate. St. Petersburg has a state-designed Enterprise Zone where businesses receive state corporate income tax, sales tax, and property tax credit. The downtown has attracted a public/private investment of more than $900 million since 1982. Unemployment in 2000 was 5.2 percent.

Help in Starting a Business: The first place to contact is the St. Petersburg Area Chamber of Commerce Business Assistance Program (727-821-4069; *www.stpete.com*). Next, check in with the city of St. Petersburg, Economic Development and Property Management (727-893-7100; *www.stpete.org*), the Small Business Development Center (727-464-7332; *www.stpete.org/bdc.htm*), and the Service Corps of Retired Executives (727-532-6800; *www.score115.org*).

Job Market: Florida ranks fourth in the nation in the number of expanding or relocating businesses. Part-time or full-time employees of quality are always in demand, and never more so than in St. Petersburg. Contact Worknet Pinellas (727-524-4344; *www.worknetpinellas.org*) for specific information.

Medical Care

Of the 20 hospitals in Pinellas County, eight are in St. Petersburg and the Veterans Administration Medical Center is at nearby Bay Pines. Bayfront Medical Center (727-893-6102; *www.bayfront.org*) is a 502-bed, nonprofit, teaching hospital. Bayfront is the Tampa Bay area's highest volume trauma facility. St. Anthony's Health Care (727-825-1100; *www.stanthonys.com*) is a not-for-profit, 405-bed hospital that was established in 1931 and currently treats the citizen's of St. Petersburg.

Services for Seniors

St. Petersburg honestly loves seniors. So many services exist that support and inform seniors, it would take too long to list them all. To make it simple, check in with one of the following, and they can steer you to whatever you desire in the way of senior services. The Office on Aging (727-893-7102; *www.stpete.org*) is a division of the city of St. Petersburg's Recreation Department. This division oversees the operations of three adult centers and two multi-service centers, one of which was the first nationally accredited senior center in the state of Florida. The Sunshine Center (727-893-7102) is a place that provides services and facilities for whatever activity you have in mind. The Area Agency on Aging (727-570-9696; *www.agingcarefl.org*) coordinates and offers services for senior citizens through state and federal resources that help older adults remain in their homes.

Continuing Education

Eckerd College (800-456-9009; *www.eckerd.edu*) has the Leadership Development Institute, which is an internationally acclaimed executive development program. Eckerd also has the Center for Leadership & Lifelong Learning, which holds seminars and workshops on retirement. Senior College offers many study-travel adventures each year. The Academy of Senior Professionals at Eckerd College, mainly retirees, is dedicated to continued learning and sharing knowledge and experience with the students, faculty, and community. Elderhostel is a week-long residential program that offers creative approaches to a wide variety of liberal arts topics. The University of South Florida (727-553-4873; *www.stpt.usf.edu*) is committed to offering a range of credit and non-credit courses to lifelong learners. Its signature program, Senior Scholars, is designed to provide adults over 50 with practical instruction in such computer applications as word processing, Internet navigation, and digital photography.

Crime and Safety

According to a St. Petersburg Police Department report, there was a 1.4 percent decrease in total index crimes from 2002 to 2003. In the same period of time, there was a 3.2 percent decrease in total index crimes for the Midtown Economic Development Area. Overall, the *www.city-data.com* crime index Website reports that St. Petersburg has an average of 762 crimes per 100,000 people. This rates well in the state of Florida, but does not stand up well against the national average, which is 330 per 100,000 people.

Getting Around Town

Public Transportation: The Pinellas Suncoast Transit Authority (727-530-9911; *www.psta.net*) operates 163 buses and 20 trolleys that serve 36 regular and six commuter routes. In addition, two express buses travel between Pinellas County and Tampa, and the popular Suncoast Beach Trolley connects to the gulf beaches.

Roads and Highways: I-275 connects to I-75 and I-4

Airports: The St. Petersburg/Clearwater International Airport (727-535-7600; *www.fly2pie.com*) is serviced by eight airlines. Tampa International Airport, (813-870-8700; *www.tampaairport.com*) is 30 minutes from downtown, and is serviced by 22 airlines.

Ports: St. Petersburg's Municipal Marina (727-893-7329; *www.stpete.org/ marina.htm*) is on the west side of Tampa Bay. You can dock in the heart of St. Pete's downtown waterfront. The marina's 500-foot transient dock can accommodate vessels up to 110 feet, for daily or weekly fees.

Let the Good Times Roll

Recreation: St. Petersburg is home to 102 city parks on 2,400 acres, including a seven-mile preserved downtown waterfront. The Pinellas Trail is a paved linear park that connects most of Pinellas County, from St. Petersburg to Tarpon Springs, for 34 scenic miles. The recreational trail is a prime example of the Rails-to-Trails program and is popular with cyclists, in-line skaters, and joggers. St. Pete boasts three municipal golf courses, of which Mangrove Municipal Golf Course is among the Top 50 in the country. Within its borders are five beaches and eight public swimming pools, and the Pier, a St. Petersburg landmark that features shops, restaurants, and a marine aquarium. Tropicana Field is a 45,360-seat, climate-controlled domed ballpark with all-dirt base paths and artificial turf, and is home to the Tampa Bay Devil Rays. The Bayfront Center facilities include the St. Petersburg Times Arena (8,400 seats), and the Mahaffey Theatre for the Performing Arts (2,000 seats), and the Coliseum Ballroom, which is a historic ballroom containing the Southeast's largest wooden dance floor and has a seating capacity of 2,000.

Culture: The St. Petersburg Folk Fair Society (727-552-1896; *www.spiffs.org*) is an umbrella group with 40 ethnic member groups. It sponsors the International Harvest, which offers international singing, dancing groups, concerts, translators, and performers. The Florida International Museum (727-822-3693; *www.floridamuseum.org*) provides entertaining experiences through diverse exhibitions. The Salvador Dali Museum has a growing collection. The Museum of Fine Arts (*www.fine-arts.org*) contains outstanding examples of world art in an elegant setting. The Museum of History (*www.stpetemuseumofhistory.org*) collects, preserves, and interprets the history of St. Petersburg and the Pinellas Peninsula. The Florida Holocaust Museum honors the millions of men, women, and children who were victims of the Holocaust.

Annual Events: Because there are over 400 annual events in St. Petersburg, it would be impossible to list them all. For seniors, you can't beat the Good Life Games (727-892-5420; *www.goodlifegames.org*) in which you must be 55 or older to compete. Then there's the Easter Egg Hunt for seniors in March, which features live entertainment, free bingo, health screenings, coffee and doughnuts, and $1,000 in prizes and giveaways. For the whole family, there are greyhound races, yacht races, dog shows,

Blues festivals, art festivals, and the Festival of States, which is a gathering of high school bands from across the country. And don't forget about Juneteenth, Oktoberfest, and local theater performances. And at Christmas, they decorate the boats and take them on parade, a truly stunning sight!

When the Grandkids Come: You can visit the Suncoast Seabird Sanctuary in Indian Rocks Beach, which rescues and rehabilitates injured pelicans, herons, egrets, and other species. Don't let the kids miss Captain Nemo's Original Pirate Cruise, where they are issued water pistols and told to make as much noise as they want. The Great Explorations Hands-on Museum (727-821-8992; *www.greatexplorations.org*) is a great museum for the kids.

More Information

Municipal

St. Petersburg Area Chamber of Commerce
100 Second Avenue North, Suite #150
St. Petersburg, FL 33701
727-821-4069
www.stpete.com

Newspaper

The Tampa Tribune
1033 Ninth Street North #100
St. Petersburg, FL 33701
727-823-7732
www.tampatrib.com

St. Petersburg Times
490 First Avenue South
St. Petersburg, FL 33701
727-893-8111
www.sptimes.com

Realty

We do not have a Realtor recommendation for St. Petersburg. As an option, check out *www.realtor.com* or *www.homegain.com.* Select a Realtor with both CRS and GRI designations after their names, since it means that these folks have gone the extra mile and are both graduates of the Realtor Institute and Certified Residential Specialists.

Bloomington, Indiana

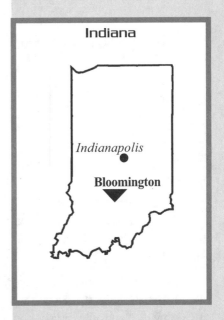

Indiana

Indianapolis

Bloomington

Bloomington at a Glance

Bloomington is a warm and friendly community nestled in the rolling hills of southern Indiana. Rand McNally's *Retirement Places* lists Bloomington among the "Top 10 Best in America." Bloomington offers many opportunities for work, recreation, leisure, and the arts. A stable economic base provides one of the lowest unemployment rates in the state. An abundance of restaurants provides a wide variety of offerings, from international and ethnic cuisine, to down-home cooking, to upscale dining. Through the facilities and resources of Indiana University, opportunities for live music and entertainment pop up almost daily. Many people already know about Bloomington's unique limestone heritage and beautiful scenery, but how about the country's only Tibetan Cultural Center, the state's oldest and largest winery, loads of antiques, and a world music festival? There are many reasons to retire here, but possibly the best is that prices aren't out of proportion. You can go to events without taking out a second mortgage. Including the student population of Indiana University's flagship campus, the area population is approximately 65,000. The city is the administrative seat of Monroe County, an area that embraces roughly 115,000 residents.

Possible Drawbacks: Well, it is the Mid-west! It gets humid in the summertime, and the ice storms in winter are fierce. And you may want to keep your car in the garage on ballgame nights, as the traffic can be rough.

▶ Nickname: The Break Away Town

▶ County: Monroe

▶ Area Code: 812

▶ Population: 69,987

▶ County Population: 120,563

▶ Percent of Population Over 65: 17%

▶ Region: Southern Indiana

▶ Closest Metropolitan Area: Indianapolis, 50 miles

▶ Median Home Price: $185,000

▶ Best Reasons to Retire Here: Rich in culture and comfortable living, it's easy to get around, and the prices are low.

Climate

39° N Latitude 89° W Longitude	Average High Temperature (°F)	Average Low Temperature (°F)	Precipitation (")	Sunshine (%)
January	36.5	18.1	3.5	40
April	64.4	42.4	4.0	54
July	85.8	65.5	3.8	66
October	67.1	44.6	3.2	61
YEAR	63.3	43.0	44.5	55

Utilities

Overview: The cost of living is a low 83, based on the national average of 100.

Gas Company: Vectren Energy Delivery (800-777-2060; *www.vectren.com*) is the natural gas provider. A typical monthly bill for a house with gas heat is $30 in summer and $100 in winter.

Electric Company: Cinergy/PSI Energy (800-521-2232; *www.cinergypsi.com*) is the local electricity provider. A typical monthly bill for a two-bedroom apartment, not including heat and air conditioning, is $30 in summer and $100 in winter.

Phone Company: Choice One (*www.choiceone.com*)

Water/Sewer Company: The city of Bloomington Utilities (812-339-1444; *http://bloomington.in.gov/utilities*)

Cable Company: Choice One (*www.choiceone.com*)

The Tax Axe

Car Registration: The Indiana Bureau of Motor Vehicles (812-336-3018; *www.in.gov/bmv*) requires that within 60 days of becoming an Indiana resident, you must obtain a certificate of title for all vehicles. The standard title fee for a vehicle title is $15, and the charge is $14 for a four year driver's license.

Driver's License: The Indiana Bureau of Motor Vehicles (812-336-3018; *www.in.gov/bmv*) maintains that you obtain a driver's license within 60 days of becoming a permanent resident.

Sales Tax: 6 percent, with food and prescription drugs exempt

State Income Tax: Flat rate of 3.4 percent of federal adjusted gross income.

Retirement Income Tax: Social Security is exempt. Persons 62 and older may exclude $2,000 from military and federal pensions or survivor benefits, minus the amount of Social Security received. It gets complicated, so check with the Indiana Department of Revenue (317-232-3777).

Property Tax: Both real and personal properties are taxed. For example, a 1,500 square foot condo within the city limits would be about $1,500 a year. Again, it's complex, so call the Indiana Department of Revenue (317-232-3777) for details.

Local Real Estate

Overview: The Bloomington real estate market is active. Single-family dwellings saw prices appreciate at a rate of 6 percent over 2004, placing Bloomington at the 145th ranking of the 265 metro areas evaluated by the Office of Federal Housing Enterprise Oversight. You can find retirement and assisted living homes that provide such services as shopping, transportation, entertainment, and recreation.

Average price of a three-bedroom/two-bath home: $150,000

Average price of a two-bedroom condo: $160,000

Common Housing Styles: There are lots of two story ranch houses and contemporary styles. Older houses are usually limestone. New construction is brick, frame, and vinyl. Most are on quarter and half acre lots. Subdivisions are rolling hills with wooded lots.

Rental Market: A large percentage of the rentals are on the part of students.

Average rent for a two-bedroom apartment: $800 per month.

Communities Popular With Retirees: Winslow Farms, Tamarron, Elm Heights area, Gentry, The Stands, Brighton Point, Sherwood Green, Peppergrass, Sycamore Village, Coppertree, Windemere, VillaGreen, and Woodcrest are all communitites that are popular with retirees in Bloomington.

Nearby Areas to Consider: Lake Monroe is a 10,000-acre manmade lake surrounded by Hoosier National Forest. It attracts those who like to boat, fish, hike, golf, play tennis, swim, sunbathe, and engage in any of a number of other outdoor activities. Nashville in Brown County has the changing seasons, especially in the fall when the cool weather transforms the countryside into a magnificent landscape. Nashville has become famous for its art and antique shops, not to mention the music scene!

Earning a Living

Business Climate: The city has made *Forbes* magazine's "Top 10 Best Small Metro Areas." Unemployment rate is low at 4.8 percent. The average travel time to work is only 15.2 minutes. For those who have suffered through a long commute, this is heaven. So the business climate in Bloomington is positive. You should be able to get a job fairly easily, and once you do, your commute will be a breeze.

Help in Starting a Business: Indiana State University's College of Business Small Business Development Center (800-227-7232; *www.indstate.edu/sbdc/start.htm*). For general business information, the chamber of commerce (*www.chamberbloomington.org*) is another resource.

Job Market: This is a fairly small college town. Jobs are sometimes tough to find, due to the relative abundance of students who are willing to work for peanuts. However, if you have experience, you'll probably do pretty well.

Medical Care

Although Bloomington is fairly modest in size, it has the full power and force of a comprehensive, full-service hospital in Bloomington Hospital and Healthcare Services, (812-336-6821; *www.bhhs.org*). In addition to acute-care, it has a fabulous referral department. For seniors, there are several programs, such as walking and balance classes, hearing and memory screenings, a discount card program, assisted living facilities, Adult Day Program, and an Alzheimer's Resource Center. Meadows Hospital (812-331-8000; *www.meadowshospital.com*) is part of the national group of Ardent hospitals. Ardent currently operates 34 hospitals in 13 states, providing a full range of medical/surgical, psychiatric, and substance abuse services. Meadows Hospital offers acute inpatient mental health care for adults. Meadows also offers a short-term day treatment program seven days a week, up to eight hours a day.

Services for Seniors

Area 10 Agency on Aging (800-844-1010; *www.area10.bloomington.in.us*) is a private, nonprofit corporation serving seniors ages 55 and older. Several services exist and deal with family issues such as respite for caregivers, home healthcare, in-home visitation, and elder abuse. For those who aren't in need, this is an opportunity to serve as a volunteer. The Evergreen Institute (812-855-4848; *www.indiana.edu/~evrgreen*) is a nonprofit organization that currently has one service, HomeShare, which matches local home providers with senior citizens seeking housing. This service is for senior citizens who are no longer interested in (or able to) care for a large home, yet do not wish to move into a nursing home or assisted-living housing.

Continuing Education

Indiana University-Bloomington (812-855 4848; *www.indiana.edu*) has a broad undergraduate curriculum, and offers ample graduate studies for the scholars among us. While there is a department called Lifelong Learning, it should be noted no references could be found to waivers for senior citizens. The Hair Arts Academy (812-339-1117) is a private, for-profit business. Have you ever wanted to do hair? Yes, you're on your feet a lot, so it's not for wimps, but closet "Steel Magnolias" exist in our crowd.

Crime and Safety

The crime index is 227.9, with the national average at 330.6. Bloomington has a sterling rate of good citizenship. On average, you are less likely to encounter crime in Bloomington than in the average city nationwide.

Getting Around Town

Public Transportation: Rural Transit (*www.area10.bloomington.in.us/ruraltransit*), a service of the Area 10 Agency on Aging, offers bus service to everyone in Monroe,

Owen, and Lawrence Counties. You can ride no matter your age or physical ability. Rural Transit offers express travel between Spencer, Ellettsville, and Bloomington Monday through Friday. County Routes offers round-trip service between specific points in the counties from one to five times a week. The county routes are on a pre-scheduled basis. To schedule a ride, call at least 24 hours in advance of your trip. Wheelchair-lift-equipped services for the disabled are available upon request. The fare varies according to the service, but monthly passes are available.

Roads and Highways: State Highways 37, 45, 46, 48, and 446 are either in or near Bloomington. I-65 is about 45 miles east of town, and the junctions of I-65, I-69, I-70, and I-74 are about the same distance to the north.

Airports: Monroe County Airport is about seven miles out of town and has a few flights. Indianapolis International Airport (*www.indianapolisairport.com*) is about 42 miles away and is served by 14 airlines.

Let the Good Times Roll

Recreation: It seems there are more things to do in Bloomington than there are people to do them. The university provides the bulk of organized activity. Many of the offerings are clubs and organizations covering such interests as biking, hiking, running, baseball, rowing, skiing, and martial arts. The long list of organized activities includes scuba, judo, yoga, rowing, fishing, football, soccer, skating, and women's triathlon, sailing on Lake Monroe, swing dance clubs, ballroom dancing clubs, spelunking club, golf, and more. Lake Lemon is great for fishing, and Griffy Lake is surrounded by wildlife trails. At the end of summer, the entire city and countryside around it dresses up in its fall colors. The Wonder of Science can be seen at the Museum of Science, Health, and Technology (our favorite). The Bloomington Speedway runs sprint-car races all summer, and it is only 50 miles to the annual Indianapolis 500 and the other races at the Indianapolis Speedway.

Culture: Most of the towns in this book offer a handsome list of cultural attractions, but none so grand in such a small community. The list of museums goes on and on, and includes the Wylie House Museum, the home of the first president of Indiana University, Wonder Lab at the Museum of Science and Technology, Mathers Museum of World cultures, Monroe County History Center, and the Indiana University Art Museum. In addition, the university provides entertainment on a grand scale, with year-round attractions to fit tastes across the board, such as live theater, art exhibits, ballet performances, musical concerts, poetry, and art lectures that cover current exhibits.

Annual Events: February brings Arts' Week, April offers the Little 500 bike race, and May is for fisher folk who want to win the "crappiethon." In June, there is the Arts Fair on the Square and National Ham Radio Kids' Day. July is the Fourth and fireworks, parade, and concerts all over the place. August ushers in the annual hot air balloon fiesta. September is the 4th Street Festival, an art exhibit for local artists. In October, the Lotus World Music & Arts Festival brings musicians and artists from around the world to Bloomington. Also in October is the Hilly Hundred bicycle event. November brings the Hoagy Carmichael Festival, and Hoosier football. December brings the much-loved tradition of the Chimes of Christmas.

When the Grandkids Come: First of all, you will want to take them out to eat. Then plan your visit to one of a very few Tibetan centers in the United States. Get out to one of the nearby lakes, Lake Monroe, Lake Lemon, or Lake Griffy. You can fish, skip stones, or just enjoy the out of doors, but the kids will want to find snack shops while you're out there. If a day-trip is on your calendar, drive the 50-odd miles to Indianapolis to the Children's Museum, the Indianapolis Motor Speedway, home to the Indy 500 race, or the Indianapolis Zoo.

More Information

Municipal
Greater Bloomington Chamber of Commerce
P.O. Box 1302
Bloomington, IN 47402
812-336-6381
www.chamberbloomington.org

Bloomington Convention and Visitors Bureau
2855 North Walnut Street
Bloomington, IN 47404
800-800-0037
www.visitbloomington.com

Newspaper
Herald-Times
1900 South Walnut Street
Bloomington, IN 47402
812-236-4200
www.heraldtimesonline.com

Realty
Shady McDonald
487 Clarizz Boulevard
Bloomington, IN 47401
812-336-7300
www.tuckerobr.com

Louisiana

23 ▶ Lafayette, Louisiana

Lafayette at a Glance

This is Cajun country. Lafayette is the hub of the eight-parish area in the heart of Acadiana, a region known for its unique Cajun and Creole heritages, French language, and Spanish cultural traditions. Acadiana is made up of 22 south Louisiana parishes that extend from south of Alexandria in the center of the state, to Lake Charles on the west, to south of New Orleans on the east. Lafayette lies 15 miles west of the Atchafalaya Basin and 35 miles north of the Gulf of Mexico, and enjoys the subtropical climate typical of southern Louisiana. The city is situated in a geographical area of forests and prairies interlaced with bayous, swamps, and marshes. Lafayette has long been known for its great food, music, and festivals. Lafayette is also a place with historic attractions, majestic plantation homes, vibrant gardens, leisurely swamp tours, and exciting museums. The unique heritage, a basically French culture, has been simmering like a gumbo for the past 200 years, making it seem like another country. You'll find festivals and celebrations of all varieties, from Mardi Gras to a Friday afternoon fais-do-do (street dance). Antebellum homes and lush tropical gardens can be found in the dark, mysterious swamps. You can tour swamplands or plantations, and visit attractions such as the Acadian Village and old Vermilionville.

Possible Drawbacks: A summer day can become quite warm and humid. Housing can be expensive.

▶ Nickname: Hub City

▶ Parish: Lafayette

▶ Area Code: 337

▶ Population: 110,257

▶ Parish Population: 190,503

▶ Percent of Population Over 65: 11.2%

▶ Region: Southern Louisiana

▶ Closest Metropolitan Area: Baton Rouge, 63 miles

▶ Median Home Price: $110,000

▶ Best Reasons to Retire Here: Cajun country lifestyle, outstanding cuisine, and great local music. The general cost of living is low. For example, health costs are only 90 percent of the national average.

Climate

30° N Latitude 91° W Longitude	Average High Temperature (°F)	Average Low Temperature (°F)	Precipitation (")	Sunshine (%)
January	59.9	41.2	5.4	46
April	78.4	58.5	4.6	62
July	90.5	73.4	6.9	58
October	79.9	57.7	3.3	64
YEAR	77.4	58.1	59.1	57

Utilities

Overview: The cost of living is slightly above average at 103.2, with a national average of 100. This is mostly because of housing, which is 120.1. Transportation is slightly high, but food, healthcare, and utilities are all well below average.

Gas Company: Entergy (800-368-3749; *www.entergy-louisiana.com*)

Electric Company: Lafayette Utilities System (337-291-8280; *www.lus.org*)

Phone Company: BellSouth (337-232-5832; *www.bellsouth.com*)

Water/Sewer Company: Lafayette Utilities (337-291-8280; *www.lus.org)*

Cable Company: Cox Communications (337-232-6323; *www.cox.com*)

The Tax Axe

Car Registration: You are required to transfer your out-of-state registration to Louisiana within 30 days. The Office of Motor Vehicles (*http://omv.dps.state.la.us*) collects a use tax based on the book value of the vehicle, and is due on all out-of-state vehicles when first registered in Louisiana. The titling fees are $29.50 plus the license plate, which can be up to $82 depending on the value of the car.

Driver's License: As a new Louisiana resident, you are required to transfer your out-of-state driver's license to Louisiana within 30 days. The fee is $24.50.

Sales Tax: The state sales tax is 4 percent. Local taxes double that to a total of 8 percent.

State Income Tax: Louisiana has an accelerated income tax that ranges from 2 percent to 6 percent. There is no state sales tax on food, electricity, or natural gas.

Retirement Income Tax: Louisiana exempts Social Security payments, public pension income, and the first $6,000 of private pension income including annuities. Deductions are also granted to residents who are disabled and for family members who care for older relatives.

Property Tax: Louisiana's property taxes are the 45th highest in the nation. Residences are assessed at 10 percent of their value, and the first $7,500 is shielded by the Homestead exemption. A homeowner living in a $75,000 home would pay no property tax. About two-thirds of the homes in Louisiana are fully exempt. The tax rate inside the city limits of Lafayette is 83.29 mills, and outside is 84.82 mills.

Local Real Estate

Overview: Lafayette is currently in a slightly upward market with sales stronger in houses under $250,000. Buyers tend to lean toward newer construction on higher-priced houses, so older houses are not selling as well. New construction is strong for houses above $200,000.

Average price of a three-bedroom/two-bath home: $135,100

Average price of a two-bedroom condo: $112,000

Common Housing Styles: This is the place for Southern style, with a balance between living and formal entertaining space. Country houses that seem to invite family gatherings with such traditional features as front porches are popular.

Rental Market: Apartments are available for rent, but rental houses are rare. You can find them, but you should start your search early so you can find the sort of home you are looking for.

Average rent for a two-bedroom apartment: $700 per month

Communities Popular With Retirees: Youngsville and Brousard. Also, the area around Cajundome and Lafitte Streets.

Nearby Areas to Consider: Opelousas, to the north of Lafayette, has a population of 20,000 and is third oldest city in Louisiana, dating back to the 1690s. Jim Bowie lived in Opelousas. It is the Zydeco Capital of the World. The annual Yambilee festival in Opelousas celebrates the harvest of yams, or sweet potatoes. Morgan City is conveniently located "right in the middle of everywhere"—70 miles west of New Orleans, 60 miles south of Baton Rouge, and 60 miles east of Lafayette. Morgan City is the gateway to the Gulf of Mexico for the shrimping and oilfield industries.

Earning a Living

Business Climate: Lafayette has a large workforce with a strong work ethic. Real estate and facilities are affordable, and there are two interstate highways, four ports, and two major airports nearby. Lafayette is now attracting large companies such as Cingular, which recently constructed a facility that created 1,000 jobs. The city is now in the process of providing high-speed fiber optic Internet connection as a utility.

Help in Starting a Business: The First Stop Shop (337-269-4036; *www.sec.state.la.us*) is a licensing information center for prospective small business owners. The First Stop Shop gives current and potential business owners a single place to go for licensing information needed to start a business in Louisiana. The regional representative for the Louisiana Economic Development of the Acadiana Region (337-232-6239; *www.lded.state.la.us*) is headquartered in Lafayette.

Job Market: The area's oil and natural gas boom contributed to a large population increase and an influx of new businesses to the city in the 1980s and 1890s. The Heymann Oil Center is headquarters for several oil companies.

Medical Care

Our Lady of Lourdes Regional Medical Center is Acadiana's leader for cardiology, oncology/cancer care, and general medical services. Our Lady of Lourdes has been named in the "100 Top Hospitals in America" for cardiovascular services, as well as in the "100 Top Hospitals in America" for orthopedic services, and in the *U.S. News & World Report*'s "Top 50 Hospitals in America" for rheumatology and respiratory services. The Lafayette General Medical Center (*www.lafayettegeneral.com*) is a short-term nonprofit hospital with 343 beds, and has the largest full-service acute-care medical center in the nine-parish area of Acadiana. Its services include heart care, cancer care, emergencies, outpatient services, home health, and older adult services. The University Medical Center (337-261-6000; *www.medschool.lsuhsc.edu*) is a 208-bed short-term hospital affiliated with the Louisiana State University School of Medicine in New Orleans. The Medical Center of Southwest Louisiana (337-981-2949; *www.medicalcentersw.com*) is a 166-bed short-term hospital. Meadowbrook Rehabilitation Hospital (337-232-1905) is a 50-bed long-term hospital and the Community Rehabilitation of Lafayette (337-234-4031) is a 38-bed long-term hospital.

Services for Seniors

The Louisiana Department of Social Services (*www.dss.state.la.us/index.htm*) provides a comprehensive list of local programs to assist elderly or disabled citizens. The department has the Strategies To Empower People program, which helps to provide transportation, hearing aids, eyeglasses, and medical exams. The department also supports the Independent Living Program, which provides rehabilitation and counseling services, among others.

Continuing Education

The University of Louisiana at Lafayette (337-482-1000; *www.louisiana.edu*) offers a total of 28 graduate degree programs in applied language and speech sciences, biology, cognitive science, English, francophone studies, mathematics, computer science, and computer engineering. The university waives the tuition costs for people over 55. Senior citizens pay $54 a quarter for instruction, a $20 one-time application fee, and a $12-a-year parking fee. Seniors get a student ID, which enables them to check out books from the library, attend entertainment events at the student price, and use many of the other facilities on campus.

Crime and Safety

Lafayette has an average reported property crime count of 7,390.1 per 100,000 people. The violent crime rate is 852.7. Both of these numbers are well above national averages.

Getting Around Town

Public Transportation: The Lafayette Transit System (337-291-8570; *www.lafayettelinc.net/LTS*) runs multiple bus routes throughout the city with senior fares of 35 cents.

Roads and Highways: State highways 10 and 49; US 90 and 167

Airports: The Lafayette Municipal Airport (*www.lftairport.com*) is served by Delta, Continental, and Northwest.

Let the Good Times Roll

Recreation: The area around Lafayette provides a number of campgrounds. Lafayette is in the heart of the sportsman's paradise of Louisiana, so there is immediate access to extraordinary fishing, hunting, water-skiing, boating, and camping. Within five miles are Charlo Lake, Grenovillieres Lake, Spreafico Lake, Lake Grande Marie, and Lake la Pointe. Other outdoor activities include charter fishing, swamp excursions, and numerous hiking trails. Cajun food and music are both hot and spicy. The city contains numerous public parks and ballparks, tennis courts, bowling alleys, and ice and roller-skating rinks. The parish has many private and public golf courses. Golfers visit Lafayette's Acadian Hills Country Club. Rafters and canoers frequent Atchafalaya River. Evangeline Downs offers an outlet for horse race fans. The university provides spectator sports with the Ragin' Cajuns athletics programs.

Culture: For an orientation to the life of the Acadians, visit the Acadian Cultural Center. The historic sites include the Alexandre Mouton House, the Cathedral of St. John the Evangelist, Chretien Point Plantation, the Acadian Village, and Maison du Co-fofil. The heritage of the city is contained in the Photographic History of Lafayette in possession of the Clerk of the Court. The museums of Lafayette shed light on early life in south Louisiana, present world-class art exhibitions, and examine many facets of the universe.

Annual Events: Every April brings the Festival International de Louisiane, which is a mixture of cultures from all over the world. It is such a large festival that they supply maps for it. The Breaux Bridge Crawfish Festival is held in May. It's mostly about food, but you have to see it to believe it. In August you'll find a sort of "Grammy-style" awards ceremony honoring the best in Cajun music, but it's mostly a two-day dance festival with award-winning Cajun bands. The Zydeco Music Festival is also held in August in Opelousas, but other things, such as a fun run, also happen. The fiddles and even more Cajun food come out for the Festivals Acadians, held each year the third weekend of September in Lafayette. "A Cajun and Creole Christmas" is celebrated the entire month of December with festivals of light, parades, tours of homes, and holiday events that will cheer you up in Southern style.

When the Grandkids Come: The Children's Museum of Acadiana is a hands-on participatory museum. All of the festivals have special areas and entertainment for kids.

More Information

Municipal

Greater Lafayette Chamber of Commerce
804 East Saint Mary
Lafayette, LA 70505
337-233-2705
www.lafchamber.org

Newspaper

The Daily Advertiser
P.O. Box 5310
Lafayette, LA 70502
337-289-6300
www.acadiananow.com

Realty

We do not have a Realtor recommendation for Lafayette. As an option, check out *www.realtor.com* or *www.homegain.com*. Select a Realtor with both CRS and GRI designations after their names, since it means that these folks have gone the extra mile and are both graduates of the Realtor Institute and Certified Residential Specialists.

Ruston, Louisiana

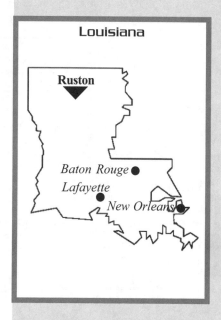

Louisiana

Ruston

Baton Rouge ●
Lafayette ●
New Orleans ●

Ruston at a Glance

Ruston is in among the rolling red hills of north Louisiana and has a down-home atmosphere intermingled with the educational atmosphere of Louisiana Tech University and Grambling University. The enrollment of Louisiana Tech University makes up more than half the population of the town, which makes it an entirely different place when school is out. Lincoln Parish offers an idyllic, old-fashioned lifestyle. The countryside is filled with peach orchards. Ruston is the parish seat of Lincoln Parish and is located in the north central part of the state, about 35 miles south of Arkansas. Peaches have been a cash crop of the area for many years. Local ownership of the main businesses is gradually being replaced by national chains and absentee owners. Ruston is becoming a retirement/college community. The surrounding forests are full of deer, wild turkeys, and game birds. There is little likelihood of significant growth for the town, but stability can be an asset for some lifestyles. The population increased only 2 percent in the entire decade of the 1990s. The population peaked in 1994 and has been slowly declining since.

Possible Drawbacks: It may be too quiet for you. This is a quiet, laidback place into which you must bring your own excitement. Starting a business in such a shrinking economy could be fruitless.

▶ Nickname: None

▶ Parish: Lincoln

▶ Area Code: 318

▶ Population: 20,546

▶ Parish Population: 42,509

▶ Percent of Population Over 65: 11.3%

▶ Region: Northern Louisiana

▶ Closest Metropolitan Area: Monroe, 37 miles

▶ Median Home Price: $80,000

▶ Best Reasons to Retire Here: With plenty of rural living, this college town could be the place if you are looking for peace and quiet in a stable surrounding.

Climate

32° N Latitude 92° W Longitude	Average High Temperature (°F)	Average Low Temperature(°F)	Precipitation (")	Sunshine (%)
January	54.0	32.4	5.4	56
April	76.3	52.5	5.0	54
July	92.5	70.2	4.3	63
October	77.4	51.4	3.7	58
YEAR	75.2	52.2	54.4	57

Utilities

Overview: The overall cost of living is 94.3, with a national average of 100. Transportation is above average because you will need your own car, and utilities are above average at 105.9. Health care is well below average at 89.8, and housing is even lower at 87.1.

Gas Company: Reliant Energy and ArkLa Gas (318-255-3014). For propane, use O'Neal Gas (318-768-2511).

Electric Company: The city of Ruston owns and operates an independent generating and distribution system (318-255-4714). Or you can use Claiborne Electric Cooperative (800-929-3504) or Entergy (888-368-3749).

Phone Company: BellSouth (318-242-0199; *www.bellsouth.com*)

Water/Sewer Company: The city of Ruston (318-251-8633) provides water and sewer service for the Ruston area.

Cable Company: Cox Communications (318-255-6594; *www.cox.com*)

The Tax Axe

Car Registration: The Department of Public Safety Motor Vehicle Office (318-251-4148) requires that, when vehicles are brought in from another state, a fee of $18.50 is paid for a Louisiana title. A use tax, based on the vehicle's value and rate of state tax already paid in the previous state, and license fee are charged.

Driver's License: A driver's license is obtained by surrendering the out-of-state driver's license and providing the DMV with a copy of your social security card and proof of insurance. Written and eye examinations are required, but the driving examination is not. The fee for an operator's license is $18 for four years.

Sales Tax: The state sales tax is 4 percent. With local taxes added, the sales tax inside the Ruston city limits is 8.5 percent.

State Income Tax: An accelerated income tax ranges from 2 percent up to a maximum of 6 percent.

Retirement Income Tax: The first $2,700 of income is deductible for persons over 65.

Property Tax: Ruston's millage rate is 87.74. The property tax rate comes out to be $12.10 per $1,000 of home value.

Local Real Estate

Overview: Ruston is very much a college town and, because of the transient nature of the population, half of all houses are rental houses. House prices are below average and it has become common for local residents to invest in and manage rental properties. This situation makes is fairly easy to sell a house.

Average price of a three-bedroom/two-bath home: $98,000.

Average price of a two-bedroom condo: $125,000

Common Housing Styles: Many houses are on large, heavily treed lots. Newer houses are mostly brick. There are a large number of older, smaller houses, although some might need to be refurbished.

Rental Market: A full-time rental is easy to find. The same situation exists for the numerous apartments around the city.

Average rent for a two-bedroom apartment: $400 per month

Communities Popular With Retirees: Dodson, Quitman, and the north side of Ruston are all communities that are popular with retirees.

Nearby Areas to Consider: The twin cities of Monroe and West Monroe, 30 miles to the east, are located along the Ouachita River, which was named one of the most beautiful rivers in the world by National Geographic. Shreveport, 65 miles to the west, has lake and river cruises, casinos, and thoroughbred racing. Shreveport is a modern city of 200,000; is only a few miles from both Texas and Arkansas; and is filled with dining hotspots, entertainment, shopping, and sports.

Earning a Living

Business Climate: Today the original industries of farming, forestry, and higher education remain, but other businesses, including some of the best retail and food chains, and large industrial employers help create a business atmosphere that offers good-paying jobs and ample opportunities for success.

Help in Starting a Business: Louisiana Tech University's Small Business Development Center (318-257-3537; *www.louisianapartnership.com/sbdc.html*) was formed to provide management and technical assistance to current and prospective small business owners; and to provide guidance or training in areas such as business plan and feasibility study preparation, marketing, advertising, finance, accounting, personnel, and production management.

Job Market: The unemployment rate is above average at 6.24 percent. Jobs are available, but you should probably secure your new position before moving. While the job market has grown slowly in the past, it is projected to change in the future.

Medical Care

Lincoln General Hospital, HealthSouth Rehabilitation Hospital, and Green Clinic, are all located within a few hundred yards of one another, and they comprise a full-service medical mall unrivaled by any community of equal stature. Lincoln General Hospital (318-254-2100; *www.lincolnhealth.com*) is a 149-bed acute-care, nonprofit facility. Next door, Green Clinic (318-255-3690) has grown to include doctors in more than 20 specialties. Green Clinic is able to handle virtually every health problem. Some of the services provided at the clinic include outpatient surgery, outpatient physical therapy, outpatient cardiac stress testing, urgent care, and the clinic pharmacy. HealthSouth Rehabilitation Hospital is a 90-bed long-term acute-care facility that provides both inpatient and outpatient services, as well as general healthcare and surgical services..

Services for Seniors

The Lincoln Council on Aging's Ruston Senior Center (318-255-1455) has an Alzheimer support group, social activities, physical fitness, income tax assistance, meals, and much more. Defiance/Ruston Senior Center (318-756-0601; *www.franketobeyjones.com/senior_center1.htm*) is a place to make new friends and share experiences, participate in fun events and activities, and stay active and healthy. It is also a Red Cross meal site. The Pecan Villa (318-251-9960) has 60 independent living units for seniors.

Continuing Education

Louisiana Tech University (318-257-021; *www.latech.edu*) waives the tuition costs for people over 55. Senior citizens pay $54 a quarter for instruction, a $20 one-time application fee, and a $12 yearly parking fee. Seniors get a student ID, which enables them to check out books from the library, attend entertainment events at the student price, and use many of the other facilities on campus. Grambling State University (318-274-3811; *www.gram.edu*), five miles to the west, is also a state university and follows the same policy.

Crime and Safety

The number of violent crimes recorded by the FBI in 2003 was 119. The number of murders and homicides was three. The violent crime rate was 5.8 per 1,000 people.

Getting Around Town

Public Transportation: There is no public transportation in Ruston.

Roads and Highways: Interstate 20 and US 80 and 167.

Airports: Monroe Regional Airport (318-329-2461; *www.ci.monroe.la.us/departments/airport*) is 30 miles to the east and is served by Northwest, Atlantic Southeast Airlines, and Continental Express, with 19 daily flights.

Let the Good Times Roll

Recreation: No matter what your preference, you will always find something in season in Lincoln Parish, where recreation and good times are a way of life. With so much nature nearby, picking the perfect spot might be tricky for camping, hiking, backpacking, fishing, and water-skiing. Mountain biking has become very popular in the hills surrounding Ruston. In particular, Lincoln Parish Park offers world-class mountain bike trails, including intermediate to advanced level technical trails, along with several picnic areas, a sandy beach and swimming area, and camping sites. The two universities present plays, operas, ballets, and guest performers. How about collegiate sports? Do the names Terry Bradshaw, Karl Malone, the Lady Techsters, and Eddie Robinson mean anything to you? Well, they definitely mean something to Lincoln Parish residents who, through the years, have watched them shine. Leon Barmore, the winningest coach in the history of college basketball (men or women), produces a Final Four caliber team year after year. And you haven't seen or heard a marching band until you've seen Grambling!

Culture: The North Central Louisiana Arts Council receives major funding and is behind many activities. The Ruston Community Theatre performs a number of plays each season and sponsors workshops for actors, directors, and stage technicians. Both Louisiana Tech University and Grambling State University play host to national and international performers, as well as local talent. The Ruston Civic Symphony Society sponsors several seasonal performances every year. Ruston is also home to a public library, two public art galleries, two museums, and several privately owned pottery and artist's studios.

Annual Events: Every October brings the Russtown Society's Annual Pumpkin Fest Carnival and the Annual Terror on James Street Haunted House. The Louisiana Peach Festival (*http://rustonlincoln.org*) is held in June, and has been celebrated for more than 50 years. It includes parades, a fishing tournament, a golf tournament, a cooking contest, photo contests, a fine arts show, bands, dances, rodeo, and a peach eating contest!

When the Grandkids Come: Kids always enjoy the downtown railroad park. The mountain bike trails in Lincoln Parish Park are graduated in levels of difficulty. Ruston is the perfect place for kids to enjoy the outdoors, and the local colleges offer opportunities for summer classes.

More Information

Municipal

Ruston-Lincoln Chamber of Commerce
P.O. Box 1383
Ruston, LA 71273
318-255-2031
www.rustonlincoln.org

Newspaper

Ruston Daily Leader
212 West Park Avenue
Ruston, LA 71270
318-255-4353
www.rustonleader.com

Realty

We do not have a Realtor recommendation for Ruston. As an option, check out *www.realtor.com* or *www.homegain.com.* Select a Realtor with both CRS and GRI designations after their names, since it means that these folks have gone the extra mile and are both graduates of the Realtor Institute and Certified Residential Specialists.

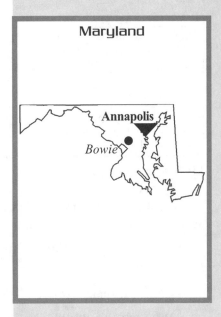

Maryland

25 ▶ Annapolis, Maryland

Annapolis at a Glance

This fabulous place will appeal to those who like to learn about our Founding Fathers. This was, for a short while, the capital of the new nation. It continues to be the capital of the state of Maryland. Several buildings survive from Colonial days and add a dimension of reality to the history they represent, making Annapolis a popular location for history buffs and those studying early America. This is a popular retirement area for graduates of the nearby Naval Academy. In 2002, *Barron's* magazine selected Annapolis as one of the Top 10 places in the world to retire. Among the reasons cited were the wide range of activities, classes, arts, and history, plus the proximity of a wider variety of recreational and educational resources and major metropolitan areas. Annapolis has a charming downtown area, complete with a dock and pedestrian walkway. Annapolis is close enough to Baltimore and Washington D.C. for big city convenience, still retains its small town accessibility and personality. Many of these elements are found in the number of programs and services made available to senior citizens.

Possible Drawbacks: This is the spot for the well-off retiree. The amenities are grand, but so is the price tag. In addition, some don't like the cool weather of winter, or the humidity of summer.

▶ Nickname: Crabtown

▶ County: Anne Arundel

▶ Area Code: 410

▶ Population: 36,178

▶ County Population: 508,572

▶ Percent of Population Over 65: 11.9%

▶ Region: Central Maryland

▶ Closest Metropolitan Area: Baltimore, 24 miles

▶ Median Home Price: $399,000

▶ Best Reasons to Retire Here: This is the place with seacoast culture, sports, historical charm, and proximity to large city conveniences.

Climate

38° N Latitude 76° W Longitude	Average High Temperature (°F)	Average Low Temperature (°F)	Precipitation (")	Sunshine (%)
January	42.3	24.6	3.2	51
April	65.7	43.9	3.4	56
July	87.4	67.6	3.6	64
October	68.7	47.8	3.3	58
YEAR	66.2	46.4	41.8	57

Utilities

Overview: The overall cost of living is rated quite high at 130.8, with a national average of 100. This is mostly due to housing costs, which are almost twice the national average at 195.2. Utilities are also high at 121.1.

Gas Company: Baltimore Gas & Electric (410-685-0123; *www.bge.com*)

Electric Company: Baltimore Gas & Electric (410-685-0123; *www.bge.com*)

Phone Company: Verizon (800-356-2355; *www.verizon.com*)

Water/Sewer Company: City of Annapolis (410-263-7953; *www.annapolis.gov*)

Cable Company: Comcast (888-266-2278; *www.comcast.com*)

The Tax Axe

Car Registration: The Maryland Motor Vehicle Administration (800-950-1682; *http://mva.state.md.us*) requires that you register your vehicle within 60 days of moving to Maryland. For vehicles less than 7 years old, vehicle(s) titled in a state with a tax rate equal to or higher than Maryland's 5 percent rate will cost $100. If the vehicle is registered in a state that imposes no tax, the tax will be assessed at 5 percent of the value of the vehicle.

Driver's License: If you are a new resident of Maryland, you have 60 days to obtain a Maryland driver's license. You will be required to pass a vision test. The fee depends on the license requested.

Sales Tax: 5 percent, with food, prescription, and non-prescription drugs exempt

State Income Tax: The state has an accelerated income tax ranging from 2 percent to 4.75 percent, Anne Arundel County adds 2.56 percent.

Retirement Income Tax: Social Security and railroad retirement income are exempt. Pensions are exempt up to $20,700, minus amount of Social Security and Railroad Retirement benefits. Out-of-state government pensions do not qualify for the exemption. Military pensioners are eligible for an additional pension exemption of up to $2,500. Up to $2,500 of retired military pay may be exempt if retiree is over 55 and meets gross income limit.

Property Tax: Property is assessed at its full cash value. Property tax rates vary widely. There are no restrictions or limitations on property taxes imposed by the state, meaning cities and counties can set tax rates at any level they deem necessary to fund governmental services. The Homeowners' Property Tax Credit Program allows credits against the homeowner's property tax bill if the property taxes exceed a fixed percentage of the person's gross income.

Local Real Estate

Overview: The real estate market prices have escalated in the past few years, making the median house value significantly above state average. The best prices are to be found in townhouses and condos. That said, the true value of some of the restored historical homes is almost beyond measure for history buffs.

Average price of a three-bedroom/two-bath home: $399,000

Average price of a two-bedroom condo: $350,000

Common Housing Styles: Victorian-Gothic, saltbox, Beaux Arts, Colonial and Tudor Revival, and Craftsman style are popular. Common features are third stories, screened-in porches or balconies, and attached garages.

Rental Market: Rentals are abundantly available. The prices cover a large range, as do the amenities. Because it's an old city, the landscaping is mature and lovely.

Average rent for a two-bedroom apartment: $1,350 per month

Communities Popular With Retirees: Senior housing is a big deal these days. Some of the independent living complexes are Arundel Woods, Bay Forest Senior Apartments, and College Parkway Place. For retirement housing, you'd be hard-pressed to beat Ginger Cove or BayWoods.

Nearby Areas to Consider: Severna Park shares much of the county's 447 miles of shoreline, furnishing waterfront living to many residential communities. The waters of the Chesapeake Bay, Severn River, and Magothy River offer not only a bountiful supply of seafood, but also a beautiful setting for sailing, fishing, crabbing, and waterfowl hunting. Bay Ridge is just outside of Annapolis, on the shores of the Chesapeake Bay, in the "land of pleasant living."

Earning a Living

Business Climate: The unemployment rate is 4.5 percent as opposed to a national average of 5.4 percent. The county's economy is supported by a diverse set of drivers, such as services, trade and distribution, the maritime industry, and the government sector. Anne Arundel County is home to the National Security Agency, which supports a growing number of defense contractors.

Help in Starting a Business: Contact the Anne Arundel County Economic Development Corporation, (410-222-7410; *www.aaedc.org*). and the Annapolis Economic Development Corporation (410-263-7940; *www.annapolis.gov*).

Job Market: Annapolis jobs are not easy to get because there is always competition. Annapolis is very near Washington D.C., and the job market fluctuates between boom and bust, depending on the national economy and government spending levels.

Medical Care

Because of the high-tech presence in Annapolis, medical care is very much up to date. Anne Arundel Medical Center (443-481-1000; *www.aahs.org*) has been named one of the nation's "Top 100 Hospitals" by Solucient, a national healthcare information and benchmarking company. It was the only large hospital in Maryland to be named to the list. For seniors, there are several special services, including emergency room services, rehabilitation, recreation, screening, surgery, and nutrition programs. North Arundel Hospital (410-787-4000; *www.northarundel.org*), a 272-bed community hospital, is an acute-care facility that is part of the University of Maryland Medical System. It serves about 80,000 patients a year in the emergency room. The hospital's Tate Cancer Center allows cancer patients to receive outpatient care on the hospital's campus. North Arundel Senior Care is a medical practice focused on the care of adults 50 years and older. Johns Hopkins Bayview Medical Center (410-550-0100; *www.jhbmc.jhu.edu*) is a member of the Johns Hopkins Health System, with more than 700 beds, and is home to one of Maryland's most comprehensive neonatal intensive care units, a sleep disorders center, an area-wide trauma center, the state's only regional burn center, and geriatrics programs that enjoy a national reputation in the field of aging.

Services for Seniors

The Annapolis Senior Center (410-222-1818; *www.aacounty.org/aging*) is a wonderful clearinghouse of information and activities, located in a shopping mall. And they are so "upper crust" that you have to make a reservation just for lunch. Check with the senior center for current events, opportunities for socializing, exercising, and intellectualizing. The Department of Aging (800-492-2499; *www.aacounty.org/Aging/index.cfm*) has under its umbrella adult evaluation and review services (410-222-4366), assisted housing (410-222-4464), senior eligibility information (410-222-4526), foster grandparent programs (410-222-4464), nutrition (410-222-4464), and transportation (410-222-4464). In addition to the Annapolis Senior Center, there are active centers all over the area with activities such as extended cruises to Cape Cod, massage/facials, and tennis lessons. Among the centers are the Arnold Senior Center (410-222-1922), Brooklyn PK Senior Center (410-222-6847), O'Malley Senior Center (410-222-6227), Pasadena Senior Center (410-222-0030), Pascal Senior Center (410-222-6680), and South County Senior Center (410-222-1927).

Continuing Education

Anne Arundel Community College (410-647-7100; *www.aacc.cc.md.us*) has a full-time enrollment of at least 6,467 students. It has several classes geared toward seniors. Students age 60 and older and disabled retirees pay only the $40 administration fee per three-month cycle, plus any supplies and/or lab fees associated with any of the classes. Midshipmen of Annapolis of the United States Naval Academy (410-293-1000; *www.usna.edu*) have been heroes in the past, and continue to make the country proud. Midshipmen volunteers visit area assisted living centers to adopt elders for activities. St. John's College (410-626.2540; *www.sjca.edu*) is located in the Historic Annapolis district, one block away from the Maryland State Capitol building. It provides several options for seniors (us older folks, not fourth year students) to participate in absolutely intriguing thematic conversations.

Crime and Safety

The number of violent crimes recorded by the FBI in 2003 was 390. The number of murders and homicides was five. The violent crime rate was 10.7 per 1,000 people. The *www.city-data.com* crime index is at 554.4.

Getting Around Town

Public Transportation: The Annapolis Regional Transportation Management Association (410-897-9340; *www.artma.org*) provides several options for public transportation using car or van pool, bus, train, plus options for walking or riding a bike.

Roads and Highways: US 50, 301, Route 295, Interstates 95 and 97

Airports: Baltimore/Washington International Airport (410-859-7111; *www.bwiairport.com*) is about 18 miles away, and is served by 18 airlines. The airport is one of the fastest growing major airports in North America, now handling over 20 million passengers annually.

Ports: The Port of Baltimore is regarded as one of America's top container terminals, providing technological advances that have transformed port operations from clipboard to keyboard. The port boasts computerized gate complexes, handheld computers, scanners, and the use of Electronic Data Interchange, all which greatly increase the port's efficiency and cost-effectiveness.

Let the Good Times Roll

Recreation: Sailing is a passion here. The richest purse prizes and world-class sailing competitions are common conversation. Although sailing is king, that doesn't mean that land-lubbers are left out. You will find several parks where you can rent a pavilion for a family gathering; watch, feed, and even adopt a duck; launch your boat; or do some serious bird-watching. For spectators, there are Navy football, lacrosse, and basketball games throughout the year.

Culture: The Banneker-Douglass Museum (*www.bdmuseum.com*) is the official repository of African-American material culture for the state. The site for the museum, the former Mount Moriah African Methodist Episcopal Church building, is a beautiful example of Victorian-Gothic architecture. The U.S. Naval Academy Museum (*www.usna.edu/museum*) is charged with collecting, preserving, and using the objects, documents, and works of art that relate the history and traditions of the United States Navy. The William Paca House and Garden is listed as one of the most elegant landmarks in Annapolis. Constructed between 1763 and 1765, the five-part Georgian residence was built as a town home for William Paca, a wealthy young planter who was a signer of the

Declaration of Independence. Among Annapolis performers are the Annapolis Opera, Annapolis Symphony Orchestra, and the Maryland Ballet Theatre.

Annual Events: January sees the end of Lights on the Bay. In March, the Footworks Percussive Dance Ensemble and the Maryland Day Celebration provide entertainment. April brings in the Great Kite Fly, the Bay Bridge Boat Show, Annual St. John's/Navy Croquet Match, Maritime Derby Day, Wednesday Night Races, and the Maritime Heritage Festival. June is bustin' out all over with the Greek Festival, the Quilt Show, Great Chesapeake Bay Swim, and the Build-A-Boat Race. In August, when it gets really warm, go outside for the Rotary Crab Feast and the Annapolis Run. In September the weather cools a bit, but not the spirit of football fun with Duke at Navy, Northeastern at Navy, and Vanderbilt at Navy. October is the West Annapolis Oktoberfest, Sailboat Show, and the U.S. Powerboat Show. November is Annapolis by Candlelight, Lights on the Bay, and the Grand Illumination. In December the holidays are in full swing with Midnight Madness I and II, Lighted Boat Parade, Annapolis New Years Eve, and First Night Annapolis.

When the Grandkids Come: The mission of Chesapeake Children's Museum is to create an environment of discovery about oneself, the people, technologies, and ecology of the Chesapeake Bay area. MEOW Bus (Museum Education On Wheels) is where the kids learn about the world around them. Included are live animals, games, crafts, stories, and experiments. Enjoy the Pirate Adventures on The Chesapeake for a wonderful time sailing the bounding main, reading a treasure map, and fighting the bad guys with awesome water-cannons.

More Information

Municipal

Annapolis Chamber of commerce
49 Old Solomons Island Road, Suite 204
Annapolis, MD 21401
410-266-3960
www.annapolischamber.com

Newspaper

Capital-Gazette Newspapers
2000 Capital Drive
Annapolis, MD 21401
410-268-5000
www.hometownannapolis.com

Realty

We do not have a Realtor recommendation for Annapolis. As an option, check out *www.realtor.com* or *www.homegain.com*. Select a Realtor with both CRS and GRI designations after their names, since it means that these folks have gone the extra mile and are both graduates of the Realtor Institute and Certified Residential Specialists.

Bowie, Maryland

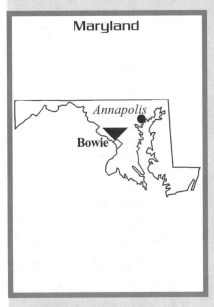

Maryland

Bowie at a Glance

Bowie was incorporated as a town in 1916 and has grown from a small railroad stop to the largest municipality in Prince George's County. In addition to all the business-related benefits of living in Bowie, there is the atmosphere. Beautiful green landscaping surrounds peaceful neighborhoods and shopping areas. Historical sites, such as the Belair Mansion, define the personality of the town. You will have good neighbors, as well as access to some of the world's best recreation, entertainment, and sports. With the addition of high-tech businesses, new homes, office space, several hotels, and shopping centers, Bowie continues to grow as a warm and prosperous community. Expanding firms are making the choice to reside in Prince George's County. Some of the factors that helped with these decisions are competitively priced land and buildings, an integrated transportation system, proximity to Washington, D.C., the Revitalization Tax Credit, a new High Technology Incentive Package, and Enterprise Zone benefits. The county also has a foreign trade zone and two state enterprise zones within its boundaries.

Possible Drawbacks: The cost of living is above the national average. It is part of a very large metropolitan area, so it has the big-city lifestyle and pace.

▶ Nickname: None

▶ County: Prince George's

▶ Area Code: 416

▶ Population: 52,123

▶ County Population: 801,515

▶ Percent of Population Over 65: 9.4%

▶ Region: Southern Maryland

▶ Closest Metropolitan Area: Washington, D.C., 18 miles

▶ Median Home Price: $225,000

▶ Best Reasons to Retire Here: Bowie has comfortable living with access to big-city amenities.

Climate

39° N Latitude 77° W Longitude	Average High Temperature (°F)	Average Low Temperature (°F)	Precipitation (")	Sunshine (%)
January	39.6	23.2	2.4	51
April	64.6	41.9	3.6	56
July	85.3	64.0	3.6	64
October	67.1	45.5	3.6	58
YEAR	64.2	44.1	42.8	57

Utilities

Overview: The cost of living is above the national average of 100 in all categories. Transportation is the highest at 120.4. Housing is 104, and food is 103. Healthcare is at 109.6 and utilities are at 106.6. The overall cost of living index is 106.5.

Gas Company: Washington Gas (800-752-7520; *www.washgas.com*)

Electric Company: Potomac Electric (202-833-7500; *www.pepco.com*)

Phone Company: Verizon (800-564-0999; *www.verizon.com*). Bell Atlantic is the sole provider for local calls. You have the option of selecting your own long-distance telephone service or cell phone company.

Water/Sewer Company: Washington Suburban Sanitary Commission (800-634-8400; *www.wssc.dst.md.us*)

Cable Company: Comcast (416-499-1980; *www.comcast.com*)

The Tax Axe

Car Registration: The Maryland Motor Vehicle Administration (800-950-1682; *www.dmv.org*) requires that you register your vehicle within 60 days of moving to Maryland. Vehicles titled in a state with a tax rate equal to or higher than Maryland's 5 percent tax rate will cost $100. The MVA may require you to submit additional documentation to substantiate the purchase price.

Driver's License: If you are a new resident of Maryland, you have 60 days to obtain a Maryland driver's license. You will be required to pass a vision test. The fee depends on the license requested.

Sales Tax: 5 percent.

State Income Tax: The accelerated tax ranges from 2 percent to 4.75 percent.

Retirement Income Tax: Social Security and Railroad Retirement income are exempt. Pensions are exempt up to $20,700, minus amount of Social Security received and Railroad Retirement benefits.

Property Tax: Real property is valued at full cash value. Property tax rates vary widely. No restrictions or limitations on property taxes are imposed by the state, meaning cities and counties can set tax rates at any level they deem necessary to fund governmental services. These rates increase, decrease, or remain the same each year. In Prince George's County, the taxes currently break down as follows: $0.960, $2.40, $2.40, for real, personal, and utility, respectively. The Maryland State Department of Assessments and Taxation (410-767-1184; *www.dat.state.md.us/sdatweb/taxrate.html*) can answer any questions.

Local Real Estate

Overview: The real estate market is changing as businesses and families move into the area to be near Washington, D.C.

Average price of a three-bedroom/two-bath home: $485,000

Average price of a two-bedroom condo: $207,500

Common Housing Styles: Cape Cods abound, with a few Colonials mixed in. A great percentage of houses for sale have full basements, second stories, custom front porches, and dormers.

Rental Market: The rental market offers a good mix of town homes, condos, and apartments, many of which are advertised for empty-nesters.

Average rent for a two-bedroom apartment: $1,200 per month

Communities Popular With Retirees: Evergreen, Somerville, and Woodward Estate

Nearby Areas to Consider: Laurel is on the bank of the Patuxent River at the northern tip of Prince George's County. Laurel is about halfway between Washington and Baltimore and is primarily residential. Upper Marlboro is among the oldest of the surviving southern Maryland towns with histories dating back to Colonial times. The remaining old homes and streets reflect the grace and beauty for which the town was known in its earlier days. Upper Marlboro now hosts the administrative bustle of a county seat by day and relaxes into a quiet country town by night.

Earning a Living

Business Climate: Maryland's business community is robust, diverse, and strong. Small businesses generate half of the economic activity and contribute more than three-quarters of the annual new job creation.

Help in Starting a Business: Prince George's County Economic Development Corporation (301-583-4650; *www.pgcedc.com*) offers several business assistance programs, including help finding a site, expediting permits and approvals, providing access to county and state business incentives, workforce assistance programs, sources of financing, and managerial and technical assistance.

Job Market: Unemployment in Bowie currently sits at 1.86 percent, so unless you have specific skills needed by the community, your best bet would be to relocate or start your own business. Many of the residents of Bowie commute to work in the capital.

Medical Care

The medical care available to residents of Bowie is impressive. Gerontology is coming into its own just in time for retirees to benefit from the results of research. Both Doctor's Community and Prince George's Hospital are award-winners. You can feel comfortable asking for specific doctors, services, or information to make the best decisions for you and your loved ones. Doctors Community Hospital (301-552-8118; *www.dchweb.org*) is an award-winning, 185-bed, acute-care medical and surgical hospital. Prince George's Hospital Center (301-618-2000; *www.dimensionshealth.org*) is an acute-care teaching hospital and regional referral center located in Cheverly. It maintains 290 beds, and is the largest nonprofit hospital in Prince George's County. As an adjunct to the hospital, seniors may qualify for healthcare through the Senior Health Center (301-927-4987).

Services for Seniors

This is merely a thumbnail of the available services for seniors. Visiting Angels Living Assistance (800-365-4189; *www.visitingangels.com*) adjusts to your schedule and keep your loved one comfortable at home. Their philosophy of home care service is never to compromise on providing high quality services to your family in Bowie. The Department of Parks and Recreation Prince George's County (*www.pgparks.com*) provides a varied program of activities including social events, day trips, health fairs, fitness programs, and classes. Senior center staff collaborate with county agencies to provide many services for the county's aging population including transportation to and from the centers and hot meals. Check in with the Bowie Senior Center (301-809-2300; *www.bowieseniorcenter.org*) for community college classes. The four senior centers in the county are Camp Springs Senior Center (301-449-0490), the Cora B. Wood Senior Center in Brentwood (301-699-1238), the Evelyn Cole Senior Center in Seat Pleasant (301-386-5525), and the Langley Park Senior Center (301-434-2900).

Continuing Education

Bowie sits in the middle of a number of fine colleges. Seniors have special rates in most. Bowie State University (301-860-4000; *www.bowiestate.edu*), with a full-time enrollment of 3,323, offers seniors of 60 years or above reduced fees for enrollment. Prince George's Community College (301-322-0864; *www.pgcc.edu*), with a full-time enrollment of 5,764, offers classes at the Camp Springs Senior Center for individuals age 60 or older, with a $50 registration fee each semester. The United States Naval Academy (*www.usna.edu*) has a full-time enrollment of 4,172. Midshipmen visit area assisted living centers to adopt elders through entertainment activities in a program called the Midshipman Action Group. Georgetown University (202-687-0100; *www.georgetown.edu*) has a full-time enrollment of 11,674. Senior citizens may enroll as auditors for a nominal registration fee of $50 per course. A transcript of previous academic achievement will be required.

Crime and Safety

Based on the national crim index that maintains 100 as the average, personal crime risk is 307 and property crime risk is 291.

Getting Around Town

Public Transportation: The Senior Citizen & Handicapped Bus Services (301-262-6200) offers several options. Among the services are Metrobus, Metrotrail (202-637-7000 *www.wmata.com*), Call-A-Bus senior citizen program (301-809-2300), Park and Ride, Commuter Connection, Connect-A-Ride, Call-A-Cab, and MARC. Every type of transport seems to be available, from individual pick-up and delivery services, to the impressive Metrorail, a train service that connects Washington, D.C. to outlying areas in Prince George's County.

Roads and Highways: US 50, 301

Airports: Baltimore-Washington International (410-859-7111; *www.bwiairport.com*), about 15 miles away, served more than 20.34 million passengers in 2004, and moved about 523.1 million pounds of freight in the same year. Ronald Reagan Washington National Airport, (703-417-8000; *www.mwaa.com*), about 22 miles away, served 15.9 million passengers in 2004.

Let the Good Times Roll

Recreation: Prince George's County has community centers and arts facilities, fitness trails, aquatic centers, peaceful open space, and sports for all ages. There's something for everyone! And you can believe this of Bowie in particular. It is a wonderful oasis of mature landscaped parks and neighborhoods, where the sunlight filters through graceful branches onto sculptured lawns and picnic areas. Baseball? How about the Baysox? And nearby Baltimore has the Orioles for your All American enjoyment. For you footballers, get yourself over to Washington and watch those Redskins. World famous horse racing is nearby at Pimlico and Laurel Park.

Culture: Must-see museums in Bowie include the Belair Mansion, the Belair Stable Museum, the Bowie Railroad Museum, and the Huntington Museum. There is also a fascinating Radio and Television Museum. Bowie has no fewer than 30 community theater production companies in its shared area with Annapolis and Baltimore.

Annual Events: The Maryland Handel Festival (*http://gfhandel.org/mhf*) Safeway National Barbecue Battle (*www.bbq-usa.com*), Pan African Festival (*www.panafricanfestival.com*), Baysox WinterWorks (*www.baysox.com*), Marlborough Day (*www.marlboroughday.com*), and Bowie Heritage Day (301-809-3089) are all a lot of fun. The Annual Leonardtown Criterium Bicycle Races in nearby Leonardtown, for those 10 and younger (410-394-2770), is a must see, as is the annual Walk for the Animals and Dog Games Day (301-645-8181), benefiting the Humane Society of Charles County.

When the Grandkids Come: Start at the Bowie Community Center (301-464-1737), where the kids can participate in recreation programs and classes. Huntington Community Center (301-464-3725) is another location where the same activities, crafts, and classes are available through the week. The South Bowie Community Center building includes a gymnasium, preschool room, warming kitchen, multi-purpose room, fitness room, computer room, art room, racquetball court, offices, and storage areas. The activities are much the same as in the Bowie Community Center and the Huntington Community Center. All three centers host tournaments, clubs, camps, special events, workshops, drop-in programs, after-school programs, and cultural activities.

More Information

Municipal

Bowie Chamber of Commerce
6911 Laurel Bowie Road, Suite 302
Bowie, MD 20715
301-262-0920
www.bowiechamber.org

Newspaper

The Bowie Blade-News
6000 Laurel Bowie Road
Bowie, MD 20715
301-262-3700
www.capitalonline.com/extras/bowieoffice.html

The Bowie Star
8201 Corporate Drive, Suite 1200
Landover, MD 20785
301-731-2100
www.gazette.net/index.html

Realty

We do not have a Realtor recommendation for Bowie. As an option, check out *www.realtor.com* or *www.homegain.com.* Select a Realtor with both CRS and GRI designations after their names, since it means that these folks have gone the extra mile and are both graduates of the Realtor Institute and Certified Residential Specialists.

27 ▶ Rochester, Minnesota

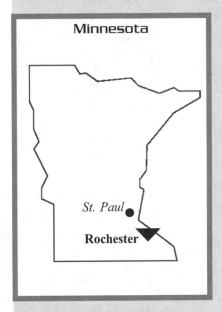

Rochester at a Glance

Rochester is one of those places you'd like to call home. The folks who first came here and settled found a comforting atmosphere in which to build their dreams. Modern Rochester citizens often draw on that pioneering vision to build new, innovative technology, as well as more effective human services. One well-respected business journal recently placed Olmsted County in the Top Five "Best Places to Live in America." In addition, Rochester's population tends to be well educated, with one study showing that 35 percent of residents are college graduates. They enjoy diverse entertainment of world-class quality, whether home-grown or imported. Minneapolis/St.Paul is not far away, where you can enjoy the symphony, art museum, and other cultural activities. For sports fans, the nearby Twin Cities offer both amateur and professional team sports. And Rochester itself boasts summer activities such as hiking, fishing, golf, and tennis. In winter, there are opportunities for great cross-country skiing. Minnesota is known as the state of 1,000 lakes for a good reason! There are plenty of opportunities for fishing, canoeing, kayaking, and camping.

Possible Drawbacks: Are you ready for cold and snow? Minnesota joins Alaska in being the ice-boxes of the nation. So, insulate your slippers and gloves, and go for it!

▶ Nickname: The Best Small City in America

▶ County: Olmsted

▶ Area Code: 507

▶ Population: 96,037

▶ County Population: 132,013

▶ Percent of Population Over 65: 11.5%

▶ Region: Southeastern Minnesota

▶ Closest Metropolitan Area: Minneapolis/St. Paul, 76 miles

▶ Median Home Price: $114,400

▶ Best Reasons to Retire Here: Remarkable senior services, and great medical care.

Climate

44° N Latitude 92° W Longitude	Average High Temperature (°F)	Average Low Temperature (°F)	Precipitation (")	Sunshine (%)
January	21.2	3.0	0.8	53
April	55.2	34.3	2.9	58
July	81.7	59.9	4.4	72
October	58.8	37.6	2.7	55
YEAR	53.6	34.2	33.3	58

Utilities

Overview: The overall cost of living is just under the national average, sitting at 99 with the national average at 100. Real estate is lower, sitting at 96.7.

Gas Company: Natural gas is provided by Peoples Natural Gas/Energy (800-303-0752).

Electric Company: Electricity is provided by a community-owned electric and water utility company, RPU Rochester Public Utilities (507-280-1500; *www.rpu.org*), and by the Peoples Cooperative Power Association (507-288-4004; *www.peoplesrec.com*).

Phone Company: Among the providers of local telephone service are AT&T (800-222-0300; *www.att.com*) and Qwest (800-244-1111; *www.qwest.com*).

Water/Sewer Company: Rochester Public Utilities is a community-owned electric and water utility company (507-280-1500; *www.rpu.org*).

Cable Company: Charter Communications (800-581-0081)

The Tax Axe

Car Registration: New residents have a 60-day grace period in which to register their vehicles. If your registration expires before the 60-day period is up, you must obtain Minnesota registration immediately. The application fees for a vehicle are $5.50 title fee, $2 to record a lien, $3.50 public safety vehicle fee, $8.50 filing fee, and a $4.25 license plate fee. Also, Minnesota has an "ad valorem" registration tax system. The age of the vehicle is a factor in determining passenger registration tax. The minimum tax for vehicles 10 years old and older is $35.

Driver's License: You have 60 days after moving into Minnesota to obtain your license. You will be required to pass a written exam and pay the fee. The fee is $37.50.

Sales Tax: There is a state sales tax of 6.5 percent. Rochester adds a local sales tax of 0.5 percent and a lodging tax of 4.0 percent. This means that for most purchases, the sales tax is 7 percent.

State Income Tax: Minnesota has an accelerated personal income tax ranging from 5.35 percent to 7.85 percent.

Retirement Income Tax: Social Security income is taxed. If your only income is Social Security, you would not be required to file an income tax return. Pensions are taxable by Minnesota regardless of where your pension was earned. Railroad retirement benefits are not taxed by Minnesota. Taxpayers 65 and older may subtract some income if federal adjusted gross income is under certain limits. Retired Military pensions are taxable. Check with the State Department of Revenue for more specific details on the military tax.

Property Tax: There is a Senior Citizen Property Tax Deferral Program that allows people 65 or older who have $60,000 or less annual income, to defer a portion of their property tax on their home. However, this is not a tax forgiveness program, it is a low-interest loan from the state. The deferred tax is paid by the State to your county. Interest is charged on any such loan. It is currently capped at 5 percent. This program attaches a lien on your property and collects later. For property tax refunds, you must apply under the Homestead program.

Local Real Estate

Overview: Real estate prices are lower than the national average, sitting at 96.7, based on a national average of 100.

Average price of a three-bedroom/two-bath home: $152,349

Average price of a two-bedroom condo: $94,500

Common Housing Styles: Older neighborhoods feature similar architecture, whether one-, one-and-a-half, or two-story frame houses. Newer structures tend to be brick, incorporating pillared or arched entries.

Rental Market: Rochester is a growing market and, at this time, is keeping up with rentals by constructing new apartments. However, because time affects the market quickly, it is well to check with a Realtor.

Average rent for a two-bedroom apartment: $550 per month

Communities Popular With Retirees: Stewartville is home to more than 5,000 citizens, and welcomes new seniors anytime. St. Charles, too, would be a fine place to live. It's even smaller than Stewartville, with around 3,500 citizens.

Nearby Areas to Consider: Kasson and Pine Island, two nearby communities, are attractive options to those who wish to move just outside the Rochester city limits.

Earning a Living

Business Climate: In every survey, Rochester ranks well above average with its business climate. With Mayo medical services and IBM anchoring employment, other endeavors, such as agribusiness and innovative technology firms and services, are well supported in an atmosphere of solid growth. At present, the annual increase in jobs is 3.5 percent.

Help in Starting a Business: Rochester Area Economic Development, Inc. (*www.raedi.org*) has as one of its mandates the support and development of new business. You should also check in with the Rochester chamber of commerce.

Job Market: As of 2004, the unemployment rate in Rochester hovered around 3.6 percent, keeping jobs a premium unless you can boast the kind of education and experience it takes to join the well-trained workforce that staffs most of this "can-do" city. That said, there is room for above-average workers in medicine, technology, and education.

Medical Care

Rochester Methodist Hospital (507-266-7890; *www.mayoclinic.org*) is one of two Mayo Foundation hospitals in Rochester. It contains 794 licensed beds and 36 operating rooms. This hospital earns its reputation as a home to cutting-edge medical practice. Saint Mary's Hospital (507-255-5123; www.mayoclinic.org) is the other of the two Mayo hospitals in Rochester. It contains 1,157 licensed beds and 53 operating rooms. Within its walls, healthcare providers offer services in nearly every medical specialty.

Services for Seniors

The Rochester Senior Center (507-287 1404) claims to be housed in the only "castle" in town. And it's true! Like senior centers all over the nation, Rochester's offers game time, conversations, hobbies, learning opportunities, advocates, health programs, and lots of social activities. Senior Net (507-287-7154; *www.seniornet.org*) is the place to become "computer savvy." They will teach you the ins and outs of basic computer functions and the terminology for it. In addition, you will learn how to get on the Internet and use e-mail. Elder Network Peer Counseling (507-285-5272) is a program of mental health support services for older adults utilizing the services of peer volunteers. Elder's self-help approaches aid them through many difficulties of aging and mental health issues. The Minnesota Department of Human Services (507-287-1362; *www.dhs.state.mn.us*) provides several options for low-income seniors, including medical assistance, in-home and nursing home care, prescription help, and low-cost health insurance.

Continuing Education

The University of Minnesota Rochester (507-280-2838) has Senior Citizen Education Program Credit Courses. Minnesota state law allows persons 62 and older to register on the second day of the class in credit (degree, certificate) courses for $9 per credit, or audit courses free of charge on a space-available basis. Under the Senior Citizen Education Program, persons 62 and older pay any required laboratory or materials fees, a special fee of $62.50 per credit for courses, and a computer lab fee. For specific information, contact University of Minnesota Rochester (507-280-2824). The Rochester Community Education Adult Enrichment Program (507-285-8350; *http://activenet1.recware.com/rochesterce*) allows any resident of District 535 who is 62 years of age or older to take most Community Education courses for half of the regular fee. In 2004, more than 14,000 adults participated in 1,200 classes that were offered by the Rochester Community Education Adult Enrichment Program. Rochester Community Technical College Learning Is

For Ever (507-285-7218; *www.rctc.edu/community/seniors/life/about.html*) is open to anyone over the age of 55. The cost to join is $25 per year, and includes the popcorn and soda you need for the quarterly foreign film showings. Small fees are charged for each event or course.

Crime and Safety

When evaluating these, or any statistics, you should keep in mind that these numbers represent crimes reported to law enforcement. The actual numbers may differ considerably. That said, this city continues to hold one of the lowest crime rates per capita in the country. Rochester comes in at a very healthy rate of 72 percent of the national average. There are, on average, 2.8 violent crimes, and 32.9 property crimes, per 1,000 people.

Getting Around Town

Public Transportation: Rochester City Lines (507-288-4353; *www.rochesterbus.com*) has senior fares available for those 65 and older. Fares are good between 8:15 a.m. and 2:15 p.m., all trips after 6:45 p.m., and all day Saturdays. ZIPS is the Zumbro Independent Passenger Service (507-287-7800; *www.rochesterbus.com*), a door-to-door transportation system for persons who cannot use Rochester City Lines bus service due to a disability. You have to qualify for this service by filling out an application.

Roads and Highways: I-90, I-35, US 14, 52, and 63, Highways 30, 40, and 296

Airports: Rochester International Airport Minnesota (507-282-2328; *www.rochesterintlairport.com*) is located eight miles south of downtown Rochester. It currently has a full schedule of flights provided by Northwest and American Airlines.

Let the Good Times Roll

Recreation: Recreation and sports keep everyone on their toes in Rochester. The Rochester Parks and Recreation Department maintains 3,500 acres of park land, more than 60 miles of trails, 56 playgrounds, tennis courts, picnic shelters, outdoor pools, horseshoe courts, dog parks, Frisbee golf courts, volleyball courts, and archery ranges. The city also offers golf and hockey camps and Red Cross swimming instruction. The Rochester Balloon Company provides hot air balloon rides including guided tours of Rochester and parts of southeast Minnesota. Quarry Hill Nature Center is surrounded by an estimated 300 acres of park land. This nature center offers visitors information about flora and fauna, which are mounted in dioramas, a 1,700 gallon live aquarium, live animals, a visible bee hive, and a bird-watching room. Outside, you'll find five miles of trails ideal for biking, cross country skiing, and snowshoeing in meadow and forest terrain.

Culture: Rochester Civic Music (507-281-6005; *www.ci.rochester.mn.us*) lists its current calendar, which has high classics to country. Rochester Civic Theater (507-282-8481; *www.rochestercivictheatre.org*) has a seating capacity of around 300, and a full year-round schedule. Mayo Civic Center (507-281-6184; *www.mayociviccenter.com*) is arguably one of the grandest buildings in the city. The Civic Center can accommodate large numbers of attendees for several different types of activities. Assisi Heights is an Italian Romanesque building, home to the Sisters of Saint Francis and the Assisi Community. The Chateau Theatre was once an elaborate theater, and is now a Barnes and Noble bookstore and Starbucks Cafe. Heritage House of Rochester is in the Historic Town Square (507-286-9208). Mayowood Mansion (507-282-9447) is a not-to-be-missed tour of Doctor Charles H. Mayo home. The Plummer House (507-281-6160) is a five-story house and the former home of Henry S. Plummer, who was considered by the medical profession to be the best clinician of his time, and immensely interested in medical education. It is notable that he taught not only male doctors, but their wives and daughters as well!

Annual Events: The number of events is enormous, from charity balls to sports events, to golf tournaments and arts festivals. Check the annual calendar (800-634-8277; *www.rochestermn.com/living/calendar.asp*) for any specific date.

When the Grandkids Come: Rochester Art Center (507-282-8629; *www.rochesterartcenter.org*) provides art classes and a variety of other activities. The Masque Youth Theatre and School (507-287-0704; *www.masque.org*) is an educational organization that allows young actors to participate in all aspects of stagecraft.

More Information

Municipal

Rochester Area Chamber of Commerce
220 South Broadway, Suite 100
Rochester, MN 55904
507-288-1122
www.rochestermnchamber.com

Newspaper

Post Bulletin News
18 SouthEast 1st Avenue
Rochester, MN 55903
507-285-7600
www.postbulletin.com

Realty

We do not have a Realtor recommendation for Rochester. As an option, check out *www.realtor.com* or *www.homegain.com*. Select a Realtor with both CRS and GRI designations after their names, since it means that these folks have gone the extra mile and are both graduates of the Realtor Institute and Certified Residential Specialists.

28 ▶ Branson, Missouri

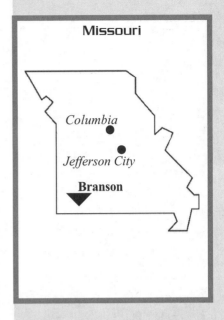

Branson at a Glance

There is no other town in the United States like this one. It's a small town in the heart of the Ozark Mountains, yet it has more than 45 theaters playing host to over 80 live shows daily with 7.5 million visitors a year. The three motivations for visitors coming to Branson are entertainment and shows, theme parks, and shopping. The average age of a visitor is 57. Many of the shows are in the evening, but some are held in the afternoon, and a few even come with breakfast. Regular names include Andy Williams, Bobby Vinton, Buck Trent, the Gatlin Brothers, the Lennon Sisters, Mel Tillis, Moe Bandy, and Ray Stevens. Several of the widely known performers are now permanent residents and are actively involved in the community. It is a small town where the neighbors care about each other and family values are important. Nearly 200 national outlet stores have opened in three malls. Hikers can enjoy the outdoors on established nature trails that wind through forests and skirt the lakes' shorelines. Spelunking is also available in the area. Bikers will find some designated trails, but cyclists are frequently seen on rural roads in the lakes area. For people who prefer to see the outdoors from the comfort of their vehicles, all roads and highways offer scenic vistas of the Ozarks.

Possible Drawbacks: It's a small town, and you could miss big-city amenities. Tourist flow sometimes creates traffic jams. Unemployment also rises sharply in the winter months.

▶ Nickname: Music Capital of the World
▶ County: Taney
▶ Area Code: 417
▶ Population: 7,500
▶ County Population: 39,703
▶ Percent of Population Over 65: 16.2%
▶ Region: Southwestern Missouri
▶ Closest Metropolitan Area: Tulsa, 188 miles
▶ Median Home Price: $123,900
▶ Best Reasons to Retire Here: Low cost of living, rural lifestyle, unlimited live music, and a beautiful natural setting with hunting, fishing, and boating.

Climate

37° N Latitude 93° W Longitude	Average High Temperature (°F)	Average Low Temperature (°F)	Precipitation (")	Sunshine (%)
January	41.7	41.7	1.9	50
April	67.8	67.8	4.2	59
July	89.6	89.6	3.5	71
October	69.8	69.8	3.3	64
YEAR	66.9	66.9	42.0	60

Utilities

Overview: The overall cost of living is below the national average of 100 at 97.8. Housing costs are above average at 105.7, but food, transportation, health care, and utilities are all below average.

Gas Company: There is no natural gas available in Branson.

Electric Company: The Empire District Electric Company (417-334-3174; *www.empiredistrict.com*) and the White River Valley Electric Cooperative (417-335-9335; *www.whiteriver.org*)

Phone Company: Verizon (417-334-9237; *www.verizon.com*)

Water/Sewer Company: City of Branson Water Department (413-334-3345; www.cityofbranson.org)

Cable Company: Cox Communications (417-334-7897; *www.cox.com*). Rural Missouri Cable TV (417-334-7897)

The Tax Axe

Car Registration: You have 30 days from the date of becoming a Missouri resident to title your vehicle. If the vehicle has been owned and operated in another state for at least 90 days prior to titling and registering in Missouri, no sales tax is due. There is an $8.50 title fee, a registration (license plate) fee (based on either taxable horsepower or vehicle weight), a $2.50 title processing fee, and $3.50 registration processing fee for a one year registration, or $7.00 registration processing fee for a two year registration.

Driver's License: Drivers who are 21 to 69 years of age receive a six-year license that expires on the applicant's date of birth. Drivers who are 70 and over receive a three-year license that expires on the applicant's date of birth. The fee is $10.00.

Sales Tax: The state sales tax is 4.225 percent. The total rate is 7.475 percent.

State Income Tax: The accelerated income tax varies from 1.5 to 6 percent.

Retirement Income Tax: Pension recipients have a $6,000 exemption.

Property Tax: The total tax rate varies locally. The state imposes a 3 cent tax per $100 of valuation. Some personal property is exempt, such as household goods and clothing.

Local Real Estate

Overview: The area continues to experience growth while remaining one of the most affordable housing markets in the country. The area offers affordable housing and excellent house values. Branson real estate is highly desirable for its affordability, location, and investment potential. Condominium time-sharing is common.

Average price of a three-bedroom/two-bath home: $109,000

Average price of a two-bedroom condo: $110,000

Common Housing Styles: Golf condos, houses, and lakefront houses. Branson is a resort area, and includes everything from stunning luxury estate houses to cozy modern single-family homes and condominiums.

Rental Market: Short-term rentals of apartments, condominiums, and houses is common because families rent for their entire vacations, so it is common to rent by the week.

Average rent for a two-bedroom apartment: $500 per month

Communities Popular With Retirees: Branson West, Kimberling City, Republic, and Thousand Hills

Nearby Areas to Consider: Springfield, 40 miles to the north, is Missouri's third largest city. It has universities, 12 golf courses, shopping, all larger city amenities, and is within easy reach of Branson's shows. Eureka Springs, just across the border in Arkansas, has its own flavor of Ozark history and year-round outdoor beauty and recreation. Eureka Springs is a Utopia for the outdoor enthusiast, whether it's hiking, fishing, caving, mountain biking, boating, golf, or just a walk in the sun.

Earning a Living

Business Climate: To say that business is booming is Branson is to put it mildly. Located at the intersecting points of commerce and travel, Branson offers a thriving business base. Branson has a very positive climate for many different types of businesses, and growth seems certain.

Help in Starting a Business: The Missouri Small Business Development Center at the University of Missouri (314-516-6121; *www.umsl.edu/~smallbus*), lends assistance to small business owners by acquainting them with helpful resources, information, and links to various agencies. The center will help with everything from evaluating your business idea to acquiring financing. They have an online startup business kit and a number of other useful documents available.

Job Market: Many jobs are available in support of the tourist businesses and the shows, but they tend to be part-time and lower paying jobs. Unfortunately, employment is seasonal, so the unemployment rate is 4.2 percent in the summer and 22 percent in the winter.

Medical Care

Skaggs Community Health Center (417-335-7000; *www.skaggs.net*) is a 132-bed community-owned and supported healthcare facility. Skaggs holds the highest national accreditation available for medical facilities from the Joint Commission on Accreditation of Healthcare Organizations. It also operates or manages 16 area healthcare clinics around the city, including Branson Cardiovascular Associates, Branson West Rehab Services, and Skaggs Urgent Care Plus. Skaggs also provides, free to the community, a 24-hour nurse advice line. St. John's Health System (417-820-2000; *www.stjohns.com*) operates an 866-bed, nonprofit hospital in Springfield. St. John's is the Ozarks' leader in cardiac care. Cox Medical Center (417-269-3000; *www.coxhealth.com*) is a 61-bed, short-term, skilled-nursing facility in Springfield.

Services for Seniors

The Southwest Missouri Office on Aging (417-862-0762; *www.swmoa.com*) provides a number of services including transportation, employment, and in-home services. It also supports the Branson Senior Center (417-335-4801). The Missouri Senior RX program assists seniors in coping with rising prescription costs. The Taney County Council on Aging (417-546-6100) offers many forms of entertainment, including tickets to many Branson shows.

Continuing Education

Southwest Missouri State University (*http://ce.smsu.edu*), about 36 miles away with an enrollment of 14,680, has a program for enrolling adult students in its regular curriculum. Adults who are 60 years of age or older are eligible to register for one to eight hours of class and have the required student fees waived. Drury University (417-873-7879; *www.drury.edu*), 40 miles away and with an enrollment of 3,125, has the Institute for Mature Learning for senior learners 50 or older. Ozarks Technical Community College (417-447-7500; *www.otc.cc.mo.us*), 44 miles away with an enrollment of 3,756, has continuing education in the non-credit division providing a wide range of educational workshops, seminars, and courses that may begin at any time and do not necessarily coincide with the college's academic calendar. All fees are waived if you are over 50 and live in the district.

Crime and Safety

The violent crime rate per 100,000 people is below the national average at 432.

Getting Around Town

Public Transportation: Ozark Mountain Transit is a tourist-oriented bus system connecting theaters, attractions, restaurants, lodging establishments, and the airport.

Roads and Highways: Missouri highway 165, US 65. The city of Branson provides maps of back roads for locals to avoid tourist traffic jams.

Airports: The Springfield/Branson Regional Airport is located 45 miles north in Springfield, and is served by five major airlines.

Let the Good Times Roll

Recreation: For 40 years, Silver Dollar City has delighted guests with an incredible variety of entertainment offering five unique festivals, 60 craft shops, 50 daily shows, and 15 rides and attractions. There is also Celebration City, a multi-themed nighttime park that highlights eras of 20th century America and features a laser production. White Water, a theme park with a tropical atmosphere, offers a large wave pool, a lazy river for relaxation, and several faster, wetter rides for the more adventurous visitor. There are 10 golf courses currently open in the Branson area. Construction has begun on the city of Branson's new 42 acre state-of-the-art sports and recreation center complex in Branson Hills that will combine fitness, recreation, and organized athletics at one convenient location. The completed 44,000 square foot recreation center will feature two gymnasiums, a fitness center, indoor track, locker rooms, community rooms, game room, and a concession area. Table Rock, Taneycomo, and Bull Shoals lakes offer some of the finest fishing in the nation and any freshwater activity you can imagine. You can enjoy boating, swimming, skiing, sailing, sunning, scuba diving, parasailing, and sightseeing.

Culture: Keeping history alive is part of the fascination of Branson. Silver Dollar City does its part in preserving Ozark history with a living demonstration of master craftsmen at work. The 1907 novel *Shepherd of the Hills* was set in Branson and started the flow of visitors to the area. The locals responded by greeting visitors with performances. Silver Dollar City was constructed to preserve and demonstrate the Ozark way of doing things. It has done nothing but grow since its inception, but the original culture is all around. The Ralph Foster Museum contains one of the greatest collections of memorabilia in existence. The Veterans Memorial Museum is a reminder of the American lives lost in the name of freedom. The Shepherd of the Hills is an elaborate outdoor production that brings the novel to life.

Annual Events: In March, the IMAX FilmFest starts a new season of giant-screen films in the Ozarks Discovery IMAX Theater. In April, at the Lawrence Welk Champagne Theatre, is the quasi start of the Branson "Theatre Season" with a five-day showcase event. Also in April, America's largest international festival, World-Fest, features performers presenting the music, dance, costumes, and culture of their native lands. April brings the Ozarks 100, a one-day road cycling event through the beautiful Mark Twain National Forest. In May are the Plumb Nellie Days, the Annual Hillbilly Festival & Craft Show. Also in May are the hydroplane races and swimsuit contest. In June is the Bluegrass Festival, a three-day event with Bluegrass bands from all over the country. A T-bucket is a highly modified and modernized Model T. More than100 of them come for the Branson 2,000 T-Bucket Run in July. In August is the Super Summer Cruise, with hot rods, street rods, classics, and roadsters displayed and cruising. The Run Wild for Habitat, a 3.1-mile run and 2-mile walk fund-raiser, is held in December.

When the Grandkids Come: The Track Family Fun Park has go-karts, mini-golf, bumper boats, and kids' rides. Getting wet is optional. Many of the shows are perfect for kids, and there is always Silver Dollar City. The city of Branson promotes itself under the banner "America's Family Destination," and it's true that all entertainment is for the entire family.

More Information

Municipal

Branson Lakes Area Chamber of Commerce
P.O. Box 1897
Branson, MO 65615
800-214-3661
www.explorebranson.com

Branson Tourism Center
220 Branson Hills Parkway
Branson, MO 65616
800-785-1550
www.bransontourismcenter.com

Newspaper

Branson Daily News
P.O. Box 1900
Branson, MO 65615
417-334-3161
www.bransondailynews.com

Realty

We do not have a Realtor recommendation for Branson. As an option, check out *www.realtor.com* or *www.homegain.com*. Select a Realtor with both CRS and GRI designations after their names, since it means that these folks have gone the extra mile and are both graduates of the Realtor Institute and Certified Residential Specialists.

29 ▶ Columbia, Missouri

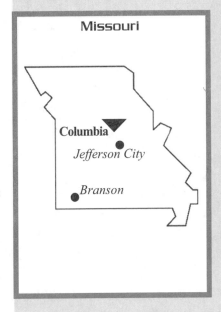

Missouri

Columbia
Jefferson City
Branson

Columbia at a Glance

Columbia has been described as "fun, funky, and surprisingly sophisticated." The presence of the University of Missouri, Stephens College, and Columbia College add shape and tone to the life in the city. Bordered on three sides by college campuses, the "District" is a continually evolving and vibrant hot spot for live performances, one-of-a-kind specialty shops, and owner-operated retail stores. It's the place to go for exciting nightlife or to meet friends for dinner. Columbia is located in gently rolling terrain midway between St. Louis and Kansas City. Residents are never more than 15 minutes away from a major shopping area. To the north of the city you will find enough forests, parks, fairgrounds, and lakes to satisfy the nature lover, while up north you'll find Cosmos Park, Oakland Park, Bear Creek Trail, and Finger Lakes. Traveling to the west of town will take you into residential areas and towards farms, forests, and rolling hills. Also west are the famous Les Bourgeois Vineyards. *Money* magazine consistently rates Columbia as one of the nation's best cities in which to live. Within 50 miles of Columbia there are an abundance of spectacular national and state parks, providing wonderful photographic moments.

Possible Drawbacks: Columbia is the healthcare center for all of central Missouri, and that can make getting an appointment difficult. It is also more than a two-hour drive to a large city.

▶ Nickname: College Town, USA

▶ County: Boone

▶ Area Code: 573

▶ Population: 89,603

▶ County Population: 135,454

▶ Percent of Population Over 65: 8.6%

▶ Region: Central Missouri

▶ Closest Metropolitan Area: St. Louis, 127 miles

▶ Median Home Price: $130,000

▶ Best Reasons to Retire Here: Small town living in the center of the country, with excellent healthcare and continuing education.

Climate

38° N Latitude 92° W Longitude	Average High Temperature (°F)	Average Low Temperature (°F)	Precipitation (")	Sunshine (%)
January	36.5	18.5	1.6	50
April	65.7	43.7	4.3	55
July	88.5	66.2	3.9	67
October	67.5	45.5	3.1	59
YEAR	64.0	43.5	40.8	56

Utilities

Overview: The cost of living is slightly above average at 101.4 based on a national average of 100. Food, transportation, utilities, and health care are all below average. Housing is above average at 106.7.

Gas Company: AmericanUE (800-552-7583; *www.ameren.com*) provides natural gas to the Columbia area.

Electric Company: Columbia Water and Light (573-474-8473; *www.gocolumbia.com/waterandlight*) is the local electricity provider.

Phone Company: CenturyTel (800-824-2877; *www.centurytel.com*) provides both local and long-distance phone service.

Water/Sewer Company: No information is currently available.

Cable Company: Mediacom (573-443-1536; *http://mediacomcc.com*) provides cable television service.

The Tax Axe

Car Registration: You have 30 days from the date of becoming a Missouri resident to title your vehicle. If the vehicle has been owned and operated in another state for at least 90 days prior, no sales tax is due. There is an $8.50 title fee, a registration fee (based on either taxable horsepower or vehicle weight) a $2.50 title processing fee, and $3.50 registration processing fee for a one year registration, or $7.00 registration processing fee for a three year registration.

Driver's License: Drivers who are 21 to 69 years of age receive a six year license that expires on the applicant's date of birth. Drivers who are 70 and over receive a three year driver's license that expires on the applicant's date of birth. The fee is $10.00.

Sales Tax: The state sales tax is 4.225 percent. County is 1.125 percent. City is 2.0 percent. The total is 7.35 percent.

State Income Tax: The accelerated income tax ranges from 1.5 to 6 percent.

Retirement Income Tax: Pension recipients have a $6,000 exemption.

Property Tax: Tax rate per $100 of value in Columbia is 4.79 percent. Other locations in the county are slightly lower.

Local Real Estate

Overview: The real estate market is strong and housing prices are inline with, or below, the national average. Some houses are quite expensive, and that brings the average price calculation up, but there is a wide range from which to choose. *Money* magazine said, "The price of an average home puts Columbia in the most affordable 15 percent of all cities."

Average price of a three-bedroom/two-bath home: $160,000

Average price of a two-bedroom condo: $110,000

Common Housing Styles: Some older Victorian homes can still be seen around town. Other styles are ranch, two-story frames, and Tudor.

Rental Market: It is a college town, so the types and prices of rental houses and apartments vary, and with the high turnover, something is almost always available.

Average rent for a two-bedroom apartment: $700 per month

Communities Popular With Retirees: The entire area of Columbia is popular.

Nearby Areas to Consider: Ashland is located in southern Boone County. It is a small town maintaining a quaint, small-town atmosphere. Ashland's folks enjoy hiking and spelunking at Rock Bridge State Park, hunting, hiking, and horseback riding at Three Creeks State Wildlife Area, along with camping at the Pine Ridge Campground in the Mark Twain National Forest. Jefferson City, to the south of Columbia, is a small town and is the capitol of the state of Missouri. Fulton, 20 miles to the east, is the home of Westminster College, where Winston Churchill made his famous Iron Curtain speech.

Earning a Living

Business Climate: Columbia is located in the center of the state, and is accessible from all parts of the state. The city has a low tax structure and offers a comfortable quality of life. The economy is based on the health and insurance industries, and the general diversity of industries in the area has made the city recession resistant. Several Fortune 500 company branches are located in Columbia, including Dana Corporation, 3M, and Quaker Oats.

Help in Starting a Business: The Regional Economic Development (573-442-8303; *www.columbiaredi.com*) is interested in helping you relocate or expand your existing business into Columbia, as is the Small Business Development Center (573-882-7096; *www.missouribusiness.net/sbdc*). The Missouri Small Business Development Center at the University of Missouri (314-516-6121; *www.umsl.edu/~smallbus*) lends assistance to small business owners and potential owners by acquainting them with helpful resources, information, and links to various agencies. The Service Core of Retired Executives (573-874-1132) is a not-for-profit association providing free business counseling. The City of Columbia Finance Department (573-874-7378) provides business licenses.

Job Market: The unemployment rate is 2.4 percent. The workforce of Columbia is highly educated, and 20 percent of all jobs are in the health insurance industry. The presence of three universities makes the competition stiff for part-time and summer jobs.

Medical Care

The city of Columbia is a medical center for most of the state and has six hospitals with a total of 1,105 acute-care beds. Columbia Regional Hospital (573-884-2100; *www.columbiaregional.org*) is a 249-bed facility providing state-of-the-art diagnostics and treatment, and has been named on of the "Top 100 Orthopedic Hospitals" in the nation. The Ellis Fischel Cancer Center (573-882-2100; *www.ellisfischel.org*) provides cancer inpatient and outpatient services and cancer screening. They are co-located with intensive care units and multiple specialty physicians. The Rust Rehabilitation Center (573-817-2703) is a 60-bed long-term hospital. The Mid-Missouri Mental Health Center (573-884-1300) provides acute psychiatric inpatient services. The Family Health Center (573-214-2314) provides comprehensive medical and dental care.

Services for Seniors

The Boone County Council on Aging (573-443-1111; *http://bcca.missouri.org*) has resources that support seniors with independence, vitality, and security. The Central Missouri Area Agency on Aging (573-443-5823; *www.cmaaa.net*) provides vital assistance and information. The Columbia Senior Center (573-874-2050) is a gathering place and a center for activities. The Retired Senior Volunteer Program (573-442-7238) and the Voluntary Action Center (573-449-6959) are connections where active seniors can volunteer.

Continuing Education

The University of Missouri-Columbia (573-882-6333; *www.missouri.edu*) has an enrollment of 23,000 and offers 250 degree programs. Columbia College (573-875-7352; *www.ccis.edu*) has more than 20,000 students on its various campuses and enrolled in online courses. Stephens College (573-442-2211; *www.stephens.edu*) is a private college, a national liberal arts college, and the second-oldest women's college in the country. These colleges are available, but they have no specific programs for seniors. The Parks and Recreation Department publishes *Leisure Times* (*www.gocolumbiamo.com*), which lists the upcoming recreation activities, including classes held online.

Crime and Safety

According to the FBI, the total number of all reported crimes per 100,000 people is 3,878.3. The violent crime rate is below the national average of 496.4 at 477.6.

Getting Around Town

Public Transportation: The Columbia Transit System (573-874-7282; *www.gocolumbiamo.com/publicworks*) runs bus routes through the city with senior fares of 25 cents. The purpose of Older Adults Transportation Services (573-449-3789; *www.oatstransit.org)* is to provide reliable transportation for transportation disadvantaged Missourians so they can live independently.

Roads and Highways: Interstate 70, US 63

Airports: The Columbia Regional Airport (573-442-9770) is a regional airport and can be used to make a connection to a major hub. Major airports can be found in St. Louis and Kansas City, each of which is more than two hours away.

Let the Good Times Roll

Recreation: The award-winning Columbia Parks and Recreation Department (573-874-7460) maintains over 42 parks and recreation facilities on more than 2,000 acres, including the Twin Lakes Recreation area, Rainbow Softball Center, MKT Trail, Battle Park, Martin Luther King Memorial Ampitheater, and the Grindstone Nature Area. The department offers enrichment classes and organizes sports leagues for all ages in softball, soccer, and volleyball. Recreation is available at the area parks, golf courses, tennis courts, swimming pools, bowling alleys, roller rinks, and athletic clubs. The Area Recreation Center has an indoor leisure pool featuring a gymnasium, basketball court, exercise room, and more. Big 12 conference football is at Missouri Univeristy, as well as NCAA Division 1 baseball, wrestling, volleyball, softball, gymnastics, and track and field. Mizzou Arena is the home court of the Big 12 MU Tiger basketball. The Mid-Missouri Mavericks is a professional Minor League baseball team. The surround area is filled with places for canoeing, swimming, hiking, biking, and off-road motorcycling.

Culture: The Stephens College Playhouse and the Warehouse Theatre are known for excellent performances by students and professions. The Missouri Symphony Society features nationally known artists and orchestra performances. The Museum of Art and Archaeology, on the campus of the University of Missouri, houses more than 14,000 artworks and archeological artifacts. The Museum of Anthropology has collections including more than 100 million artifacts. The State Historical Society of Missouri maintains references and manuscripts, in addition to paintings, sculpture, and prints.

Annual Events: In March is the Taste of Mid Missouri. In April is the Moo Day Parade, when things and people go sort of nuts. In June is the Summer Art Festival, and September brings the Boone County Heritage Festival.

When the Grandkids Come: The Parks and Recreation Department has the Active Kids Club (573-874-7642) for fun and fitness for youth. Games include basketball, floor hockey, soccer, kickball, flag football, dodgeball, and four square.

More Information

Municipal

Columbia Missouri Chamber of Commerce
300 South Providence Road
Columbia, MO 65203
573-874-1132
http://chamber.columbia.mo.us

Columbia Convention and Visitors Bureau
300 South Providence Road
Columbia, MO 65203
800-652-0987
www.visitcolumbiamo.com

Newspaper

The Columbia Missourian
221 South Eighth Street
Columbia, MO 65201
573-882-5700
www.digmo.org

The Columbia Daily Tribune
P.O. Box 798
Columbia, MO 65205
573-815-1700
www.columbiatribune.com

Realty

We do not have a Realtor recommendation for Columbia. As an option, check out *www.realtor.com* or *www.homegain.com.* Select a Realtor with both CRS and GRI designations after their names, since it means that these folks have gone the extra mile and are both graduates of the Realtor Institute and Certified Residential Specialists.

Bozeman, Montana

30

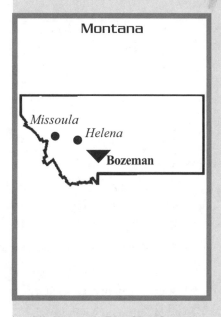

Bozeman at a Glance

Bozeman has the shortest vision statement around, it's only four words long: "The most livable place." And it certainly lives up to that vision! Bozeman is the county seat of Gallatin County, which is located in southwest Montana. It was established in 1863. The county includes 2,517 square miles of Montana. To put this into perspective, Gallatin County is larger than the states of Rhode Island and Delaware combined. Most of the county is fertile farm fields, however, more than 40 percent of the land is forested and managed by the U.S. Forest Service, which provides an excellent, and very large, recreational area. Bozeman is near world-class downhill ski runs, blue ribbon trout streams, Yellowstone National Park, and a multitude of other outdoor activities. Although the winters can be cold and snowy, if you are interested in an active retirement, Bozeman could be the perfect place for you. They don't call Montana the Big Sky Country for nothing! If you look up, you can almost kiss the sky.

Possible Drawbacks: This wonderland comes at a price. The cost of living composite index in the fourth quarter of 2003 was 106.8, based on a national average of 100, which means it's a little more expensive to live in Bozeman than in other parts ot he country, but it's not so bad that you won't be able to afford your dreamhome.

▶ Nickname: Big Sky Country
▶ County: Gallatin
▶ Area Code: 406
▶ Population: 30,000
▶ County Population: 71,206
▶ Percent of Population Over 65: 8%
▶ Region: Southwest Montana
▶ Closest Metropolitan Area: Great Falls, 127 miles
▶ Median Home Price: $212,900
▶ Best Reasons to Retire Here: The people are Montana's most precious asset. No one is a stranger, and all are welcome at suppertime.

Climate

45° N Latitude 111° W Longitude	Average High Temperature (°F)	Average Low Temperature (°F)	Precipitation (")	Sunshine (%)
January	28.8	6.3	0.6	46
April	54.1	28.8	1.3	59
July	84.2	49.5	1.1	78
October	58.1	29.5	1.1	60
YEAR	55.4	28.4	14.3	59

Utilities

Overview: The utilities in Bozeman will cost less than an in other places around the country. In a system that rates such costs across the nation, with the average at 100, Bozeman comes in at a reasonable 60.

Gas Company: NorthWestern Energy (888-467-2669; *www.northwesternenergy.com*)

Electric Company: NorthWestern Energy (888-467-2669; *www.northwesternenergy.com*)

Phone Company: Qwest Communications (800-244-1111); *www.qwest.com*) provides local and long-distance phone service.

Water/Sewer Company: City of Bozeman (406-582-3200; *www.bozeman.net/water*)

Cable Company: Cable television service is provided by Bresnan Communications (406-587-8922; *www.bresnan.com*).

The Tax Axe

Car Registration: You must register your vehicle within 90 days of moving in, or as a soon as you get a job. You can do this with the Gallatin County Treasurer's Office(406-582-3084).

Driver's License: You must get a Montana driver's license within 120 days of moving in, if you're getting a non-commercial license. If you want a commercial license, you need to apply no later than 30 days after moving to Bozeman.

Sales Tax: There is no state sales tax in the state of Montana.

State Income Tax: For information, contact the State Department of Revenue (406-444-6900; *www.state.mt.us/revenue*). Montana has an individual income tax that is progressive, meaning the more you make, the higher percentage you pay within a range from 2 percent to 11 percent of taxable income. All income, no matter its source, is taxed.

Retirement Income Tax: All income, no matter its source, is taxed. Therefore, retirement income is also taxed on the progressive scale.

Property Tax: All property, except agricultural land, has an assessed value that is equal to its market value. Property is "statutory classified" for determining taxable value. It's complex, so call the Gallatin County Classification and Appraisal Office (406-582-3400) and ask for the pamphlet titled "Understanding Property Taxes."

Local Real Estate

Overview: The local real estate market is affected by the local university, although you should still have an adequate selection to meet most of your needs. Houses are commonly rented on a year lease, while apartments might be month-to-month, seasonal, or only during the school-year.

Average price of a three-bedroom/two-bath home: $212,936

Average price of a two-bedroom condo: $110,000

Common Housing Styles: Bozeman offers many different home styles. They vary from early Victorian "spreads" to 1920s practical, and from smaller homes to elegant modern ranch styles.

Rental Market: The rental market in Bozeman is mercurial, due to the large number of tourists and university students who make their destination or school-year home in town. While ample facilities exist most of the year, it is a good idea to check out the availability in advance.

Average rent for a two-bedroom apartment: $650 per month

Communities Popular With Retirees: Belgrade and Livingston are both well-eqipped for active retirees, as well as folks who might need a little extra help.

Nearby Areas to Consider: Just 10 miles northwest of Bozeman, Belgrade is one of the fastest growing cities in the state. With a population of more than 10,000, Belgrade is a quiet yet lively town in the heart of the Gallatin Valley. West Yellowstone is a rustic mountain town nestled between National Forest lands and Yellowstone National Park. The area is filled with wildlife, breathtaking views, and activities for people of all ages. Within the world's First National Park, 10,000 thermal features and 2.5 million acres of nature's best offer days of exploration, adventure, and learning.

Earning a Living

Business Climate: From the *American City Business Journal*, which recently published a study titled "Where to go for America's hottest small biz market," Bozeman ranked number one in the nation for small-sized markets. Bozeman has a ratio of 5,262 small businesses per 100,000 residents, as well as a two-year growth rate of 10.7 percent. This makes Bozeman very attractive for business. Agriculture, tourism, and government drive the economy in Bozeman. Technology has done away with some sections of farm jobs, but farming is still a major element, with the county consistently ranking in the Top 10 in the state for dairy and hay, barley, winter wheat, livestock, and crop production. Because it's so close to Yellowstone National Park, Bozeman benefits from the annual influx of tourists, making that industry an important one in the community. And the University of Montana Bozeman employs more than 3,200 faculty and staff, and caters to 2,500 students. Good transportation, high quality of life, and resources from Montana State University, are some of the reasons many entrepreneurs elect to establish a presence in the Bozeman area.

Help in Starting a Business: Gallatin Development Corporation (406-587-3113; *www.bozeman.org*) is billed by the locals as the lead economic development organization in Gallatin County. The corporation also helps businesses relocate to Bozeman. You can access SCORE through the Chamber Center (406-586-5421). The Business Information Center is also housed in the chamber of commerce building.

Job Market: Gallatin Valley continues to have significant growth in new jobs, ranging from service and retail, to technology and manufacturing. Although the recent data affirm the unemployment rate at an admirable low of 2.5, there is room for good workers.

Medical Care

In addition to acute care, Bozeman Deaconess Hospital (406-585-5000; *www.bozemandeaconess.org*) provides In-Home Care and Companions as well as Hospice and Healthcare Connections, all of which are available for in-home delivery. Under the Deaconess umbrella are the Same Day Surgery Center plus two walk-in urgent-care centers.

Services for Seniors

The Area 4 Agency on Aging (406-447-1680), located in Helena, covers Gallatin County. The Montana Department of Health and Human Services, Division of Seniors and Long-term Care (406-444-7783) is also in Helena. RSVP, part of the Human Resource Development Council (406-587-5444; *www.rsvpmt.org*) is on the second floor of the Bozeman senior center. Its purpose is to facilitate volunteering for individuals 55 and older. Volunteers are matched with public and nonprofit organizations ranging from education centers to police departments to hospitals.

Continuing Education

Montana State University has a Montana Senior Citizen Fee Waiver, which exempts in-state students from incidental and registration fees if they are 62 years or older. Contact Montana State University, Information Services (406-994-0211; *www.montana.edu*).

Crime and Safety

During 2003, Bozeman reported 82 violent crimes and 1483 property crimes. *CityData.com* places the crime index at 365.1. You are safer in Bozeman than in many other places around the country.

Getting Around Town

Public Transportation: Bobcat Transit (409-586-8567) provides bus service for all residents of Bozeman and Belgrade. The fee is $1 per ride, and runs during the school semester with 17 scheduled stops. Galavan (406-587-2434) is a senior/disabled transit program with wheelchair accessibility. It runs daily in Bozeman, and on Tuesdays it even goes to Belgrade and back. You can arrange ground transportation to Yellowstone Park by calling West Yellowstone Foundation (406-646-7600). West Yellowstone also serves both seniors and disabled folks. Karst Stage (406-586-8567; *www.karststage.com*) offers local shuttle service to the airport and other destinations.

Roads and Highways: US 191; State Highway 10, Interstate 90

Airports: Gallatin airport (406-388-8321) is the closest airport to Bozeman. From there you can catch a flight to the larger state airport.

Let the Good Times Roll

Recreation: There is a lot of stuff to do in Bozeman, and none of it includes sitting around! There's fishing in nearby mountain lakes and rivers, hunting, as well as hiking and biking. Have you seen photos of this place? It's absolutely fabulous! If you are into rock climbing, Bozeman provides spots for many levels of derring-do. Then there's skiing, of course, both alpine and cross-country. Bozeman also boasts spectator sports, although I doubt you will stay seated the whole game. Football, women's and men's basketball, women's volleyball, tennis, golf, track and rodeo are a few highlights. Hockey has a presence in the Bozeman IceDogs. Get your tickets early, though, as they sell out early. You can swim indoors or out, either at the Bogert Pool or the local high school.

Culture: Bozeman hosts a treasure trove of theatrical talent and events, including the Vigilante Theatre Company, Shakespeare in the Parks, and the Equinox Theatre that will keep you entertained with comedy, tragedy, and drama. Bozeman also prides itself musically with performances by the Bozeman Symphony. Both the Symphony and the Intermountain Opera combine talents from the local area with guest artists from around the world. The "Nutcracker Ballet" highlights the holiday season, but the Montana Ballet dances the year round, featuring talented dancers, as well as invited guest dancers from national companies. For art, you can't beat the Emerson Center for the Arts and Culture, which houses the work of several artists and provides facilities for several arts and crafts displays. The downtown area of Bozeman is home to many galleries.

Annual Events: February brings the International Food Bazaar. April brings the American Indian Pow Wow at Montana State University. May brings the Intermountain Opera, Downtown Gallery Walks, and the Bozeman Second Friday of the month, which runs through September. June is the Garden Tour and Shakespeare in the Park. July brings the Gallatin County Fair, Music on Main Street, and Lunch on the Lawn at the Emerson Center for Arts and Culture. August sees the Bite of Bozeman, Sweet Pea Festival of the Arts and the annual Quilting in the Country quilt show. In September, the Fall Farm Festival and the Lewis and Clark Marathon take center stage. October displays the Bridger Raptor Festival, and the MSU Homecoming festivities. November is jazzy with the Jazz Festival, and the Holiday Festival of the Arts. December, of course, is Christmas and the *The Nutcracker* ballet production, along with the Bridger Bowl

Torchlight Parade and Fireworks Display. For the winter sports enthusiast, downhill skiing, snowboarding, and cross-country skiing begin in earnest in December.

When the Grandkids Come: This is a great "get back to nature" place, so take the kids hiking, fishing, and backpacking. The Montana Outdoor Science School provides age-appropriate studies indoors and out for preschoolers up to fifth grade. Depending on their interests, the kids might also be interested in the Museum of the Rockies at Montana State University, home to the largest collection of dinosaur fossils in the United States. And don't forget about Yellowstone Park! It's just down the road!

More Information

Municipal
Chamber of Commerce
2000 Commerce Way
Bozeman, MT
406-586-5421
www.bozemanchamber.com

Newspaper
Bozeman Daily Chronicle
P.O. Box 1190
Bozeman, MT 59771
406-587-4491
http://bozemandailychronicle.com

Realty
Jon Bertelsen
612 West Main Street
Bozeman, MT 59715
406-581-0630
www.inbozeman.com

Missoula, Montana

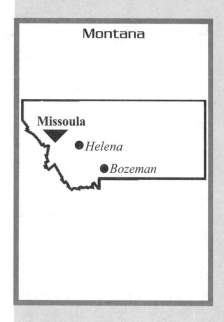

31

Montana

Missoula

●Helena

●Bozeman

Missoula at a Glance

Missoula lies in a mountain forest setting where five valleys converge. It is home to more and more retirees every year. But the population growth and dynamism of the business community haven't stifled the sense of being a small town, for which this remarkable city is known. Resources abound, from the mountains and rivers, to downtown shopping, to excellent medical facilities and staff. But the real resource, the best-kept secret, is the people. Many have moved in from other places for no other reason than they fell in love with the place. For seniors, according to a representative Realtor, "There is an abundance of senior retirement housing." The cost of living is an issue for most retirees, and Missoula shines in this department, coming in at a composite index of 101.7 according to a chamber of commerce reporting agency, with housing (98.5) and utilities (94.9) under the country-wide average of 100. Missoula started out as a settlement called "Hell Gate" with a trading post to accommodate travelers. The settlement was later renamed Missoula, taken from a Salish Indian word meaning "near the cold, chilling waters."

Possible Drawbacks: It gets nippy in the winter. Also, Missoula sits at 3,199 feet above sea level, and the air is thin up there. For most, this is not an issue, but if you have any concerns, check with your doctor.

▶ Nickname: The Garden City

▶ County: Missoula

▶ Area Code: 543

▶ Population: 60,768

▶ County Population: 98, 616

▶ Percent of Population Over 65: 10.4%

▶ Region: Western Montana

▶ Closest Metropolitan Area: Spokane, 198 miles

▶ Median Home Price: $165,000

▶ Best Reasons to Retire Here: Scenic grandeur, four distinct seasons, abundant housing, and a low cost of living.

Climate

46° N Latitude 114° W Longitude	Average High Temperature (°F)	Average Low Temperature (°F)	Precipitation (")	Sunshine (%)
January	36.3	18.3	1.4	33
April	59.0	30.9	1.0	57
July	84.7	47.7	0.9	81
October	62.1	32.5	1.1	55
YEAR	59.9	32.5	15.8	55

Utilities

Overview: The national average of the cost of living is set at 100, and Missoula comes in at 66.

Gas Company: Gas is provided by the Northwestern Energy Company (888-467-2669; *www.northwesternenergy.com*)

Electric Company: Energy is provided by the Northwestern Energy Company (888-467-2669; *www.northwesternenergy.com*) and the Missoula Electric Cooperative (406-541-4433; *www.missoulaelectric.com*).

Phone Company: Local telephone service is provided by Blackfoot Communications (406-541-5000; *www.blackfoot.net*) and by Qwest Communications (800-244-1111; *www.qwest.com*).

Water/Sewer Company: Water is provided by the Mountain Water Company (406-721-5570). The Missoula Public Works Department (406-543-3157; *www.ci.missoula.mt.us/publicworks*) is responsible for sewer.

Cable Company: Comcast Communications (800-266-2278; *www.comcast.com*)

The Tax Axe

Car Registration: You must register your vehicle within 90 days of moving in, or as a soon as you get a job. A vehicle cannot be titled in Montana without also being registered. Check in with Missoula County Motor Vehicle Office (543-258-4747; *http://doj.state.mt.us/department/motorvehicledivision*) for more information.

Driver's License: You must get a Montana license within 120 days of moving in. If you want a commercial license, you need to apply no later than 30 days after moving to Missoula. Contact the Montana State Government Drivers License & Exam office (406-329-1350) for details.

Sales Tax: There is no sales tax in Montana.

State Income Tax: An accelerated tax rate varies from 2 percent to 8 percent.

Retirement Income Tax: Montana taxes military retirement pay.

Property Tax: Taxes are based on property assessments completed, on average, every five years. The rates vary depending on your particular school district.

Local Real Estate

Overview: The Missoula real estate market is currently strong, with plenty of available homes and folks anxious to move in. With the prices and the availability, a retiree is able to fulfill home-ownership dreams on a grander scale than he or she might suspect.

Average price of a three-bedroom/two-bath home: $200,000

Average price of a two-bedroom condo: $200,000

Common Housing Styles: In Missoula you are apt to run into any style home, including Victorian, ranch, Cape Cod, Spanish, ultra-modern, log cabin, and modular. Also, you will find an abundance of senior retirement housing.

Rental Market: Several rental properties have been built in recent years, adding approximately 2,000 new units, and creating a good selection of modest to upscale apartments.

Average rent for a two-bedroom apartment: $600 per month

Communities Popular With Retirees: Grizzly Peak Retirement Residence, Hunter's Glen Assisted Living, Missoula Manor Homes, and the Village Senior Residence

Nearby Areas to Consider: There are several rural communities outside Missoula proper, including Lolo, Florence, Frenchtown, and Bonner. Each is about 15 to 20 minutes from Missoula's central city area. For extended fun and a possible alternative to Missoula, the Bitterroot Valley (just down the road) deserves a look. There is plenty of room per house, and you will find lots of horse properties. There is plenty of bare land to drive a stake and claim it for your own.

Earning a Living

Business Climate: Business is very good, indeed, and employment is the same. Missoula holds unemployment at 4 percent against a 5.1 percent rate for the entire state of Montana for the same time period.

Help in Starting a Business: The Missoula office of the Small Business Development Centre (406-728-9234; *www.mtcdc.org/sbdc.html*). The Montana Secretary of State has posted information on how to launch a new business (*www.sos.state.mt.us/css/BSB/New_Business*). This same Web page has links to other helpful online sites, such as business services and records management. For help with small business counseling, funding, marketing, international trade, and other public programs, contact Buzgate (*www.buzgate.org/mt*).

Job Market: The job market is flexible, and job listings plentiful, with everything from entry-level retail, to jobs requiring advanced degrees. The Website of choice is the official state workforce services division of the Montana Department of Labor and Industry *(https://jobs.mt.gov/jobs/login.seek)*.

Medical Care

The Community Medical Center (406-728-4100; *www.communitymed.org*) is licensed for 146 acute-care beds, and offers such diverse services as traumatic brain injury rehabilitation, good nutrition lessons, and joint reconstruction. The center houses the Montana Heart Center, which provides testing for heart health . St. Patrick Hospital and Health Sciences Center (406-543-7271; *www.saintpatrick.org*) is a nonprofit medical center under the sponsorship of the Sisters of Providence. It has 195 acute-care beds and 18 transitional-care beds. The hospital's cardiovascular surgeons perform the only heart surgeries in western Montana. The emergency department treats more than 24,000 people annually, and the Life Flight air ambulance and fixed-wing transport flew 767 missions in 2001. It provides cancer treatment and addiction treatment. Big Sky Surgery Center (406-542-6559) specializes in outpatient same-day surgery.

Services for Seniors

Missoula Aging Services (406-728-7682; *www.missoulaagingservices.org*) provides typical community-based programs. The Missoula Senior Citizens Center (406-543-7154; *www.missoulaagingservices.org*) is one of several such organizations located in the surrounding communities, and provides a number of services for rural senior citizens. The Choices Bank (*www.choicesbank.org*) allows you to specify your choices for the possible future day when you are not able to speak for yourself. And you don't have to be old to take advantage of this sensible solution to illness-related decisions. Caring Circles (406-728-1613; *www.caringcircles.org*) is a group of volunteers working together to provide practical, emotional, and spiritual support to individuals and families with health concerns or other special needs. Partners In Home Care, Inc. (406-728-8848; www.partnersinhomecare.com) provides hospice care. Home Instead Senior Care (406-523-9909; *www.homeinstead.com*) provides non-medical companionship for the elderly at home. Western Montana Chapter for the Prevention of Elder Abuse (406-327-7886; *www.westernmontanachapter.org*) gives training in spotting elder abuse, so we can help others.

Continuing Education

Located at the base of Mount Sentinel and on the banks of the Clark Fork River is the University of Montana (406-243-0211; *www.umt.edu*). The 200-acre campus is one of the most beautiful in the nation and is home to 12,000 students. Students who are 62 years old are called non-traditional, and may attend school for a reduced rate. Further, senior citizens may qualify for a registration and incidental fee waiver if they are classified as in-state residents. The univeristy also offers online courses.

Crime and Safety

The FBI's Uniform Crime Index consists of the combined rate of murder and non-negligent manslaughter, forcible rape, robbery, assault, burglary, larceny, and auto theft per 100,000 population. Missoula's overall index 4,729. You are safer in Missoula than in a lot of other places, but not so safe that you want to leave your house unlocked.

Getting Around Town

Public Transportation: Missoula has no public transportation system.

Roads and Highways: I-90, US 90, 93, and 12

Airports: Missoula International (406-728-4381; *www.msoairport.org*) is about six miles out of town and is served by four major airlines.

Let the Good Times Roll

Recreation: Three major rivers run through the area. The famous Blackfoot River to the northeast, the beautiful Bitterroot River to the south, and the Clark Fork of the Columbia River, which flows through the city. The Rocky Mountain Elk Foundation Wildlife Visitor Center features a world-record elk display with full mounts of grizzly bears, mountain lions, lynx, wolves, bighorn sheep, mountain goats, bison, a cow elk and her newborn calf, and more. The Rocky Mountain Museum of Military History, Fort Missoula, promotes the commemoration and study of the U.S. armed forces, from the frontier period to the present, drawing upon a collection of military artifacts and documents. The Smokejumper Visitor Center features exhibits on wildland fire ecology and behavior, current wildland firefighting gear and several videos on smoke jumping and aircraft in fighting wildland fire. Historic Downtown Missoula features classic early-century buildings and offers unique shops, galleries, fine dining, cultural activities, and an exciting nightlife.

Culture: The summer series "Broadway in the Rockies" brings professional theater to Missoula June through August. The Art Museum of Missoula manages the Missoula County Art Collection, as well as its own collection, which is distinguished by the Contemporary American Indian Art Collection, and works from regional and local artists. The Montana Museum of Art and Culture at the University of Montana (*www.umt.edu/partv/famus*) organizes traveling exhibits and maintains a permanent collection of more than 9,500 American, Native American, Asian, and European historical and contemporary works. The Historical Museum at Fort Missoula (543-728-3476; *www.montana.com/ftmslamuseum*) preserves the history of Missoula County and western Montana. The Museum of Mountain Flying is in a new 19,000-square-foot hangar on the east side of Missoula's International Airport. The museum contains artifacts relevant to the history of mountain flying in the Rocky Mountains and several restored antique airplanes.

Annual Events: Regular events include the International Wildlife Film Festival, Out to Lunch, Downtown ToNight, International Choral Festival, Farmer's Market, Saturday Arts and Crafts Market, and First Night Missoula. First Night Missoula is a community New Year's Eve celebration of the arts, featuring hundreds of performing, visual, and literary artists. Missoula's theaters, schools, dance halls, churches, and businesses are transformed into showcases for the diverse talents of Montana's artistic, ethnic, and cultural communities. First Night is open to the entire community. Irish Cultural Celebration, Germanfest, and numerous other community events are held each year.

When the Grandkids Come: The Missoula Children's Theatre provides a full season of community theater, as well as local children's productions. It also operates a performing arts summer camp at Flathead Lake, which gathers more than 200 young people from around the world.

More Information

Municipal

Missoula Cultural Council
First Interstate Plaza Building
127 East Front, Suite 212
Missoula, MT 59807
406-721-9620
www.missoulacultural.org

Missoula Area Chamber of Commerce
825 East Front Street
Missoula, MT 59802
406-543-6623
www.missoulachamber.com

Newspaper

Missoulian (daily)
PO Box 8029
Missoula, MT 59807
406-523-5200
www.missoulian.com

Realty

Diane Beck, Realtor
Gillespie Realty Company
1020 South Avenue West
Missoula, MT 59801
406-721-4141
www.homesinmontana.net

32

Las Cruces, New Mexico

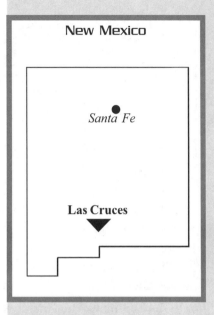

Las Cruces at a Glance

When you think "Southwest Style," you're thinking of Las Cruces, even if you don't know it! With its varied terrain, from desert to the fertile valley, from the foothills to the Organ Mountains, Las Cruces conjures visions of strolling troubadours, strumming guitars, lace mantillas, and white sand. Las Cruces is the fastest growing city in New Mexico and the 11th fastest in the nation. This book is not alone in proclaiming this sweet place a wonderful place to live—the Milken Institute and *Money* magazine do, too. The Rio Grande flows through the middle of the valley, bringing both moisture and opportunities for watersport. The gorgeous Organ Mountains rise to the east of the city, and encourage residents to go hiking, camping, or biking. The surrounding agricultural land yields pecans, onions, and other produce, but it is renowned for growing the best-tasting green chili in the world. If you like things spicy, you'll love Las Cruces!

Possible Drawbacks: It *is* a desert. Some people will miss the high-speed lifestyle of a big city. A friend who moved there several years ago said that in the spring she spends extra time sweeping sand from the front door because of the wind. But overall, she reports that her husband is happy; her children are healthy; she loves the festivals, food, and people; and she is not moving!

- Nickname: City of the Crosses
- County: Dona Ana
- Area Code: 505
- Population: 75,786
- County Population: 174,682
- Percent of Population Over 65: 13.1%
- Region: South central New Mexico
- Closest Metropolitan Area: El Paso, 45 miles
- Median Home Price: $197,950
- Best Reasons to Retire Here: Las Cruces has an absolutely enchanting cultural entertainment, which gives you a recipe for the good life.

Climate

32° N Latitude 106° W Longitude	Average High Temperature (°F)	Average Low Temperature (°F)	Precipitation (")	Sunshine (%)
January	56.3	19.6	0.5	78
April	76.5	36.5	0.2	89
July	95.2	61.9	1.8	82
October	77.4	39.7	1.0	84
YEAR	76.1	39.2	9.5	84

Utilities

Overview: The cost of living index is 100.3, which is virtually at the national average of 100. Housing is high at 105.6, and food is slightly above average at 101.8. Transportation, utilities, and healthcare are all below normal. The city of Las Cruces Customer Service (505-541-2111) administers service connections, billings, and accounts for City of Las Cruces gas, water, wastewater, and solid waste utilities. They also provide these services for Rio Grande Natural Gas customers.

Gas Company: Rio Grande Natural Gas (505-541-2111)

Electric Company: El Paso Electric (915-543-5970; *www.epelectric.com*)

Phone Company: Qwest (505-556-6040; *www.qwest.com*)

Water/Sewer Company: City of Las Cruces (505-541-2111)

Cable Company: Qwest (800-573-1311), and US Sprint (800-521-0579)

The Tax Axe

Car Registration: The New Mexico Motor Vehicle Division (888-683-4636) requires a registration fee for passenger vehicles is based on the weight, year, and model of the vehicle. Registration fees range from $25.50 to $60.50 for a one year registration, or $50.50 to $120.50 for a two year registration. Registration fees for trucks range from $36.50 to $205.50 for a one year registration or $72.50 to $410.50 for a two year registration.

Driver's License: You must apply for a New Mexico driver's license within 30 days of moving into the state. You will only have to pass a vision test. You must surrender your out-of-state license when applying for a new one. For a four year license, the cost is $16, and for eight years, it's $32.

Sales Tax: 6.5 percent. Exemptions include prescription drugs.

State Income Tax: New Mexico has an accelerated income tax ranging from 1.7 percent to 8.2 percent. Taxpayers 65 and older may be eligible for a deduction from taxable income up to $8,000.

Retirement Income Tax: Taxpayers 65 and older may exempt $8,000 (single), or $16,000 (joint) from any income source if their income is under $28,000 (individual) or $51,000 (married, filing jointly).

Property Tax: Las Cruces residential properties are taxed at a rate of $27.53 per $1,000 on 33.3 percent of appraised value. Mesilla residential property tax rate is $22.61 per $1,000 on 33.3 percent of appraised value.

Local Real Estate

Overview: Real estate in Las Cruces ranges from the very modest mobile home, to million-dollar estates covering several acres. The supply of available, affordable housing is good.

Average price of a three-bedroom/two-bath home: $132,000

Average price of a two-bedroom condo: $115,000

Common Housing Styles: Southwest, mission, adobe hacienda, xeriscaped yards, fireplaces, and mountain-views are all popular styles of construction, both in houses and condominiums. There is a lot of variety, so you should be able to find exactly what you're looking for.

Rental Market: Rentals are available throughout the year. Some owners rent homes during the summer months only, returning in the fall. There are condo rentals as well. Apartments are available in several price ranges, with amenities to match.

Average rent for a two-bedroom apartment: $750 per month

Communities Popular With Retirees: Sonoma Ranch and the Village at Northrise are all popular communitees with retirrees.

Nearby Areas to Consider: Deming is rich with history, atmosphere, and sunshine. The state parks are diverse, from the desert to the mountains of the Black Range. The water and the agricultural influence make Deming an oasis in the desert. The City of Truth or Consequences is the water wonderland of New Mexico, with geothermal hot springs, lakes, and rivers. The surrounding county has laid claim to some of the most beautiful mountain and desert terrain in the entire state. They also have exclusive rights to the largest lake in the southwestern region, Elephant Butte.

Earning a Living

Business Climate: Las Cruces has been ranked by the Milken Institute and *Money* magazine as both the best small-metro area in the nation in which to do business, and a great place to retire.

Help in Starting a Business: Three top-notch resources are available, including the Greater Las Cruces Chamber of Commerce (*www.lascruces.org*), High Tech Consortium of Southern New Mexico (*www.hightechnm.org*), and Mesilla Valley Economic Development Alliance (*www.mveda.com*).

Job Market: There are jobs aplenty in the Las Cruces area. We found almost 400 jobs listed within 20 miles, and nearly 900 jobs within 50 miles. The downside is that the unemployment rate is currently 6.67 percent.

Medical Care

Las Cruces offers several medical centers. The newly opened Mountain View Regional Medical Center (505-556-7600; *www.mountainviewregional.com*) is a 168-bed acute-care hospital, and provides a full-service emergency room, specialized woman's center, comprehensive intensive-care services, surgical care, and specialized cardiology center. Memorial Medical Center is a full-service hospital and serves as the acute-care facility for the county. Memorial Medical Center (505-521-5374; *www.mmclc.org*) is a 286-bed acute-care facility offering services in several areas, including cancer , emergency, family care, health education and wellness, home health, imaging services, laboratory services, medical/surgical services, heart and vascular care, orthopedics, outpatient surgery, pastoral service, and women's health and wellness. In addition, the Heritage program offers psychiatric services for senior adults age 55 or older.

Services for Seniors

The city of Las Cruces administers senior services including home-delivered meals, lunch at the senior centers, seniors volunteering in the community, in-home services, and transportation. Dial-A-Ride is a special transportation service offered by the city of Las Cruces Transit Department, to provide curb-to-curb, on-demand transportation for qualified Americans with Disabilities Act individuals and senior citizens 60 years of age and older. Senior programs are available at four centers within the city of Las Cruces, the Eastside Community Center (505-524-1632), Mesilla Park Community Center (505-524-2657), Munson Senior Center (505-528-3000), and the Benavidez Community Center (505-528-3000).

Continuing Education

At Dona Ana Branch Community College (505-527-7500; *http://dabcc.nmsu.edu*), seniors can broaden their horizons through Elderhostel and the Academy of Learning. Both programs are part of the Community Education Program. New Mexico State University (505-646-0111; *www.nmsu.edu*), based in Las Cruces, is the state's land-grant institution, with more than 23,000 graduate and undergraduate students on the main campus and four branch campuses. For seniors, the university offers a break in tuition fees. Normally the fee per credit is $163.25, but the fee per credit for senior citizens is $48.75.

Crime and Safety

Historically, towns this close to the Mexican border have struggled with bandits ripping through town and causing all kinds of mischief. Luckily, this is no longer the case, but the crime rate is still higher than the national average at 701.5 for violent crime, and 8,429.0 for non-violent crime (incidents per 100,000 people). Little of either violation type involves law-abiding citizens in Las Cruces.

Getting Around Town

Public Transportation: Roadrunner Transit (505-541-2777; *www.las-cruces.org*) administers the Senior Transportation Dial-A-Ride service. Fares are 75¢ per one-way trip, with a punch card available which provides 30 rides for $22.50.

Roads and Highways: I-10, I-25, Highway 70

Airports: Serving 2.8 million passengers per year, the El Paso International Airport (915-780-4700; *www.elpasointernationalairport.com*) is located approximately 45 miles southeast of Las Cruces via Interstate 10. Direct shuttle service (505-525-1784) is available from various locations around Las Cruces. The airport is one of the most charming and colorful of facilities in the United States. Las Cruces International Airport (505-541-2471; *www.las-cruces.org/airport*) provides in-state commuter services, and services private and charter aircraft.

Let the Good Times Roll

Recreation: Begin with 55 parks; one public, one semi-private, and two private golf courses; 18 public tennis courts; three swimming pools; and a lake. Add hiking, biking, swimming, camping, dancing, sky-gazing, and touring, and Las Cruces can satisfy the most particular sports and recreation tastes. In addition, the Las Cruces area is a haven for birds and bird-watchers. Fabulous differing biotic provinces offer attractive food and shelter for more than 200 species. And don't forget about the ghost towns! Here are some intriguing choices: Chloride, 60 miles north of Las Cruces on Highway 52, settled in 1881 by miners after silver chloride ore was discovered nearby. Hillsboro, 70 miles north of Las Cruces on Highway 152, was founded in 1877 as a gold town. Today, Hillsboro's fortunes rest on apples, not gold. There are quaint gift shops, restaurants, the Black Range Museum, and the remains of the Sierra County Courthouse. The annual Hillsboro Apple Festival is held the first weekend in September. Winston, located 100 miles north of Las Cruces on Highway 52, first settled in 1881, grew to a population of 3,100 within three years. Other ghost towns include Chise, Cuchillo, Monticello, Placita, and Kingston. For the adults only, go on a tour of the local vineyards, including the Blue Teal Vineyards & Tasting Room, La Viña Winery, Mademoiselle, and St. Clair Winery. You don't have to go abroad to sample excellent vintages!

Culture: The majority of annual events pertain to, or celebrate, cultures that meet, shake hands, and oftentimes blend in Las Cruces. From fiestas to art and antique shows, from Superbowl Sunday to an International mariachi concert, you will have to work hard to keep up with the community calendar.

Annual Events: In January is the Sky Safari and the Mesilla Valley Balloon Rally. In February, visit the For the Love of Art Fiesta, Las Colcheras Quilt Show, Las Cruces Roadrunners Wheels Downtown, and Love Songs in Celebration of Valentine's Day. In March, see the Cowboys for Cancer Team Roping, and Nostalgia Antique & Collectible Show. In April, catch the 101 Gold Spring Fest Egg Hunt, American Indian Week, and

Rhythm Nights Dinner and Show. In May, go on the Lake Lucero Tour, La Fiesta de San Ysidro, and the Southern New Mexico Wine Festival. In June, Raft the Rio, Mesilla Valley Serra Club Antique and Collectible Show, and San Juan Fiesta are all a lot of fun. In July, you can go to Discover the Desert, Full Moon Nights, or Missoula Children's Theatre. In August is the National Night Out Event, Bluegrass in the Desert, and Friday Night Star Talks. In September, visit the Franciscan Festival of Arts, Hatch Chile Festival. In November, go to the International Mariachi Conference and Spectacular Concert. In December, see the Holiday Hoopla Tournament and Luminarias on the Plaza.

When the Grandkids Come: Take the kids to White Sands National Monument. Other day trips include Ruidoso, which has an American West museum, or check out Caballo Lake or Elephant Butte Lake State Park, both of which are only an hour's drive from Las Cruces. To the west of Las Cruces, and within an hour and a half drive, is the Gila National Forest, City of Rocks State Park, and Rockhound State Park.

More Information

Municipal

Las Cruces Convention & Visitors Bureau
211 North Water Street
Las Cruces, NM 88001
505-541-2444
www.lascrucescvb.org/index.html

City of Las Cruces
P.O. Box 20000
Las Cruces, NM 88004
505-541-2000
www.las-cruces-new-mexico.org

Newspaper

Las Cruces Sun-News
256 West Las Cruces Avenue
Las Cruces, NM 88005
505-541-5400
www.lcsun-news.com

Realty

We do not have a Realtor recommendation for Las Cruces. As an option, check out *www.realtor.com* or *www.homegain.com.* Select a Realtor with both CRS and GRI designations after their names, since it means that these folks have gone the extra mile and are both graduates of the Realtor Institute and Certified Residential Specialists.

33

Santa Fe, New Mexico

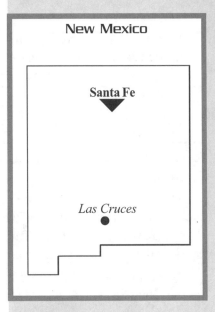

New Mexico

Santa Fe

Las Cruces

Santa Fe at a Glance

Santa Fe is not only the capital of the state of New Mexico, it is also a golfer's paradise, offering a climate that makes golf a year-round sport. And with the high altitudes, you can hit a golf ball about 10 percent farther than at sea level. Within driving distance there are 12 ski areas in the Southern Rockies. In the summer, numerous lakes and streams beckon anglers for the thrills of hooking trout, bass, walleye, and catfish. Water enthusiasts can windsurf, water-ski, jet-ski, swim, or scuba dive. Yes, there's that much water around, even in this high desert! Let's not forget the professional end of things. Business, as they say, is booming. The visual and performing arts also help define this "City Different." From handcrafted Native American art to high opera, Santa Fe has it. The city's low skyline profile—itself a visual delight—traces to a 1957 city law limiting construction to traditional adobe architectural styles in the Historic Zone. Santa Fe was recently rated number one on the "Healthy Cities" list by *Organic Style* magazine.

Possible Drawbacks: Real Estate prices are formidable. Also, folks who have difficulty slowing down best look elsewhere. Santa Fe is laid-back—in a big way. So, excuse me while I take a brief siesta!

▶ Nickname: The City Different

▶ County: Santa Fe

▶ Area Code: 505

▶ Population: 69,299

▶ County Population: 138,000

▶ Percent of Population Over 65: 13.9%

▶ Region: Northern New Mexico

▶ Closest Metropolitan Area: Albuquerque, 60 miles

▶ Median Home Price: $365,000

▶ Best Reasons to Retire Here: Healthy atmosphere, fabulous sports, arts, and folk.

Climate

35° N Latitude 105° W Longitude	Average High Temperature (°F)	Average Low Temperature (°F)	Precipitation (")	Sunshine (%)
January	42.3	14.4	0.4	72
April	64.8	30.6	0.5	77
July	87.3	53.4	1.2	76
October	67.8	32.9	1.2	79
YEAR	65.3	32.9	12.2	76

Utilities

Overview: The cost of living index is very high at 153.2, compared to the national average of 100. This is because of the extremely high housing cost index of 256.4. Food is slightly above average at 104.8. Transportation is also above average at 107.4, and health-care is at 104.4. Utilities are quite low at 89.9.

Gas Company: PNM (505-950-1830; *www.pnm.com*) provides gas and electricity for the Santa Fe area.

Electric Company: PNM (505-950-1830; *www.pnm.com*) provides gas and electric-ity for the Santa Fe area.

Phone Company: Qwest (800-898-9675; *www.qwest.com*) offers both local and long-distance phone service.

Water/Sewer Company: Sangre De Cristo Water (505-954-7199; *www.santafenm.gov/public-utilities*)

Cable Company: Comcast (505-438-2600; *www.comcast.com*) provides cable tele-vision service, as well as cable internet connections.

The Tax Axe

Car Registration: The New Mexico Motor Vehicle Division (888-683-4636) re-quires a registration fee for passenger vehicles based on the weight, year, and model of the vehicle. Registration fees range from $25.50 to $60.50 for a one year registration, or $50.50 to $120.50 for a two year registration. Registration fees for trucks range from $36.50 to $205.50 for a one year registration or $72.50 to $410.50 for a two year registration.

Driver's License: You must apply for a New Mexico driver's license within 30 days of moving into the state. You will only have to pass a vision test. You must surren-der your out-of-state license when applying for a new one.

Sales Tax: 6.5 percent. Exemptions include prescription drugs.

State Income Tax: New Mexico has an accelerated income tax ranging from 1.7 percent to 8.2 percent. Taxpayers 65 and older may be eligible for a deduction from taxable income of up to $8,000. Unreimbursed and uncompensated medical expenses may be eligible for a tax deduction.

Retirement Income Tax: Taxpayers 65 and older may exempt $8,000 (single), or $16,000 (joint) from any income source if their income is under $28,000 (individual) or $51,000 (married, filing jointly).

Property Tax: Santa Fe County is separated into four school/tax districts. The school districts are identified as Moriarty, Santa Fe, Pojoaque, and Espanola. All properties in Santa Fe County are taxed at a third of their market value. The actual rate changes each year, and you can contact the County Tax Assessor's office (505-986-6300; *www.co.santa-fe.nm.us/assessor/tax*) for the current rates.

Local Real Estate

Overview: The term "affordable housing" may seem like an oxymoron in Santa Fe, where the median price of a single-family home is 80 percent above the national average. Still, if you can afford it, this is a fabulous choice.

Average price of a three-bedroom/two-bath home: $365,000

Average price of a two-bedroom condo: $435,000

Common Housing Styles: Single-story, Mexican adobe haciendas, and Spanish Colonials are common. Buff-colored exteriors, ceilings with exposed beams, and earth-toned interiors mark the Santa Fe home. Features include xeriscaped landscaping, yards defined by low walls, and wonderful, long-distance views to the mountains.

Rental Market: Lots of apartment housing is available in Santa Fe and the surrounding areas. Although single family dwellings are expensive, the apartments are modest by comparison.

Average rent for a two-bedroom apartment: $625 per month

Communities Popular With Retirees: Tesuque and Las Campanas

Nearby Areas to Consider: Los Alamos is a small mountain community with a world-wide reputation for scientific and technological achievement. Located about 35 miles from Santa Fe, Los Alamos offers easy access to cultural activities and, acccording to a study by the American City Business Journals, offers the best quality of life anywhere in America. *Money* magazine has included Rio Rancho as the only New Mexican city on its list of the best places to live in America.

Earning a Living

Business Climate: A central location, clean air, great weather, and numerous cultural amenities all combine to make Santa Fe the ideal place to do business. Unemployment sits at 3.1 percent, low by any standard, and less than the national average by more than a full percentage point. Here's an interesting note: Santa Fe is first in the United States for telecommuters, with 4.9 percent of workers telecommuting each day.

Help in Starting a Business: One of the best sources for information is Santa Fe Economic Development (505-984-2842; *www.sfedi.org*). The Santa Fe Community

College's Small Business Development Center (505-428-1343; *www.sfccnm.edu*) is also a great place to get business support.

Job Market: The tourist trade is still king, but with the area growth, increasing economic base, and diverse population, jobs may be found across the board.

Medical Care

St. Vincent Hospital (505-983-3361; *www.stvin.org*) is a 248-bed, full-service hospital, priding itself on its many departments and services, including behavioral health services; a cancer center; cardiology; dermatology/dermatopathology; ear, nose and throat; emergency department; gastroenterology; geriatrics; internal medicine; family practice; infectious disease; laboratory services/pathology; nephrology; neurology; ophthalmology; and pediatrics; as well as the Pojoaque Primary Care, which offers services to Los Alamos National Laboratory commuters and the residents of Santa Fe, Rio Arriba, and Los Alamos counties. St. Vincent also has a sexual assault response team, sleep disorder center, surgical services, and urology and women's services departments. This hospital accepts both Medicare and Medicaid patients. The Santa Fe Indian Hospital (505-988-9821; *www.ihs.gov/medicalprograms*) is a 40-bed hospital and clinic serving the people of the Eleven Pueblo Tribes and urban Native Americans of northern New Mexico.

Services for Seniors

The Division of Senior Services offers a variety of programs to older adults at 11 senior centers throughout the city and county of Santa Fe. They offer transportation, nutrition, home delivered meals, information and referral, outreach, case management, preventive health education, and volunteer programs to any of those residents over 60. The Santa Fe government (*www.santafenm.gov*) provides links to everything a senior citizen will want to have access to in Santa Fe. El Castillo Retirement Residences (505-988-2877; *www.elcastilloretirement.com*) provides independent living. Ventana de Vida (877-893-9836) is also a community for independent living

Continuing Education

Santa Fe Community College (505-428-1000; *www.sfccnm.edu*) has a full-time enrollment of 1,760. For seniors, there is a handsome discount for tuition. You pay space-available tuition of only $5 per credit up to six credits. Beyond six credits, you pay regular tuition (early-bird rate is $28.20 per credit). This school has an active community service program including Continuing Education in art, crafts, creative writing, dance, fitness and wellness, home and garden, kid's stuff, languages, leisure, money matters, music, photography, southwest explorations, computer skills, and nonprofit management. College of Santa Fe (505-473-6011; *www.csf.edu*), with a full-time enrollment of 1,146, is a private, not-for-profit school offering 20 undergraduate majors, two graduate programs, and several certificate programs. The Senior Citizens Program is available at

$336 per credit hour, or you can audit for $674 per credit hour. In addition there are fees that may apply to your particular class. St. Johns College (505-984.6000; *www.sjcsf.edu*), with a full-time enrollment of 486, is a nonprofit college. St. John's offers a classic liberal arts curriculum in its strictest sense. All classes are taught in a conversational, or Socratic Seminar, style. Lectures are a thing of the past. Students engage the class material with professors guiding the conversation.

Crime and Safety

Forget all those things you've heard about the southwest. This is a safe place to live. Statistically, Santa Fe shines, with only 272 reported incidents per year on the violent side, and 2,470 non-violent incidents, both of which are around half the national average.

Getting Around Town

Public Transportation: Transit services are provided Monday through Friday from 8 a.m. to 5 p.m. and Tuesday from 8 a.m. to 3 p.m. for grocery shopping, doctor appointments, and social service agency appointments. Transportation reservations must be made 24 hours in advance. Transit coupons are available for a suggested donation per ride.

Roads and Highways: I-25 and I-40

Airports: The Santa Fe Municipal Airport (505-955-2908; *www.airnav.com/airport/SAF*) serves commercial airlines, corporate jets, and small private planes. The Albuquerque International Sunport (505-842-4366) is located about an hour south of Santa Fe on Interstate 25. Sandia Shuttle Service (505-474-5696) provides transportation between both airports and Santa Fe.

Let the Good Times Roll

Recreation: From the Sangre de Cristo Mountains in the north to the high desert in the south, the area offers ample terrain for hiking, biking, skiing, and other outdoor sports. The Senior Olympic Program is alive and well in Santa Fe. If you enjoy old ruins, take a day trip to the Bandelier National Monument, where you'll see some of the most unusual and interesting ancient ruins in the Southwest, steep narrow canyons with plentiful wildlife, mountains rising to 10,000 feet, many acres of unspoiled back country, plus a colorful section of the Rio Grande River valley.

Culture: The Santa Fe Opera (505-986-5900; *www.santafeopera.org*) Santa Fe Stages (505-982-6683; *www.santafeez.com*), Santa Fe Chamber Music (505-983-2075; *www.sfcmf.org*), Santa Fe Festival Ballet (505-983-3262), The Santa Fe Concert Association (800-905-3315; *www.musicone.org*), and the Museums of New Mexico (505-827-6548) all give Santa Fe a rich cultural atmosphere.

Annual Events: In January, the Museums of New Mexico host the Costume Workshops. In February is the Carnaval Mardi Gras Party, Guatemalan Textile Sale, and Star

Gazing Party at Fort Sumner State Monument. In April is Frontier Day, and Fabric of Life. In May is Japanese Children's Day with Origami Samurai helmets and Koi-Nobori, and the Last Ride of Billy the Kid. May also brings Mother's Day, All Natural Fiber Festival, and the Small Wonders Annual Show and Sale. In June, listen to Latin World Music, and Navajo Treaty Day. In July is Santa Fe Bandstand, Santa Fe Indian Market, Carnival Santa Fe, Swiss Carnival Weekend, Annual Traditional Spanish Market, Spanish Market, Frontier Days, and Fiesta de Santa Fe. In September, there is Fiestas de los Ninos and Searching for Other Life Forms. October brings Harvest Festival, San Marcos Studio Tour, and the Halloween Feature Presentation. In November is Ski Santa Fe and the La Cienega Studio Tour. December has the Santa Fe Film Festival, Winter Spanish Market, and the El Rancho de las Golondrinas Benefit Auction.

When the Grandkids Come: Not to be missed is the Museum of International Folk Art (*www.moifa.org*), famous for its collection of children's toys from around the world. Or you can get your hands dirty in an Earthworks Activity at the Santa Fe Children's museum (*www.santafechildrensmuseum.org*). The Santa Fe National Forest (*www.fs.fed.us/r3/sf*) is almost always available for exploration, camping, hiking, picnics, fishing, and in winter, snowmobiling, cross-country skiing, and snowshoeing.

More Information

Municipal

Santa Fe Convention Bureau
P.O. Box 909
Santa Fe, NM 87504
505-955-6200
www.santafe.org

Santa Fe Chamber of Commerce
8380 Cerrillos Road, Suite 302
Santa Fe, NM 87507
505-988-3279
www.santafechamber.com

Newspaper

New Mexican
202 East Marcy Street
Santa Fe, NM 87501
505-983-3303
www.freenewmexican.com

Albuquerque Journal
328 Galisteo
Santa Fe, NM 87501
505-988-8881
www.abqjournal.com/cs

Realty

We do not have a Realtor recommendation for Santa Fe. As an option, check out *www.realtor.com* or *www.homegain.com*. Select a Realtor with both CRS and GRI designations after their names, since it means that these folks have gone the extra mile and are both graduates of the Realtor Institute and Certified Residential Specialists.

34 ▶ Asheville, North Carolina

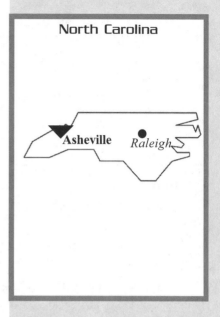

North Carolina

Asheville Raleigh

Asheville at a Glance

Asheville is undoubtedly one of the loveliest towns. It's one of those places where people come to visit, and decide to stay. The Asheville area is having a lasting effect on Hollywood, because so many films are now being shot in its beautiful local scenery. Within a short distance of Asheville is Mount Mitchell, which is the highest point in the United States east of the Mississippi River. More than 10 million visitors make their way along the 469-mile-long Blue Ridge Parkway that cuts through Asheville and the 14 other counties that comprise greater western North Carolina. Asheville is famed for its collection of art deco buildings, left intact in large part because city fathers refused to default on Depression-era debt, earning Asheville the nickname "The City That Suffered Most." The Blue Ridge Parkway, famed for its autumn fireworks and sumptuous twists, should be used whenever possible to get from place to place. Glorious summer brings warm days for outdoor adventures and cool nights for enjoying the hours after dark. Autumn cloaks the Blue Ridge Mountains with every shade of red, orange, and yellow imaginable. You can also enjoy mild winter days in Asheville with easy access to the higher elevations that are dusted in snow.

Possible Drawbacks: Some of the summer days do get quite hot, but it always cools down in the evening. Also, the town is beginning to attract more and more tourist traffic.

▶ Nickname: Land of the Sky

▶ County: Buncombe

▶ Area Code: 828

▶ Population: 68,889

▶ County Population: 206,330

▶ Percent of Population Over 65: 18.3%

▶ Region: Western North Carilina

▶ Closest Metropolitan Area: Greenville, 65 miles

▶ Median Home Price: $125,000

▶ Best Reasons to Retire Here: The best of all possible senior lifestyles for a city of its size, fabulous four-season climate and scenery, and the green mountainous area.

Climate

35° N Latitude 82° W Longitude	Average High Temperature (°F)	Average Low Temperature (°F)	Precipitation (")	Sunshine (%)
January	48.6	24.8	3.1	55
April	69.4	41.9	3.9	66
July	84.4	60.4	4.2	60
October	70.0	42.8	3.9	61
YEAR	68.2	43.0	48.8	59

Utilities

Overview: The overall average cost of living is slightly above the national average of 100 at 103.1. This is mostly because of housing at 112.4. Transportation is also high, at 106.7. The cost of food is at the national average while utilities are low at 96.5 and healthcare is quite low at 90.9.

Gas Company: North Carolina Natural Gas Corporation is a division of Piedmont Natural Gas Company (800-275-6264; *www.ncng.com*).

Electric Company: Progress Energy (800-452-2777; *www.progress-energy.com*)

Phone Company: BellSouth (888-757-6500; *www.bellsouth.com*) provides both local and long-distance phone service to the Asheville area.

Water/Sewer Company: City of Asheville Water Resources Department (828-251-1122; *www.ci.asheville.nc.us/water/services.htm*)

Cable Company: Charter Communications (800-955-7766)

The Tax Axe

Car Registration: The Division of Motor Vehicles (919-715-7000; *www.ncdot.org/DMV*) has all the information you need to register your vehicle.

Driver's License: The Division of Motor Vehicles (919-715-7000; *www.ncdot.org/DMV*) requires new residents to get a driver's license within 30 days. Both vision and written tests are required. The license is issued for five years at a fee of $3.05 per year.

Sales Tax: The state tax is 4.5 percent. The county is 2.5 percent, for a total of 7 percent.

State Income Tax: The accelerated income tax ranges from 6 to 8.25 percent.

Retirement Income Tax: Social Security is exempt. Government pensions are exempt up to $6,400. Private pensions are exempt up to $2,000. Certain military retirees are permanently exempt.

Property Tax: Property is appraised at 100 percent of its value. The amount of Homestead and over 65 exemption depends on income compared to the value of the property.

Local Real Estate

Overview: In a recent study, the American Associated of Retired Persons identified 15 towns that are the best for Baby Boomers who are looking to revitalize their lives, and Asheville was high on the list. Asheville also made a recent list of cities for buying a second home, because the properties, while still at good prices, have increased by 10 percent or more per year for the last five years.

Average price of a three-bedroom/two-bath home: $188,600

Average price of a two-bedroom condo: $103,251

Common Housing Styles: Houses typically have 2 bedrooms and 3 bathrooms, sit on level ground, have an attached garage, and have a fireplace in the living room. Lots are generally large, most houses have basements, and almost all have gardens.

Rental Market: Rent costs are extremely competitive with other cities. The apartment vacancy rate runs around 9 percent.

Average rent for a two-bedroom apartment: $650 per month

Communities Popular With Retirees: Grove Park, Lakeview Park, Biltmore-Forest, Biltmore Park, and Reems Creek in Weaverville

Nearby Areas to Consider: Brevard, in the mountains to the south along the Blue Ridge Parkway, has arts, music, and the surrounding majestic mountains, which have 250 waterfalls. Balsam Mountain Preserve, to the west, is an exclusive residential community. Less than 10 miles away are the mountain towns of Waynesville, Dillsboro, and Sylva, each with its own classic Main Street charm.

Earning a Living

Business Climate: Businesses that elect to move their operations to Asheville clearly have quality of life in mind. Residents enjoy the availability of numerous local resources, and at the end of the day they face little traffic and congestion. Instead, they can sit outside, enjoy the Great Smokies and the cool, clean, mountain air.

Help in Starting a Business: The Asheville Small Business and Technology Development Center (828-251-6025) has the primary focus of providing management counseling to established firms, high-growth companies, and later-stage start-up businesses. Score Counselors to America's Small Business Asheville Office (828-271-4786) is a national nonprofit association and resource partner with the U.S. Small Business Administration and offers a seasoned source of professional business counseling at no charge for business owners and start-up ventures.

Job Market: The region's major employers include J. Crew Group, K-Mart, Bell-South Telecommunications, BASF Corporation, and Kimberly-Clark Corporation. The local economy continues to diversify and prosper as more corporations relocate to the area.

Medical Care

Memorial Mission Hospital (828-213-1111; *http://missionhospitals.org*) is a 773-bed short-term hospital with many specialties, including cancer, oncology, cardiac care, diabetes services, high blood pressure, cholesterol, and trauma services. Memorial Mission Hospital is the regional medical referral center for the western quarter of North Carolina and parts of several adjoining states. The quality of the medical care is one of the factors in *Modern Maturity* magazine ranking Asheville as one of the Top Five "Most Alive Places to Live." Thoms Rehabilitation Hospital is a 100 bed rehabilitation hospital. Park Ridge Hospital, (828-684-8501; *www.parkridgehospital.org*) is a 103-bed short-term hospital about 11 miles away in Fletcher. The Margaret R. Pardee Memorial Hospital is a 20-bed short-term acility about 21 miles away in Hendersonville.

Services for Seniors

Memorial Mission Hospital offers several quality services and programs for seniors, such as Golden Care, a membership program that provides medical claim filing assistance and predictable out-of-pocket hospital costs. Lifeline is a 24-hour home monitoring service for those who live independently but may need emergency assistance. Health Education Programs help area seniors remain active and well informed about their health. The Buncombe County Council on Aging (828-277-8288; *www.coabc.org*) is a private, nonprofit corporation, providing services to older people.

Continuing Education

The University of North Carolina at Asheville (828-251-6600; *www.unca.edu*) has a full-time enrollment of 2,759. The College for Seniors program has courses that are non-credit, with no tests or grades, and open to all interested adults. Members collaborate with staff to teach, learn, design curricula, and arrange special events. Asheville Buncombe Technical Community College (828-254-1921; www.*abtech.edu*) has a full-time enrollment of 2,728, has continuing education courses built on the concept of lifelong learning and, for convenience, they are offered at a variety of times and locations

Crime and Safety

The reported crime rate is above the national average. The reports of property crimes, per 100,000 people, is 6,647.7 compared to a national average 4,532.5. The violent crime reporting rate is at 979.9 compared to a national average of 496.4.

Getting Around Town

Public Transportation: The Asheville Transit Service (904-389-4949; *www.ci.asheville.nc.us/transit.htm*) provides transportation to all parts of the city of Asheville and the surrounding area, including downtown, the hospitals, schools, malls, universities, and residential areas. The senior citizen fare is 35 cents.

Roads and Highways: Interstate highways 26, 40, and 240. US 19, 23, 25, 70, and 74. State highways 63, 81, and 251. The Blue Ridge Parkway curves through the city.

Airports: Asheville Regional Airport (*www.flyavl.com*) is served by Northwest, Delta, USAirways, and Continental airlines.

Let the Good Times Roll

Recreation: The summer of 2005 marked the 75th anniversary of the Blue Ridge Parkway, one of America's most popular scenic drives. It follows the crest of the mountains for 469 miles and provides access to stunning sights, including Mount Mitchell, the highest peak in the eastern United States. Asheville's varied terrain and mountains makes for exciting cycling. The Bent Creek Experimental Forest is filled with bike trails of various levels of difficulty. Or you can go boating on the river. Relax on a gentle float trip while you soak up the scenery, or get onto a challenging white water run. The minor league baseball team, the Tourists, plays at McCormick Field. Or watch the Asheville Splash, a team of the Women's United Soccer League. For football, there is the Asheville Grizzlies and the women's team the Asheville Assault. The Great Smoky Mountains Railroad offers tours through mountainous terrain and tunnels. Take a ride on a 12-passenger jet boat on Lake Fontana. You will find eight golf courses in and around Asheville.

Culture: The Biltmore House, the nation's largest residence, is located in Asheville. Built in the late 19th century, this French-style, 250-room castle sits on more than 7,500 acres and is open to the public. Your tour will include a visit to the estate's 35-acre gardens, designed by Frederick Olmsted, best known for his role in planning New York City's Central Park. Stroll around downtown Asheville and look at the architecture. Faces look down from intricately designed friezes, since Art deco is everywhere. Other things to see are the North Carolina Arboretum; former home of author Thomas Wolfe; the Western North Carolina Nature Center; and the Folk Art Center on Blue Ridge Parkway, where you'll find handmade mountain crafts made of wood, glass, ceramics and more. In downtown Asheville, and you'll find plenty of opportunities for antique shopping.

Annual Events: In January is the annual Big Band Swing Dance Weekend and the Asheville Fringe Festival of Performing Arts. In March, the Victorian Easter Celebration in Asheville's first mansion and oldest surviving structure, now restored as a history museum. In April is the Festival of Flowers, and Arbor Day Weekend Celebration at the North Carolina Arboretum. The Mountain Sports Festival is held at the end of April. Shakespeare in the Park runs most of June. June 2005 was the 81st annual Singing on the Mountain. The "Singing" is a day-long gathering held out-of-doors in a meadow at the base of Grandfather Mountain. Music begins at 8:30 a.m. and features performances by top Southern Gospel groups. Starting in July, spontaneous jam sessions of mountain music spring up on Saturday night around sundown all through the city plaza. July 2005 was the 50th annual Grandfather Mountain Highland Games and the 58th annual Craft

Fair of Southern Highlights. August 2005 was the 77th annual Mountain Dance and Folk Festival. Also in August, visit the Asheville Quilt Competition and Exhibit and the Asheville Antiques Fair. October has the City Art Walks and the annual Carolina Bonsai Exposition. Many movies are shot around Asheville, and the Asheville film festival is in October.

When the Grandkids Come: The Tweetsie Railroad is Carolina's original theme park. Pan for gold, visit the deer, and ride on the amusement park rides. Several nationally known puppet artists have created the Asheville Puppetry Alliance and perform at the Diana Wortham Theatre.

More Information

Municipal

Asheville Area Chamber of Commerce
P.O. Box 1010
Asheveille, NC 28802
800-257-1300
www.exploreasheville.com

Newspaper

Asheville Citizen-Times
14 O'Henry Avenue
Asheville, NC 28801
828-252-5611
www.citizen-times.com

Realty

We do not have a Realtor recommendation for Asheville. As an option, check out *www.realtor.com* or *www.homegain.com.* Select a Realtor with both CRS and GRI designations after their names, since it means that these folks have gone the extra mile and are both graduates of the Realtor Institute and Certified Residential Specialists.

Raleigh, North Carolina

35 ▶

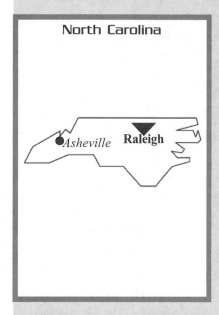

North Carolina

Asheville   Raleigh

Raleigh at a Glance

Raleigh is becoming one of America's most talked-about cities, located in one of the South's most intriguing areas. It is overflowing with history, culture, and natural beauty. The city is filled with majestic oaks, magnolias, dogwoods, and azaleas. The area around this city of gardens is filled with 156 beautiful parks and lakes. Raleigh is the capital of North Carolina, and is the largest city in the metropolitan area known as the Triangle, which has a population quickly approaching the 1 million mark. Visitors to the Greater Raleigh area can experience first-hand why, in a pair of recent national studies, the Triangle was named the number one place in America to live and do business. An interesting historical fact: The first English attempts at colonization in the New World, sponsored by Sir Walter Raleigh in 1585, were at this location and was named Fort Raleigh. Although the colony prospered for a number of years, it ended with the complete disappearance of 116 men, women, and children. The fate of this "lost colony" remains a mystery to this day.

Possible Drawbacks: Much of the Southern charm is in the history rather than in lots of activities. And the entire area is quite populous, so if you are looking for a rural lifestyle, you will be a bit crowded.

▶ Nickname: The City of Oaks

▶ County: Wake

▶ Area Code: 919

▶ Population: 276,093

▶ County Population: 627,846

▶ Percent of Population Over 65: 8.3%

▶ Region: Central North Carolina

▶ Closest Metropolitan Area: Durham, 23 miles

▶ Median Home Price: $164,200

▶ Best Reasons to Retire Here: The medical care is outstanding and the scenery is beautiful.

Climate

35° N Latitude 78° W Longitude	Average High Temperature (°F)	Average Low Temperature (°F)	Precipitation (")	Sunshine (%)
January	50.7°	30.2	3.7	52
April	72.7	47.5	3.0	63
July	88.7	67.5	4.2	60
October	72.9	49.3	3.1	60
YEAR	71.4	49.1	45.3	58

Utilities

Overview: The cost of living is above average at 114.9 where the national average is 100. This is primarily because of housing costs at 146. Healthcare is at 102.1 and utilities are at 108.3. Food at 99.5 and transportation at 89.5 are both below average.

Gas Company: North Carolina Natural Gas Corporation, a division of Piedmont Natural Gas Company (800-275-6264; *www.ncng.com*)

Electric Company: Progress Energy (800-452-2777; *www.progress-energy.com*)

Phone Company: BellSouth (888-757-6500; *www.bellsouth.com*)

Water/Sewer Company: City of Raleigh Water/Sewer Service (919-890-3245; *www.raleighnc.gov*)

Cable Company: Time Warner Cable (866-489-2669; *www.timewarnercable.com*)

The Tax Axe

Car Registration: The license is issued for 5 years at a fee of $3.05 per year. License plates must be purchased within 30 days. The city of Raleigh's vehicle decal fee is $15 per vehicle.

Driver's License: The Division of Motor Vehicles (919-715-7000; *www.ncdot.org/ DMV*) requires new residents to get a driver's license within 30 days. Both vision and written tests are required.

Sales Tax: State 4.5 percent. The county is 2.5 percent, for a total of 7 percent.

State Income Tax: The accelerated income tax ranges from 6 to 8.25 percent.

Retirement Income Tax: Social Security is exempt. Government pensions are exempt up to $6,400. Private pensions are exempt up to $2,000. Certain military retirees are permanently exempt.

Property Tax: Each year the city council establishes a tax rate that is used to establish property taxes for the next fiscal year. The 2005 tax rate for Wake County was $0.604 for each $100 in value. The city tax rate was $0.395 per $100 valuation.

Local Real Estate

Overview: The higher income in the Raleigh area has helped fuel a strong housing market, and prices are well above the national average. The area offers something for everyone. Wake County is a unique mix of urban and rural areas, medium-sized cities, and small towns. A house sells in two to three months. The number of higher priced houses above $400,000 is increasing, causing the average housing cost figure to move up.

Average price of a three-bedroom/two-bath home: $197,770

Average price of a two-bedroom condo: $130,438

Common Housing Styles: You can find almost any style. Ranches and two-story houses are both popular. Closer into town you will find older Victorians, while further out you find houses with brick exteriors and patios, decks, European kitchens, and split-level floor plans.

Rental Market: The area is growing rapidly, and this normally puts pressure on the availability of rental properties. But Raleigh, with a vacancy rate at or above 10 percent, rents remain favorable. Another factor is the large college population, so there is a seasonal demand for apartments.

Average rent for a two-bedroom apartment: $715 per month

Communities Popular With Retirees: Cary, Durham, and Chapel Hill

Nearby Areas to Consider: Chapel Hill, centered around the University of North Carolina, is the largest municipality in Orange County and has been nicknamed the "Southern Part of Heaven," having the best of small-town living in a unique cosmopolitan environment. High Point, the "Home Furnishings Capital of the World," is home to the International Home Furnishings Market held each April and October. High Point also boasts more than 125 furniture plants, over 60 retail discount furniture stores, great golf, and many lake recreation opportunities.

Earning a Living

Business Climate: The area is growing in almost every way, so business opportunities are there. Raleigh is an excellent place for small and home-based businesses, as well as being excellent for corporate relocations. While the high technology of Research Triangle Park gets a lot of the attention, North Carolina State University's Centennial Campus has also lured major corporate relocations and generated thousands of local jobs. Centennial Campus is a unique technology community that blends public, academic, and private sector research, and is the only public-private partnership of its kind.

Help in Starting a Business: Wake Technical Community College's Small Business Center (919-851-5193; *www.waketech.edu*) has a small business consulting service that offers seminars and business education with the local SCORE. Raleigh SCORE (*www.raleighscore.org*) has executives ready to help in planning, managing, purchasing, franchising, and more. The North Carolina Small Business and Technology Development Center (919-715-7272; *www.sbtdc.org*) helps small business owners, and those interested in starting a business, meet the challenges of today's business environment.

Job Market: Each year in Raleigh and Wake County, thousands of new jobs are created, providing a wide range of opportunities for employment and advancement. Raleigh and the Triangle are world leaders in knowledge-based industries, and the region is home to major employers in numerous fields.

Medical Care

The Triangle area ranks sixth in the number of physicians per capita nationwide. WakeMed (919-350-8000; *www.wakemed.com*) is a 752-bed private, nonprofit healthcare system with a network of medical centers, ambulatory care centers, outpatient facilities, and other health resources. It has been named by *Modern Maturity* magazine as having one of the Top 10 cardiovascular surgery programs and one of the Top 50 hospitals in the nation. Rex Healthcare (919-784-3100; *www.rexhealth.com*) is a private, nonprofit healthcare system that has provided superior care to Wake County and the surrounding area since 1894. The Rex Hospital campus is the heart of the network of services, including a 394-bed acute-care hospital, cancer center, convalescent care center, same day surgery center, heart and vascular center, and wellness center. Duke Health Raleigh Hospital (919-954-3000; *www.dukehealthraleigh.org*), previously known as Raleigh Community Hospital, is now a member of the Duke University Health System family.

Services for Seniors

The Retired Senior Volunteer Program (919-831-6295) provides volunteer placement for retired citizens who want to contribute their time and talents in service to others. The Retired Senior Volunteer Program (919)-831-6295; *www.seniorcorps.org*) is part of Senior Corps, a network of national service programs that provides older Americans the opportunity to apply their life experiences to meeting community needs. The North Carolina Senior Games, the SilverLiners, SilverStriders, and the SilverClassic all provide opportunities for seniors to get physical activity and companionship.

Continuing Education

The area has a number of colleges, offering continuing education in one form or another. North Carolina State University has the McKimmon Center for Extension and Continuing Education (919-515-3373; *www.mckimmon.ncsu.edu*) and is certified to award Continuing Education Units by the International Association for Continuing Education and Training. Shaw University (800-214-6683; *www.shawuniversity.edu*), founded in 1865, is the oldest historically black college of the South, and is a private, coeducational, liberal arts university affiliated with the Baptist Church. It offers a number of continuing education programs. St. Augustine's College (800-948-1126; *www.st-aug.edu*) is a private, accredited, historically black, coeducational college. Meredith's College (919-7608600; *www.meredith.edu*) is an independent private women's college. Peace College (800-732-2347; *www.peace.edu*) is a baccalaureate college for women. Wake

Technical Community College (919-662-3500; *www.waketech.edu*) offers, in addition to its continuing education program, several degrees online.

Crime and Safety

Reported incidents of property crime per 100,000 people is above average at 6,196.8 compared to the national average of 4,532.5. Also, reported violent crimes reporting is above average at 826.3 compared to the national average of 496.4.

Getting Around Town

Public Transportation: Capital Area Transit provides extensive bus service throughout the city. Accessible Raleigh Transport provides subsidized door-to-door transportation service through participating taxi companies within a 3/4 mile boundary of CAT fixed routes. The trolleys are bus replicas of the streetcars that traveled the streets of Raleigh until 1932.

Roads and Highways: Interstate 40, 85, and 95; US 1, 64, 70, 401; State 50 and 51

Airports: The Raleigh-Durham International Airport (*www.rdu.com*) is about 11 miles from the city, and is served by nine major airlines and 12 regional carriers.

Let the Good Times Roll

Recreation: Several parks and lakes offer fishing, biking, hiking, canoeing, rowboating, and picnicking. The William B. Umstead State Park also offers horseback riding. Lake Johnson is known for its large mouth bass and crappie fishing, and has a 300-acre park. Lake Wheeler is contained within an 800-acre park. The Tar Heel Regatta is held each spring, and bass tournaments are held throughout the summer. Shelley Lake is a 50-acre lake. Falls Lake State Recreation Area has a 12,000-acre lake and 26,000 acres of forest. Jordan Lake Recreation Area has nine individual recreation areas. Dead Broke Farm and J&H Stables have horseback riding on the scenic trail rides of Raleigh. The Pullen Aquatic Center is an Olympic-sized pool, and Millbrook Exchange Tennis Center features 23 lighted, hard surface courts. In addition, Raleigh offers the Wake County Speedway and the Capital City Bicycle Motorcross Race Track. Also available are the Fred G. Bond Metro Park, Durant Nature Park, Hemlock Bluff's Nature Preserve, Raleigh Municipal Rose Garden, the J.C. Raulston Arboretum, Pullen Park, the North Carolina State University Solar House, and the Historic Tours of Raleigh.

Culture: The Alltel Pavilion presents concerts, and the BTI Center for the Performing Arts presents opera and ballet. The long list of museums include the Raleigh City Museum, the North Carolina Museum of Art, the North Carolina Museum of Natural Sciences, the North Carolina Museum of History, Mordecai Historic Park, Artspace, the African American Cultural Complex, the North Carolina Sports Hall of Fame, and Wake Forest College Birthplace Museum.

Annual Events: In January is the Antique Extravaganza. In February is the Run for the Roses, a 5K race. March brings the North Carolina Renaissance Faire. In April is the Umstead 100 Mile Endurance Run and the Great Raleigh Road Race. In May is the Brookhill Steeplechase. July has the Farmers Market Festival. August brings the Jimmy V Celebrity Golf Classic. With September comes the Eurosport Fall Soccer Showcase. October is the North Carolina State Fair. In November there are many performances of *The Nutcracker* and December brings the annual production of *A Christmas Carol.*

When the Grandkids Come: The Triangle Metro Zoo, Adventure Landing, Hill Ridge Farms, Playspace, Silver Lake Waterpark, and Bullwinkle's Family Food 'N Fun, are all great options for the kids. The Dream Sports Center offers classes, clinics, camps, and facilities for baseball, soccer, roller hockey, and lacrosse.

More Information

Municipal

Greater Raleigh Convention & Visitors Bureau
421 Fayetteville Street Mall, Suite 1505
Raleigh, NC 27601
800-849-8499
www.visitraleigh.com

Newspaper

The News and Observer
215 South McDowell Street
P.O. Box 191
Raleigh, NC 27602
919-829-4500
www.newsobserver.com

Realty

We do not have a Realtor recommendation for Raleigh. As an option, check out *www.realtor.com* or *www.homegain.com.* Select a Realtor with both CRS and GRI designations after their names, since it means that these folks have gone the extra mile and are both graduates of the Realtor Institute and Certified Residential Specialists.

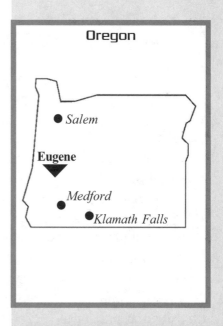

Oregon

• Salem

Eugene

▼

• Medford

• Klamath Falls

Eugene, Oregon

36 ▶

Eugene at a Glance

The laid-back living style is noticeable right away, which causes many visitors to change their plans and stay! Eugene is a college town. The Pacific Ocean is one hour in one direction, and the Cascade Mountains are one hour in the other, so you can experience the best of both worlds. Eugene is at the southern end of the Willamette Valley, and is known for biking, walking, hiking, and jogging. Eugene is Oregon's third largest city. It covers approximately 41.5 square miles, and the Willamette River runs through the heart of the city, with the McKenzie River joining the Willamette River at the north end of town. The elevation is 426 feet above sea level. The city's topography features are Skinner Butte to the north of downtown and Spencer Butte to the south, creating a nice protected area for the city. The city is known for a mix of art, culture, education, scenic attractions, and a passion for recreation. Eugene is also noted as being a home to alternative lifestyles, and reminders of the 1960s and 1970s can be seen throughout the city.

Possible Drawbacks: Medical costs are well above average. Air pollution is historically a problem for the area because of traditional industry, but that seems to be changing.

▶ Nickname: Green Eugene
▶ County: Lane
▶ Area Code: 541
▶ Population: 137,893
▶ County Population: 322,959
▶ Percent of Population Over 65: 12.1%
▶ Region: Western Oregon
▶ Closest Metropolitan Area: Portland, 110 miles
▶ Median Home Price: $178,500
▶ Best Reasons to Retire Here: Slow and easy lifestyle, mountain and ocean area, with great education opportunities.

Climate

44 °N Latitude 123 °W Longitude	Average High Temperature (°F)	Average Low Temperature (°F)	Precipitation (")	Sunshine (%)
January	46.4	35.1	7.4	28
April	60.4	40.5	3.1	52
July	81.7	52.7	0.4	69
October	64.6	43.3	3.3	44
YEAR	63.1	43.3	46.6	48

Utilities

Overview: The overall cost of living is above the national average of 100 at 109.8. Housing is at 122 and health care is at 122. Transportation is 115. Food costs are at the national average, while utilities are quite low at 70.9.

Gas Company: Northwest Natural Gas (800-422-4012; *www.nwnatural.com*) provides natural gas to the Eugene area.

Electric Company: Water/Electric Board (541-484-2411; *www.eweb.org*) is owned and operated by the city of Eugene.

Phone Company: Qwest (800-491-0118; *www.qwest.com*)

Water/Sewer Company: Water/Electric Board (541-484-2411; *www.eweb.org*)

Cable Company: There is no information currently available.

The Tax Axe

Car Registration: The Oregon Department of Transportation (503-945-5000; *http://egov.oregon.gov*) requires an emissions test and a VIN certification to register a car.

Driver's License: For a driver's license, those over 50 are required to take a vision test. Contact the Oregon Department of Transportation (503-945-5000; *http://egov.oregon.gov*) for more information.

Sales Tax: There is no sales tax in Oregon.

State Income Tax: Oregon State income tax ranges from 5 to 9 percent.

Retirement Income Tax: Your pension income, along with all other income regardless of the source, will be taxed by Oregon. Depending on your age and income, you may be entitled to a retirement income credit on your Oregon return.

Property Tax: Assessments are based on a percentage of market value (referred to as *assessed value*). Real property is constitutionally restrained to no more than a 3 percent annual growth in assessed value, and property values in Eugene have been growing faster than that. The county's permanent tax rate is $1.28 per $1,000 in property value. The city of Eugene is at $7.

Local Real Estate

Overview: Eugene is considered to be one of the Top 10 locations in the nation for a second home because of the setting and the availability of lower priced houses. Eugene was at the slow end of the annualized home appreciation in 2002, but since then prices have firmed up. The population of Eugene is now increasing. New employment is causing prices to rise. In 2005, prices were up 10 to 15 percent over the previous year. Houses are on the market less than 30 days.

Average price of a three-bedroom/two-bath home: $204,000

Average price of a two-bedroom condo: $130,000

Common Housing Styles: Houses are built with large windows and skylights to allow light, which can be important in the winter. Contemporary and ranch houses are common.

Rental Market: With the increase in population, and increased enrollment in the local university, rental conditions are tight in the Eugene-Springfield area. Vacancy rates of 3 percent or below are common. A low level of new multi-family construction has also contributed to the tight rental market.

Average rent for a two-bedroom apartment: $700 per month

Communities Popular With Retirees: Springfield and Cresswell

Nearby Areas to Consider: Springfield is the sister city to Eugene. Springfield is the gateway to the McKenzie River National Recreation Area, and there are many outdoor recreation opportunities. Corvallis home of Oregon State University. In 2004, Harvard Business Review placed Corvallis 15th in the nation for creativity. *Men's Journal* magazine voted Corvallis "the 8th best place in the nation to live."

Earning a Living

Business Climate: The population of Eugene is growing because of large employers moving into the area, so a booming economy for retail and services should follow. While this will help the overall economy, it could tighten the job market and raise salaries.

Help in Starting a Business: The Oregon Small Business Development Center Network Office (541-463.5250; *www.bizcenter.org*) has trained business counselors and staff, and has helped thousands of Oregonians with their small business endeavors. The Lane Community College Business Development Center (541-463-5255; *www.lanebdc.com*) holds a "Going Into Business" Series every term. The 10 week class covers the A-to-Zs of owning and operating a small business.

Job Market: Big employers are moving in and the population is increasing to fill jobs. Projections call for 15 percent employment increase by 2014.

Medical Care

Sacred Heart Medical Center is a 432-bed short-term hospital, and the largest between Portland and San Francisco. Key services include cardiology, rehabilitation, adult intensive care, newborn intensive care, orthopedics, neurology, and general surgery. The hospital also provides outpatient services ranging from physical therapy to home health and hospice, and emergency care in a Level II Trauma Center. McKenzie-Willamette Hospital (541-726-4400; *www.mckweb.com*) is a 114-bed hospital about seven miles away in Springfield. The McKenzie-Williamette program called Active Advantage, for those 50 and older, is an extensive senior discount membership program with the specific needs of seniors in mind. The program includes health screenings and seminars, and the discounts extend to local merchants. Lane County Psychiatric Hospital is a 15-bed psychiatric hospital.

Services for Seniors

Eugene houses a number of social services of a caliber usually found only in very large cities. The services range from information referral, senior centers, escort transportation, and in-home counseling, to delivered meals and home health care. With focus on community-based care, assistance is also available to assess an individual's need for institutional care. Help can even be obtained for those within institutions who have the desire and the capacity to return to a less-restricting setting. Your contact for all of these services is through the Lane Council of Governments (541-682-4435; *www.lcog.org*).

Continuing Education

The University of Oregon (541-346-1000; *www.uoregon.edu*), with an enrollment of close to 20,000, has academic programs, professional development programs, and other lifelong learning programs for seniors. It offers distance education and a Community Education Program, which provides access to credit courses without formal admission to the university. There is no charge to Oregon residents 65 years of age and older. Charges may be made for any special materials. Lane Community College (*www.lanecc.edu*), with an enrollment of 5,900, is closely tied to the community and offers a number of services. The reduced tuition benefit for senior citizens has been discontinued, but they offer distance learning courses online for anyone who finds it difficult to attend on-campus classes.

Crime and Safety

The number of violent crimes reported each year is 546.5 per 100,000 people, which is slightly above the national average of 496.4. The number of reported property crimes is 8,466.9, which is well above the national average of 4,532.5.

Getting Around Town

Public Transportation: Lane Transit District (800-248-3861; *www.ltd.org*) offers a full bus system throughout the city. Their EZ Access program offers an array of products and services to senior citizens and people with disabilities.

Roads and Highways: Interstate 5 and 105; US 58 and 99; Route 126

Airports: The Eugene Airport, Mahlon Sweet Field (541-682-5430; *www.eugeneairport.com*) is the fifth-largest airport in the Pacific Northwest. It is served by four air carriers: America West Express, Horizon Air, Delta Connection, and United Express.

Let the Good Times Roll

Recreation: Rated as one of the Top 10 cycling cities, Eugene has miles of biking, walking, and jogging paths. The paths are built along the Willamette River, through parks and gardens, and even next to shopping centers. Canoes and kayaks can be rented for a pleasant day boating on the Willamette River. For picnicking, camping, swimming, water-skiing, or sailing, Fern Ridge Lake is just outside of town. Fern Ridge Lake is also great for anglers, supplying trout, crappie, bass, and catfish in the spring. If you prefer white-water rafting, Eugene is close to the McKenzie River, with class II and III rapids. Located in the heart of downtown Eugene, the Hult Center theater cluster is surrounded by wonderful galleries and restaurants. Many of the downtown restaurants offer substantial discounts to Hult Center ticket holders. The Eugene Saturday Market is the oldest weekly open air crafts festival with more than 300 artisans selling handcrafted goods. Eugene's University of Oregon, a member of the PAC-10 athletic conference, provides a variety of sports events, frequently world-class, for everyone's entertainment during each season.

Culture: The Hult Center for the Performing Arts is host to eight resident companies including the Dance Theatre of Oregon, the Eugene Ballet Company, Eugene Concert Choir, Eugene Opera, and the Eugene Symphony Orchestra. The Hult Center attracts top name performers from around the world. The Oregon Bach Festival has grown out of the university and is now held in the Hult Center every summer.

Annual Events: June brings the Oregon Bach Festival. July is the Oregon Country Fair, which has been described as having a "primitive ecotopian atmosphere." The Oregon Festival of Music is held in July and August. The Saturday Market is held April through November. Contact the chamber of commerce for a complete listing of community events.

When the Grandkids Come: The Science Factory Children's Museum & Planetarium is dedicated to playful learning, scientific exploration, and hands-on/minds-on activity. At the National Oregon Trail Interpretive Center museum there is a very large rattlesnake and a big ox. Kids can dress up, visit the theater, or hike on trails.

More Information

Municipal

Eugene Area Chamber of Commerce
1401 Willamette Street
Eugene, OR 97401
541-484-1314
www.eugenechamber.com

Convention & Visitors Association of Lane County Oregon
754 Olive Street
Eugene, OR 97401
541-484-5307
www.cvalco.org

Newspaper

The Register-Guard
P.O. Box 10188
Eugene, OR 97440
541-485-1234
www.cvalco.org

Realty

We do not have a Realtor recommendation for Eugene. As an option, check out *www.realtor.com* or *www.homegain.com.* Select a Realtor with both CRS and GRI designations after their names, since it means that these folks have gone the extra mile and are both graduates of the Realtor Institute and Certified Residential Specialists.

37 Klamath Falls, Oregon

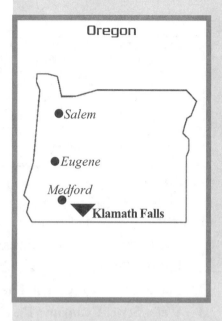

Klamath Falls at a Glance

Klamath Falls sits on the southern shore of Upper Klamath Lake, and is on the eastern slopes of the Cascade Mountains. While Oregon is often known for rain, the Klamath Falls region enjoys nearly 300 days of sunshine each year. Just 60 miles south of Crater Lake, and 70 miles north of Mt. Shasta, south central Oregon is unsurpassed for beauty and diversity of activities. From class IV white-water rafting on the Klamath River, to the Ross Ragland Theatre, to spelunking in the Lava Beds National Park, to the largest northern United States population of wintering bald eagles, the region boasts landscapes, climates, and activities for you and your family that are dramatically varied. Klamath Falls has scenic beauty teeming with wildlife. There are mountain lakes and rivers renowned for fishing. There are four distinct seasons, yet the weather is mild because of the 4,340-foot altitude and the abundant sunshine. Most of the precipitation falls as snow in the middle of winter. The real estate is cheaper, and the climate is drier and sunnier, than the Oregon towns west of the Cascade Mountains.

Possible Drawbacks: The rural lifestyle. It may be too rural and too remote for those more accustomed to an urban lifestyle. The altitude is rather high and the thin air may irritate breathing problems in some.

▶ Nickname: City of Sunshine
▶ County: Klamath
▶ Area Code: 541
▶ Population: 19,315
▶ County Population: 63,775
▶ Percent of Population Over 65: 12.8%
▶ Region: Southern Oregon
▶ Closest Metropolitan Area: Portland, 235 miles
▶ Median Home Price: $123,000
▶ Best Reasons to Retire Here: Rural lifestyle, beautiful settings, relaxed, outdoor activities, four distinct seasons with generally mild weather.

Climate

42° N Latitude 121° W Longitude	Average High Temperature (°F)	Average Low Temperature (°F)	Precipitation (")	Sunshine (%)
January	38.7	20.3	1.8	52
April	57.9	31.1	0.8	69
July	84.6	50.7	0.3	85
October	63.7	34.3	1.0	72
YEAR	60.6	34.3	13.3	68

Utilities

Overview: Klamath Falls is just below the national average in cost of living with an index of 99.6 compared to a national average of 100.

Gas Company: Avista Utilities (800-227-9187; *www.avistautilities.com*)

Electric Company: Avista Utilities (800-227-9187; *www.avistautilities.com*)

Phone Company: Oregon Telecom (541-779-7004; *www.oregontelecom.com*)

Water/Sewer Company: The city's water supply (541-883-5383; *www.ci.klamath-falls.or.us*) comes from deep isolated aquifers that are free of impurities or contaminates that are typically present in surface water systems.

Cable Company: Charter Communications (541-884-6880; *www.charterlink.net*)

The Tax Axe

Car Registration: To register a car in Oregon, you will need emissions test and VIN certification. Contact the Department of Motor Vehicles for more information (*http://egov.oregon.gov/ODOT/DMV*).

Driver's License: License and registration are required immediately on establishing residency. Contact the Department of Motor Vehicles for more information (*http://egov.oregon.gov/ODOT/DMV*).

Sales Tax: There is no sales tax in the state of Oregon.

State Income Tax: Oregon State income tax ranges from 5 percent to 9 percent.

Retirement Income Tax: Your pension income, along with all other income regardless of the source, will be taxed by Oregon. Depending on your age and income, you may be entitled to a retirement income credit on your Oregon return.

Property Tax: The property tax rates and assessments are limited by voter referenda. The maximum is $15 per $1,000 of assessed value, and assessed values are limited to a 3 percent increase per year, with some exceptions. This limit does not include local levies, and the overall property taxes are higher inside the city limits of Klamath Falls.

Local Real Estate

Overview: Several areas within a 30 minute drive of Klamath Falls offer mountain and lake living in homes with smaller acreage. Starting in the late 1990s, many retirees, second-home buyers, and cyber-commuters have moved into Klamath Falls, a situation that has created a great deal of growth in upper and custom home developments. The opening of Running Y Ranch in 1997 was a key to the discovery of Klamath Falls by retirees, especially from California. This upper-end growth has generated developers' interest in the area, and plans for several neighborhoods are in the design/approval stage.

Average price of a three-bedroom/two-bath home: $140,000

Average price of a two-bedroom condo: $102,900

Common Housing Styles: The styles of homes vary. The more vintage areas around downtown have many classic homes. Suburban areas include both new and older developments with many one-level ranch style homes.

Rental Market: A two bedroom house rents for $500 to $600, but there is a low vacancy rate and good rentals are hard to find.

Average rent for a two-bedroom apartment: $550 per month

Communities Popular With Retirees: Try Keno for open spaces, or Rocky Point and Chiloquin for a rural atmosphere.

Nearby Areas to Consider: Many retirees want one-level ranch style homes, and these are available in all suburban areas, and some of these neighborhoods have great views. A number of new development areas are in the works, or opening up, within the urban growth boundary of Klamath Falls, and these provide easy access to services.

Earning a Living

Business Climate: Oregon-based businesses enjoy financial benefits designed to make running a company easier and more successful. The Oregon compensation rate has lowered every year for the past 12, and is now 65 percent lower than California's. There's no sales tax, inventory tax, state business, or occupations tax. Energy costs are also low. Oregon is in the lowest 25 percent of overall business costs in the nation.

Help in Starting a Business: The Klamath Falls BizCenter (541-885-1760; *www.bizcenter.org*) provides practical information for your business success. The Klamath County Economic Development Association (541-882-9600; *www.sobusi.com/kceda*) is a private, nonprofit corporation chartered to foster and develop responsible industrial activities in the Klamath Region.

Job Market: The town is small, so the number of jobs is also small. It would be best to seek employment before you move here.

Medical CAre

The Merle West Medical Center is a 176-bed hospital, with a full range of services including cancer and heart centers. It has a family practice residency center, and a kidney dialysis center. There are a number of general and specialty clinics, as well as urgent-care facilities, throughout the city. Two regional healthcare facilities are located in nearby Medford.

Services for Seniors

Rogue Klamath River Adventures provides rafting trips for today's adventurous and energetic seniors. The Klamath Falls Multiple Service Office (800-442-0341) has services for seniors and people with disabilities. The Senior Citizen's Council (541-883-7171) provides transportation, hot meals, home delivered meals, and social activities for seniors mostly on low, fixed incomes.

Continuing Education

The Oregon Institute of Technology offers associate, undergraduate, and graduate degree programs at the main campus in Klamath Falls. The Klamath Community College (541-882-3521; www.kcc.cc.or.us) is a small two-year public college with half the students attending part time. Southern Oregon University (541-552-7672; www.sou.edu) is located in Ashland, 70 miles to the west, and offers the Continuing Education Unit, which was designed to award credit for short programs of education.

Crime and Safety

Klamath Falls reported a crime instance of 4198.49 per 100,000 people, compared to the national average of 4,118.8.

Getting Around Town

Public Transportation: A shuttle bus (541-883-2609) links Klamath Falls with the nearby communities of Lakeview, Bly, Beatty, and Dairy. You need to call for times and reservations. The city is also served by Amtrak (www.amtrak.com).

Roads and Highways: Highway 97, Oregon Highways 140 and 39

Airports: The Klamath Falls Airport and Kingsley Field (541-883-5372; www.klamathfallsairport.com) is served by Horizon Airlines with several non-stop flights to Portland. Rogue Valley International, about 76 miles away, serves the city of Medford and is served by four airlines with approximately 56 flights a day.

Let the Good Times Roll

Recreation: The 300 days of sunshine each year invites you outside, and makes it easy to schedule activities. Rafting the Klamath River is like visiting a playground overflowing with amazing white-water. The incredibly blue water of Crater Lake is truly inspiring. At 1,932 feet deep, it is the deepest lake in the country, and the seventh deepest in the world. Currently, 21 caves have been opened for spelunkers at the Lava Beds National Monument. These lava tubes include Hopkins Chocolate, named for the rich chocolate glaze covering the ceilings; and Skull Ice Cave, named for the ice chamber, which has a large ice floor, and the skulls of bighorn sheep once found at its entrance. Big Painted Cave and Symbol Bridge contain some of the best examples of pictographs in the area. Upper Klamath Lake is the largest lake in Oregon. The 25-mile-long lake is the best bird-watching area in the state. The Klamath Basin has six National Wildlife Refuge Areas. The Klamath Basin Snowdrifters are a nonprofit organization is for promoting snow-mobiling and trail grooming in southern Oregon.

Culture: The Ross Ragland Theater is a visual and performing arts center committed to providing culturally diverse events and related educational opportunities. Klamath Falls has several fine museums. The Favell Museum has an extensive collection of Indian artifacts and western art. The Klamath County Museum has exhibits depicting the history of the Klamath area. Exhibits range from fossils, geology, minerals, and wildlife of the area, to exploration and the hardships of settlement. The Baldwin Hotel Museum offers a depiction of the general history of the area back to 1911. The Klamath Tribes Museum, about 22 miles north, has exhibits on artifacts, baskets, and historical items of the Klamath and Modoc Indian tribes.

Annual Events: The Crater Lake Rim Run at Crater Lake National Park is held in June. The Downtown Walkabout is held in August, where you can enjoy art of all types, street music of classical, blues, rock, and bongo beats. There are children's activities, dancers, refreshments, and wine and beer tasting. Each August is the Annual Civil War Days and Old Fashioned Country Faire at the Fort Klamath Military Post. The annual Blues, Brats, and Brews is held at the Klamath Yacht Club with a German bratwurst dinner, Basin Microbrews, and Blues Music. It is a charity for Hospice Children's Bereavement Camp.

When the Grandkids Come: If you are up to it, there is a jet-boat service at the KOA Campground. There's also the Children's Museum of Klamath Falls, an outdoor experience for young and old to share. And if you haven't grown tired of it yet, take the kids out to Crater Lake. The lake is beautiful in every season! If the weather requires you to keep them indoors, check out the Northwest Youth Theater (*www.nwyouththeatre.org*) for performance and class schedules.

More Information

Municipal

Klamath County Chamber of Commerce
706 Main Street
Klamath Falls, OR 97601
541-884-5193
www.klamath.org

Newspaper

The Herald & News
P.O. Box 788
Klamath Falls, OR 97601
541-885-4410
www.heraldandnews.com

Realty

Sherry McManus
3815 South Sixth Street
Klamath Falls, OR 97603
541-884-1343
www.soldonklamath.com

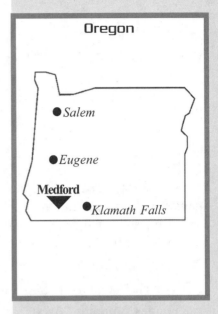

Oregon

● *Salem*

● *Eugene*

Medford
● *Klamath Falls*

Medford at a Glance

Medford, the center of Rogue Valley, is famous in the United States for its succulent pears. Bosc, Comice, d'Anjou, Bartlett, and Winter Nellis pears are all grown in Medford. Medford is about midway between Portland and San Francisco. Medford is just 27 miles north of the California border, 118 miles east of the Pacific Ocean, and 75 miles west of Klamath Falls. The economy is centered on agriculture and timber products, and you will see miles and miles of fruit and timber trees in the area. Medford is also in a central location to access recreational areas such as the Oregon Caves National Monument and the Rogue River Valley. There are five covered bridges in the Medford area. Bear Creek is the site of two city parks with nature trails, bike paths, and picnic areas. Crater Lake National Park, just 80 miles northeast of Medford, is the deepest lake in the United States. Oregon Caves National Monument is located 80 miles southwest of Medford. You can spend your days fishing, golfing, skiing, hiking, exploring the mountains, or lounging on the coast. You can relax and enjoy the beautiful scenery, wildlife, and tranquility, or shoot over rapids and splash through waves by rafting and kayaking. There is so much to see and do, you may find yourself spending hardly any time at home.

Possible Drawbacks: Life passes at a slower pace in a small town. Large cities are far away, and so are large airports. This may or may not be a good idea, depending on the atmosphere you are looking for.

▸ Nickname: The Pear City

▸ County: Jackson

▸ Area Code: 521

▸ Population: 63,154

▸ County Population: 181,269

▸ Percent of Population Over 65: 16.5%

▸ Region: Southwestern Oregon

▸ Closest Metropolitan Area: Portland, 221 miles

▸ Median Home Price: $118,500

▸ Best Reasons to Retire Here: Beautiful settings, relaxed attitude, many opportunities for continuing education, and four distinct seasons with mild weather.

Climate

42° N Latitude 122° W Longitude	Average High Temperature (°F)	Average Low Temperature (°F)	Precipitation (")	Sunshine (%)
January	45.7	30.6	2.6	52
April	64.6	37.9	1.1	69
July	90.5	55.0	0.3	85
October	69.3	40.3	1.5	72
YEAR	67.1	41.2	18.2	68

Utilities

Overview: The cost of living is close to the national average of 100 at 101. The highest index is healthcare at 117.6. Housing at 106.0 and transportation 104.7 are both above average, but food is very close to the national average at 100.9, and utilities are well below the national average at 74.9.

Gas Company: Avista Utilities (509-495.4817; *www.avistacorp.com*)

Electric Company: Pacific Power and Light (503-813-5000; *www.pacificorp.com*)

Phone Company: QWest (800-491-0118; *www.qwest.com*)

Water/Sewer Company: Medford Water (541-774-2430; *www.medfordwater.org*)

Cable Company: TCI Cablevision (541-779-1814; *www.tci.com*)

The Tax Axe

Car Registration: The Oregon Department of Transportation (503-945-5000; *http://egov.oregon.gov*) requires an emissions test and a VIN certification to register a car.

Driver's License: For a driver's license, those over 50 are required to take a vision test. Contact the Oregon Department of Transportation (503-945-5000; *http://egov.oregon.gov*) for more information.

Sales Tax: There is no sales tax in Oregon.

State Income Tax: Oregon state income tax ranges from 5 to 9 percent.

Retirement Income Tax: Your pension income, along with all other income regardless of the source, will be taxed by Oregon. Depending on your age and income, you may be entitled to a retirement income credit on your Oregon return.

Property Tax: The property tax rate in Medford is $11.60 per $1,000 of home assessed value.

Local Real Estate

Overview: Over the five year period ending in 2005, house values in Medford increased 76 percent. Real estate speculation accounts for more than 20 percent of all purchases in only five cities in the United States, and Medford is one of them.

Average price of a three-bedroom/two-bath home: $165,000

Average price of a two-bedroom condo: $110,000

Common Housing Styles: These are typically large lots in rural areas, with plenty of trees. Log houses are popular in some rural areas.

Rental Market: The rental market is Medford is tight for renters. But you should contact a realtor, because they often have information on availabilities that is not published elsewhere.

Average rent for a two-bedroom apartment: $800 per month

Communities Popular With Retirees: Sun Oaks, Rogue Valley Manor, Anna Maria Creekside, and Arbor Place.

Nearby Areas to Consider: The city of Ashland has become increasingly popular, having been nominated as one of the nation's most attractive communities by several publications and recently ranked by the American Association of Retired Persons as the second-best small town in America for retirees. Located approximately 15 miles north of the California border on Interstate 5, Ashland is close to Crater Lake National Park and the headwaters of the Rogue River. Grants Pass is just one hour north of the California border. Grants Pass is a classic Oregon river town on the legendary Rogue River, and is one of the best places in the western United States for white-water adventures, forest trails, and fly-fishing.

Earning a Living

Business Climate: Medford is the professional and retail trade and service center for eight counties in Southern Oregon and Northern California. *Inc.* magazine's "Best Places for Doing Business in America 2005" ranked Medford among the top five.

Help in Starting a Business: The Medford BizCenter (541-772-3478; *www.bizcenter.org/Medford*) provides practical information for your business success by assisting the expansion of existing firms, assisting business start-ups, and providing services to high growth businesses. The Microenterprise Development Center (541-779-3992; *www.sowac.org*) promotes economic development by providing hands-on assistance to help you start a business or expand your current business to the next level through classes, training workshops, round table discussion groups, counseling, and loan assistance programs.

Job Market: From 1990 to 2000, nonagricultural employment had an average growth of 3 percent annually. Non-manufacturing employment grew by 41 percent as a result of increases in retail trade and health services. Currently, one in 10 non-farm jobs in the area are in health services. The unemployment rate is above the national average at 7.61 percent.

Medical Care

Providence Medford Medical Center (*www.providence.org/medford*) is a 168-bed short-term hospital, and is one of 19 Providence acute-care hospitals. It offers diabetes services, cancer care, home services, a rehabilitation center, and emergency services.

Seniors have access to a full range of health education programs and personal assistance through Providence Senior Services. The free program assists individuals in maintaining active, independent, and healthy lifestyles through seminars, clinics, forums, and classes featuring an eclectic variety of health, fitness, legal, and specific medical topics. Ashland Community Hospital (541-482-2441; *www.ashlandhospital.org*), about 21 miles away, is a 49-bed short-term hospital. The Rogue Valley Medical Center is a 16-bed religious non-medical healthcare institution.

Services for Seniors

The Department of Human Services Area Agency on Aging (800-282-8096; *http://egov.oregon.gov/DHS/spwpd*) has senior services for employment, food, health, long-term care, prescription, and other services. The Rogue Valley Council of Governments (541-664-6674; *www.rvcog.org*) is for those needing information about any program for seniors or adults.

Continuing Education

Southern Oregon University (541-552-8100; *www.sou.edu*) has an enrollment of more than 5,500. The university holds a 20-year track record of success in the growing field of older adult education. Southern Oregon Learning in Retirement offers its members of retirement age opportunities to pursue current intellectual interests and to explore, with an academic approach, new areas of learning. Elderhostel is the nation's first and world's largest educational and travel organization for older adults. Southern Oregon University has been a part of this network since 1980. Senior Ventures is Southern Oregon University's own program, offering educational adventures combined with housing on the university's campus in Ashland. The university offers Community Education classes, which are open to all interested adults, as a way to follow your interests, learn new skills, or gain personal fulfillment. You can return to college with the special Degree Completion Program, where it's never too late to fulfill your dream of earning a bachelor's degree.

Crime and Safety

The reported incidents per year per 100,000 people is well below the national average of 496.4 at 397.5. The number of reported property crimes is above the national average of 4,532.5 at 7,933.1.

Getting Around Town

Public Transportation: Rogue Valley Transportation District (541-779-2877; *www.rvtd.org*) provides public transportation to all of Rogue Valley, including Medford and the surrounding communities.

Roads and Highways: Highway 62 is the Crater Lake Highway.

Airports: Rogue Valley International (*www.airnav.com/airport/MFR*), about three miles outside of Medford, serves the surrounding area with flights to eight hub airports. Four air carriers serve the airport with approximately 56 arriving and departing flights daily.

Let the Good Times Roll

Recreation: Outdoor living and recreation is encouraged by the warm summers and mild winters. Within an 80 mile radius of Medford there are 153 stocked streams for fishing, 17 lakes, and hunting and camping in 56 forest camps. Visit the Rogue River for fishing, boating, jet boat trips, camping, picnicking, guided raft trips, and rentals for rafting on your own. Sample the local harvest of pears, berries, and nuts at Harry & David's Country Store, and then follow your nose to the Jackson & Perkins store. Minor league baseball is in the form of the Southern Oregon Timberjacks, an Oakland A's affiliate. Sunrise Balloon Adventures presents scenic and special event flights. The Southern Oregon Speedway is just outside of Medford at the Jackson County Sports Park in White City. Cross-country skiing and snowmobiling are great on Mount Ashland and Hyatt Lake.

Culture: The Schneider Museum of Art is a regional fine arts museum. The museum offers a variety of educational programs directed to a broad segment of the community. The museum features visual works of Shakespeare, corresponding with the Oregon Shakespeare Festival plays. It is open April to October. The Rogue Opera presents three full-scale productions each year. The Rogue Valley Symphony offers concerts October through May. The Southern Oregon Traditional Jazz Society holds monthly concerts, and the musicians also perform during various musical events, often featuring well-known guest artists and regional jazz groups.

Annual Events: The Shakespeare Festival is a repertory theater that offers 15 different plays in three different theaters nine months out of the year. Chamber orchestra features "Baroque & More" at popular holiday Candlelight Concerts in December with performances in Grants Pass, Medford, and Ashland. The Britt Festival was the Northwest's first outdoor music festival and now is the largest. The hillside estate of pioneer photographer Peter Britt forms a natural amphitheater, where world-renowned artists perform classical, folk/county, jazz, musical theatre, and dance from mid-June through early September.

When the Grandkids Come: The Medford Railroad Park is a great place for train buffs. The historic park features a vintage Medford Corp logging train and other rolling stock. There are rides available on scale model trains. It's easy to keep kids interested on the short Fall Creek hiking trail, from the wooden bridge to the viewing platform at the falls.

More Information

Municipal

The Chamber of Medford/Jackson County
101 East 8th Street
Medford, OR 97501
541-779-4847
www.medfordchamber.com

Medford Oregon Visitors and Convention Bureau
101 East 8th Street
Medford, OR 97501
800-469-6307
www.visitmedford.org

Newspaper

Medford Mail Tribune
P.O. Box 1108
111 North Fir Street
Medford, OR 97501
541-776-4411
www.mailtribune.com

Ashland Daily Tidings
1661 Siskiyou Boulevard
Ashland, OR 97520
541-482-3456
www.dailytidings.com

Realty

We do not have a Realtor recommendation for Medford. As an option, check out *www.realtor.com* or *www.homegain.com*. Select a Realtor with both CRS and GRI designations after their names, since it means that these folks have gone the extra mile and are both graduates of the Realtor Institute and Certified Residential Specialists.

39

Wayne, Pennsylvania

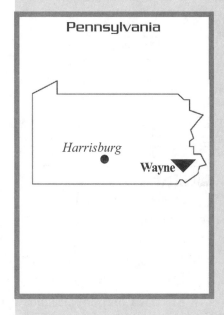

Pennsylvania

Harrisburg

Wayne

Wayne at a Glance

For more than 100 years, Wayne has been considered one of the best places in the western suburbs of Philadelphia to live. The median income is very high and the crime rate is very low, making it a relatively safe and secure community. A large percentage of the residents have higher degrees of education and work in executive or professional occupations. Wayne has an active business community and is within close proximity to many golf courses, colleges, parks, libraries, shopping areas, restaurants, and entertainment. The seashore and mountains are both about two hours away, and 30th Street Station in Philadelphia is only a 30-minute train ride from Wayne Station. From 30th Street Station you can catch trains on SEPTA, New Jersey Transit, Amtrak, and bus service to areas throughout Philadelphia. The "Main Line" is what the immediate western suburbs of Philadelphia are often called, and boasts of dwellings from mansions to affordable housing. Located here are a number of prestigious colleges and universities, including Villanova University, Haverford College, Bryn Mawr College, and Rosemont College.

Possible Drawbacks: It gets hot in the summertime, and the cost of housing is exceptionally high. But if you are looking for a quiet city, Philadelphia might be a little too close for comfort.

▶ Nickname: The Main Line

▶ County: Delaware

▶ Area Code: 613

▶ Population: 32,051

▶ County Population: 555,040

▶ Percent of Population Over 65: 12%

▶ Region: Southeastern Pennsylvania

▶ Closest Metropolitan Area: Philadelphia, 25 miles

▶ Median Home Price: $422,750

▶ Best Reasons to Retire Here: Your neighbors will be nice folks, guaranteed. And you're really close to all the amenitites of Philadelphia!

Climate

39° N Latitude 75° W Longitude	Average High Temperature (°F)	Average Low Temperature (°F)	Precipitation (")	Sunshine (%)
January	37.8	22.8	3.2	49
April	62.6	42.1	3.5	56
July	86.0	67.1	4.3	61
October	66.2	46.4	2.6	60
YEAR	63.3	45.0	41.1	56

Utilities

Overview: The utilities are a bit more expensive in this area. On a scale where the national average is 100, Wayne sits at 137.

Gas Company: Gas and electric service are combined in the Philadelphia Electric and Gas Company (215-841-4000; *www.peco.com*). New customers must go to the local office, present proof of identification, and fill out a credit report.

Electric Company: Radnor/Wayne distinguished itself by purchasing 62 percent of their electrical power from a totally pollution-free wind-generated electrical company in 2003. Contact Community Energy, Inc. (866-946-3123; *www.newwindenergy.com*).

Phone Company: When you sign up with Verizon, (800-660-2215; *www.verizon.com*) be sure to ask about Metropolitan Service, which enables you to call the Philadelphia suburban region without incurring extra fees. Local Service covers only the immediate Main Line area.

Water/Sewer Company: Most properties, except in the extensive estate areas, have public water and sewer facilities. Water service is provided by the Philadelphia Water Company with annual residential rates generally ranging between $150 and $200. Sanitary sewer service is provided by the Radnor-Haverford-Maple Sewer Authority, which is part of the regional system of the Delaware County Regional Water Quality Control Authority.

Cable Company: The Main Line suburbs are serviced by Comcast Cable (215-389-1944; *www.comcast.com*).

The Tax Axe

Car Registration: Any car dealer, notary public, or 24-hour auto license tag service will be able to register your car. You will need the title or title release authorization form from your bank or lending institution, proof of Pennsylvania car insurance, mileage, and tracing of serial number or verification from a licensed mechanic. The fee to register your vehicle in Pennsylvania is $24 for a passenger car, and cars must be inspected once a year at a licensed Pennsylvania inspection garage or gas station.

Driver's License: The closest Pennsylvania Department of Transportation facility to the Main Line area is the Island Avenue Center (215-937-1351). When you go, take your out-of-state license and your Social Security card. Be prepared to take a vision test and to answer questions from the Pennsylvania Drivers Manual. The fee is $24. New residents must file for licenses and registration within 60 days of moving to the commonwealth.

Sales Tax: Pennsylvania has a state sales tax of 6 percent with food, clothing, text books, heating fuels, and drugs exempt. Other taxing entities may add 1 percent.

State Income Tax: Personal income is taxed at a flat rate of 3.07 percent. There are no deductions.

Retirement Income Tax: At age 59 and a half, Social Security, civil service, government, and private pensions are exempt. IRAs are exempt, as are out-of-state government pensions.

Property Tax: Radnor Township, Radnor Township School District, and Delaware County all levy taxes on Wayne. The taxes are set each year. In 2005, the millage rates on which real estate taxes were paid was 2.79 for Radnor Township and 4.45 for Delaware County; the millage rate for the Radnor School District was 15.64. All property is taxed at 100 percent of fair market value as decided by County's Board of Assessment.

Local Real Estate

Overview: Radnor Township, which includes the village of Wayne, has some available housing, and the market is fairly stable.

Average price of a three-bedroom/two-bath home: $560,074

Average price of a two-bedroom condo: $197,000

Common Housing Styles: There are many styles and amenities available in Wayne, including colonials, contemporaries, two- and three-story homes, single-story, and split-level homes. As you drive around, you are apt to see lots of gracious older homes, as well as some brand-spanking new ones. The new homes may feature vinyl siding, but stone, brick, and stucco will appear on both old and new construction.

Rental Market: Estimated cost would be around $1,200 to $1,500 where rental houses are available.

Average rent for a two-bedroom apartment: $1,000 per month

Communities Popular With Retirees: Rosemont, St. Davids, and Mill Ridge

Nearby Areas to Consider: Chester County, home of the Brandywine Valley, is 30 miles west of Philadelphia. In the heart of Pennsylvania Dutch Country you'll find the Amazing Maize Maze, which has more than 10 acres of fun for the family. The 24 villages of Hershey's Mill make up a gated, adult community located in the gentle hills of central Chester County. On 772 acres of premium land, Hershey's Mill features quality construction, innovative design, a spectacular clubhouse for its 18-hole golf course, and a planned shopping area.

Earning a Living

Business Climate: Although small, the business community is active and community-minded. Part of the town's charm can be found in the numerous mom-and-pop retail shops that line the avenues, and have been operating there for several generations.

Help in Starting a Business: Wayne has its own SCORE chapter, which is housed in the Main Line Chamber of Commerce (610-687-6232). Doing business in Wayne/Radnor requires knowledge of local tax laws. For information on starting your own business, contact William Martin, the township's assistant director of finance (610-688-5600).

Job Market: While Wayne is an excellent place to retire, it is small. It has a moderate call for full-time employees, but has more opportunities for part-timers, and still more for volunteering.

Medical Care

Excellent hospitals and healthcare facilities are located either within or close to Radnor Township. They include the Penn Medicine at Radnor and Paoli Memorial Hospital (610-648-1000). In 2005, Paoli Hospital was named to the Top 100 Hospitals list for the second year in a row by Solucient, a leading national healthcare data and consulting firm. Out of more than 1,000 medium-sized community hospitals, Paoli Hospital was one of only 20 in the nation to achieve this honor, and the only hospital of any size in southeastern Pennsylvania to be so recognized. Penn Medicine at Radnor (800-789-7366; *www.pennhealth.com*) is part of the University of Pennsylvania Health system. *U.S. News & World Report* magazine ranked the University of Pennsylvania Health system the highest in the region for geriatric medicine.

Services for Seniors

Surrey Services for Seniors (610-647-6404; *www.surreyservices.org*) offers a wide variety of programs from transportation to in-home services, to a full range of activities. It's for all seniors age 55 and older, regardless of income. The Wayne Senior Center (610-688-6246; *www.radnor.com*) was incorporated in 1980 as a full-service senior center run by paid and volunteer staff who are experts in gerontology, social work, fitness, exercise physiology, marketing, placement, and counseling.

Continuing Education

Many opportunities are available for personal development through lifelong learning. Choices of interest can include music, physical fitness, dance, creative writing, and even computer literacy or programming. At Villanova University (610-519-4300; *www.parttime.villanova.edu*), senior citizens are eligible to enroll in undergraduate courses for personal enrichment only, but they are not charged tuition. The Senior Associates Program at the University of Pennsylvania (215-746-6907; *www.sas.upenn.edu/CGS/senior*) allows people aged 65 and older to be silent auditors in undergraduate lecture classes in Penn's School of Arts and Sciences. Senior Associates pay a $20 membership fee to be retained on the Senior Associates mailing list and to be eligible to participate in Senior Associate activities. The registration fee is $180 per class for a maximum of two classes.

Crime and Safety

The crime rate in Wayne and the surrounding area is very low. According to the best current estimate, the crime rate is just over one half the national average.

Getting Around Town

Public Transportation: The Southeastern Pennsylvania Transportation Authority. also known as SEPTA (215-580-7145; *www.septa.org*), operates a trolley line through the township and direct bus service to nearby points. An extensive train service runs throughout southeastern Pennsylvania, and connects to several cities in New Jersey.

Roads and Highways: The township is traversed by an extensive network of roads, most notably I-476, also known as the Blue Route. Smaller roads include US Route 30 and PA Route 320.

Airports: Philadelphia International Airport (*www.phl.org*) serves the fifth largest metropolitan population in the country. Located approximately seven miles from downtown Philadelphia, the airport is easily accessible from Interstate highways 76, 95, and 476. In addition, rail service to the airport is available on SEPTA'S High Speed Rail Line train that operates from 5:25 a.m. until 11:25 p.m. daily, every 30 minutes, with easy connections to Amtrak and SEPTA at 30th Street Station.

Let the Good Times Roll

Recreation: Valley Forge National Historic Park is located about 10 minutes away, and contains a wealth of American History. This park could be listed in all three categories: (1) Recreation, for trail hiking and biking; (2) Culture, for all the history contained here; and (3) When the Kids Come, because it provides two special kids' programs. The first is the Saturday Morning Kids Corner at Valley Forge, a series focusing on different topics and including a range of activities from storytelling to hands-on projects. The second is the Junior Ranger Program, in which Junior Rangers learn about the Valley Forge encampment by completing an activity booklet as they follow the park tour. Three golf courses are located in Wayne—the Glenhardie Country Club, Golf Association of Philadelphia, and St. Davids Golf Club.

Culture: The Wayne Art Center (610-688-3553; *www.wayneart.org*) is unique in that it focuses on local people. In addition, Wayne provides the site for the Radnor Historical Society (610-688-2668; *www.radnor.com*), which currently owns a fully-equipped Conestoga wagon, a children's wagon, and a milk sleigh, along with a house containing a wonderful collection of period furniture. The Wayne Ballet Theatre (610-688-3904; *www.wbcda.com/wel.htm*) is a well-staffed training ground for dancers and teachers. Their performances and demonstrations in and around Wayne are worthy additions to the cultural life of suburban Philadelphia. And speaking of Philadelphia, it sits 25 miles to the east, and adds much to the American experience and culture.

Annual Events: The Devon Horse Show & Country Fair (610-688-2554) in May and June has, for more than 100 years, been a place where champions meet. The Radnor Hunt Steeplechase Races (610-388-2700) are held in May, as is the annual "Race for Open Space" and benefits the Brandywine Conservancy's regional environmental programs. Then there's the Wayne Flower Fest in April, the Main Line Jazz and Food Festival in June, Radnor's Fall Festival in September, and the Christmas Parade in December. In June, kids from age 9 to 14 race in the soap box derby.

When the Grandkids Come: The Claws and Paws Wild Animal Zoo is a zoo-in-the-woods with 120 species, where kids can feed the giraffe and the parrots, and hunt for dinosaur bones. In nearby Scranton, stables rent horses for rides in the Pocono Mountains, and you can see the Houdini Museum.

More Information

Municipal
The Main Line Chamber of Commerce
175 Strafford Avenue, Suite 130
Wayne, PA 19087
610-687-6232
www.mlcc.org

Newspaper
Suburban and Wayne Times
134 North Wayne Avenue
Wayne, PA 19087
610-688-3000
www.zwire.com

Realty
Mark Rocktashel
Coldwell Banker, Inc.
2100 Darby Road
Havertown, PA 19083
610-446-2300
www.markrealtor.com

40

Charleston, South Carolina

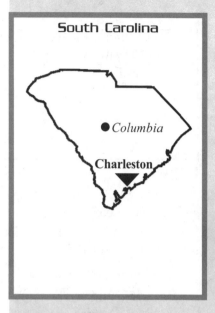

Charleston at a Glance

Charleston embodies class. This gracious city maintains its traditions and rich, historic charm. It has antebellum homes dating back to the 1600s. Charleston is also one of the fastest growing cities in the Southeast. Charleston has 90 miles of Atlantic beach and is within hours of the Blue Ridge Mountains. Between 1997 and 2000, the region's population grew by 3 percent, outpacing the national rate of 2 percent. The area's diverse economic blend includes the largest cargo seaport on the South Atlantic and Gulf Coasts, an enormous tourism industry, world-class medical care, manufacturers, and a military presence. Ft. Moultrie was the site of the first decisive patriot victory of the American Revolution, and Ft. Sumter was the scene of the first shots of the Civil War. The first laws of the Carolinas guaranteed the widest measure of religious liberty in all of the 13 colonies, thus the nickname the "Holy City." By 1704, Charles Towne was a picture of religious freedom with members of the English, French, Quaker, Anabaptist, and Independent churches worshiping peacefully together in a small community.

Possible Drawbacks: It gets really humid. The region is known as the "Low Country." Along with that affectionate appellation comes the proximity to some nasty weather from time to time.

- ▶ Nickname: The Holy City
- ▶ County: Charleston, Berkeley, and Dorchester
- ▶ Area Code: 843
- ▶ Population: 106,412
- ▶ County Population: 717,228
- ▶ Percent of Population Over 65: 13%
- ▶ Region: South central South Carolina
- ▶ Closest Metropolitan Area: Savannah, 110 miles
- ▶ Median Home Price: $147,000
- ▶ Best Reasons to Retire Here: Mild temperatures, an abundance of coastal waterways, arts, and antiques.

Climate

32° N Latitude 80° W Longitude	Average High Temperature (°F)	Average Low Temperature (°F)	Precipitation (")	Sunshine (%)
January	57.7	37.6	3.5	56
April	75.7	53.8	2.8	72
July	90.1	72.7	7.1	67
October	77.2	56.3	3.0	63
YEAR	75.4	55.6	51.8	63

Utilities

Overview: The cost of living is above the national average of 100 at 105.8. Utilities are well above average at 118.4, and healthcare is also above average at 110.4. Housing is also above average at 107.5. Food costs are average, and transportation is below the national average at 91.0.

Gas Company: South Carolina Electric and Gas (803-217-9000; *www.scana.com*)

Electric Company: South Carolina Electric and Gas (803-217-9000; *www.scana.com*). Also Berkley Electric Cooperative (843-553-5020; *www.becsc.com*) and Edisto Electric Cooperative (843-563-3292; *www.edistoelectric.com*).

Phone Company: Bell South (888-757.6500; *www.bellsouth.com*) provides local and long-distance servce to the Charleston area.

Water/Sewer Company: Berkley County Water and Sanitation Authority (843-572-4400; *www.co.berkeley.sc.us*). In the City of Charleston, contact the Commissioners of Public Works (843-727-6800; *www.charlestoncpw.com*).

Cable Company: Comcast Cablevision (843-266-3248; *www.comcast.com*). Also Time Warner Cable (843-871-8710; *www.timewarnercable.com*).

The Tax Axe

Car Registration: The Department of Motor Vehicles (800-442-1368; *www.scdps.org/dmv*) requires all new residents of South Carolina to file a motor vehicle tax in the county. After taxes are paid, you can apply for South Carolina motor vehicle tags.

Driver's License: You must obtain a driver's license within 90 days. You will be obliged to take a written test. Contact the Department of Motor Vehicles (800-442-1368; *www.scdps.org/dmv*) for more information.

Sales Tax: 5 percent, prescription drugs are exempt

State Income Tax: An accelerated income tax ranges from 2.5 to 7 percent.

Retirement Income Tax: Retirement income is taxed. Social Security is exempt. Deductions vary. After age 65, for example, if married filing jointly, there is a deduction of $30,000.

Property Tax: There is no state property tax; however real and personal property taxes are levied by local governments. For homeowners 65 and older, the state's Homestead exemption is $50,000 of fair market value.

Local Real Estate

Overview: A local boom in real estate is continuing, thanks to growing numbers of Baby Boomers. Many major homebuilders are developing new residential areas. This means more neighborhoods and more choices for the homebuyer. Sellers are in a bidding war in certain locations, and they are obtaining more than the asking price.

Average price of a three-bedroom/two-bath home: $260,000

Average price of a two-bedroom condo: $249,000

Common Housing Styles: You can see everything from antebellum plantations to ultra-modern, efficient one-story homes. The seafront boasts contemporaries, with colonial and Cape Cod styles inland. Porches are popular, as are swimming pools. Newer homes feature cathedral ceilings and gracious master suites. Of course, at about eight feet above sea level, there are no basements.

Rental Market: Rentals abound, with many styles, locations, amenities, and prices. With the influx of business and industry, even more options are opening up. Especially charming are some of the newer apartment complexes with lovely views, fountains, and swimming pools.

Average rent for a two-bedroom apartment: $795 per month

Communities Popular With Retirees: Goose Creek and Hanahan

Nearby Areas to Consider: Hilton Head Island is a barrier island 100 miles south of Charleston and only 30 miles from Savannah. Hilton Head Island is a great place with miles of beautiful beaches, the best group of golf courses in the east, terrific restaurants, and friendly people. Mount Pleasant is located on South Carolina's central coast, just East of Charleston and North Charleston. It is the home of Shem Creek (known for its shrimp boats and seafood restaurants), and the Patriots Point Naval and Maritime Museum. The State Ports Authority's Wando River terminal is also in Mount Pleasant.

Earning a Living

Business Climate: Charleston has progressed solidly into the 21st century in commercial terms. Over the past six years, for example, its employers have created more than 30,000 new jobs. This is due in large measure to the virtual flood of new business and industry in the area.

Help in Starting a Business: SCORE, the Small Business Administration's Service Corps of Retired Executives (843-727-4778; *www.score285.org*), operates an office in the area. Contact the Small Business Development Center (843-740-6160

www.mooreschool.sc.edu). The Minority Business Development Center (843-937-0011; *www.mbda.gov*) offers a lot of information for new business owners. Trident Technical College provides consulting services to improve the competitiveness and quality of area businesses.

Job Market: The current job market in Charleston is very good, and is reflected in its unemployment rate of only 3.3 percent. If you want to explore this further, contact the Charleston Chamber of Commerce and request their job-hunting packet. *Employment Review* has ranked Charleston in the Top 20 of "America's Best Places to Live and Work."

Medical Care

Bon Secours St. Francis Xavier Hospital (843-577-1000; *www.carealliance.com*) is a 141-bed short-term local hospital. Roper Hospital (843-724-2000; *www.carealliance.com*) is a 453 bed short term hospital. Roper Hospital North is a 104-bed short-term hospital. Charleston Memorial Hospital (843-577-0600; *www.musc.edu/medcenter/cmh*) is a 113-bed short-term hospital. Charter of Charleston (843-747-5830) is a 102-bed psychiatric and rehabilitation hospital. Medical University of South Carolina (843-792-2300; *www.muschealth.com*) is a 596-bed hospital with 8,000 employees. The R.H. Johnson VA Medical Center (843-577-5011; *www.med.va.gov*) is a 105-bed hospital.

Services for Seniors

The Mayor's Office on Aging (843-722-4127; *www.ci.charleston.sc.us*) focuses attention on senior issues. The office seeks to act as an advocate for the aging population and develop public policy to improve the lives of the aging citizens of the city of Charleston. And check in with the Area Agency on Aging/Elderlink (843-745-1710). The Website of the South Carolina Department of Health and Human Services (*www.dhhs.state.sc.us/Programs/default.htm*) lists more services than one person could possibly use. Some include not only services, but providers, recipients, a resource library, and how it all works together to get you what you need.

Continuing Education

The College of Charleston/University of Charleston (843-953-5507; *www.cofc.edu*) has adult programs for both degree and non-degree students. They may enroll full-time or part-time, and adult students attend the same classes as other students. Limestone College (843-745-1100; *www.limestone.edu*) has the Block Program, which offers courses for evening adult students. Trident Technical College (843-574-6111; *www.tridenttech.edu*) has a Division of Continuing Education and Economic Development, which promotes economic development through a variety of training opportunities to include licensure and certification. Miller Motte Technical College (843-574-0101; *http://mmtccharleston.com*) is job oriented and concentrates on skills needed for a career. Charleston Southern University (843-863-0700; *www.csuniv.edu*) is a four-year liberal arts university with an enrollment of approximately 3,000. Webster University (843-760-1324; *www.webster.edu*) has several campuses around the country with a total enrollment of more than 20,000.

Crime and Safety

Charleston has its share of crimes per year. According to the latest figures from the FBI, Charleston has 7,071.2 crimes per 100,000 people, well above the 4,118.8 per 100,000 national average. The good news is that the Charleston Police Department, (*www.charlestoncity.info/dept*) has initiated neighborhood watch programs, and has a number of suggestions for seniors to avoid becoming victims.

Getting Around Town

Public Transportation: The Charleston Area Regional Transportation Authority (843-724-7420; *www.ridecarta.com*) has bus routes that run throughout the city.

Roads and Highways: With 25 highways, you are sure to find an easy way to get from here to there. The three Interstate highways are 26, 526, and 95. The five US highways are 17, 52, 78, 176, and 701. There are also 17 South Carolina primary highways.

Airports: Charleston International Airport (843-767-1100; *www.chs-airport.com*) is served by seven airlines and serves more than 1.6 million passengers per year.

Ports: The Port of Charleston is the second largest container port on the Atlantic and Gulf Coasts, and fourth largest in the United States. For cruise ship information, contact the port (800-979-8687; *www.allcruising.com/charleston.htm*).

Let the Good Times Roll

Recreation: Charleston is the site of numerous year-round outdoor activities. You can enjoy the magnificent beaches while boating, swimming, skiing, snorkeling, fishing, or just catching some sun. If you would enjoy a round of golf, Charleston has several nationally-ranked courses. If you are a nature lover, you can hike the trails in the Francis Marion National Forest. Along with the basketball, football, hockey, and baseball, there is drag racing at the Cooper River Dragway (*www.crdragway.com*), boxing at the Plex (*www.theplexonline.com*), and horse shows/competitions at Mullet Hall Equestrian Center (*www.ccprc.com*). For more information, visit the city of Charleston Recreation Department (843-724-7327; *www.ci.charleston.sc.us/dept*).

Culture: C'mon down and see all the lovely plantations and historic homes. There is the Boone Hall Plantation, Middleton Place, Magnolia Plantation, Cypress Gardens, and the Edmondston-Alston House, as well as the Aiken-Rhett House and the Nathaniel-Russell House. If all that doesn't satisfy, you may want to attend museums, fine arts, and performing arts festivals, concerts, or the ballet, theater, and opera.

Annual Events: Festivals begin in January with the Low Country Oyster Festival. In March, it's Houses and Gardens. Later on it's the World Grits Festival, and the Spoleto Festival in May and June. July sees the Fourth celebrated with style, and in September is the Annual Fall Candlelight, Scottish Games, and Highland Gathering. November hosts the Charleston Cup, and the beginning of the Festival of Lights that lasts into January. And in December it's Christmas in Charleston, the Holiday Parade of Boats, and First Night Charleston. For more information, contact the Charleston Area Convention and Visitors Bureau (800-868-8118; *www.charlestoncvb.com*).

When the Grandkids Come: For preschool through high-school ages, take them to Art at Your Place, a great place for art instruction. Or perhaps you could introduce them to yoga at the Holy Cow Yoga and Holistic Center. Or you could expose them to birds at the South Carolina Center for Birds of Prey.

More Information

Municipal

Charleston Metro Chamber of Commerce
2750 Speissegger Drive Suite 100
North Charleston, SC 29405
843-577-2510
www.charlestoncvb.com

Newspaper

Post and Courier
134 Columbus Street
Charleston, SC 29403
843-577-7111
www.charleston.net

Realty

We do not have a Realtor recommendation for Charleston. As an option, check out *www.realtor.com* or *www.homegain.com*. Select a Realtor with both CRS and GRI designations after their names, since it means that these folks have gone the extra mile and are both graduates of the Realtor Institute and Certified Residential Specialists.

41

Austin, Texas

Austin at a Glance

The Texas Colorado River, the largest river completely contained in Texas, runs through the middle of town. Lake Travis lies on the western edge of the city. Lake Austin and Town Lake are situated in the heart of the city. Austin is the state capital of Texas and home to the University of Texas, the country's largest public university. Austin is a center for academics, politics, and technology, as well as music, entertainment, art, and cultural activities. Plus there is the surrounding terrain, with a number of lakes for fishing and boating. You will see rolling farm land, and pine forests perfect for hiking and biking. The *Wall Street Journal* ranked Austin in the "Top Four American Cities for Livability." Austin is a friendly, unpretentious, and smart town with countless amenities. With restaurants from funky to fine, great venues for live music, outdoor sports, and local arts. According to the American Booksellers Association, Austin residents buy more books per capita than residents of any other city in the nation. Within 200 miles are three of the nation's 10 largest cities. Austin's reputation as a center for movie production is increasing, and filmcrews can be seen around town on a relatively frequest basis.

Possible Drawbacks: Summers can be quite warm, and it seldom rains to cool things off. So be sure to pack that air conditioner!

▶ Nickname: Silicon Hills

▶ County: Travis

▶ Area Code: 512

▶ Population: 680,899

▶ County Population: 1,377,633

▶ Percent of Population Over 65: 6.7%

▶ Region: Central Texas

▶ Closest Metropolitan Area: San Antonio, 80 miles

▶ Median Home Price: $156,700

▶ Best Reasons to Retire Here: Austin is a university town, so expect lots of college students. It also has a high-tech economy, and there is no end to the outdoor entertainment.

Climate

30° N Latitude 97° W Longitude	Average High Temperature (°F)	Average Low Temperature (°F)	Precipitation (")	Sunshine (%)
January	58.8	38.5	1.9	62
April	79.3	59.7	3.0	72
July	95.0	73.8	1.9	80
October	82.0	59.9	3.5	72
YEAR	78.8	58.1	32.5	70

Utilities

Overview: The cost of living is slightly above the national average of 100 at 102.9. The highest costs are healthcare at 112.3 and housing at 111.2. Food costs are below the national average at 94.3 and transportation is 91.1. Utilities are slightly above average at 103.9.

Gas Company: Texas Gas Service (800-700-2443; *http://txgas.com)*

Electric Company: The City of Austin (512-322-6514; *www.austinenergy.com*) provides electricity to the Austin area.

Phone Company: For information contact SBC Communications (800-464-7924; *www.sbc.com*).

Water/Sewer Company: The City of Austin (512-972-0101; *www.ci.austin.tx.us/water*) provides water and sewer city for the residents.

Cable Company: Time Warner (512-485-5555; *www.timewarnercable.com*) or Heartland (888-990-4327)

The Tax Axe

Car Registration: Your vehicle must first pass a vehicle safety inspection and an inspection of the vehicle identification number at a state-approved Safety Inspection Station. The form then must be submitted to the county tax office (512-854-9473), along with an application for certificate of title and the registration fees. Liability insurance is required. The fee is a minimum of $52, but it goes up for newer and/or heavier cars.

Driver's License: New residents have 30 days after entry into the state to secure a Texas license from the Department of Public Safety (512-424-2000). You will need to provide proof of identity, Social Security number, Texas vehicle registration and liability insurance, pass a vision exam, and surrender your out-of-state license. The cost is $24 and it expires in six years.

Sales Tax: Total of 6.25 percent; city 1 percent, transit authority 1 percent

State Income Tax: There is no income tax in Texas.

Retirement Income Tax: There is no retirement income tax in Texas.

Property Tax: $2.68 per $100 of assessed value.

Local Real Estate

Overview: Strong media attention focused on Austin's job growth and expanding housing market made 2005 a busy home-buying and -selling season. Austin is shifting from a buyer's to a seller's market. There are usually multiple offers on the more desirable homes. Inventory is down to a less than six month supply. Waterfront properties are a small part of the overall Austin real estate market, and are almost a market of their own.

Average price of a three-bedroom/two-bath home: $125,100

Average price of a two-bedroom condo: $126,000

Common Housing Styles: Most houses are on concrete slabs, and almost all of them have air conditioning. Siding is usually stone or brick. Porches and patios are common because of the weather.

Rental Market: The occupancy rate is high because of the growth of the city and the large university population.

Average rent for a two-bedroom apartment: $700 per month

Communities Popular With Retirees: Cobblestone Court, Sun City Texas, Eberhart Place, the Heritage at Gaines Ranch, and the Summit at Westlake Hills

Nearby Areas to Consider: Dripping Springs, in the beautiful Texas Hill Country about 25 miles west of Austin, has a rural Texas lifestyle. Something is always happening in Wimberly, which has authentic hill country charm. The Wimberly Market Days are a bargain hunter's paradise for the unusual, while Pioneer Town is a historic recreation of an 1890s village of the Old West, the VFW Rodeo, and an outdoor walk-in theater under the stars.

Earning a Living

Business Climate: *Expansion Management* magazine ranked Austin as the 14th best place to relocate a business. *Forbes* magazine put Austin number one on the list of the best places in which to do business and advance your career. Austin ranks second only to Silicon Valley in the number of patents issued each year. Among the high-tech benchmark regions, Austin received one of the highest levels of venture capital funding.

Help in Starting a Business: Austin Small Business Development Center of the Austin Community College (512-225-9888; *www.business.swt.edu/sbdc*) works with existing and start-up small companies to help in every phase of the business cycle, including financing. The City of Austin Small Business Development Program (512-474-7800; *www.ci.austin.tx.us/sbdp*) offers training and technical assistance to anyone starting, expanding, or managing a small business. The Austin Public Library maintains a list of these and other entities that may be help in starting a business (*www.ci.austin.tx.us/library/funding_for_businesses.htm*).

Job Market: Employment is available for just about every industry possible. Austin is a large high-tech city, the capital of Texas, and entertains 16 million visitors per year.

The population is growing and jobs are always available. Among the major employers are ACS Healthcare, Apple Computer, Dell Computer, IBM, State Farm Insurance, and the state of Texas.

Medical Care

Many of the local medical facilities are affiliated with either the St. David's Health Care System or the Seton Healthcare Network. The area contains 52 medical facilities of various kinds. The Austin Diagnostic Clinic (512-442-5566; *www.adclinic.com*) employs 130 doctors and has two locations in the city. The Austin Regional Clinic (512-272-4636; *www.austinregbionalclinic.com*) is one of the largest multi-specialty healthcare groups in central Texas with 13 locations. Breckenridge Hospital (512-324-7000; *www.seton.net/breckenridge*) is a major center for central Texas with a 115 year history and major renovations in the past few years. Breckenridge is a teaching hospital affiliated with two universities.

Services for Seniors

Information Referral for Older Adults (512-450-0844) is a good source of information. Also, the *Senior Advocate* (512-451-7433) is published monthly. Austin Groups for the Elderly (512-451-4611) is a consortium of 12 agencies providing services to senior citizens. The services include Alzheimer's information and support, adult daycare, adult education, and respite care.

Continuing Education

University of Texas at Austin (512-471-3434; *www.utexas.edu*), with an enrollment of 52,261, is a leader in American higher education and has a number of "third age" programs. Their Learning Activities for Mature People (*www.utexas.edu/cee/thirdage/utlamp.html*) is an annual membership organization limited to persons at least 55 years of age. The program offers 36 morning lectures per session. Each series of lectures is given by experts in their fields, including history, science, fine arts, education, foreign policy, government, travel, economics, engineering, health, politics, and other areas of interest. UT also has Seminars for Adult Growth and Entertainment, an annual membership organization with no age restriction. UT's Elderhostel is the nation's first and the world's largest educational and travel organization for older adults.

Crime and Safety

The number of violent crimes reported per 100,000 peoplen is 540.4, which is above the national average of 496.4.The non-violent crime reporting rate is 6,461.4 compared to the national average of 4,532.5.

Getting Around Town

Public Transportation: The Capital Metropolitan Transportation Authority (512-474-1200; *www.capmetro.org*) provides transportation throughout the city.

Roads and Highways: Interstate 35; US 290 and 183; Texas 71.

Airports: The Austin-Bergstrom International Airport is served by eight airlines providing direct service to 113 destinations.

Let the Good Times Roll

Recreation: More than 150 miles of highland lakes wind through the Texas hill country into Austin for sailing, rowing, fishing, and canoeing. The Austin area has more than 60 golf courses. The city has 34 golf courses (15 municipal and 19 private or semi-private), over 200 tennis courts, 32 miles of hike and bike trails (18 surfaces, 14 of which are natural). Austin has produced a number of Grammy winning performances with its 105 live music venues and a host of professional recording studios. There is unlimited opportunity to participate in line dancing, square dancing, and round dancing. Austin is home to the world's largest urban bat colony, and bat-watching has become a regular activity. There are a number of live theaters in town, three of which specialize in comedy. In the towns surrounding Austin you will find no end of festivals of different types.

Culture: The city contains seven historic districts and 210 historic structures. The city ranks first in Texas in the number of artists and musicians per capita. The locally produced television program "Austin City Limits" is viewed by more than 5 million people worldwide. Filmmakers from around the world come to Austin to make movies. And Austin has more than 150 theater companies, nearly 70 art galleries, and dozens of museums.

Annual Events: Each spring brings the Capital 10K race. In the spring and fall is the Old Pecan Street Festival. Also in the spring is the Austin Fine Arts Festival, Star of Texas Rodeo, Texas Wine and Food Festival, Cinco de Mayo, South by Southwest Music and Film Conference, UT baseball, swimming, tennis, and track and field. In spring and summer the Austin Lone Stars Soccer Team plays. In June is the Juneteenth celebration. July brings the Austin Symphony Fourth of July Concert. Fall brings the Austin City Limits Music Festival and University of Texas football, soccer, and volleyball. In the winter you can see the Austin Ice Bats hockey team play, UT basketball, and Yulefest.

When the Grandkids Come: The 351-acre Zilker Park near downtown includes Barton Springs Pool, a children's playscape, miniature railroad, soccer fields, botanical gardens, and the Austin Nature Science Center. Local parks and playgrounds include McKinney Falls State Park. There is also the Schlitterbahn Water Park and Texas Paintball.

More Information

Municipal

Austin Convention and Visitors Bureau
209 East Sixth Street
Austin, TX 78701
866-462-8784
www.austintexas.org

Greater Austin Chamber of Commerce
210 Barton Springs Road, Suite 400
Austin, TX 78704
512-478-9383
www.austinchamber.org

Newspaper

Austin American-Statesman
P.O. Box 670
Austin, Texas 78767
512-445-4040
www.statesman.com

Realty

We do not have a Realtor recommendation for Austin. As an option, check out *www.realtor.com* or *www.homegain.com*. Select a Realtor with both CRS and GRI designations after their names, since it means that these folks have gone the extra mile and are both graduates of the Realtor Institute and Certified Residential Specialists.

42 ▶ Plano, Texas

Plano at a Glance

Plano is located just 20 miles north of downtown Dallas, and is considered a part of the Dallas/Fort Worth metroplex. Plano was chosen as one of the six best places to live by *Money* magazine. *Men's Health* named Plano as the fifth best city for men, while the *Ladies' Home Journal* ranked Plano as the ninth best city for women. Mild winters and hot summers provide opportunities year round for outdoor activities. At Lake Lavon, just east of Plano, fishing, boating, camping, and water sports can be enjoyed most of the year. You could go to a different restaurant every night of the year—that's how many restaurants there are. The elevation of Plano is 675 feet. The name Plano was chosen in error. It was thought to be the Spanish word for "plain," but it actually means "flat." Luckily, it is that also. In Plano and the neighboring cities of the metroplex, you will find almost unlimited museums, concerts, night life, theaters, amusement parks, and more.

Possible Drawbacks: Even though there is almost open country to the north, Plano is still part of a very large city complex. It is hot enough in the summer that you must take that into consideration. Plano is also along the southern edge of tornado alley.

▶ Nickname: Balloon Capital of Texas

▶ County: Collin

▶ Area Codes: 214, 972, and 469

▶ Population: 222,030

▶ County Population: 491,675

▶ Percent of Population Over 65: 4.9%

▶ Region: North central Texas

▶ Closest Metropolitan Area: Dallas, 15 miles.

▶ Median Home Price: $140,000

▶ Best Reasons to Retire Here: Superior theater, art, and leisure. Plano also enjoys mild winters, and has a very low crime rate.

Climate

32° N Latitude 96° W Longitude	Average High Temperature (°F)	Average Low Temperature (°F)	Precipitation (")	Sunshine (%)
January	54.5	34.3	1.8	52
April	77.0	56.1	4.1	61
July	95.5	75.9	2.2	75
October	78.3	57.0	3.9	63
YEAR	76.3	55.9	36.1	61

Utilities

Overview: The general cost of living is below the 100 average at 96.1. Housing, groceries, and utilities are below average, but transportation and medical are above average.

Gas Company: Natural gas is provided by Lone Star Gas (214-741-3720), which is now known as Enserch.

Electric Company: TXU Energy (972-791-2888; *www.txu.com*) and the Denton County Electric Cooperative (817-383-1671; *www.dcec.com*)

Phone Company: Verizon (972-516-0888; www.verizon.com) and SBC Communications (800-464-7928; *www.sbc.com*)

Water/Sewer Company: The City of Plano Engineering Department (972-424-6531; *www.planoengineering.org*) is responsible for water, sewer, streets, and drainage.

Cable Company: Comcast Cable (800-266-2278; *www.comcast.com*)

The Tax Axe

Car Registration: Your vehicle must pass a vehicle safety inspection and an inspection of the vehicle identification number at a state-approved Safety Inspection Station. The form then must be submitted to the county tax office (972-881-3010) along with an application for certificate of title and the registration fees. Liability insurance is required. The fee is a minimum of $52, but it goes up for newer and/or heavier cars.

Driver's License: New residents have 30 days after entry into the state to secure a Texas license from the Department of Public Safety (972-867-4221). You will need to provide proof of identity, Social Security number, Texas vehicle registration and liability insurance, pass a vision exam, and surrender your out-of-state license. The cost is $24 and it expires in six years.

Sales Tax: The state sales tax is 6.25 percent. The county adds to it for a total rate of 8.25 percent.

State Income Tax: There is no income tax in Texas.

Retirement Income Tax: There is no income tax in Texas.

Property Tax: Generally, it is 2.3 percent to 2.9 percent of assessed value. A Homestead exemption reduces the assessed value.

Local Real Estate

Overview: Plano began a growth spurt in about 1970 that has varied a bit now and then, but it is still going strong. The market is brisk, with a healthy appreciation in sales. Buyer confidence is high, and housing prices should still be a bargain compared to prices in other major metropolitan areas.

Average price of a three-bedroom/two-bath home: $250,000

Average price of a two-bedroom condo: $125,000

Common Housing Styles: Swimming pools and fenced backyards are common. Plano has expanded to its current size by adding almost exclusively brick veneer houses, but you will find a few wood-sided houses.

Rental Market: The average occupancy rate of apartments hovers around 95 percent, but there are so many of them there are always plenty from which to choose. The typical older apartment now costs about $690 per month. The average rent for a unit built during the past decade is $928.

Average rent for a two-bedroom apartment: $900 per month

Communities Popular With Retirees: North Dallas, Frisco, Allen, Southlake, Carrollton

Nearby Areas to Consider: McKinney is a semi-rural community of rolling hills and lush trees to the north of Plano, but it is still close enough to the metroplex that it could be considered a part of it. It is a mix of traditional values and contemporary vision, making it a unique and desirable place to live, conduct business, and explore. The city of Colleyville is located between two major cities.

Earning a Living

Business Climate: Plano is home to many thriving businesses, because it's on the north end of the communications corridor. It is the corporate home of telephone equipment manufacturers, satellite communication systems, and computer manufacturers. About 94 percent of the workforce has some college education, and 53.3 percent has at least an undergraduate degree.

Help in Starting a Business: The Courtyard Center for Professional & Economic Development (972-985-3770; *www.ccccd.edu/bc/buscomm.html*) works with start-up and existing business owners, providing free counseling services on issues such as business planning, registering a business, financing, regulations, licensing, and so on. The North Texas Certified Development Corporation is a nonprofit corporation that provides growing businesses with long-term, fixed-rate financing for major fixed assets, such as land and buildings.

Job Market: Plano is home to more that 6,000 businesses, including EDS, JCPenney, Frito-Lay, Countrywide Home Loans, Dr. Pepper/7-Up, Network Associates, Crossmark, and Advanced Neuromodulation. Texas is a right-to-work state. The unemployment rate is about 4.2 percent.

Medical Care

The spectrum of medical care available is enormous. Presbyterian Hospital of Plano is a 91-bed short-term hospital. Healthsouth Plano Rehabilitation Hospital is a 62-bed long-term facility. IHS Hospital at Plano is a 30-bed long-term facility. Nearby Dallas has 26 hospitals, including the Baylor University Medical Centers, scattered around the metroplex with more than 1,700 beds. One of the facilities is the Baylor Heart and Vascular Center. Among the others are the Dallas Southwest Medical Center, a 107-bed short-term hospital, Medical City Dallas Hospital, Methodist Medical Center, and Parkland Health and Hospital System.

Services for Seniors

The Collin County Committee on Aging (972-562-4275; *www.cccoaweb.org*) supports Meals on Wheels and the Nutrition Centers located throughout Collin County, which provide a place where people age 60 and over can share a meal and participate in activities such as exercise, games, and music. The Plano Senior Center (972-941-7155) provides a variety of activities and friendships to appeal to a wide variety of seniors. A monthly newsletter is available and can be mailed for a small fee. Lunch is served on premise by Collin County Committee on Aging's nutrition program. The Senior Citizens Police Academy (972-941-2135; *www.planopolice.org*) is sponsored by the Plano Police Department and is designed to educate the senior citizens of Plano on the operations of their police department. Bart Peddicord Community Center, Senior Services Program (972-442-8119) serves lunches Monday through Friday, and serves other meals daily for those attending other senior activities.

Continuing Education

Collin County Community College (972-985.3751; *www.ccccd.edu*) is a two year college with six campuses located in the county and has a Continuing Education and Workforce Development Division for adults. The University of Texas at Dallas (972-231-5362; *www.utdallas.edu*), on the southern edge of Plano, offers undergraduate, graduate, and postgraduate degrees. Its math, science, and engineering programs are rated among the best. Area colleges that have satellite campuses in Plano are Southern Methodist University, Texas Women's University, and Dallas Baptist University. Plano's position in the metroplex places it in close proximity to other universities, such as the University of Texas at Arlington, University of North Texas, Texas Christian University, and the University of Texas Southwestern Medical School.

Crime and Safety

Plano ranks as one of the Top 25 safest cities in the country. The crime rate is a below-average 241.8, with the national average being 330.6. The 337 police officers work closely with hundreds of neighborhood crime watch groups. The police hold education seminars, some especially for senior citizens.

Getting Around Town

Public Transportation: Dallas Area Rapid Transit, known locally as DART (214-979-1111; *www.dart.org*), provides bus, light rail, and train service throughout the city and into the neighboring communities. They also have tours to the arts district, Fair Park, and other areas of interest.

Roads and Highways: Interstate 35. US 75. Dallas North Tollway. State highways 289, 121, 190.

Airports: The Dallas/Fort Worth Airport (*www.dfwairport.com*) is in the center of the metroplex between Dallas and Fort Worth. It is a major hub with five terminal buildings served by 21 airlines. The terminals and the parking areas are all linked by an automated rail system. Love Field (*www.dallas-lovefield.com*) is in Dallas, and is the home of Southwest Airlines.

Let the Good Times Roll

Recreation: The city contains 80 parks on more that 3,600 acres of land, and maintains 47 miles of hiking and biking trails. There are also six recreation centers, five swimming pools, more than 150 athletic fields, and a variety of seasonal classes that are offered by the recreation department. The city has three public golf courses and 79 tennis courts, including the 21-court tennis center. Active entertainment is available around town for everything from skating to bumper car basketball. The options for shopping seem unlimited, from the enormous new Collin Creek Mall to the Lakeside Market shopping center, from Plano's historic downtown district with its cobblestone streets to Plano Market Square. The rest of the metroplex holds the Dallas Cowboys football, Texas Rangers baseball, Dallas Stars hockey, Dallas Mavericks basketball, and the Mesquite Championship Rodeo.

Culture: The Plano Symphony Orchestra is one of the premier orchestras in the area. The Plano Repertory Theatre presents classics, musicals, dramas, and comedies. The city maintains five excellent public libraries. The Artcentre of Plano offers a wide array of local and national exhibits. The Heard Natural Science Museum and Wildlife Sanctuary is a 25,000 square foot museum, a 289-acre sanctuary, and more. The Heritage Farmstead Museum is a restored 1890s pioneer sheep farmer's home.

Annual Events: You often see brightly colored hot air balloons over Plano, but the September sky fills with them as the city hosts the annual Plano Balloon Festival, (*http://planoballonfest.org*), which is a balloon race and has a full weekend of activities, including performing arts stages, children's activities, and more. Also in September is the Texas State Fair. In January is the Very Special Arts Festival. In February is Daddy's Little Sweetheart Dance. April brings the Blackland Prairie Festival, where the downtown cobbled streets fill with costumed performers, artists, food, and fun. In June is the Juneteenth celebration and the Picnic in the Parks Concert series. The American Girl's Fashion Show is in November, and in December is Dickens in Historic Downtown Plano.

When the Grandkids Come: You can play miniature golf in a jungle. A number of arcades are filled with video games and more. Dave & Buster's in Dallas has every electronic game imagined. Race your friends on go-kart tracks, or zap them in a laser tag course. At WhirlyBall, you and your four teammates will try to score as many points as possible while maneuvering your WhirlyBug and scooping the ball into your goal. And there is no end to the high flying fun at Six Flags over Texas. One roller coaster goes under water, another has multiple loops in the air, and yet another is of the huge wooden kind.

More Information

Municipal

Plano Texas Convention & Visitors Bureau
2000 East Spring Creek Parkway
Plano, TX 75074
800-817-5266
www.planocvb.com

Plano Chamber of Commerce
1200 East 15th Street
Plano, TX 75074
972-424-7547
www.planocc.org

Newspaper

Plano Star Courier
624 Krona Drive Suite 170
Plano, TX 75074
972-424-6565
www.zwire.com

Realty

Kay Cheek
5013 Plano Parkway, Suite 100
Plano, TX 75093
972-733-8025
www.kaycheek.com

43 ▶ San Antonio, Texas

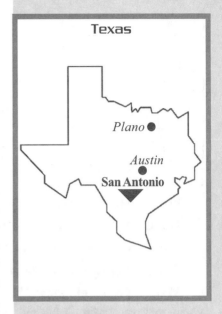

Texas

Plano ●

Austin ●
San Antonio ▼

San Antonio at a Glance

San Antonio is a graceful and beautiful city, and she moves at a slower pace than you would expect for a city of her size. Now the eighth largest city in the United States, San Antonio has retained its sense of history and tradition while carefully blending in cosmopolitan progress. Sounds and flavors of Native Americans, Old Mexico, Germans, the Wild West, African-Americans, and the deep South mingle and merge. The actual founding of the city came in 1718 by Father Antonio Olivares, when he established Mission San Antonio de Valero, which became permanently etched in the annals of history in 1836 as the Alamo. Market Square is the largest Mexican marketplace outside of Mexico. In the middle of the busy metropolitan downtown, 20 feet below street level, is one of San Antonio's jewels, the Paseo del Rio, better known as the RiverWalk. Cobblestone and flagstone paths border both sides of the winding San Antonio River as it meanders through the business district. Dining options include French, Chinese, Cajun, but the one not to miss is Tex-Mex. Tex-Mex is a passion with local residents of all ethnic backgrounds, and numerous restaurants are open 24 hours.

Possible Drawbacks: It is hot in San Antonio. Although it is easier to manage transportation than in most large cities, San Antonio is a large metropolitan area and it can be hard to get around.

▶ Nickname: The Alamo City
▶ County: Bexar
▶ Area Code: 210
▶ Population: 1,144,646
▶ County Population: 1,392,931
▶ Percent of Population Over 65: 10.4%
▶ Region: South central Texas
▶ Closest Metropolitan Area: Austin, 79 miles
▶ Median Home Price: $129,500
▶ Best Reasons to Retire Here: The sun shines most of the time, there is excellent healthcare, and a lower cost of living than average.

Climate

29° N Latitude 98° W Longitude	Average High Temperature (°F)	Average Low Temperature (°F)	Precipitation (")	Sunshine (%)
January	60.8	37.8	1.6	47
April	80.2	58.3	2.9	56
July	95.0	74.8	2.1	74
October	81.7	58.6	2.8	64
YEAR	79.3	57.6	29.2	60

Utilities

Overview: The cost of living is below average, at 93 on a scale of 100.

Gas Company: Public Service (210-353-2222; *www.citypublicservice.com*)

Electric Company: Public Service (210-353-2222; *www.citypublicservice.com*)

Phone Company: SBC Communications (210-821-4105)

Water/Sewer Company: The San Antonio Water System (210-704-7297; *www.saws.org*) has multiple sources for water.

Cable Company: Time Warner (210-244-0500; *www.timewarnercable.com*)

The Tax Axe

Car Registration: Your vehicle must first pass a vehicle safety inspection and an inspection of the vehicle identification number at a state-approved Safety Inspection Station. The form then must be submitted to the County Tax Office (210-615-1776), along with an application for certificate of title and the registration fees. Liability insurance is required. The fee is a minimum of $52, but it goes up for newer and/or heavier cars.

Driver's License: New residents have 30 days after entry into the state to secure a Texas license. You will need to provide proof of identity, social security number, Texas vehicle registration and liability insurance, pass a vision exam, and surrender your out-of-state license. The cost is $24 and it expires in six years.

Sales Tax: The state sales tax is 6.25 percent. The city and county add 1.75 percent. The total is 8 percent.

State Income Tax: There is no income tax in Texas.

Retirement Income Tax: There is no income tax in Texas.

Property Tax: The tax rate is $2.53 per $1,000 of assessed value, but that varies with the neighborhood, school district, and so on, and it changes every year. There are exceptions for Homestead, people over 65, and those with disabilities.

Local Real Estate

Overview: While home values are still a bargain when compared to the rest of the nation, San Antonio's residential real estate market is maturing and the prices are moving up. Entry-level homes are in short supply and are selling quickly at or near list prices. Mid-range homes are almost as active, but with a slightly greater supply. The upper end poses more of a challenge to sellers.

Average price of a three-bedroom/two-bath home: $123,600

Average price of a two-bedroom condo: $108,700

Common Housing Styles: Houses tend to be open to the sunshine, situated on large lots, and have patios and swimming pools. There is lots of Mexican-type tile and stucco work.

Rental Market: Apartments are being constructed at the rate of 3,000 to 4,000 per year, and plenty are always available. The rental occupancy rate is 94 percent, but that is expected to drop.

Average rent for a two-bedroom apartment: $1,000 per month

Communities Popular With Retirees: Leon Valley, Alamo Heights, Converse, and Kirby

Nearby Areas to Consider: New Braunfels, about 25 miles away, is a little bit of old Germany smack dab in the middle of the Texas hill country. New Braunfels is the kind of old-fashioned town that makes folks feel right at home. And you can dine at biergartens and dance to polka music! San Marcos is located between Austin and San Antonio, and is home to Texas State University.

Earning a Living

Business Climate: San Antonio, the second fastest growing city of one million or more, provides a dynamic environment for business in a community. San Antonio was selected by *Forbes* magazine as eighth out of the Top 15 "Best Places to Put Your Business" in the United States. San Antonio has developed thriving trade and services, especially with Mexico. One of the primary economic development strategies has been the development and promotion of San Antonio as an inland port and center for trade processing activities. It has a bilingual and bicultural workforce, and a low cost business climate.

Help in Starting a Business: The San Antonio Small Business Development Center (210-458-2020; *www.iedtexas.org/sasbdc*) assists current and potential small business owners in achieving success by providing professional business advice in a consistent, efficient, and friendly manner. The Economic Development Foundation (800-552-3333; *http://saedf.dcci.com*) is an independent, nonprofit organization, responsible for recruiting business and industry to San Antonio. The City of San Antonio Economic Development (210-207-8080; *www.sanantonio.gov/edd*) provides a full range of business services. The South Texas Business Fund (210-207-3932; *www.sotexbizfund.com*) provides small business loans.

Job Market: There has been stable and continuous growth in the job market over the past several years. San Antonio is accounting for a growing percentage of the states technology employment. From the 1.8 million-square-foot, $800 million Toyota plant that's rising on the South Side to the shops at La Cantera and the PGA Tour resort in the north, the city is experiencing a boom. In 2004, San Antonio added about 15,000 new jobs, and that growth is continuing as hiring picks up this year with new companies relocating and more corporations eyeing San Antonio as a possible site for expansion.

Medical Care

More than 36 hospitals exist in the city of San Antonio. Founded in 1961, the Southwest Texas Medical Center (*www.southtexasmedicalcenter.com*) has expanded from one medical school and a teaching hospital on less than 150-acres to 45 associated institutions, medical, dental, and nursing schools, 12 hospitals, and five specialty institutions on almost 700-acres. The complex employs more than 25,000 with over 12,000 volunteers, and serves nearly 4.5 million patients each year. It has made significant contributions to world medical research. Other institutions include the Baptist Health System (210-297-7000; *www.baptisthealth.org*), which is a 1,245-bed short-term system of hospitals with a number of locations around the city. The Methodist Health Care System (800-333-7333; *www.sahealth.com*) operates 22 healthcare facilities of various types and employs 7,000 people.

Services for Seniors

The San Antonio Seniors Guide (512-257-7607; *www.seniorsguide.net*) is a reference to local senior resources, businesses offering senior discounts, delivery services, and senior living. The Senior Community Service Employment Program (210-822-7640; *www.twc.state.tx.us*) assists eligible individuals age 55 and older to gain competitive job skills through employment and training. Bexar Area Agency on Aging (210-362-5217; *www.aacog.com*) is one of 28 area agencies on aging in the state.

Continuing Education

The University of Texas at San Antonio Office of Extended Education (210-458-2411; *www.utsa.edu/VPEE*) offers a wide variety of workshops and courses in both classroom and online forms. San Antonio College Continuing Education Training Program (210-733-2000; *www.accd.edu/sac/ce*) offers senior citizens 65 and older enrollment free of tuition and fees on a space available basis. St. Philips College Continuing Education (210-531-3200; *www.accd.edu/spc/ce*) offers both credit and non-credit courses. St Mary's University (210-436-3011; *www.stmarytx.edu/continuingstudies*) offers a program of lifelong education.

Crime and Safety

The number of all types of crimes reported per 100,000 people is well above average at 7,873.3.

Getting Around Town

Public Transportation: VIA Metropolitan Transit (210-362-2020; *www.viainfo.net*) runs 78 bus routes, offering five different levels of service. Most routes are either frequent (every 15 minutes) or metro (every 30 or 60 minutes). VIA offers express Special Event Park 'n Ride service to many San Antonio events, such as Fiesta, Folklife, or a Spurs game.

Roads and Highways: Interstate 10, 35, 37 and loop 410. US 90 and 281. Texas 151 and loop 1604.

Airports: The San Antonio International Airport (210-207-3411; *www.sanantonio.gov/airport*) is about seven miles from the center of town, and is served by 14 airlines. It averages 250 daily domestic and international departures and arrivals.

Let the Good Times Roll

Recreation: The Riverwalk stretches through the city and is a great place to stroll. Rio San Antonio Cruises, the river's floating transportation system, provides a novel method of sight-seeing. Rivercenter is a dazzling three-level glass shopping, dining, and entertainment complex. San Antonio is home to Sea World San Antonio, the world's largest marine life park, and Six Flags Fiesta Texas, a town built just for fun! The first public golf course in Texas was built in San Antonio in 1916, and the city has been busy building courses ever since, with at least one additional public course opening every year since 1993. Golf Digest named La Cantera Golf Club the best new public course in the United States in 1995. Working ranches throughout central and south Texas are available as hunting leases for wild game, while dude ranches offer a taste of the old West, complete with horseback riding. Numerous state parks offer opportunities for hiking in the rugged terrain of the hill country. The Senior Games of San Antonio, with many different kinds of sports competition, is open to everyone over age 50.

Culture: The McNay Art Museum is set in a Mediterranean-style mansion and has wide-ranging collections, including post-impressionist and modern art, theater art, medieval art, Native American art, and more. The San Antonio Museum of Art is housed in the castle-like former headquarters of the Lone Star Brewery. Two centers for contemporary artistic expression include the Blue Star Contemporary Art Center in Southtown, and the ArtPace on Main Avenue. Another is the Southwest School of Art and Craft, a beautiful complex built by French nuns in 1848, which served as the first girls' school in the city. The Guadalupe Cultural Arts Center provides a venue for Hispanic artistic endeavors. Signature events of the center include the San Antonio CineFestival, a celebration of conjunto music, a South Texas original. The Carver Jazz Festival is famous for presenting the hottest new stars and the masters of American Jazz each year. The Majestic Theatre downtown, built in 1929, is often a setting for touring Broadway shows and concerts, but is mainly the permanent home of the San Antonio Symphony, now in its 54th season.

Annual Events: Fiesta San Antonio (*www.fiesta-sa.org*) happens in April. Fiesta is a 10-day, city-wide, multicultural, family-oriented celebration. Fiesta has grown into an elaborate celebration featuring more than 150 events, including a parade where "floats" really float down the San Antonio River through the center of the city. An Asian New Year is celebrated in January. The two-week San Antonio Stock Show & Rodeo is held in February. Dawn at the Alamo, in March, includes reenactments of the battle. In May, the Return of the Chili Queens is held in Market Square. Charreada, a Mexican rodeo with traditional dress, is held in June, and again in August. The Annual Guadalupe Festival & Street Parade, with floats, marching bands, and more, is held in September. Greater San Antonio Senior Men's Amateur Match Play Championship is a golf tournament held in October. The German-flavored Oktoberfest San Antonio and Wurstfest are both held in October.

When the Grandkids Come: At the San Antonio Children's Museum, kids are encouraged to explore a miniature version of the city. The Magik Theatre provides family, professional theater. The Downtown All-Around Playground at HemisFair Park and the newly renovated Milam Park provide excellent stops for kids. The Tower of the Americas offers a spectacular view of San Antonio from 750 feet above the ground. The Plaza Theatre of Wax houses more than 225 life-like characters. Ripley's Believe it Or Not! has more than 500 unique curiosities from around the world. Brackenridge Park is a 433-acre refuge in the heart of the city. The San Antonio Zoo, with a collection of more than 3,000 animals, is ranked as one of the best in the country. The Witte Museum is for hands-on learning, with exhibits exploring science and Texas history.

More Information

Municipal

The San Antonio Convention and Visitors Bureau
203 South St. Mary's Street, 2nd floor
San Antonio, TX 78205
210-207-6700
www.sanantoniocvb.com

Newspaper

San Antonio Express News
Avenue E & 3rd
San Antonio, TX 78205
210-225-7411
www.mysanantonio.com

Realty

We do not have a Realtor recommendation for San Antonio. As an option, check out *www.realtor.com* or *www.homegain.com.* Select a Realtor with both CRS and GRI designations after their names, since it means that these folks have gone the extra mile and are both graduates of the Realtor Institute and Certified Residential Specialists.

St. George, Utah

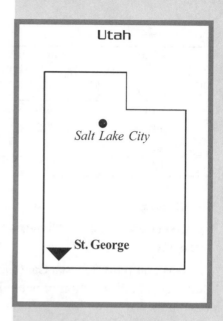

Utah

Salt Lake City

St. George

St. George at a Glance

St. George has a temperate climate filled with sunshine, red rock mountains, green carpeted valleys, and miles of trails for hiking, biking, and running. You will find at least 10 top-rated golf courses within 15 minutes of each other, with at least five more in development. All of this, along with the temperate climate, the new state-of-the-art medical center, symphony orchestra, state college, and friendly people, has made St. George one of the most desirable retirement communities in the country. A spring-fed pond at one end of Main Street supplies water for a meandering stream, with a waterfall and other water features. The city has 25 parks encompassing 210 acres. Quail and Gunlock are wonderful places to take your boat to water-ski or just enjoy the water. The town is only an hour and a half from Las Vegas, and less than three hours from several national parks, including the Grand Canyon. Zion National Park is only 45 minutes away. Bryce Canyon is only two hours away, where skiing and other sports are available in the winter. The city got its "Dixie" nickname not only because of its southern location in the state, but because cotton was grown in the area during the Civil War, when it was a scarce commodity.

Possible Drawbacks: St. George is small, but it is rapidly growing. Right now it has certain small-town limitations that might feel constraining if you are used to a big city.

▸ Nickname: Utah's Dixie
▸ County: Washington
▸ Area Code: 435
▸ Population: 54,049
▸ County Population: 90,354
▸ Percent of Population Over 65: 17%
▸ Region: Southwestern Utah
▸ Closest Metropolitan Area: Las Vegas, 125 miles
▸ Median Home Price: $259,725
▸ Best Reasons to Retire Here: St. George offers continuous sunshine, a low cost of living, booming economy, natural scenery, year-round golf, and great outdoor recreation and living oppurtunities.

Climate

37° N Latitude 113 °W Longitude	Average High Temperature (°F)	Average Low Temperature (°F)	Precipitation (")	Sunshine (%)
January	53.8	27.3	0.9	58
April	76.5	44.2	0.5	69
July	102.2	68.9	0.6	77
October	80.8	45.7	0.6	76
YEAR	78.1	46.4	8.1	70

Utilities

Overview: The cost of living is exceptionally low at 94.2, where the national average is 100.

Gas Company: Questar Gas (435-674-6157; *www.questargas.com*) provides transportation and distribution of natural gas for residential, commercial, and industrial customers.

Electric Company: The city Utilities Department (435-674-4270; *www.sgcity.org/utilities*) supplies power, water, sewer, and garbage collection. They require a $125 deposit from renters. There is no connection fee.

Phone Company: South Central Communications (435-986-0838)

Water/Sewer Company: The city Utilities Department (435-674-4270; *www.sgcity.org/utilities*) supplies power, water, sewer, and garbage collection. They require a $125.00 deposit from renters. There is no connection fee.

Cable Company: Charter Communications (435-888-1053; *www.charter.net*)

The Tax Axe

Car Registration: The Utah Department of Motor Vehicles (800-DMV-UTAH; *http://dmv.utah.gov/register.html*) requires all vehicles to be registered. You must present the most recent registration, title, a Utah safety inspection certificate, a Utah emission certificate, and a serial number inspection. The amount of the tax is determined by the make and year of the vehicle.

Driver's License: The Utah Department of Public Safety (801-965-4437; *http://driverlicense.utah.gov*) requires that a driver's license be obtained immediately by those entering the state with the intention of making Utah their home. The fee is $20.

Sales Tax: The state sales tax is 4.75 percent. Washington County adds 1.25 percent for a total of 6 percent.

State Income Tax: The state has an accelerated income tax that ranges from 2.3 percent to 7 percent. Half of the federal taxes are deductible.

Retirement Income Tax: All income is taxed regardless of source.

Property Tax: The rate is 1.13 percent. A 45 percent discount can be taken on residences.

Local Real Estate

Overview: A wide range of real estate is available, including horse properties, large acreage properties, condos, golf course homes, and many styles of single-family homes.

Average price of a three-bedroom/two-bath home: $239,319

Average price of a two-bedroom condo: $110,039

Common Housing Styles: Houses are built with outdoor living in mind. Prevalent in most new construction is the "Southwest" feel. You will also find Mediterranean, Tuscan, and Santa Fe types.

Rental Market: Houses, condos, and apartments are widely available. Rentals range from small studio apartments to million dollar homes. Fully furnished and kitchen-equipped vacation apartments are common by the day, week, or month.

Average rent for a two-bedroom apartment: $700 per month

Communities Popular With Retirees: Snow Canyon and StoneCliff. English Oaks is a 55 and older community, Sunbrook, Coral Canyon, Green Springs, and Entrada are golf communities.

Nearby Areas to Consider: Pine Valley is at an elevation of 6,500 feet in the Pine Valley Mountains. The Pine Valley area has thick forests of ponderosa pine and offers cooler summer temperatures than the surrounding desert areas. Toquerville is along the banks of Ash Creek at an elevation of 3,394 feet. The town today has a population of about 900.

Earning a Living

Business Climate: The economy of Washington County has been the fastest growing metropolitan statistical area in the nation for the last decade. Job growth continues to outpace the rest of the state and the nation with a double digit percentage increase annually. It has a workforce of more than 50,000. Electrical rates and worker compensation insurance are both low. The trade area of St. George extends into Nevada and part of Arizona.

Help in Starting a Business: The chamber of commerce (435-628-1658; *www.stgeorgechamber.com*) can put you in touch with a number of helpful organizations. The Economic Development Corporation of Utah (800-574-UTAH; *www.edcutah.org*) can provide you with a wealth of information about doing business in the state. The Dixie Business Alliance (435-652-7741) provides seminars and other training opportunities. The Washington County Economic Development Council is part of the chamber of commerce and actively supports value-added businesses to help bring new facilities from the drawing board into production.

Job Market: With the constantly expanding economy, the job opportunities are also expanding. Jobs of all types are always available. The average commute time is 17.2 minutes. The unemployment rate is 4.4 percent. The wages in Washington County are lower than average for the state.

Medical Care

The Dixie Regional Medical Center (435-251-1000; *www.ihc.com*) is a 196-bed fully-capable hospital in two locations in the city. It is part of the Intermountain Health Care system. It has an acute rehabilitation center, providing specialty care for stroke and other neurologically impaired patients. It is the smallest fully-accredited cancer center in the nation. It has a world-class heart program and performs open heart surgery. Most other acute-care services are available. There is an extensive program for seniors, including home care, and a health care library for seniors with information about heart services, cancer, asthma, diabetes, high blood pressure, and preventative health.

Services for Seniors

Red Rock Center for Independent Living (800-649-2340; *www.rrci.org*) is all about independent living for those with disabilities. The *Senior Sampler* (435-673-7604; *www.seniorsampler.com*) is a weekly newspaper for seniors. The Five County Area Agency on Aging (435-673-3548; *www.fcaog.state.ut.us/dep/aging*) provides community planning, training, and services to assist older persons in remaining independent and living in their own homes. Events, meetings, and services are organized at the St. George Senior Citizen's Center (435-634-5716). In-Home & Community Based Aging Services (435-673-3548) is also a good resource.

Continuing Education

Dixie State College (435-652-7500; *www.dixie.edu*) has the Institute for Continued Learning, specifically for learners in retirement. It presents non-credit programs including lectures, study and discussion groups, educational trips, and other special events. A partnership for adult education has been formed between DSC and the new Dixie Applied Technology College to offer several special programs. The University of Utah, on the campus of DSC, (435-652-7892; *http://extension.usu.edu*) makes a variety of graduate and postgraduate degrees available in St. George. Classes are presented live through an interactive satellite link. The Mohave Community College (928-692-3031; *www.mohave.edu*) is in Kingman, Arizona, and provides corporate training and customized training programs on productivity, workplace skills, and technical skills.

Crime and Safety

The City of St. George has a violent crime rate of 2.4 per 1,000 residents, far below the national average. Over 95 percent of all crimes committed are non-violent in nature.

Getting Around Town

Public Transportation: Suntran (435-673-8726; *www.sgcity.org/suntran*) is the new public transit system that runs three bus routes throughout the city. The buses have bike racks so you can ride to the bus stop and then take your bike with you. The St.

George Shuttle (800-9933-8320; *www.stgshuttle.com*) provides van service to and from Las Vegas, and to and from Salt Lake City.

Roads and Highways: I-15 connects St. George to both Salt Lake City and Las Vegas. I-70 to Denver joins I-15 approximately 125 miles to the north.

Airports: St. George Municipal Airport, about one mile to the south, is served by Skywest Airlines (435-634-3000; *www.skywest.com*), which is headquartered in St. George and provides daily flights to Salt Lake City.

Let the Good Times Roll

Recreation: St. George is a great for golfers. You will also find tennis courts, hiking trails, horseback riding, rock climbing, biking, walking, skating, and any other outdoor activity you could think of. The St. George Recreation Department presents programs year round to promote active and healthy living. You will find paved walking paths within half a mile of every resident living in the city. The ghost town of Silver Reef, an abandoned silver mining boom town, is 20 miles to the north. Another ghost town, Grafton, has been abandoned since 1868. Local helicopter tours are available for scenic rides. There are two primary urban fishing ponds inside St. George—Tawa near the Softball complex, and the Skyline Drive facility—giving anglers a couple of choices close to home. Bird watchers come to St. George year-round, but the wide variety of birds is exceptional in the winter when the "snowbirds" arrive. You can swim at the Sand Hollow Aquatic Center, which features a three-lane pool, indoor water-slide, two diving boards, family locker rooms, and multi-play unit. Other pools, such as the Dixie College Nautical Center, St. George City Pool, Hurricane City Pool, and the Veyo City Pool, are also are available to help you cool off and exercise. The true treasure of St. George is the surrounding countryside with the mountains, parks, national monuments, and canyons.

Culture: A crowded schedule of concerts, plays, art shows, and more are offered throughout the year with music and theater under the stars at several outdoor venues during warmer months, and performances at indoor facilities through cooler months. The area is filled with historic sights and museums that display artifacts of the area's past. You can spend a day in early-day St. George by taking a walking tour of old St. George, where many buildings from the 1800s still stand as public buildings and private homes. Tours through many of these buildings are available from Memorial Day through Labor day. The Daughters of Utah Pioneers Museum was constructed next to the pioneer courthouse for the purpose of preserving pioneer relics. The St. George Dinosaur Track Site is at the Johnson Farm and is home to hundreds of early Jurassic era dinosaur footprints.

Annual Events: Each October, the Huntsman World Senior Games are held. It's a competition for thousands of seniors from all over the world. The age groups range from 50 to 95, and includes golf, tennis, table tennis, and just about anything else you can imagine, such as pickleball, horseshoes, and bowling. Besides sporting events, the Games sponsor lifestyle seminars that promotes peace, friendship, and health. From May through August, Sunsational Days of Summer is a celebration of all the programs provided by the city of St. George. In January is the Winter Bird Festival sponsored by Red Cliffs Audubon. In February is the Dixie College Invitational Art Show, which is one of the finest art shows in the west. The Annual St. George Art Festival in March is known as the "Friendliest Festival in the West." In April, the Dixie Downs Horse is sponsored by the St. George Lions Club. In July is the Blue Moon Festival & Pottery Sale. In August, the Enterprise Corn Festival is held, featuring fresh, succulent corn on the cob; games; selling crafts; exhibiting quilts; and plain old-fashioned fun. In September is the annual rodeo celebration at the Sun Bowl in St. George. October brings more than 4,000 runners from all over the world to participate in the 13th largest marathon in the United States.

When the Grandkids Come: Fiesta Fun-Family Fun Center is where you can find something for everyone. This includes a driving range, miniature golf, batting cages, a Soft Play center, go-karts, video arcade, bumper boats, and the Back Porch Cafe. The St. George Recreation Center is where you will find racquetball courts, a fitness center, gymnasium, hobby and craft center, game rooms, and more.

More Information

Municipal

St. George Chamber of Commerce
97 East St. George Boulevard
St. George, UT 84770
435-628-1658
www.stgeorgechamber.com

Newspaper

The Spectrum
275 East St. George Boulevard
St. George, UT 84770
435-674-6200
www.thespectrum.com

Realty

Dave Ellis
1224 South River Road #A-200
St. George, UT 84790
435-862-9199
www.davidellisrealtor.com

45 ▶ Burlington, Vermont

Burlington at a Glance

One of America's most livable cities, Burlington is located on the eastern shore of Lake Champlain between the Adirondack and Green Mountains. Lake Champlain is the sixth largest freshwater lake in the United States, with 88 miles of coastline in Chittenden County. Burlington has a covered downtown pedestrian and shopping mall. Battery Street, near the waterfront and site of a ferry landing since the early 1800s, is known for its historic commercial and industrial buildings. More than 200 houses in the King Street Neighborhood Historic District have been restored. Around City Hall Park, originally set aside in the 1790s for a courthouse, are public and commercial buildings, including the Colonial Revival style City Hall, the old Ethan Allen Firehouse, and several banks. A magnificent restoration of the Art Deco Flynn Theater (a significant success for the arts community) is now the site of performances of all types, including concerts, plays, and musical theatre. *Maturity* magazine named Burlington one of the "50 Best Places to Live." The Arts and Entertainment network named Burlington number one on its list of "Top 10 Cities to Have It All."

Possible Drawbacks: You must enjoy winter. It gets cold up there, and it stays cold for a long time. The average annual snowfall is an amazing 81 inches.

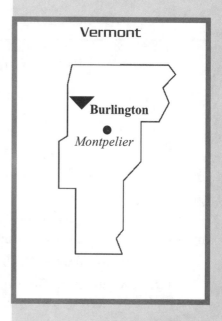

Vermont

Burlington ▼

● Montpelier

▸ Nickname: New England's West Coast
▸ County: Chittendon
▸ Area Code: 802
▸ Population: 39,466
▸ County Population: 146,571
▸ Percent of Population Over 65: 12.4%
▸ Region: Northwestern Vermont
▸ Closest Metropolitan Area: Montreal, 50 miles
▸ Median Home Price: $287,000
▸ Best Reasons to Retire Here: Four distinct seasons, excellent healthcare, clean air, proximity to Montreal, and beautiful Lake Champlain.

Climate

44° N Latitude 73° W Longitude	Average High Temperature (°F)	Average Low Temperature (°F)	Precipitation (")	Sunshine (%)
January	25.2	17.5	1.8	41
April	53.6	34.2	2.8	49
July	81.1	59.5	3.6	64
October	56.8	38.5	3.0	47
YEAR	54.0	35.1	34.2	49

Utilities

Overview: The cost of living is 90, compared to a national average of 100. This means that it's cheaper to live in Burlington than in other areas of the country.

Gas Company: Vermont Gas Systems (802-863-4511; *www.vermontgas.com*)

Electric Company: The Burlington Electric Department (802-658-0300; *www.burlingtonelectric.com*) provides electricity to the Burlington area.

Phone Company: Verizon (*www.verizon.com*) provides local and long-distance phone service in Burlington.

Water/Sewer Company: The Department of Public Works (802-863-4501; *www.dpw.ci.burlington.vt.us*) provides water and sewer services for Burlington.

Cable Company: The city cable television franchise is held by Adelphia (802-447-1534; *www.adelphia.com*). The city provides discounts for low income seniors and disabled customers.

The Tax Axe

Car Registration: The State of Vermont Department of Motor Vehicles (802-828-2000; *www.aot.state.vt.us/dmv*) requires that cars and motorhomes be registered at the main office in Montpelier. Basic registration is $50.00 a year.

Driver's License: To obtain a license, Vermont law requires that out-of-state applicants must pass a vision test. The road test and written test may be waived by the examiner if the applicant holds a valid out-of-state license, but the $5 exam fee must be paid. A four year license is $35.

Sales Tax: The state sales tax is 6 percent. Certain items, including medicine and food, are exempt.

State Income Tax: Vermont has an accelerated income tax with the rate varying from 3.6 percent to 9.5 percent.

Retirement Income Tax: There are no exemptions, except for railroad retirement benefits. Out-of-state government pensions are fully taxed.

Property Tax: The rate is $2.59 per $100 of valuation, but plans are in the works to raise it.

Local Real Estate

Overview: From 1998 to the present, the area has sustained a seller's market, leading to a low inventory of houses for sale, and a low number of days on the market. Most recently, houses were selling with an average of 33 days on the market. This is decidedly down from the mid-1990s when the average was 90 days.

Average price of a three-bedroom/two-bath home: $274,000

Average price of a two-bedroom condo: $224,000

Common Housing Styles: Ranch, Cape Cod, contemporary, Colonial, and Victorian are all fairly common housing styles in Burlington.

Rental Market: A two- or three-bedroom single family house will rent for about $1,500 per month.

Average rent for a two-bedroom apartment: $1,000 per month

Communities Popular With Retirees: All of northwest Vermont is becoming more popular with retirees.

Nearby Areas to Consider: Stowe can only be described with superlatives. It is a world famous historic village nestled next to Vermont's highest peak, Mt. Mansfield. It is where you will find legendary fall foliage, spectacular skiing, stunning summers, and beautiful mountains. Shelburne is located on the shores of Lake Champlain just a few minutes south of Burlington. Shelburne contains Vermont's largest retirement community and includes some of the more popular Vermont attractions, such as the Vermont Teddy Bear Company, Shelburne Farms, and the best historical museum in New England, the Shelburne Museum.

Earning a Living

Business Climate: The metropolitan area of Burlington features unmatched benefits for businesses, including top-notch telecommunications, transportation, and educational systems, a highly educated labor force, innovative business/education partnership programs, and more. *Inc.* magazine named Burlington as one of the "10 Best Small Cities" in which to do business.

Help in Starting a Business: The Vermont Department of Economic Development (802-828 3080; *www.thinkvermont.com*) has economic data, information on doing business in Vermont, what the regional resources are, and general business news. The Small Business Development Center (802-728-9101; *www.vtsbdc.org*) provides affordable high quality training programs for start-up businesses.

Job Market: The unemployment rate is 3.6 percent. The Website *www.monster.com* named Burlington as one of America's best places to live. This means that there is less competition for an opening, and that the jobs are good. The Vermont Department of Employment and Training (802-828-4000; *www.det.state.vt.us*) is part of the state effort to provide services, information, and support so individuals are able to obtain and keep good jobs.

Medical Care

Fletcher Allen Health Care (802-847-0000; *www.fahc.org*) has 526 beds and is an academic medical center affiliated with the University of Vermont College of Medicine. It is a Level I Trauma Center, serving a population of 850,00 throughout Vermont and northern New York. Fletcher Allen Health Care provides care at more than 40 patient care sites and 100 outreach clinics in Vermont and upstate New York.

Services for Seniors

Champlain Senior Center (802-658-3585; *www.champlainseniorcenter.org*) has multiple locations and exists to provide nutritional, educational, recreational, social programs, and activities for older Vermonters, helping make it possible for seniors to live in dignity and independence. They provide a variety of activities including art, gardening, exercise, education, health programs, and meals. Senior Citizens Having Fun (802-425-3176) meets the first and third Wednesday of each month. The Champlain Valley Agency on Aging (802-865-0360) coordinates a number of senior community meal sites in the county. These meals are available to anyone age 60 or older. Meals on Wheels (802-862-6253) is a program for residents of Burlington, South Burlington, Shelburne, and Charlotte. Vermont residents age 65 or older can get a permanent hunting and fishing license for $14 from Vermont Fish and Wildlife (802-241-3703; *www.vtfishandwildlife.com*). A Golden Age Passport is issued for people age 62 or older by the United States Forest Service as a lifetime entrance permit to national parks.

Continuing Education

The University of Vermont (800-639-3210; *www.uvm.edu*) has a continuing education program designed to fulfill the university's commitment to lifelong learning through the development and delivery of courses and programs that connect the resources with students in Vermont. These innovative courses and programs are for pre-college, college, and postgraduate students, as well as working professionals. The continuing education program delivers relevant and timely educational opportunities to more than 8,000 individuals in the Vermont region. Champlain College (802-860-2700; *www.champlain.edu*) is a private nonprofit college with a Center for Online and Continuing Education where you can take individual courses or work toward a degree.

Crime and Safety

The violent crime rate is 3.5 instances per 1,000 people. The overall crime rate is below average with a crime index of 282.5, where the national average is 330.6.

Getting Around Town

Public Transportation: The Chittenden County Transportation Authority (802-864-CCTA; *www.cctaride.org*) operates the region's public transit buses and connects Burlington with the airport, South Burlington, and the other communities in the county.

Roads and Highways: US 7 and US 2. I-89 connects to I-91.

Airports: Burlington International Airport (*www.vermontairports.com/btv.html*) is three miles east of the city and is served by seven airlines.

Ports: Lake Champlain Transportation (*www.ferries.com*) operates passenger and vehicle ferries across the lake, one of which is the scenic cruise between Burlington and Port Kent.

Let the Good Times Roll

Recreation: Vermont has the greatest variety of high-quality freshwater fishing in the Northeast, according to the Vermont Fish & Wildlife Department. There are more than 20 golf courses in the Champlain Valley. You will want to check out the specialty cruises and charters with Lake Champlain Cruises. The ski resorts nearest to Burlington are Smugglers Notch, 18 miles away, with a vertical drop of 2,610 feet, and Bolton Valley, 17 miles away, with a vertical drop of 1,634 feet. A six mile paved recreational trail, mostly on a former railroad and close to the lakeshore, runs from one end of the city to the other. It passes through the revitalized waterfront, the city beaches/campground and residential areas, and connects at its south end to a similar path through South Burlington. A movement is underway to provide a means at the north end to continue across the Winooski River into Colchester and eventually all the way to the Canadian border, crossing Lake Champlain into South Hero via "The Fill" (a former railroad causeway). The drive from Burlington to the Canadian border is about 45 miles. The Burlington Community Boathouse is the centerpiece of Burlington's beautiful and ever growing waterfront, offering boaters a full service marina with power, water, showers, and pump-out facilities. Also at the Boathouse are Splash Cafe and Catering, diving registration for local historic wrecks, sailing charters, and the always fantastic sunset over the Adirondack Mountains of New York.

Culture: The Vermont Symphony Orchestra is the oldest state-supported orchestra in the United States and performs 50 concerts a year in more than 20 communities across Vermont. The Dorset Theatre Festival, an award-winning professional theater company, presents eight plays from June to September in the historic, newly restored, air-conditioned Dorset Playhouse. The Shelburne Museum is one of the nation's premiere museums of art, folk art, Americana, and New England heritage with more than 150,000 works exhibited in a beautiful setting of gardens, landscaped grounds, and historic New England buildings. The Southern Vermont Arts Center is a 400-acre arts campus featuring 10 galleries of fine art. National and international traveling exhibitions can be seen in the Elizabeth de C. Wilson Museum. Vermont Cultural Heritage Month is held from mid May to mid-June. It's a month of events exploring Vermont's people, history, artistry, inventiveness, community, and humor.

Annual Events: The annual Vermont City Marathon, ranked "One of the Top 20 Best Marathons" in the country by *Runner's World* magazine, is held in May. It is a 26.2-mile running event held on the city streets and bike paths of Burlington. Pre-race activities include a two-day Sports and Fitness Exposition with vendors and a buffet dinner. The Discover Jazz Festival, held in August, has evolved into the most eclectic celebration imaginable, ranging from the progressive to the traditional, with an array of venues from the clubs and the courtyards, to the theatre and the auditorium. The Burlington Winter Festival is two weeks in February, including music and drama at the Burlington Community Boathouse, mounds of snow and playground activities, snowshoes on an obstacle course, a broomball tournament, wagon rides, a snow sculpture competition, and a Mardi Gras parade.

When the Grandkids Come: Circus Smirkus is Vermont's award-winning international youth circus, which tours Vermont and New England every year. All the stars are kids. It is a nonprofit organization with a year-round circus school, summer camps for kids, and a school residency program in addition to the Big Top Tour. Kid's Town, a children's department store, is in South Burlington. At Kids in Kayaks (802-253-2317), kids learn how to paddle, play river games, and explore the Winooski River.

More Information

Municipal

Lake Champlain Regional Chamber of Commerce
60 Main Street, Suite 100
Burlington, VT 05401
802-863-3489
www.vermont.org

Newspaper

The Burlington Free Press
P.O. Box 10
Burlington, VT 05402
802-863 3441
www.burlingtonfreepress.com

Realty

Mike Gannet
346 Shelburne Road
Burlington, VT 05401
800-451-5004
www.burlingtonvermonthomes.com

Virginia

46 Charlottesville, Virginia

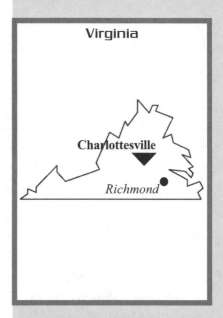

Charlottesville at a Glance

Charlottesville is located between the flatlands of the east coast and the peaks of the Blue Ridge Mountains. Charlottesville is the small city many other American cities would like to be; it is a small city with big city sophistication. Monticello is the former home, gardens, and plantation of Thomas Jefferson. James Monroe's 550 acre estate is named Ash Lawn. James Madison's home, Montpelier, is also in Charlottesville. You will find spectacular scenery and championship golf courses designed by some of the industry's top architects. The many beautiful parks offer wonderful settings for sports, picnics, relaxation, and adventure. The area is rich in antique shops, charming boutiques, distinguished local wineries, antique bookstores, and small towns filled with pleasant surprises. The array of entertainment opportunities was only one factor that led to Charlottesville being named *Money* magazine's "Number One Small City in the South." Charlottesville has a thriving retirement community, a culturally diverse population, and a wide range of activities for mature living. The population of Charlottesville and surrounding counties is growing overall at a rate faster than Virginia; the increase is taking place in the surrounding counties while the city population remains static.

Possible Drawbacks: The humidity in the summer will tend to keep you indoors. It's a small town with large city costs.

▶ Nickname: None
▶ County: Albemarle
▶ Area Code: 434
▶ Population: 45,048
▶ County Population: 79,236
▶ Percent of Population Over 65: 11.6%
▶ Region: Central Virginia
▶ Closest Metropolitan Area: Richmond, 70 miles
▶ Median Home Price: $442,855
▶ Best Reasons to Retire Here: Southern hospitality, small city sophistication, distinctive architecture, spectacular scenery, a great deal of history, and the beauty of the Blue Ridge Mountains.

Climate

38° N Latitude 78° W Longitude	Average High Temperature (°F)	Average Low Temperature (°F)	Precipitation (")	Sunshine (%)
January	43.3	25.5	3.3	54
April	67.6	45.0	3.3	66
July	86.5	65.8	5.4	68
October	68.4	47.7	4.0	63
YEAR	66.4	46.4	46.5	63

Utilities

Overview: The overall cost of living index is a respectable 102.5 based on a national average of 100.

Gas Company: The City of Charlottesville gas utility (434-970-3340; *www.charlottesville.org*)

Electric Company: Virginia Power (888-667-3000; *https://service.vapower.com/cssresconn.asp*)

Phone Company: Sprint (*www.sprint.com*)

Water/Sewer Company: City of Charlottesville at (434-970-3330; *www.charlottesville.org*)

Cable Company: Adelphia (434-979-7571)

The Tax Axe

Car Registration: The Department of Motor Vehicles (*www.dmv.state.va.us*) lists the current wait time for each office online, and you are encouraged to check it before showing up. Emissions tests are required for some northern Virginia communities, but not in the city of Charlottesville.

Driver's License: Contact the Virginia Department of Motor Vehicles (*www.dmv.state.va.us*) for information about getting a Virginia driver's license.

Sales Tax: State sales tax is 3.5 percent and local tax is 1 percent, for a total of 4.5 percent.

State Income Tax: 5.75 percent. An age deduction applies for those 65 or over.

Retirement Income Tax: Taxpayers age 65 and over are elegible for a deduction of $12,000. Contact a tax specialist to find out the income limitations.

Property Tax: Real estate is taxed at the local level, based upon 100 percent of fair-market value. Effective true tax rates on real estate vary and are set by locality. In 1997, the effective true tax rate on real estate ranged from a low of $0.31 per $100 of value in a rural county to $1.42 in northern Virginia. The average effective rate for all counties and cities in the state, exclusive of town levies, was $0.72 per $100 of fair-market value. This comes to 11.9 percent per $1,000 of home value for Charlottesville.

Local Real Estate

Overview: The real estate market is consistently good. The area has controlled growth, making it difficult at times for folks moving in from outside Charlottesville. Prices tend to be a bit higher than might be expected for a small town.

Average price of a three-bedroom/two-bath home: $319,500

Average price of a two-bedroom condo: $422,855

Common Housing Styles: The home styles tend to be Colonial; however, there are some of all styles, depending on the area.

Rental Market: Rental housing in Charlottesville is a big part of the city's economy, driven in large part by the increasing demands of student housing off-campus. Be sure to contact a real estate agent for other options.

Average rent for a two-bedroom apartment: $1,000 per month

Communities Popular With Retirees: Branchlands, the Cottages of Jefferson Heights, Dunlora Village, Lake Monticello, and Glenmore Cottages

Nearby Areas to Consider: Are you looking for a little less density in your life? Well, new homes are sprouting up like daffodils in Fluvanna and Louisa Counties. They're all less than an hour from downtown Charlottesville. Fluvanna County planners are trying to find ways to preserve the lifestyle long enjoyed by residents, which means preparing for growth while maintaining that rural character. Two upscale senior residential subdivisions are in the works in Ruckersville, and county officials are hoping the retirees will stay in Greene County to spend on entertainment and shopping. The Madison County Street Project has given the business center a facelift.

Earning a Living

Business Climate: The region's long tradition of innovation continues with the presence of a base of technology-oriented businesses, small manufacturers, companies emerging from the research being conducted at the University of Virginia, organizations, new programs that support business development, and a general entrepreneurial spirit driven by the creative people who come to the area for its recognized quality of life. *Forbes* magazine and the Milken Institute have ranked Charlottesville as the "12th Best Small Place for Business and Career" in the United States. Charlottesville has a well-educated workforce, including access to talent and resources at the university. There is a state-of-the-art telecommunications infrastructure with an extensive fiber optic network and digital switching capability, and a strategic location near Washington, D.C. and Richmond.

Help in Starting a Business: The Small Business Development Center (434-295-8198; *http://avenue.org/sbdc*) offers free business consulting services, assists with feasibility studies and business planning, sponsors seminars and training, and provides information and other services to area small and mid-sized businesses. The Department of Economic Development (434-970-3117; *www.charlottesville.org*)

offers free business training seminars, and other services to assist new and expanding businesses. SCORE, the Service Corps of Retired Executives (434-285-6712; *www.score-494.org*), provides free consulting services to both start-up and existing small businesses.

Job Market: The unemployment rates are 2.7 percent in the city and 3.9 percent in the state. Because of the students at the University of Virginia, the job market is tight at both the low end (student jobs) and the high end (graduates who decide to remain). You should probably try to arrange for a job before you move.

Medical Care

The University of Virginia Health System (*www.healthsystem.virginia.edu*) is a major academic medical center, and provides an entire spectrum of geriatric services. It is one of the nation's Top 100 hospitals. The main University Hospital consists of 632 beds on eight floors, is organized along the service center concept, and employs a staff of 4,255 people in addition to the 2,500 faculty and students.

Services for Seniors

The Senior Center (434-974-7756; *www.seniorcenterinc.org*) is nationally accredited, and has been an integral resource for the community for more than 40 years. Charlottesville Recreation and Leisure Services (434-970-3261) has special programs for senior citizens. The Jefferson Area Board for Aging (434-817-5222; *www.jabacares.org*) was founded in 1975, and provides daycare, healthcare, housing, referrals, and many other services.

Continuing Education

The offices of Continuing Education of the University of Virginia (804-982-5313) provide conferences, seminars, and workshops throughout the year. They provide credit, non-credit, and certificate programs. The Citizen Scholar Program is a part-time, non-degree program administered through Continuing Education. This program allows adults in Charlottesville and surrounding communities to be admitted to the regular credit courses at the university.

Crime and Safety

In 2003 there were 70 robberies, one homicide, 41 sex offenses, 199 burglaries, 1,315 thefts, 128 motor vehicle thefts, 13 abductions, and 995 incidents of vandalism.

Getting Around Town

Public Transportation: There is a free trolley from downtown to the University grounds. The Charlottesville Transit Service (434-296-RIDE; *www.charlottesville.org/transit*) provides bus service throughout Charlottesville and Albemarle County.

Roads and Highways: I-64, US 29 and 250, Virginia 20 and 302

Airports: The Charlottesville-Albemarle airport has 60 flights daily by United Express, US Airways Express, and Delta Connection.

Let the Good Times Roll

Recreation: Charlottesville and surrounding Albemarle County are ideal for nature lovers. The nearby Blue Ridge Mountains provide ample opportunities for hiking, mountain biking, fishing, and camping. Shenandoah National Park (*www.nps.gov/ shen*) is in the midst of a beautiful section of the Blue Ridge Mountains, which form the eastern rampart of the Appalachians that run between Pennsylvania and Georgia. Within or near the city are 10 golf courses. The Outdoor Adventure Social Club (*www.outdoorsocial.com*) organizes hiking, backpacking, biking, canoeing, caving, kayaking, rock climbing, and many other outdoor adventures and social activities. You will find plenty of parks with playgrounds inside the city, as well as hiking trails and picnic areas. Hike around the city on Rivanna Trail and have your picnic in McIntire Park. The city also has public tennis courts and swimming pools. Many interesting organizations are sponsored by the various departments of the University of Virginia, including everything from Astronomy to Zoology. Fridays After Five and other concerts by national artists are held at the open-air Charlottesville Pavilion.

Culture: Because of the presence of a large university, cultural events and organizations of all possible types exist. The performing arts are active, including a number of live theatres of different types in and around the city, and the University Symphony Orchestra. While it isn't a big city, Charlottesville has a surprisingly full schedule of dance.

Annual Events: The annual Virginia Film Festival of the College of Arts and Sciences of the University of Virginia (*www.vafilm.com*) runs for a week. The annual Virginia Festival of the Book (*www.vabook.org*) is five days in March of free literary events featuring readings, panels, and discussions with authors, illustrators, and publishers. Bring your summer music plans to life with the best concerts of the season. The annual Charlottesville Vegetarian Festival is held in Lee Park in September. The festival draws more than 100 exhibitors and 6,000 visitors. The downtown Dogwood Festival and Parade (*www.dogwoodfestival.org*) happens every year when the trees bloom.

When the Grandkids Come: Shenandoah National Park has the Junior Ranger Explorer Notebook, which provides 15 activities for children age 7 and older with the opportunity to have fun learning about the park as they work toward becoming Junior Rangers.

More Information

Municipal

Charlottesville Regional Chamber of Commerce
P.O. Box 1564
Charlottesville, VA 22902
434-295-3141
www.cvillechamber.org

Newspaper

The Daily Progress
685 Rio Road West
Charlottesville, VA 22902
434-978-7264
www.dailyprogress.com

Realty

Tara Savage
1524 Insurance Lane, Suite B
Charlottesville, VA 22911
866-437-3629
http://wesellcharlottesville.com

Bellingham, Washington

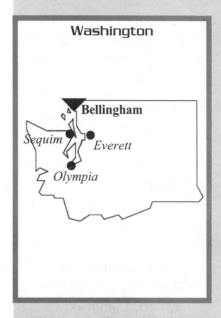

Washington

Bellingham

Sequim   Everett

Olympia

Bellingham at a Glance

Bellingham is where the mountains meet the sea. Halfway between Seattle and Vancouver, it is convenient to both. The city of Bellingham is the hub of activity for a region offering unspoiled recreational opportunities. Bellingham is a coastal city built around the deep water of Bellingham Bay, and is only 23 miles south of the Canadian border. Washington has no state income tax. Transportation links connect the community to the nearby San Juan Islands and Victoria on Vancouver Island. Squalicum Harbor is the second largest in Puget Sound, where 1,900 pleasure and commercial boats are moored. From Bellingham's ports, passenger ferries leave for whale watch cruises, tours to Victoria on Vancouver Island, and cruises to the San Juan Islands. Visitors bound for Alaska depart on the Alaska Marine Highway System ferries from the Bellingham Cruise Terminal in the Historic Fairhaven District. The cultural district includes the respected Whatcom Museum of History and Art, originally built in 1892 as the city hall. The imposing brick building is the centerpiece of a four-building campus, including a children's museum. Bellingham is home to Western Washington University on Sehome Hill, from which you have a view across the bay.

Possible Drawbacks: The winters tend to be mostly cloudy. The local government has not kept up with the growth.

▶ Nickname: City of Subdued Excitement
▶ County: Whatcom
▶ Area Code: 360
▶ Population: 67,171
▶ County Population: 166,814
▶ Percent of Population Over 65: 12.4%
▶ Region: Western Washington
▶ Closest Metropolitan Area: Vancouver, 60 miles
▶ Median Home Price: $250,000
▶ Best Reasons to Retire Here: Bellingham offers beautiful scenery, relaxed life style, and friendly neighbors.

Climate

48° N Latitude 122° W Longitude	Average High Temperature (°F)	Average Low Temperature (°F)	Precipitation (")	Sunshine (%)
January	43.2	31.8	4.5	28
April	55.8	39.9	2.6	52
July	70.9	53.3	1.2	65
October	58.3	42.1	3.5	43
YEAR	57.2	42.1	35.3	47

Utilities

Overview: Based on a national average of 100, the cost of living in Bellingham is slightly high at 106. The cost of healthcare is high throughout the state, and is the factor that raises the index above average.

Gas Company: Cascade Natural Gas Corp (360-733-5980; *www.cngc.com*) provides natural gas across Washington and Oregon.

Electric Company: Puget Sound Energy (888-225-5773; *www.pse.com*)

Phone Company: Local telephone service is provided by Qwest (*www.qwest.com*) and by Verizon (*www.verizon.com*).

Water/Sewer Company: City of Bellingham Water & Sewer at (360-676-6900; *www.cob.org*)

Cable Company: Comcast (800-266-2278; *www.comcast.com*)

The Tax Axe

Car Registration: Your vehicle must be licensed by the Department of Licensing (360-902-3600; *www.dol.wa.gov*) within 30 days of becoming a Washington resident. A number of fees can apply, such as a filing fee of $7, a basic license fee of $30, a license service fee of 75 cents, a title application fee of $5, an emergency medical services fee of $6.50, and the standard license plate or decal fee ranges from 50 cents to $3. There is also a $15 out-of-state fee. The amount of tax charged partially depends on the amount of tax paid in the other state, so you will need that information.

Driver's License: You must apply for a license within 30 days of becoming a Washington resident. Normally, only the written examination is required. The fees are $10 for the examination and $25 for a five-year license.

Sales Tax: The state sales tax is 6.5 percent. In Bellingham, the total sales tax rate is 8.2 percent.

State Income Tax: There is no income tax in Washington.

Retirement Income Tax: There is no income tax in Washington.

Property Tax: Properties in the county are reassessed roughly once every four years. In Bellingham, the tax rate is roughly 1.25percent of the assessed value. Nearby areas are slightly more or less.

Local Real Estate

Overview: The market is out of balance, with more buyers than sellers. This has caused the norm to be multiple offers with escalator clauses. Most of the growth is being met with new houses, but some pre-war houses are becoming available. Condo purchases are up as an affordable alternative to a house. Overall, prices are increasing at the rate of 20 percent a year.

Average price of a three-bedroom/two-bath home: $292,000

Average price of a two-bedroom condo: $169,000

Common Housing Styles: Bellingham likes two-story houses, but offers a few ranch style properties as well. There are lots of mature landscaping and uneven lots provide a good mix of street-front appearance.

Rental Market: Home ownership is under 50 percent of the population, attributed largely to the student population. The rental vacancy rate has been low for some years, but is rising, causing competition among landlords.

Average rent for a two-bedroom apartment: $600 per month

Communities Popular With Retirees: Sudden Valley to the northwest has a natural feel. Fairhaven is good for the condo life. A number of neighborhoods on the north side of town are new and have a homogenous look and feel. The rest of the neighborhoods are a good mix.

Nearby Areas to Consider: Blaine, the Peach Arch City, has a population of 4,000 and is in the far northwest corner of the state, on the Canadian border. Some gated retirement communities are near Blaine. Lynden is also on the Canadian border, but is further inland. It is making a conscious effort to retain the community spirit and small town atmosphere of its agricultural roots. The people are determined that the quality of life in Lynden will not diminish with the increase in population.

Earning a Living

Business Climate: Downtown Bellingham has been enjoying a renaissance with an increase in the number of businesses, including major employers. With Western Washington University, Bellingham has an educated workforce and, because of this, many small to medium-sized businesses. Bellingham's waterfront is host to a major shipping operation, and is the southern terminus of the Alaska state ferry system. Restaurants, parks, and trails surround Bellingham Bay, making it one of the state's best tourist draws. Mining is gone, and the timber and fishing industries continue to have dwindling resources and increasing regulation. However, agriculture, light manufacturing, education, retail, and healthcare have all taken hold, giving Bellingham a very stable economic foundation. Canadian commerce's effect is mostly seen in retail, but there has been a lot of interest by Canadian businesses in establishing a presence in Whatcom County.

Help in Starting a Business: The Bellingham office of the Small Business Development Center (360-733-4014; *www.cbe.wwu.edu/sbdc*) works with start-up and existing business owners, providing free counseling services on issues such as business planning, registering a business, financing, regulations, and licensing. Bellingham SCORE (360-676-3307; *www.scorechapter591.org*) provides counseling, loan information, and workshops for start-up businesses.

Job Market: Because of the presence of the Western Washington University, competition is stiff for jobs that require an education. Employment is good in the area, because there are many new start-up businesses. The unemployment rate is about the same as the national average. Contact the Whatcom County WorkSource Center (360-671-1660) for more information.

Medical Care

St Josephs Hospital (360-734-5400; *www.peacehealth.org/Whatcom*) is a 253-bed, two-campus medical center, and level II trauma center in Bellingham. As Whatcom County's only hospital, St. Joseph's Hospital provides a full range of inpatient and outpatient services, including 24-hour emergency and trauma care, neurosurgery, total joint replacement, the cardiovascular center, and the community cancer center.

Services for Seniors

The Bellingham Senior Activity Center (360-676-1450; *www.co.whatcom.wa.us/parks/seniors*) is a multipurpose drop-in facility that offers a variety of services, programs, and activities that encourages independent, healthy, active living, resulting in positive physical and emotional wellness. The Whatcom Volunteer Center (360-734-3055; *www.whatcomvolunteer.org*) is a one-stop center linking people of all ages who want to contribute their talents and time to directly assist agencies in meeting community needs.

Continuing Education

Western Washington University (360-650-3000; *www.wwu.edu*) has a tuition waiver program for those over 60. Courses are open to anyone during the academic year through the Space Available to Non-matriculated students (SPAN) program. Western Washington University is one of six state-funded, four-year institutions of higher education in Washington. It maintains nearly 73 buildings on a 215-acre campus. Whatcom Community College (360-676-2170; *www.whatcom.ctc.edu*) offers associate's degrees and provides support services to students who have never been to college, or have been away from college for a number of years.

Crime and Safety

The number of crimes reported is 5,237.4 per 100,000 people. Crime is not a predominant factor of life in Bellingham. Most victims of violent crime know their attacker as a relative, associate, friend, or acquaintance.

Getting Around Town

Public Transportation: The Whatcom Transportation Authority (360-676-7433; *www.ridewta.com*) runs busses with routes throughout the city. The cost is 50 cents per ride, or, for those over 60, a quarterly pass can be purchased for $20.

Roads and Highways: I-5, SR 542, 539

Airports: Bellingham International is served by the three regional carriers: Horizon Air, Allegiant Air, and San Juan Airlines. The closest major airport is Seattle.

Ports: The port of Bellingham has a shipping terminal, four marinas, and a cruise terminal that is the southern connection of the Alaska Marine Highway.

Let the Good Times Roll

Recreation: The slopes of the Mt. Baker ski area is a laid-back ski destination that boasts of having the most snowfall ever in a single season: the world record of 1,140 inches! You might want to try some challenging ice climbing on a glacier flanking the mountain. Bellingham was named "Trail Town U.S.A." nearly 10 years ago by the National Park Service and American Hiking Society because of the miles of trails and thousands of stunning views. If you would rather be seated for your adventure, rent a sailboat or kayak. You can paddle a kayak around the uncrowded coves along Chuckanut Drive. Join a charter trip to the stunning San Juan Islands, or go visit Victoria. Take a raft trip on the Nooksack River and watch the mighty Orca whales. Recreational boaters enjoy easy access to the San Juan Islands and the Canadian Gulf Islands. The Bellingham Mt. Baker region has more public golf courses than any area in Oregon, Washington, and Idaho, according to *Golf Digest* magazine. The Parks and Recreation Department provides park facilities, classes, special events, trails, nature centers, museums, and historical sites. You can spend the day in Bellingham's renowned district of Victorian-era buildings, where you will find shops offering hand-crafted products, local restaurants that serve fresh seafood, and art galleries featuring Northwest artisans.

Culture: You are never far from a museum or art gallery in Bellingham, including the American Museum of Radio and Electricity (*www.americanradiomuseum.org*). You will also find the Bellingham Railway Museum and the Lynden Pioneer Museum here. The Mindport Exhibit is a blend of art and interactive exhibits. Whatcom Museum of History & Art (*www.whatcommuseum.org*) is composed of four buildings, featuring exhibitions of contemporary art and regional history.

Annual Events: The Birch Bay Polar Bear celebration and quick swim is held on January 1st. The Bellingham Festival of Music (*www.bellinghamfestival.org*) is a series of concerts presented in August. The annual Bike to Work and School Day is held in May. Also in May, the Ski to Sea relay, starting in the heights of Mt. Baker, ends for racers as a final dash is made to ring to the bell in Boulevard Park, concluding 82.5 miles of skiing, running, biking, and paddling. The Skywater Festival of June is filled with parades, food, arts and crafts, and music. The Mt. Baker Blues Festival is held at the end of July. The Mt. Baker Bicycle Hill Climb is 24.5 miles and 4,300 feet of the best road climb in Washington is held in September.

When the Grandkids Come: The Children's Museum holds a Wonder Workshop each Saturday afternoon. Kids are always fascinated by whale watching, and paddling a kayak.

More Information

Municipal

Bellingham/Whatcom Chamber of Commerce & Industry
1201 Cornwall Avenue Suite 100
Bellingham, WA 98225
360-734-1330
www.bellingham.com

Bellingham Convention and Visitors Bureau
904 Potter Street
Bellingham, WA 98229
360-671-3990
www.bellingham.org

Newspaper

The Bellingham Herald
1155 North State Street
Bellingham, WA 98225
360-676-2600
www.bellinghamherald.com

Realty

Richard Baila
913 Lakeway Drive
Bellingham, WA 98229
360-961-1873
www.rbaila.com

48 ► Everett, Washington

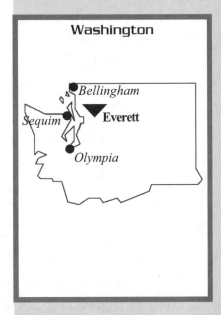

Everett at a Glance

Everett is a bayside community between the beautiful Cascade Mountain Range to the east, Puget Sound to the west, and the Snohomish River. Everett is consistently rated as one of the best places to live by the national media. Everett is an "All-American" city, an award given by the National Civic League annually to 10 cities in the United States. At 10,541 feet, Glacier Peak is one of the highest mountains in the country. About 68 percent of the county is forest land, 19 percent is rural, 8 percent is urban, and 5 percent is agricultural. The Olympic Mountains to the west, across Puget Sound, shelter the area from excessive precipitation coming off the Pacific Ocean. Naval Station Everett is the Navy's most modern facility. Everett is the site of the world's largest building, Boeing's final assembly plant. Also, Everett is home to the second largest marina on the West Coast. You can watch the activity on Port Gardner Bay from the waterfront brew pubs, restaurants, or hotels. A farmer's market operates June through September. Narbeck Wetland Sanctuary lies within the city limits of Everett, only 20 miles north of the heart of downtown Seattle, the region's largest city.

Possible Drawbacks: This is not a place for hot, dry, or sunny weather. The cost of living, particularly housing and healthcare, are both above the national average.

► Nickname: None.

► County: Snohomish

► Area Code: 425

► Population: 96,643

► County Population: 606,024

► Percent of Population Over 65: 9.1%

► Region: Western Washington

► Closest Metropolitan Area: Seattle, 25 miles

► Median Home Price: $225,000

► Best Reasons to Retire Here: The beautiful scenery, relaxed life style, and employment opportunities are great reasons to retire in Everett.

Climate

47° N Latitude 122° W Longitude	Average High Temperature (°F)	Average Low Temperature (°F)	Precipitation (")	Sunshine (%)
January	44.8	33.3	4.4	28
April	56.8	40.5	2.5	50
July	72.1	53.4	1.0	64
October	59.4	42.4	3.4	40
YEAR	58.5	42.6	35.1	45

Utilities

Overview: The cost of living index is 117.4, which is well above the national average of 100. This is primarily because of housing at 134.4 and healthcare at 130. Transportation is also high at 125.5. Food is also above average at 109.9, but utilities are very cheap at 66.1.

Gas Company: Puget Sound Energy (888-225-5773; *www.pse.com*)

Electric Company: Puget Sound Energy (888-225-5773; *www.pse.com*)

Phone Company: Verizon (425-261-5321; *www.verizon.com*) offers both local and long-distance phone service in Everett.

Water/Sewer Company: City of Everett (425-257-8800; *www.everettwa.org*)

Cable Company: Comcast (800-266-2278; *www.comcast.com*)

The Tax Axe

Car Registration: Your vehicle must be licensed by the Department of Licensing (360-902-3600; *www.dol.wa.gov*) within 30 days of becoming a Washington resident. A number of fees can apply, such as a filing fee of $7, a basic license fee of $30, a license service fee of 75 cents, a title application fee of $5, an emergency medical services fee of $6.50, and the standard license plate or decal fee ranges from 50 cents to $3. There is also a $15 out-of-state fee. The amount of tax charged partially depends on the amount of tax paid in the other state, so you will need that information.

Driver's License: You must apply for a license within 30 days of becoming a Washington resident. Normally only the written examination is required. The fees are $10 for the examination and $25 for a five-year license. Contact the Department of Licensing (360-902-3600; *www.dol.wa.gov*) for more information.

Sales Tax: The state imposes a 6.5 percent sales tax. With the local taxes added, the total rate is 8.6 percent.

State Income Tax: There is no income tax in Washington.

Retirement Income Tax: There is no income tax in Washington.

Property Tax: The property tax amount is $12.40 per $1,000 of assessed value.

Local Real Estate

Overview: The market in Everett varies with employment, and Boeing is the major employer. Major cutbacks at Boeing have created a seller's market, except at the low end of the price scale. The recent economic boom has created an active real estate market with the average time on market for sales being less than 60 days.

Average price of a three-bedroom/two-bath home: $216,000

Average price of a two-bedroom condo: $200,000

Common Housing Styles: Colonial and contemporary with wood exteriors and open floorplans. Cedar is a common building material.

Rental Market: There is a lot to choose from among the rental houses, apartments, houses, duplexes, townhouses, and condos for rent.

Average rent for a two-bedroom apartment: $660 per month

Communities Popular With Retirees: Clinton, Lake Stevens, Langley, Mabana, and Machias

Nearby Areas to Consider: During the 1920s, Marysville earned the nickname "The Strawberry City" in recognition of the area's overabundance of the sweet fruity berries, which are celebrated annually in June with the Strawberry Festival and the Grand Parade. The city of Lake Stevens was primarily a resort community through the 20th century. By 2000, the city had grown to a population of 6,361 because of its natural beauty and changes in the economy of the surrounding area. The lake remains the focal point of the greater Lake Stevens community for recreation and as a symbol of the need to provide for a sustainable existence that will protect a natural environment.

Earning a Living

Business Climate: Snohomish is one of the fastest-growing counties in the nation. Washington state's Puget Sound region is one of the world centers for technology in aerospace, biomedicine, and computer software, represented by such global names as Boeing, Immunex, and Microsoft.

Help in Starting a Business: The Small Business Administration (509-353-2811; *www.sba.gov/wa*) provides business start-up assistance with access to state, local, and federal resources. SCORE, the Service Core of Retired Executives (206-553-7320; *http://seattlescore.org*), provides business counseling services from seasoned experts who have retired. The Small Business Development Center at Edmonds Community College (425-640-1459; *http://workforce.edcc.edu*) has additional information.

Job Market: The fastest growing occupations in Snohomish County are medical science, veterinary, survey research, dental, computer software, assembly line, technical writing, architecture, and photography. Of these, medical science is the fastest growing, while computer software is the largest.

Medical Care

Providence Everett Medical Center (425-261-2000; *www.providence.org/everett*) is a short-term, 257-bed hospital and has been working to build a healthcare system that can meet all of your needs. From acute, inpatient hospital care, to outpatient surgery and wellness promotion, Providence Everett Medical Center offers a full spectrum of services at four campuses. Stevens Hospital (425-640-4000; *www.stevenshealthcare.org*) is a 217-bed short-term hospital about 14 miles away, and provides a network of quality primary care physicians, specialists, resources for health education, and health and wellness programs. Evergreen Hospital Medical Center (425-899-1000; *www.evergreenhealthcare.org*) is a 129-bed short-term hospital about 17 miles away, and provides primary care, home care, hospice, and many other services. Fairfax Hospital is a 133 psychiatric hospital about 17 miles away.

Services for Seniors

The mission of the Everett Senior Activity Center (425-257-8780; *www.everettwa.org*) is to offer programs of continued learning, physical health, and social interaction in a safe and caring environment. Membership is open to any person 55 years or older, and there is no membership fee. Senior Services of Snohomish County (425-290-1257; *www.sssc.org*) provides senior information and assistance, transportation, nutrition, housing, adult daycare, home repair, and a monthly newsletter.

Continuing Education

A 10-student state-of-the-art computer lab is available at the Everett Senior Activity Center. Training emphasis is on basic computer skills, leading to Internet access and word processing. Everett Community College, as part of its continuing education, has Lifelong Learning (425-640-1459; *http://workforce.edcc.edu*), which is committed to linking college and community resources to provide quality enrichment programs to people of all ages. Also at Everett Community College is the Creative Retirement Institute (*http://new.cri.edcc.edu*), which is a member-driven, self-supporting organization whose mission is to provide quality, affordable educational opportunities for adults in a supportive environment. Henry Cogswell College (866- 411-4221; *www.henrycogswell.edu*) reduces registration fees to almost one-third of the normal for the non-credit registrants.

Crime and Safety

The number of violent crimes recorded by the FBI in 2003 was 546. The number of murders and homicides was two. The violent crime rate was 5.6 per 1,000 people.

Getting Around Town

Public Transportation: Everett Transit (425-257-8803; *www.everetttransit.org*) has buses that provides seven-day-a-week service over several routes throughout the city. Transit service to Everett Station is timed to connect with Sound Transit Express rail service to Lynnwood and Seattle. Quick Coach provides affordable and reliable transportation from Seatac Airport and other locations.

Roads and Highways: Interstate 5; State 522, 525, 526

Airports: Snohomish County Airport Paine Field (425-353-2110; *www.painefield.com*) is home to more than 500 aircraft, including the new Boeing widebody 777, 747, 767s, and business, corporate, and recreational aircraft. Goodrich provides repair and maintenance services for air transport aircraft for major airlines. Today, Snohomish County Airport is home to more than 55 on-site businesses providing over 30,000 jobs to the community.

Ports: The Port of Everett (800-729-7678; *www.portofeverett.com*) is located 25 miles north of Seattle on Puget Sound, operating eight berths on 100 acres of land and handling approximately 1 million tons of cargo per year.

Let the Good Times Roll

Recreation: Jetty Island is a two mile long, manmade island with sandy beaches and shallow warm water. The free Jetty ferry departs from the 10th Street Boat Launch and Marine Park, located at 10th and West Marine View Drive. City of Everett residents with a current resident card or current driver's license with an Everett address may make advance reservations. Grab your blanket, your lawn chair, and a bag of popcorn for Cinema Under the Stars. Music in the Parks provides free music all summer, from jazz and salsa to rockin' blues and folk, you can hear diverse musical styles performed by the Northwest's most popular musicians as Everett Parks and Recreation presents the annual Music in the Parks Summer Concert Series. The Mosquito Fleet is a leading wildlife adventure company in Washington state, operating naturalist-guided Orca whale watching tours in the San Juan Islands, Puget Sound, and areas north of Seattle. The Everett Silvertips are major junior hockey in the Western Hockey League. Island Wood is a one-of-a-kind school on Bainbridge Island. Spencer Island is more than 1,400-acres of the Snohomish River estuary, where the waters of the river meet the salt water, and is a home for more than 300 birds. At the summit of Mount Pilchuck is the historic lookout cabin that the Everett Mountaineers have restored and established as a museum.

Culture: The Everett Performing Arts Center is managed by the Village Theatre. The Village Theatre provides the area with quality theater for all ages with many shows geared toward the entire family—both musicals and non-musicals that are accessible, entertaining, and educational. Everett Symphony Orchestra (*www.everettsymphony.org*) performs in different locations around the city and performed its 67th concert year in 2005.

Annual Events: The General Aviation Appreciation Days festival is held at Paine Field in May. Also in May is the the Annual Hebolb Pow Wow at Everett Community College with Native American Plains dancing, drumming, singing, and arts and crafts. The Everett Area Chamber of Commerce Annual Golf Tournament is held in July.

When the Grandkids Come: Visit the largest building in the world by volume (472,000,000 cubic feet) and see airplanes in various stages of flight test and manufacture. See the Imagine Children's Museum of Snohomish County.

More Information

Municipal

Everett, Washington Area Visitors Bureau
1710 West Marine View Drive
Everett, WA 98206
425-252-5181
www.everettwa.org

Everett Washington Chamber of Commerce
2000 Hewitt Avenue, Suite 205
Everett, WA 98201
425-257-3222
www.everettchamber.com

Newspaper

The Everett Herald.
1213 California Street
P.O. Box 930
Everett, WA 98201
425-339-3017
www.heraldnet.com

Realty

We do not have a Realtor recommendation for Everett. As an option, check out *www.realtor.com* or *www.homegain.com*. Select a Realtor with both CRS and GRI designations after their names, since it means that these folks have gone the extra mile and are both graduates of the Realtor Institute and Certified Residential Specialists.

Olympia, Washington

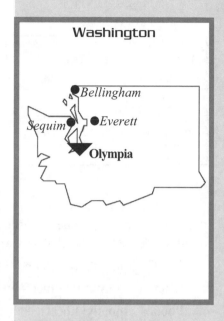

Washington

Olympia at a Glance

Olympia, at the lower end of Puget Sound, provides everything for both the land lubber and the boating enthusiast. Olympia is thought of as having a lot of rain, but there is actually less rain than Houston or Atlanta. On a clear day, Mount Rainier is visible from almost anywhere in town (the city was named because of its view of the Olympic range). And Puget Sound is always a beautiful sight to see. Olympia is a quiet and safe community without the headaches and traffic of a big city. It is less than two hours to beaches, and about three hours to the Vancouver ski resorts or the more desert-like weather of eastern Washington. Downtown you will find shops and a wonderful farmer's market, with only homegrown and homemade items. The summer highs seldom require the use of air conditioning, and the winters average only one snowfall per year. Tree filled areas and natural settings are designated as parks in the middle of town, so it never has an urban or sterile feeling. It is both a college town and the state capitol, so the city is continuously active. If you are looking for a slow pace with a big city culture, and close to recreation, Olympia could be just what you're looking for.

Possible Drawbacks: Olympia is definitely not hot and dry! Also, look elsewhere if you want to see snow in the winter. The winter skies are usually filled with clouds and rain.

▶ Nickname: City on the Sound

▶ County: Thurston

▶ Area Code: 360

▶ Population: 42,514

▶ County Population: 207,355

▶ Percent of Population Over 65: 12.4%

▶ Region: Southwestern Washington

▶ Closest Metropolitan Area: Tacoma, 30 miles

▶ Median Home Price: $205,000

▶ Best Reasons to Retire Here: Proximity to Mount Rainier offers residents lots of outdoor recreation opportunities.

Climate

46° N Latitude 122° W Longitude	Average High Temperature (°F)	Average Low Temperature (°F)	Precipitation (")	Sunshine (%)
January	44.2	31.6	7.5	28
April	58.6	36.1	3.3	47
July	76.5	49.1	0.8	63
October	60.4	38.7	4.6	37
YEAR	60.1	39.2	49.3	43

Utilities

Overview: The cost of living in Olympia is above average at 103 where the national average is 100. The lowest cost indexes are in housing and utilities, while the highest index is the cost of healthcare.

Gas Company: Puget Sound Energy (888-225-5773; *www.pse.com*)

Electric Company: Puget Sound Energy (888-225-5773; *www.pse.com*)

Phone Company: Local telephone service is provided by Qwest (*www.qwest.com*)

Water/Sewer Company: City of Olympia (360-753-4444; *www.ci.olympia.wa.us*)

Cable Company: Comcast (800-266-2278; *www.comcast.com*)

The Tax Axe

Car Registration: Your vehicle must be licensed by the Department of Licensing (360-902-3600; *www.dol.wa.gov*) within 30 days of becoming a Washington resident. A number of fees can apply, such as a filing fee of $7, a basic license fee of $30, a license service fee of 75 cents, a title application fee of $5, an emergency medical services fee of $6.50, and the standard license plate or decal fee ranges from 50 cents to $3. There is also a $15 out-of-state fee. The amount of tax charged partially depends on the amount of tax paid in the other state, so you will need that information.

Driver's License: You must apply for a license within 30 days of becoming a Washington resident. Normally only the written examination is required. The fees are $10 for the examination and $25 for a five-year license. Contact the Department of Licensing (360-902-3600; *www.dol.wa.gov*) for more information regarding getting a Washington license.

Sales Tax: The state sales tax is 6.5 percent. In most of Olympia, the total sales tax rate is 8.0 percent.

State Income Tax: There is no income tax in Washington.

Retirement Income Tax: There is no income tax in Washington.

Property Tax: The tax rate varies depending on the exact area, but it is approximately 1.5 percent of value, and the evaluations are typically 25 percent to 30 percent below market value.

Local Real Estate

Overview: Olympia is an easy commute to such places as Fort Lewis, Madigan Army Hospital, and McChord AFB, which is keeping the market as strong as ever, even in the face of rising prices. If a house is being sold for under $200,000, you can expect multiple offers and a bidding war in this hot seller's market.

Average price of a three-bedroom/two-bath home: $235,000

Average price of a two-bedroom condo: $235,000

Common Housing Styles: There is a mix of urban styles near the state capital and close to downtown. There is a bit of suburbia because of the proximity of Seattle and Tacoma. There are rural properties with acreage and privacy. Waterfront homes are on both lakes and salt water.

Rental Market: The average rent for a two-bedroom house is $744 per month, and for a three-bedroom house is $1,045. Rents increase an average of 4.5 percent per year.

Average rent for a two-bedroom apartment: $800 per month

Communities Popular With Retirees: Indian Summer, Stratford Lane Condos, Jubilee, East Bay Condos, and Capitol Towers

Nearby Areas to Consider: Centralia is an historic railroad town located near I-5, midway between Seattle and Portland, just one mile east of the freeway. Most of the buildings in the area were built shortly before and after 1900. If you like antique shopping, Centralia has 350 antique dealers located in its 11 antique malls, and holds a giant flea market every July. The city of Aberdeen is located on the southern edge of the Olympic Peninsula at the confluence of the Wishkah and Chehalis Rivers. Historically, Aberdeen's economy has been based on logging and fishing, but there is now a concerted effort to replace these with tourism.

Earning a Living

Business Climate: A Deloitte & Touche report gave Washington state an "advantage" rating for business in labor availability, education, port access, character of life, and climate, but a "disadvantage" rating in labor costs, unemployment insurance, workers' compensation, construction costs, state and local tax rates, environmental permitting, and overall business climate.

Help in Starting a Business: The Business Information Center is a joint venture between the SBA, the SCORE Counselors to America's Small Business, and the Washington Small Business Development Center. The center can give you the preliminary information and advice you are looking for, and provide you with on-site counseling, access to training, and a national electronic bulletin board. Individuals who are interested in starting a small business, or who already have a small business, can use the center as often as they wish at no charge. The Business and Project Development (360-725-

4100; *http://choosewashington.com*) assists manufacturing, processing, and call center businesses with site location and expansion needs.

Job Market: Employment was slow the first three years of the century, but it has since been on the rise. The unemployment rate dropped to a four-year low of 4.6. Government employment stands at 35,200 people in Thurston County.

Medical Care

Providence St. Peter Hospital (360-491-9480; *www.providence.org*) is a 390-bed, not-for-profit regional teaching hospital offering comprehensive medical, surgical, and behavioral health services. They have been named one of the 100 Top Hospitals in the nation for cardiology, orthopedics, and stroke. Their outpatient surgery center has received national benchmark awards for its work in cataract surgery, knee arthroscopy, and many other procedures. Capital Medical Center (360-754-5858; *www.capitalmedical.com*) is a 119-bed hospital, with one general family practice clinic, serving Thurston and surrounding counties. Among others, it provides services for cardiac rehabilitation, diabetes, emergency, gynecology, surgery, laboratory, joint treatment, nuclear medicine, outpatient diagnostics, outpatient surgery, radiation therapy, surgical specialties, and trauma services.

Services for Seniors

The Senior Activity Center (360-943-6168; *www.wsasc.org*) is a key part of a comprehensive community strategy to meet the needs of older adults by offering services and activities within the center and linking participants with resources offered by other agencies. The numerous center programs are made up of a variety of individual and group services and activities. They teach classes, print a newsletter, perform health screenings, hold photo and essay contests, and organize trips to the mountains and to other cities. Adult Day Services Centers (888-609-2372; *www.adultday.org*) provide safe, quality care for older adults. The Senior Citizens' Lobby (360- 754-0207; *www.waseniorlobby.org*) works through elected officers, a board of directors, executive committee, and a nominations & review committee.

Continuing Education

South Puget Sound Community College (*www.spscc.ctc.edu*), with a full time enrollment of 2,908, offers online classes, adult basic education, a center for continuous learning, and several other special programs. Evergreen State College (360-867-6000; *www.evergreen.edu*) is a liberal arts and sciences college with a full time enrollment of 3,749.

Crime and Safety

The crime rate is 4,183.5 annual reported crimes per 100,000 people. The crime rate dropped sharply in 2003, but has been rising since.

Getting Around Town

Public Transportation: Intercity Transit (360-786-1881; *www.intercitytransit.com*) runs bus routes throughout the city. Seniors can ride at a reduced fare of 35 cents, and you can buy passes for the day, week, month, and year.

Roads and Highways: I-5,US 101, SR 8, 121, 510

Airports: Olympia Regional Airport (360-528-8079; *www.portolympia.com*) is a regional and corporate aviation facility. Olympia is less that one hour from the Seattle-Tacoma airport.

Ports: The port's 60-acre terminal consists of three modern, deepwater berths, on-dock rail, a customs bonded warehouse, and a complete container yard.

Let the Good Times Roll

Recreation: You can rent canoes and kayaks for outings on the Black River. Tumwater Falls is a great place to watch salmon leap as they move upstream. A walk along the shore of Puget Sound is one of the most beautiful walks anywhere. The viewing platforms and photo blinds of the Nisqually Flats National Wildlife Refuge bring many visitors to see the migrating birds. Olympia has an excellent marina with numerous parks. At least 10 city parks offer tennis, picnics, boating, and nature trails for jogging and hiking. Olympia is less than an hour from Seattle and the Pike Place Market, Mariners Baseball, Sonics Basketball, and Seahawks Football. Nearby Mt. Rainier is the highest single-peak glacier system in the U.S., and is perfect for skiing, snowboarding, snowmobiling, camping, fishing, and hiking through rugged terrain. There are 10 golf courses close to Olympia. Madison Scenic Park provides a territorial view of the city set against the dark backdrop of the rumpled Black Hills and is an excellent place to watch sunsets.

Culture: The Yashiro Japanese Garden is a traditional Asian garden, designed in the ancient hill and pond style, honoring Olympia's sister city Yashiro, Japan. Classic gates, built without nails, open into a walled world where splashing water muffles the sound of the city. Smooth stones contrast with lacy maples and spiky clumps of iris. Percival Landing Waterfront Park has a growing collection of outdoor public arts and historic interpretive sites. The Bigelow House Museum, built during the 1850s, is one of the oldest homes still standing in the Pacific Northwest. The Bigelow House has been home to a single family who saved things, so it contains a remarkable collection of original furnishings. Harlequin Productions is a small nonprofit theater in the historic State Theater, and was founded with the mission of producing new works, neglected works of merit, and unconventional treatments of classics. The Washington Center for the Performing Arts hosts the Olympia Symphony Orchestra and dozens of other community theater, music, and dance groups.

Annual Events: The Olympia Film Society offers innovative films throughout the year and an acclaimed film festival each November. Music in the Park is Olympia's summer outdoor concert series, held Fridays at noon in Sylvester Park from mid-July through August. Arts Walk is Olympia's bi-annual arts celebration showcasing the quality and diversity of South Puget Sound's artistic and cultural resources in April and again in October. Super Saturday at Evergreen State College in June is the largest one-day arts, crafts, and music festival in the state. The Boatswap & Chowder Challenge occurs in May, featuring clam chowder from several Olympia restaurants. The Capital City Marathon is held the 3rd Sunday in May. Capital Lakefair is a five-day festival and the Dixieland Jazz Festival is in early July. Music in the Park is in July and August. Olympia Harbor Days is held during Labor Day weekend. The Procession of the Species occurs the fourth Saturday in April. Sand in the City, in August, has more than100 competitors, thousands of spectators, great food, live entertainment, hands-on art and science activities, master sand sculptors, and 240 tons of sand.

When the Grandkids Come: The hands-on Children's Museum was voted "Best Place to Take Kids" six years in a row in the Olympian's Best of South Sound reader's poll. The museum has five exhibit galleries filled with more than 55 exciting, interactive exhibits. Wolf Haven International is a friendly, beautifully landscaped, wolf sanctuary.

More Information

Municipal
Thurston County Chamber
1600 East 4th Avenue
Olympia, WA 98507
360-357-3362
www.thurstonchamber.com

Olympia Thurston County Visitors and Convention Bureau
1600 4th Avenue East
Olympia, WA 98506
360-704-7544
www.visitolympia.com

Newspaper
The Olympian
111 Bethel Street North East
Olympia, WA 98506
360-754-5454
http://news.theolympian.com

Realty
Vonna Madeley
3333 Capitol Boulevard South
Olympia, WA 98501
360-561-7888
www.coldwellbankerteam.com

Sequim, Washington

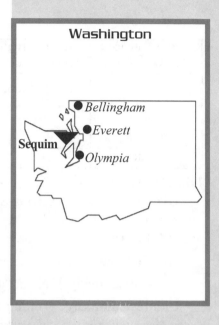

Washington

Sequim at a Glance

You may hear the name pronounced in different ways, but the locals say "skwim." Sequim is a very special place; a place unlike any other in the world. Sequim lies in the Dungeness Valley, nestled between the Olympic Mountains and the Strait of Juan de Fuca. Sequim is famous for Dungeness crab, the Olympic Game Farm, Dungeness Spit, and the endless sun. This region has become a very well-known and often talked about retirement area, and that's a primary cause of the aging population. The residents claim there's something about the area that keeps them young. You may have heard that Washington state has lots of rain, but Sequim has been dubbed "the blue hole" by pilots, because when they fly over, there is always a patch of blue in contrast to the clouds all around it. The sun shines more in Sequim than anywhere else in western Washington. Sequim is the nation's lavender capital because several farms in the area grow it in purple, fragrant fields. The enthusiasm of the new residents has formed a perfect blend with the history and experience of the old-timers to make Sequim an active and caring community with a friendly small-town flavor. Sequim is a place for nature lovers, who can enjoy the nearly 1 million acres in Olympic National Park, the gorgeous San Juan Islands, and the dense fishing waters of the Strait of Juan de Fuca.

Possible Drawbacks: The highway through Sequim is the main access to vacation spots on the peninsula, and the traffic can get heavy in the summer.

- Nickname: The Banana Belt of the Northwest
- County: Clallam
- Area Code: 360
- Population: 4,334
- County Population: 64,525
- Percent of Population Over 65: 44.5%
- Region: Western Washington
- Closest Metropolitan Area: Seattle, 70 miles
- Median Home Price: $155,100
- Best Reasons to Retire Here: You'll love the small-town life and the scenic area. The city moves at an elderly pace, because about half the population is over 50. This is a good place to relax and enjoy!

Climate

48° N Latitude 123° W Longitude	Average High Temperature (°F)	Average Low Temperature (°F)	Precipitation (")	Sunshine (%)
January	40.6	30.7	8.6	38
April	55.8	36.7	3.4	57
July	72.9	49.5	0.8	73
October	56.8	40.3	4.9	47
YEAR	56.8	39.6	54.8	53

Utilities

Overview: The cost of living is above the national average of 100 at 118.6. Housing is quite high at 137.9 and health care has an index of 130. Transportation is also high at 124.5. Food is 109.3, but utilities are quite low at 65.9.

Gas Company: There is no natural gas service.

Electric Company: Clallam Public Utility (360-452-9771; *www.clallampud.net*)

Phone Company: Among the local telephone companies are Verizon (*www.verizon.com*), Vonage (*www.vonage.com*), and MCI (*www.mci.com*).

Water/Sewer Company: Clallam County Public Utility District (360-452-9771; *www.clallampud.net*)

Cable Company: There is currently no cable television in Sequim.

The Tax Axe

Car Registration: Your vehicle must be licensed by the Department of Licensing (360-902-3600; *www.dol.wa.gov*) within 30 days of becoming a Washington resident. A number of fees can apply, such as a filing fee of $7, a basic license fee of $30, a license service fee of 75 cents, a title application fee of $5, an emergency medical services fee of $6.50, and the standard license plate or decal fee ranges from 50 cents to $3. There is also a $15 out-of-state fee. The amount of tax charged partially depends on the amount of tax paid in the other state, so you will need that information.

Driver's License: You must apply for a license within 30 days of becoming a Washington resident. Normally, only the written examination is required. The fees are $10 for the examination and $25 for a five-year license.

Sales Tax: Sales tax is collected on all non-food purchases.

State Income Tax: There is no income tax in Washington.

Retirement Income Tax: There is no income tax in Washington.

Property Tax: Property tax is a little over 1 percent of assessed value.

Local Real Estate

Overview: Real estate development has kept up with the demand for houses for the newcomers. There is a variety of lifestyle choices, including in-town for convenience, a wooded spot in the hills for seclusion, a condo on the golf course, or a mobile in a care-free park. Prices are continuing on a slight, but continuous upward trend. There seem to be few good offerings under $100,000.

Average price of a three-bedroom/two-bath home: $160,000

Average price of a two-bedroom condo: $245,000

Common Housing Styles: Most lots are large and covered with trees. Most houses are split plan or ranch.

Rental Market: Rents increase dramatically for houses and apartments that are on the water.

Average rent for a two-bedroom apartment: $900 per month

Communities Popular With Retirees: Port Angeles and Carlesborg

Nearby Areas to Consider: Port Townsend has the Olympic Mountains on one side, Port Townsend Bay on another, and the Strait of Juan de Fuca to the north. So with access to both salt- and fresh-water bodies, Port Townsend is in a unique location. A regular ferry schedule runs from Port Townsend to Widbey Island. From Dungeness, the Dungeness Spit extends five miles into the Strait of Juan De Fuca and is the longest natural sand spit in the United States. Dungeness Spit has grown about 15 feet per year for the past 120 years. The spit shelters a large inner bay, tideflats, and an estuary.

Earning a Living

Business Climate: Retirees are still moving-in to the Sequim area, and as a result, the business community now includes several corporate chains such as Costco, Ernst, and Payless. Sequim has a strong and growing workforce; is easily access by road, water, and air; and Clallam County has an abundance of online connectivity.

Help in Starting a Business: The Clallam County Economic Development Council (360-457-7793; *http://clallam.org*) is a private, nonprofit organization that helps local agencies build business.

Job Market: The unemployment rate of Clallam Count in 2005 was 6.3 percent. The average annual growth rate of personal income was 4.9 percent, while the statewide average was 5.7 percent and the national average was 5.1 percent. The community is small, so it would be best to look for a job before you move.

Medical Care

Olympic Medical Center (360-417-7000; *www.olympicmedical.org*) is about 22 miles away in Port Angeles and is a 126-bed short-term hospital with a cancer center, as well as cardiac, imaging, nutrition, outpatient, physical therapy services. The center performs more than 5,000 surgeries per year. Olympic maintains other facilities including a cancer center, a laboratory, and a rehabilitation center all in Sequim. Jefferson General Hospital, about 22 miles away in Port Townsend, is a 22-bed critical-access hospital that specializes in walk-in/urgent care for such things as colds, coughs, flu, respiratory problems, sore throat, earaches, headaches, allergies, infections nausea, and rashes. Whidbey General Hospital, about 32 miles away in Coupeville, is a 51-bed short-term hospital.

Services for Seniors

Sequim has more than 160 service, fraternal, and special interest groups in the area. Sequim Senior Services Center (360-683-6806; *http://olypen.com/sequimsr*) provides recreation, entertainment, trips, and tours. Bridge Builders (360-683-8334; *www.bridgebldrs.com*) provides senior and disabled services, information, referral, professional guardian services, and acts as a point of contact in case of an emergency. Rainshadow Home Services (360-681-6206; *www.rainshadowhomeservices.com*) is a licensed home health agency with nursing, physical therapy, occupational therapy, and home health aides. Visiting Angels (360-417-9828) is in-home, non-medical care for seniors. Prairie Springs (360-681-3385) and Sherwood (360-683-3348) are both assisted living centers.

Continuing Education

Peninsula College (360-452-9277; *www.pc.ctc.edu*) has an enrollment of 10,418 and is 17 miles to the west of Sequim. It offers several adult courses in Sequim, as well as at the main campus in Port Angeles. Some four-year degrees are offered through an arrangement with Western Washington University. The college also offers a broad selection of courses online as an extension of the classroom courses. There are some sample courses online, so you can try one before you register.

Crime and Safety

The number of reported violent crimes is below the national average. Violent crimes are reported at the rate of 364 per 100,000 perople, compared to a national average of 496.4. The property crime reporting rate is 4,600 compared to a national average of 4,532.5.

Getting Around Town

Public Transportation: The Clallam Transit System (360-452-4511; *www.clallamtransit.com*) provides bus service to customers throughout Clallam County. Jefferson Transit (360-385-4777; *www.jeffersontransit.com*) runs multiple local routes and is a connection among Port Angeles, Bremerton, Silverdale, and the Seattle area.

Roads and Highways: Highway 101 is the main road passing through town.

Airports: William R Fairchild International (*www.portofpa.com/airports/fairchild-international-airport.html*) is about 27 miles away in Port Angeles, and is the largest airport on the Olympic Peninsula. Kenmore Air currently links Port Angeles to the Seattle/Tacoma airport.

Ports: The Port of Angeles provides fully equipped, efficient marine facilities with a variety of cargo services. Each of the various marinas has offerings for both commercial and casual boaters.

Let the Good Times Roll

Recreation: The Olympic Peninsula is surrounded by salt-water on three sides. In addition, there are many streams and rivers coming out of the Olympic Mountains and coursing over the valley as they run to the Strait of Juan de Fuca. The native freshwater fish include rainbow, cutthroat, brook trout, and whitefish. Fishing can be enjoyed from private or charter boats in the strait, bays, and ocean. Salmon and cod fishing are both good at Dungeness Spit. Walking the spit's sandy stretches far into the strait, you get the sensation that you're leaving the mainland for your own private marine observatory. The Olympic Game Farm is a family-run business and is home to many animal species. Olympic National Park has been selected to be a world heritage site. The Sequim Aquatic Recreation Center has an Olympic-sized pool, a shallow pool, a sauna, and a hydro-therapy pool.

Culture: At the Sequim Museum you can learn all about the Manis Mastadon excavation as well as the changing exhibits, S'Kallam tribal exhibit, and pioneer history displays. At the Olympic Coast Marine National Sanctuary you can learn about protecting the coast of Washington state and see a great slideshow of the sanctuary. The Audubon Center has scientific exhibits, hands-on displays, and physical specimens. The Port Angeles Fine Arts Center has changing exhibits of contemporary solo and thematic art. The Port Angeles Symphony Orchestra is a volunteer orchestra of about 85 members.

Annual Events: The annual Irrigation Festival is held in May. From May through October is the Sequim Open Aire Market. The Sunbonnet Sue Annual Quilt Show is in June. The Lavender Festival is held every July and features the lavender growers of the Sequim-Dungeness Valley, lavender fields tours, and a street fair. In October is the Dungeness Crab and Seafood Festival. The Harvest Celebration and Farm Tour is in October.

When the Grandkids Come: The Sequim Aquatic Recreation Center has a wild, wonderful waterslide. The Olympic Game Farm is a fun way to learn more about animals in their natural environments.

More Information

Municipal

Sequim-Dungeness Chamber of Commerce
P.O. Box 907
Sequim, WA 98382
800-737-8462
www.cityofsequim.com

North Olympic Peninsula Visitors and Convention Bureau
338 West 1st Street Suite 104
P.O. Box 670
Port Angeles, WA 98362
360-452-8552
www.northwestsecretplaces.com

Newspaper

Sequim Gazette
147 West Washington
Sequim, WA 98382
360-683-3311
www.sequimgazette.com

Peninsula Daily News
305 West First Street
Port Angeles, WA 98362
360-452-2345
www.peninsuladailynews.com

Realty

We do not have a Realtor recommendation for Sequim. As an option, check out *www.realtor.com* or *www.homegain.com.* Select a Realtor with both CRS and GRI designations after their names, since it means that these folks have gone the extra mile and are both graduates of the Realtor Institute and Certified Residential Specialists.

To arrive at the list of 50 cities included in this book, it was necessary to go through data and descriptions of many, many areas. At first it was fairly easy to eliminate one place in favor of another, but as time went along, and the list got shorter, it got harder to do. The nine cities listed here were the last on our list to be removed to get us down to the final 50. It wasn't easy! Any one of these would make an excellent addition to our 50 Fabulous.

Fort Myers, Florida

Fort Myers is known as the "City of Palms." Fort Myers is located on the banks of the Caloosahatchee River in southeast Florida. Here you will find the sunshine and beaches of Florida, as well as numerous golf courses. You can enjoy an atmosphere that's a little quieter, a little less hurried, and a lot less like the rest of the world. This is a place of exotic tropical wildlife, white sandy beaches, and hundreds of uninhabited islands. You can spend your time searching for sea-

shells, enjoying family, or just lounging on a beach.

The city has a full calendar of annual events including the Swamp Cabbage Festival, All-Florida Championship Rodeo, Annual Tarpon Fishing Competitions, Offshore Grand Prix Boat Races, Annual Oktoberfest, and the Caloosahatchee Cracker Festival and Civil War Reenactment. Each summer from May through August, the loggerhead sea turtles leave the water during the night and crawl ashore to lay eggs in a sandy nest.

The Fort Myers Miracle is the local minor league baseball team. The City of Palms Park (in Fort Myers) has been the home of the Boston Red Sox spring training since the early 1990s. The Minnesota Twins also do their spring training in Fort Myers, at Hammond Stadium at the Lee County Sports Complex.

The overall cost of living is below the national average at 96.9. Housing is particularly low at 89.9. Healthcare is also below the national average. The population of the city itself is 46,254.

Gainesville, Florida

The Gainesville area is aptly known as "The First Coast." The Spanish founded the first European settlement in St. Augustine in the 1560s. In Gainesville, you can find many fun things to do, including tennis, golf, sight-seeing, fishing, or just visiting the beautiful beaches. The land is divided by the meandering waters of the St. Johns River, one of only a few north-running rivers in the world. Cool mineral springs, shimmering lakes, and verdant forests offer enchanting natural beauty. City-lovers will enjoy the cosmopolitan activities. Major sites in Gainesville include the Devil's Millhopper Geological State Park, the Florida Museum of Natural History, and the historic downtown area.

Gainesville is home to the University of Florida. It blends the stimulation of a university town with the small-town flavor of Florida's heartland. *Popular Science* magazine ranks Gainesville the most technologically advanced city in Florida, and 30th in the nation. In Gainesville and the surrounding areas, you can explore the beautiful rivers and lakes, cool natural springs and unspoiled wilderness parks of a subtropical region. Along its back ways, roadside vendors sell boiled peanuts, country towns sell antiques, barbecue pork and pine forests scent the air, and crystal-clear springs make the landscape sparkle.

The population of Gainesville is 92,291. The cost of living is below the national average at 91.5. Housing costs are particularly low at 81.6.

Jacksonville, Florida

Jacksonville is "where Florida begins." Jacksonville offers the St. Johns River, the Florida Theatre, La Cruise Casino, the Jacksonville Symphony Orchestra, Fort Caroline National Memorial, and the Alhambra Dinner Theatre. The area museums include the Alexander Brest, Kareles Manuscript Library, American Lighthouse and Maritime Museum, Cummer Museum of Art and Gardens, and the Jacksonville Museum of Contemporary Art.

The City of Jacksonville ranks as the 14th largest city in the United States. The metropolitan area, which includes the beach cities of Clay, Baker, Nassau, and St. Johns, has a population of more than 1 million residents. Located in northeast Florida, Jacksonville is the largest city in the contiguous United States in land area, including a major port, the insurance and financial center of Florida, site of U.S. Navy bases, and the home of the National Football League's Jacksonville Jaguars.

A significant part of Jacksonville's growth has come from the presence of naval bases in the region. Naval Air Station Jacksonville is the third largest navy installation in the country and employs more than 23,000 civilian and active-duty personnel. Jackson-ville is one of the few cities on the eastern seaboard that have been spared from the wrath of numerous hurricanes. The only major hurricane to hit the city has been Hurri-cane Dora, in 1964.

Jacksonville is home to the Florida Community College and Jacksonville University. The cost of living is slightly above the national average at 104.7. This is primarily due to the cost of housing, where the index is 115.6.

Wayzata, Minnesota

Wayzata has a thriving business community and beau-tiful residential neighborhoods. Planning ahead has allowed the city to maintain open space and park lands, giving it a small-town feel that makes the city a special and pleasant place to live. It covers about three square miles on the north and east shore of Lake Minnetonka. Wayzata is pri-marily a residential suburb, with services and businesses found along the highway 12 corridor and along downtown Lake Street.

Lake Minnetonka is 14,310 acres in size. It is a series of small lakes connected by short canals, heavy milfoil, boat docks, rocks, and deep water. It ranks as one of the nation's better bass fisheries, and Lake Minnetonka is located only a dozen miles from Minneapolis. Both largemouth and smallmouth bass are present in huge numbers and very respectable sizes.

Wayzata is the jewel of Lake Minnetonka, just 11 miles west of Minneapolis, which makes Wayzata the best place to access Minnesota's most popular lake. Here you'll find the latest in lakeside fashions, artwork, antiques, and collectibles. You'll find an eclectic assortment of restaurants that range from casual to elegant. Most offer lakefront views and none are more than a stone's throw away from the water. You can watch the cruisers drift by or look out at lazy clusters of sailboats.

The population of the city itself is 4,113. It has a healthy retirement community with 20.8 percent of the population 65 or over. The cost of living is a bit above average at 106.5, with healthcare costs leading the way at 131.5.

Biloxi, Mississippi

The Gulf Coast has sand, sun, deep-sea fishing, casi-nos, and plenty of nightlife along the strip. There are more than enough varied and world-class attractions in this part of Mississippi to fill any itinerary. The strip along the beach includes 12 elegant casinos, and you'll also find some of the finest golf courses anywhere.

Growing numbers of retirees are discovering the ad-vantages of retirement living in Mississippi. The state does not tax pensions or retirement benefits. This popular coastal area has long been noted for its mild climate and fresh seafood. Plus there are plenty of things to keep you busy! Music industry headliners perform to sellout crowds at the Mississippi Coast Coliseum & Convention Center. Professional hockey, major college basketball tournaments, and rodeos also make regular appearances at the Coliseum. Museums and community theaters abound, and the Gulf Coast Symphony is well attended.

You can enjoy touring antebellum mansions, learning history at military forts, and browsing art, sculpture, and ceramics at noted museums. Trace the past of the fishing industry while observing modern Gulf Coast shrimping fleets or taking a deep-sea fishing expedition of your own. Highway 90 runs along the sandy beach separating the city from the Gulf of Mexico. New Orleans is only about 83 miles to the west, and Mobile is about the same distance to the east.

The Mississippi coast boasts of 26 miles of white sand, and Biloxi is only one of several small cities on the beach. Among the practical benefits of living here are housing prices 29 percent below the national average, violent crime 23 percent below the national average, and healthcare cost 13 percent below the national average. The city of Biloxi has a population of 50,644.

Liberty, Missouri

Named for the principle that Americans hold most dear, Liberty offers a freedom of choice for contemporary living rivaling that of any community in the country. Ideally located at the northeast threshold of the Kansas City region, Liberty enjoys easy access to the amenities of metropolitan life while maintaining all the advantages of a small hometown.

Liberty is in Clay County. Clay County is one of 13 counties that comprise the Kansas City metropolitan area. It is the third most populated county in the metropolitan area. Major employers in Liberty include the Hallmark distribution warehouse. Liberty is also the base for Ferrellgas, the largest retail provider of propane in the United States.

The climate for Liberty has four distinct seasons, with no severe weather in any of them. The Martha Lafite Thompson Nature Sanctuary is one mile from downtown, and has five nature trails and an interpretive center. The Liberty Fall Festival is held in September each year. Smithville Lake, northwest of Liberty, is a 7,200 acre lake with fishing, boating, sailing, and waterskiing. Liberty is the home of William Jewell College with a full time enrollment of 1,254.

The 2000 census reports a population of 26,232. The overall cost of living is below the national average at 94.9. This is primarily because the cost of housing is exceptionally low at 75.

Reno, Nevada

The "Biggest Little City in the World," Reno has something for everyone inside its 85.2 square miles. Plus it's a mere 45 minutes away from Lake Tahoe and some of the country's best ski resorts! Reno rests at a comfortable 4,400 feet above sea level, and gets more than 300 sunny days each year. The scenery is breathtaking and you will find yourself spending many hours exploring. The city gets about 12 inches of precipitation annually. Reno is "America's Adventure Place," the center of commerce and culture in northern Nevada, where 200,000 residents enjoy life in a high desert valley on the eastern slope of the Sierra Mountains.

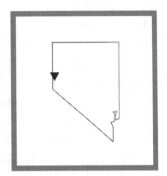

Reno has over 5 million visitors each year. Among the reasons for this popularity are the wide range of restaurants, gaming in Reno, top-notch entertainment, arts and culture, outdoor activities, and the Reno Events Center. The Truckee River Kayak Park Course is located in the heart of Reno's bustling downtown hotel-casino and booming arts district.

In a survey conducted in December of 2004, the average rating for the quality of one's neighborhood was 4.16 on a scale of 5, and the average rating for the city as a place to live was 4.23 on a scale of 5. The same survey showed that four out of five residents are satisfied with their opportunities to interact with their local government.

The population of Reno in the 2000 census was 166,650. The overall cost of living is quite high with an index of 120. Housing costs have an index of 139.1 and healthcare is at 118.2.

Kerrville, Texas

Kerrville is located in the heart of the Texas hill country northwest of San Antonio. Kerrville is one of state's most popular health and recreation centers. The Kerrville area is believed by many to have the most ideal climate in the nation. More than two dozen area boys' and girls' camps, and scores of hotels, motels, dude ranches, and religious encampments attract thousands annually. Kerrville is blessed with rugged cedar and live oak-covered hills, picturesque green valleys, and beautiful streams edged by towering cypress. White-tailed are deer so numerous that motorists are cautioned to be on the alert for them.

If you like golf, you will love Kerrville. In 1923, a $28,000 subscription was raised to build the first nine holes of the Municipal Golf Course. Three years ago, the city of Kerrville invested more than $1 million to redesign and improve the 18-hole Municipal

Golf Course. Local resident Byron Nelson, member of the PGA and winner of the Masters, along with friend and neighbor Joe Finger, designed and built the beautiful 18-hole golf course at Riverhill Country Club. Comanche Trace (a 1,180 acre golf course) has been referred to "as a slice of paradise in a meadow of perfection."

Kerrville is a 22 mile drive from Fredericksburg, Texas, which is known for its many festivals and unique shops. Bandera, the Cowboy Capital of the World, is a 25 mile drive to the south. Kerrville's outdoor activities include numerous city parks, a municipal tennis center, horseback riding, camping, bicycling, shopping, and more. Many "Winter Texans" make Kerrville their home for half of the year.

The cost of living is well below the national average at 92.9. The cost of living index is below average in all categories, with housing costs at 87 and food at 92.1. The highest is healthcare, but it is below the national average at 99.

Provo, Utah

Provo is Utah's third largest city with about 105,000 people. It is a clean, pleasant city beautifully situated between the Wasatch Mountains and 250-square mile Utah Lake. Provo's main claim to fame is Brigham Young University, a 30,000 student university founded and run as the leading Mormon institution of higher learning. It is the largest church affiliated university in the country, and its cultural offerings and sports programs play an integral role in Provo. Provo is a community based on strong family values with safe neighborhoods and an abundance of resources.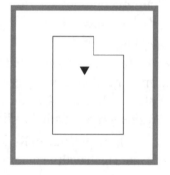

The mountains surrounding Provo provide good hiking, mountain biking, and fishing opportunities among beautiful alpine scenery. In winter there is downhill and cross-country skiing Also near town is the Mt. Timpanogos Cave National Monument and Bridal Veil Falls.

Business Week magazine, in the Special Report "Best Cities for Entrepreneurs," named Provo as a prime site. The article refers to Provo's scenic beauty, competitive tax rates, affordable homes, low crime rates, and the city's investment in fiber-optic infrastructure.

Provo is located in the middle of the state, just off I-15, about 45 miles south of Salt Lake City. It is one of several cities that form a sprawling urban area along the western base of the Wasatch Mountains. The overall cost of living index is below average at 99.1. Transportation has the highest cost of living index at 111.3. Housing and food are both slightly above average. Utility costs are exceptionally low at 79.8.

About the Authors

Arthur Griffith

Arthur Griffith was born and raised in rural Louisiana. He worked for several years as a radio and television announcer, moving from place to place. He then became a computer consultant. His experience ranges from machine language to COBOL, and he worked in software dealing with embedded systems, dynamic graphical displays, nuclear power plant design, telephone company call analysis, and missile guidance systems. After working for 25 years as programmer and software development project manager, he became a writer of computer books and articles in 1997. He has written thirteen computer programming books including *GCC: The Complete Reference*, and *COBOL for Dummie*s.

Mary Griffith

Mary Griffith was born in the Mojave Desert, raised in Santa Barbara, and has lived in or traveled the west, the middlewest, the northeast, and the southern United States. She has written on and off most of her life, producing a few minor published pieces. She takes greatest pride in her three major productions, however: Julie, John, and Joanne, her grown children. *50 Fabulous Places to Retire* is her first work co-authored with her husband. They currently live nine miles back on the North Fork, a notorious 18 mile mountain loop outside Homer, Alaska. They share living space with two cats: Miss Effie and Captain Editor. With all due respect to our co-workers in the writing industry, it should be noted that they put the Captain out at night.

How to Use the Interactive CD

First, it's important to understand what's on the interactive CD. You'll find the following:

- A folder called "50 Fabulous Places to Retire," which contains a folder called "Install," which contains a file called **setup.exe**. This file is used to install the program on your computer, allowing you to search data included in *50 Fabulous Places to Retire*.

- A "Chapters" folder, containing chapters for each of the 50 Fabulous Places to Retire. These are in PDF format, which requires Adobe Acrobat Reader, version 6.0 or higher.

- Adobe Acrobat Reader, version 7.0, which you can install on your computer by double-clicking the icon named "AdobeReader70.exe," found in the CD's main directory, which is displayed when you view the CD on your computer. This version of Adobe Acrobat reader is for Windows XP users only. To get a version that works with other versions of Windows, go to *www.adobe.com*. If you already have Adobe Acrobat Reader version 6, you don't need to install or download anything.

- This "**How to Use**" document, which you can print or re-display as needed.

Now, let's talk about how to use the CD to set up our database search tools.

1. When you put the CD in your CD drive, the Autorun program should kick in after a few moments, and automatically run the Setup program to install the database search tools. If this doesn't happen (the use of Autorun may be disabled on your computer), choose **Run** from the Windows **Start** menu.

2. Click the **Browse** button.

3. The Browse dialog box opens. Go to the drive letter for your CD drive (this is often drive D:) and **click once on the drive letter**.

4. Click the **Open** button.

5. The **50 Fabulous Places to Retire** folder is displayed. **Double-click** it.

6. The **Install** folder is displayed. **Double-click** it.

7. See a **Setup** file displayed in the Install folder. **Double-click** it.

8. Back in the **Run** dialog box, click **OK**. The installer program will start on its own, and you can respond to the prompts, inserting your name/company name, and then choosing "**Typical**" for the type of install you want to do.

That's all there is to it—the installation will take a few minutes, and you'll see both a Desktop and a Programs menu icon appear (in the Windows Start menu) when the process is complete.

To run the Search program, simply double-click the **50 Fabulous Places to Retire** icon on your Desktop or Start menu, and follow the instructions on the form that appears. **Note** that depending on the anti-virus or security software you may be using on your computer, you may be prompted about the safety of opening this program—choose Yes and/or Open (depending on the prompt/s that appear) and go ahead and open the program. There are no viruses or spyware included in this program, *guaranteed*.

If you ever want to uninstall this program, just go to the Control Panel (via your Windows Start menu) and double-click the Add/Remove Programs icon. Select "Search: 50 Fabulous Gay-Friendly Places to Live" from the list, and then click the Remove button. The un-install process begins and prompts you when it's completed—it's that simple.

If you have any **questions** about this program, its installation or use, please e-mail us at help@limehat.com.